The
Christian Life
Series

The
Christian Life
Series

Rayola Kelley

authorHOUSE®

AuthorHouse™
1663 Liberty Drive
Bloomington, IN 47403
www.authorhouse.com
Phone: 1-800-839-8640

Published by AuthorHouse   04/29/2013

ISBN: 978-1-4817-4455-3 (sc)
ISBN: 978-1-4817-4452-2 (e)

Library of Congress Control Number: 2013907401

The material is part of the series of information being offered by Gentle Shepherd Ministries for the purpose of the edification of the Body of Christ.

Except where otherwise indicated, all Scripture quotations in this book are taken from the King James Version of the Bible.

Contents

ACKNOWLEDGEMENT

I want to acknowledge the editing
work of Anna Schwery. Thank you
for the commitment, sacrifice,
and friendship you have displayed
towards us by helping to make this
book a reality.

INTRODUCTION

Have you ever struggled as to what you would call a particular project or work? I encounter this dilemma when it came to the different writings in this book. I saw a need to address some of the important spiritual subjects of our day. First hand I had witnessed people of different backgrounds and spiritual maturity struggle in their spiritual lives because they did not understand how the basic aspects of the Christian life would actually manifest themselves in their own lives. Granted, they had some concepts of these subjects, but most remained elusive or shrouded because of the lack of discipleship or lifeless teachings surrounding them. Granted, some of these teachings or messages sounded good, but had no personal affect on their actual lives.

As I began to write on these subjects I wanted to keep them simple in presentation, while organized enough for those struggling with these issues to come out with a living picture of how they would work within their lives. The presentations of each subject were not big enough to refer to them as a book, and I did not want to put them in various booklets. Hence enter the struggle as to the manner in which I would present these different subjects.

While preparing this work, patterns emerge that connected each presentation to a particular theme. Combined together you now hold, *The Christian Life Series* in your hands. As you will see, each writing was connected to a theme which eventually comprised three different books. Each book revealed a different aspect of the Christian life in respect to maturity. In your possession is the final product of these works. For example, the first book is called, *What Matter is This?* The subjects in this book comprise those matters that relate specifically to salvation such as what it means to be saved, and how the love of God, grace, faith, and holiness identifies us to the work of His salvation in our lives.

The second book is called, *The Challenge of It*. The presentations in this book reveal that the Christian life entails having a relationship with God. The concept of relationship with God seems simple enough, but in reality to have an actual relationship with Him is what presents the greatest challenge to our Christian walk. It is so easy to lose sight of having a viable relationship with our Lord because many fail to come to a real knowledge or intimacy with God. This lack of understanding has to do with the dynamics of healthy relationships. Even though we each have received an invitation to know and experience a personal relationship with God, for many of us in our Christian walk, our misconceptions, along with the worldly attractions surrounding us, and the traps of the past, keep us from entering into a satisfying bond with our Creator. As a result, we often take detours away from the simplicity of the life we can have in Christ. Detours also make the Christian life into a burdensome weight that causes confusion, doubt, and despair about God's real intentions and desires towards us in regard to having an intimate rapport with each of us.

The third and final book is called, *The Reality of It*. The reality of the Christian life is that it will bring distinction to those who truly believe. The reason for such a distinction is because we accept and walk according to the excellent ways of the life we are being called to. The excellent way involves becoming the spiritual man that gives way to the life of discipleship that each of us as believers are being called into. As we deny self and give way to the work of a personal cross to adhere to Christ's call to follow Him into our new life, we will discover what it means to walk in His light. As we walk in His light, we will be conformed to His image.

It is my prayer that *The Christian Life Series* will present the simplicity of the Christian life that has been clearly outlined in Scripture in order to bring people back to center and a realistic understanding of what the Christian walk is all about. It is when we come back to center to God's truth about these subjects, in regard to what He wants us to understand, that He can cause us to know and experience this life in a personal way. In the end, it is my hope that the reader will possess a clear picture as to how these subjects comprise the extraordinary life that is available to all saints of God.

WHAT MATTER IS THIS?

Book I

1
A MATTER OF SALVATION

INTRODUCTION

One of the most confusing matters in relationship to the kingdom of God is salvation. Although the plan of salvation is clearly laid out in the Bible, it is surrounded by diverse variables that can cause confusion as to what it means to be truly saved. In fact, this issue regularly comes up in discussions when I have had to contend with those who are struggling with the validity of their Christian life and testimony.

Admittedly, I struggled with this matter in the past. I have questioned the legitimacy of my salvation when I found myself entangled in the destructive ways of sin. In my struggle I discovered how sin robs a believer of his or her joy of salvation, kills the power of his or her testimony to stand steadfast in such salvation, and destroys the hope of finishing the spiritual course to know the fruition of salvation. King David said it best in Psalm 51:10-12 in his prayer of repentance, "Create in me a clean heart, O God, and renew a right spirit within me. Cast me not away from thy presence, and take not thy holy Spirit from me. Restore unto me the joy of thy salvation, and uphold me with a free spirit."

As I watch the matter of salvation become even more shrouded by a "modern watered-down" version of the Christian life, I feel the need to clarify what it means to be saved. My goal for this presentation is to honestly address this issue with the intent of bringing people back to the center of what has been clearly established in the Word of God.

The Bible assures us that we can know whether we are saved or not. If the issue is not clear it is not because the criterion for salvation is illusive, but that something such as sin is causing confusion about this matter.

It is vital that we come back to the simplicity of the Bible and allow it to clear up any questions or uncertainty about this subject. If there is something causing doubt in our minds about our personal salvation, then we must allow the Word of God to reveal what we must do to dash such doubts in our lives. After all, we cannot afford to enter into eternity without this matter being settled once and for all!

WHAT IS SALVATION?

As a Christian it is not unusual to take the matter of salvation for granted. Since it is not abnormal for each of us as Christians to be surrounded by references, sermons, and teachings on salvation, we assume this matter has been settled. However, as I contend with people in the Christian realm, such assumptions prove to be sick presumptions. Presumption on these people's part amounts to wishful thinking that all is well with their spiritual lives, when in reality there are indications that something is really amiss. Such inconsistencies in people's lives can and will often create doubt in their own minds as to the credibility of their salvation.

Let us begin with the meaning of salvation. *Strong's Exhaustive Concordance* identifies "salvation" as being an act that has happened (rescued), is happening (need help for the sake of preservation), or will happen in the future (coming to a place of safety). It entails deliverance from something that is destructive, as well as deliverance to something such as a state or place that will result in safety, healing, and protection, ultimately producing well-being or spiritual wholeness.

Clearly, salvation occurs because someone is in some type of danger. A good example of salvation would be a person who is in the ocean and is aware that he or she is about to drown or to be attacked by a shark. Such a person is in danger of losing his or her quality of life or the essence of it altogether. Clearly, such a person has no means to save him or herself; therefore, any deliverance must come from outside of the individual. Such deliverance will also come from above. After all, how can one save a person if he or she is in the same situation? Someone must reach down from a stable place of safety in order for the person to be lifted up and out of present danger.

One of the problems that people have is understanding what they need to be saved from. Some people are actually looking for relief from certain uncomfortable situations in their lives, but they do not see that they are in any real danger. In such cases a person really wants relief from an unpleasant situation, and not true deliverance.

This brings us to what we need to be delivered from. Most Christians know the answer to this question but they fail to understand in what way they need to be delivered. We know that because of our fallen condition of sin and death, Jesus came to deliver us from the dictates of sin and the claims of death upon our souls. However, most people associate their spiritual problems with the happenings taking place in their environment. Due to a gospel that has often been adjusted to attract people to be saved from unpleasant circumstances in order to experience a self-serving life, people seek Jesus for relief and not deliverance. They seek Jesus out to save them *in* their sin by alleviating the tormenting, vain fruits of it, but they do not have any desire or recognize the need to be delivered *from* the entanglement of sin and its fruit of death.

Since people are looking for relief, rather than deliverance, they often become disillusioned in their Christian life. The harsh reality is that any relief from the tormenting ways of sin will only prove at best to be temporary. Even though sin may not appear to be destructive, it harbors the fruit of death. A good example of how deceptive sin is can be found in the Garden of Eden.

The tree of knowledge of good and evil looked pleasant to the eyes, while the serpent claimed it offered incredible possibilities. It all looked harmless enough, but the deadly power was not in considering the tree and its fruit, it rested in partaking of the fruit. Granted, its physical attraction was a tempting lure and its possibilities caught the attention of the imagination of the heart, but none of these carried death. It was partaking of the fruit that allowed death to enter into the human race.[1]

Sin can prove to be an attractive, tempting lure for us to justify partaking of its deadly fruit. The vain imagination of a prideful heart can justify such actions at the prospect of what it might gain in the end.

---

[1]   Genesis 3:1-6; Hebrews 3:13

However, both serve as points of temptation. James 1:14-15 explains how it works, "But every man is tempted, when he is drawn away of his own lust, and enticed. Then when lust hath conceived, it bringeth forth sin; and sin, when it is finished, bringeth forth death."

When Jesus walked on this earth, He clarified the extent and entangling ways of sin when He stated that if a man looked upon a woman to lust after her, he would be committing adultery. The truth is the fruit of death begins when a person starts to covet in his or her heart that which he or she has no right to possess. Such covetousness is a form of idolatry, which is a type of spiritual agreement that is considered fornication or harlotry.[2]

Spiritual fornication occurs when the soul is ready to come into agreement with the unholy by first toying with it with the eyes or imagination. Since the person's imagination is already stirred up, he or she will trespass into forbidden areas to consider the possibilities of the pleasure such fruit will add to his or her life. Once the person actually partakes of the forbidden fruit, mentally, emotionally, or spiritually, aspects of death begin to work within his or her soul. It not only brings a separation from that which constitutes life, but it will separate the individual from the author of life, the Lord.

Jesus did not die on the cross to save us *in* sin, but He died so we could be saved *from* the consequences of sin, that of death and separation from God. He did not die so that we could partake of sin and live in it, forever tormented by the vanity and useless of it all; rather, He died so we could have eternal life and partake of heavenly fruit.

Sadly, people want the right to partake of different aspects of sin without paying the ultimate consequences. They want to put a band-aid on the real problem instead of submitting to major surgery that entails dealing with the spiritual cancer of the soul. They do not want to agree with God's evaluation of it that every aspect of sin will result in death. Clearly, our natural tendency is to give way to deception about its deadly sting, while living in denial that once sin injects its deadly ways into a matter, spiritual death is inevitable unless we honestly confront it in our lives.[3]

---

[2]   Matthew 5:27-28; 1 Corinthians 6:15-20

[3]   Romans 6:23; Hebrews 3:13

4

Unless people realize the urgency of their spiritual condition, they will not see the need to be delivered from their fallen state of death or the unmerciful dictator of sin. We all need to be rescued from sin's claims on us, saved from its present working in our lives, and saved from its future judgment of spiritual death and damnation upon our souls.

God has clearly made the first move to save us, but we must embrace His attempt to save us. We must locate the life-saver that was provided by heaven. We must reach up and grab hold of the hand of mercy and compassion that is reaching down, and allow ourselves to be lifted above the tumultuous waters of the world.

At this point it would behoove us to understand what God had to do to save us. Perhaps if we come to terms with this, we can also come to terms with what it means for us to be saved from damnation.

REDEMPTION

Redemption is an incredible word. Unless we understand it, we will not recognize the mercy that has been extended to us or the grace that has been made available. Since redemption has been interchanged with salvation in some languages we need to understand the concept of redemption. Redemption and salvation are two distinct acts. Granted, they may point to liberty or a different existence, but their actual acts are not the same.

As previously pointed out salvation points to being delivered, rescued, or spared from some type of state of ruin or destruction, whether it is physical or spiritual. "Redemption" points to the act of something being bought back or ransomed from that which has improperly taken possession of it. Such possession points to captivity or enslavement.

It is important to point out that in redemption someone must actually take responsibility for what it is being redeemed. For example, the one who pays the ransom for someone is willing to take full responsibility for that person's welfare.

To buy or ransom something back from some form of captivity is one aspect of redemption. However, there is another important facet of it. A person is redeemed with the intent of restoring him or her back to his or her original inheritance, lifestyle, or purpose.

An example of people being redeemed are the children of Israel. They were unfairly taken into slavery by Egypt. Their slavery lasted for over 400 years. After crying to heaven in their unbearable bondage, God stepped on the scene to redeem them from their tyrannical captivity.

Before God could redeem the people of Israel, He had to send a leader in who would lead them away from their bondage into the inheritance that God had promised to their great patriarch, Abraham. Once again we must be reminded that deliverance is not the same as redemption. God would first have to redeem the people before He could deliver them into the capable leadership of Moses. Moses in turn would lead the children of Israel to their promised inheritance.

Redemption involves some type of exchange for a ransom. God had to ransom all the children of Israel. What would it cost God to ransom His people from the tyranny of Pharaoh?

The first step towards setting the people of Israel free was negotiation. The Lord sent Moses to the court of Pharaoh. On His behalf, Moses set forth the conditions to secure the ransom of the descendants of Abraham. These conditions began with a declaration, "Let my people go." The Lord was laying claim to the people of Israel.[4]

The Lord's claim on Israel is very important. He was declaring that these people did not rightly belong to Egypt. It was at this point that the Lord was declaring His full ownership for them, and that He was about to take complete responsibility for them. Regardless of their slavery, the people did not belong to Pharaoh or Egypt. They had been unjustly taken into bondage; therefore, they had to be set free to be restored to their inheritance.

The Lord's claim of ownership also brought the matter into the realm of legality. Since the people of Israel belonged to Him, He did not have to purchase them to claim such ownership. Granted, He would have to take steps to ransom them in some way from captivity, but not necessarily purchase them.

The concept of redemption works from both angles. It can involve the purchasing of something that is valuable from a store or its original owner, or it might entail paying a ransom for something that has been

---

[4]   Exodus 4:21-23

stolen and taken into captivity. Regardless of the angle you approach this subject, redemption entails taking ownership.

As we follow the negotiations taking place between Pharaoh and Moses in regard to the children of Israel, we must realize that God was their original owner. He never sold them into bondage. It was the first man, Adam, who sold all mankind into various bondages of slavery.[5] God had to reclaim and release the people of Israel. In the end, His intervention would humble the powerless gods of Egypt. It would also cost the lives of innocent lambs, along with the first born of the males among every household and flocks of Egypt. The price would ultimately prove to be very high for the Egyptians, not God.

The Lord did redeem or ransom His people in an unusual, but miraculous way. Egypt had no claims on them; therefore, it could not rightfully hold onto them. After losing the first born son of every household, the Egyptians were ready to pay the children of Israel to leave with the spoils of their personal abundance to avoid greater loss.[6]

The children of Israel could not redeem or deliver themselves from Egypt. It took the outside intervention of God to unlock the chains of slavery, and lead them away from the entanglements of it.

Like the children of Israel during this period of time, everyone has been born into captivity to the tyrannical dictates of sin. The negotiation for our release occurred before the foundation of this world was ever laid. Who would pay the price and take personal responsibility for our release and well-being? It is interesting to understand that the payment was officially revealed on Mount Sinai as to what would be required to ransom us. The Holy Law of God that was given to Moses on Mount Sinai was what revealed the payment that had to be made to release each of us from the tyranny of sin and the claims of death. It declared that the only way that we could be redeemed was through sacrifice that would result in the death of that which was innocent, pure, and without blemish.[7]

The Law pronounced that the wages for our sin was spiritual death or separation from God.[8] This sentence may not be immediately carried out,

---

[5]   Romans 5:8-19

[6]   Exodus 12:29-36

[7]   Hebrews 10:3-18; 9:11-22

[8]   Romans 6:23

but each of us were born under this death penalty. When people pass from this world into eternity, lost souls will begin to pay these wages in hell.

The Law also revealed that man had to be redeemed in another way to be identified with his earthly inheritance. He had to be redeemed or properly purchase from his true owner. We see how this redemption was to take place in Exodus 30:11-16.

When a census was taken in Israel, the people had to be redeemed back from the Lord with a half of a shekel. Clearly, in redemption the same price had to be paid for those being purchased. It did not matter how rich or poor a person was, he or she stood equal as to the price that had to be paid to his or her owner. It was at this time that the people of Israel were reminded of their true owner.

In the Bible "silver" became the official payment for redemption. Interestingly, silver has been referred to as "the poor man's gold." It puts a just, equal price on those being redeemed. Clearly, there is no partiality when it comes to redemption. We are all "poor in spirit", incapable of redeeming ourselves. Therefore, when it comes to salvation, all of us had the same price paid for us. God redeemed us by the work of the cross of Jesus. Jesus' life was offered as the same price for each of us. Since life is in the blood, His blood became the payment for our redemption.[9]

Jesus brought this important equality out in His parable in Matthew 20:1-16. Even though there are those who have worked in the harvest field of humanity longer than others, their wage will be the same as those who begin their work later in the day. The wage that will be paid to each of us in full at the end of this age is our redemption, regardless of how much work we did in the harvest field.[10]

Silver even represents redemption in the New Testament. We see this in the case of Jesus. After agreeing with the religious leaders to betray Jesus, Judas Iscariot received thirty pieces of silver, the price of a servant in Jesus' age bracket. Jesus became poor when in His humanity He took on the status of a servant so we could be made spiritually rich.[11]

---

[9]   Leviticus 17:11; Matthew 5:3; Colossians 1:14

[10] Ephesians 1:10-14

[11] Matthew 26:14-16; 2 Corinthians 8:9

This brings us to the final aspect of redemption: that of being released. Redemption releases the person from oppression or captivity. The question is what will we do with such liberty?

Every Sabbatical year, which came every seven years, Jews who were indebted to a Jewish master were released from their debt. From this point they could choose to go back to their inheritance, or decide to serve their master the duration of their life. It is hard to believe that someone would exchange his or her freedom for lifetime servitude.[12]

The truth is people are indebted to something. What they choose to serve in that state is what will determine whether they are in captivity or have liberty as servants. Some masters were so gracious and kind that the Jewish servants saw it as a great honor and sign of love to become indebted to them the rest of their lives. In such service, these individuals found the greatest type of liberty. For this reason, the Apostle Paul instructs us to pay every debt but the debt of love that is clearly owed to our precious Lord.[13]

As Christians we have been release from former bondages to decide who we will serve. We cannot serve two masters.[14] Since we have been redeemed from our former masters, we should willingly choose to faithfully love and serve our Lord as a bondservant the duration of our time on earth.

Redemption ultimately points to a complete change of ownership. Most people do not even consider the significance of this change of guard. As believers we have been bought with a precious price. We do not belong to ourselves.[15] Therefore, we should not be living for ourselves, pursuing the present world, and hoping for the best in the next as we cast our crumbs at God along the way. We have been saved from the tyrannical ways of the old life and the world. Why would we want to run back into such despicable slavery when we can know true liberty under the benevolent auspice of our compassionate and loving Lord?

Jesus said that He came to preach the acceptable year of the Lord. He came inviting us to partake of the time of Jubilee. Keep in mind, that

---

[12]   Deuteronomy 15

[13]   Romans 13:8-10

[14]   Matthew 6:24

[15]   1 Corinthians 6:20; 7:21-23

at the time of Jubilee, which was to be celebrated every fiftieth year, all property attached to inheritance would be returned back to its original owner. Even though the children of Israel could redeem themselves every seventh year from the slavery of debt to other Jewish brethren, on Jubilee, as a people, they would be officially returned to their original owner, Jehovah God.

When it comes to each of us as believers, the realization of the fullness of our redemption will mark the last and final jubilee. We will be released to know and experience the fullness of our inheritance in Christ. The Apostle Paul summarized it best in Colossians 1:27, "To whom God would make known what is the riches of the glory of this mystery among the Gentiles, which is Christ in you, the hope of glory."

Let us now consider what it means for us to embrace redemption and receive God's salvation from our hopeless plight.

REPENTANCE

"Repent or perish" were Jesus' very words in response to those who had witnessed the murder of the people of Galilee.[16] What did such actions say about these poor individuals? Did it imply they were terrible sinners who were simply receiving their just reward for their deeds?

Clearly, the witnesses were trying to make sense out of such an event. The problem with most people is that they think like the world. In other words, they work from the premise that happenings reveal the so-called "karma" of a person as to what he or she has done in the past.

We see this same premise in John 9:1-34. Jesus encountered a blind man from birth. His disciples asked Jesus a question. Was this man's blindness caused by the sins of the man or the sins of his parents? The Lord's answer was neither had this man or his parents had sin; rather, it was about God manifesting Himself through the situation. The truth is things happen. The rain falls on both the just and unjust, and the sun shines on both types of people as well.[17]

---

[16] Luke 13:1-5
[17] Matthew 5:45

I refer to this type of premise as a *meritorious perspective* where life is judged or measured on the basis of merit. If the bad outweighs the good then the happenings that befall us will be in accordance to the measure of bad we have done.

This premise is man's way of trying to avoid the bitterness of the bad. The problem is that the measure man weighs all matters according to is based on a perverted perception that all he does will ultimately be regarded as clean and right.[18] Clearly, no one sets out to be wrong, foolish, and unfair. For this reason, man's ways seem right in his own eyes. Such a perception often blinds such people to their real spiritual condition, while unmercifully illuminating the deviate failures or inconsistencies of those around them. The fact that these people are divorced from recognizing their spiritual plight often causes them to weigh or judge others by unrealistic, hypocritical standards that they are likewise failing to adhere to.

The real truth is that it does not matter what weights we use to measure ourselves, the reality is that we are falling short of who we were designed to be. We were designed to reflect the glory of God.[19] In spite of the good, the bad is what causes us to personally continue to miss the mark. As long as we miss such a mark, we will remain unacceptable to our Creator who is the One who will ultimately weigh us in His balance.

This harsh reality is clearly brought out by the Gospel message. It declares that we have sinned, leaving us without any recourse other than to pay the wages for our sin, which is death or separation from God. However, this message identifies the problem in light of the solution. Granted, man may be void of changing his spiritual lot in life, but nothing is impossible with God. He provided the necessary payment so that man could be pardoned and live, thereby, escaping the death sentence. It is for this reason that the Apostle Paul declares that the Gospel message is the power of God unto salvation.[20]

A man by the name of Belshazzar learned the truth about his spiritual condition the hard way.[21] He was the king of Babylon. He not only fell

---

[18]   Proverbs 16:2

[19]   Romans 3:23

[20]   Romans 1:16; 1 Corinthians 15:1-4

[21]   Daniel 5

short of the mark set in eternity, he actually stepped over what I would refer to as the line of absurdity, causing God to immediately weigh his actions in front of others.

God's balance found Belshazzar wanting. "Wanting" in this text is an interesting word to consider. It points to complete failure.[22] The king proved to fail the test when measured. He had arrogantly demeaned the things of God, and when he was weighed in God's balance he was about to be abated or brought down to his real status. Even though he held a high position in the empire, he was about to be decreased. The balance proved he had caused great bereavement.

Since Belshazzar was found lacking in his character and ways, he was about to be made lower. We know this king not only lost his position and kingdom the very night he was weighed in the balance, but also his life. It had to be a sobering reality that proved to be too late for him to change the outcome.

This brings us to what it takes to change the outcome of what has transpired in our lives. We may possess some goods according to the world's perspective, but when weighed in God's righteous balance, we will always be found wanting because we are missing His mark in relationship to our spiritual potential. This has clearly caused bereavement to our Lord. As our righteous judge, it will require Him to be just and honest in dealing with the deviance that has caused His balance to unveil just how far away from the mark of His holiness we each have fallen.[23]

As believers, we also know what God's balance looks like that He will use to weigh each of us. It is His holy Law. The Law reveals that we have all transgressed it, making us wretched sinners or transgressors before God. Since we have broken the Law, it has passed judgment on all of us. The sentence every person is under is the sentence of death.[24]

Obviously, we cannot change or pervert the righteous balance of God. However, God has provided a weight that can change our outcome. As a reminder, this weight will not be applied on judgment day to make a last minute change, for it is appointed for man to die once, and then

---

[22] Strong's Exhaustive Concordance of the Bible; #2627
[23] John 5:27-30
[24] Romans 3:19-20; 6:23

12

face judgment.[25] Rather, the weight has already been offered on behalf of each of us, but we must receive it as the only solution that will satisfy the judgment hanging over our heads. The weight I speak of is the Lord Jesus Christ.

Jesus Christ fulfilled, satisfied, and silenced the Law on behalf of those who flee to Him, seeking forgiveness for sin, salvation from death, and reconciliation with God. Upon confession of Him as Lord, and believing in our heart that He was raised from the dead, we shall be saved from the sentence of death. Upon salvation, Jesus becomes our blessed ark in which God will place us, to serve as our wisdom, righteousness, sanctification, and redemption. There our life becomes hid in His death and resurrection so that we can take on His life. On the day we are weighed in the balance, it will be Jesus who will be weighed in our place, for like Enoch, we will have ceased to be. The balance will reveal Jesus' righteousness and not our sin. As a result, we will stand justified before God. It will be as though we never sinned.[26]

This brings us to receiving Jesus. We cannot receive Jesus until we repent. "Repentance" is an about face. It is turning away from the present life and turning to face God in humility to agree with Him about our miserable plight. We know we deserve to die in our sins and be forever cast into the bowels of hell. Such knowledge also makes us realize that God does not have to forgive us. He can choose to leave us in our miserable state. He has no real reason to save us, except He desires to do so out of love and compassion. He chooses to pity us, show mercy, and offer grace to us in our great time of need, but we must truly repent to receive such compassion.

We can see the right type of repentance in the prodigal son in Luke 15:11-32. In this parable we see a righteous father who worked hard to secure an inheritance for his two sons. Consider the younger son's attitude towards his inheritance. First of all he failed to see that he had no real right to it. The father could have given it away to great causes or used it for himself.

---

[25]   Hebrews 9:27

[26]   Genesis 5:22-24; Matthew 5:17-18; Romans 5:1-8; 6:3-10; 10:4-10 1 Corinthians 1:30; 2 Corinthians 5:18-20; Colossians 3:3

This brings us to the attitude behind rebellion. It is ingratitude. The foolish young man had no appreciation for the hard work or sacrifices his father had made on his behalf. He simply coveted his inheritance for the purpose of selfishly heaping it upon himself. He was so impatient about it that he went to his father and basically asked him to pretend, or play dead, so he could have his inheritance. Remember, inheritance is only passed down upon the death of the benefactor.[27]

What a wretched soul this young man possessed. He had no sense of value. He did not appreciate sacrifice, desire wisdom, prefer character, or have any respect or recognition for what his father had secured. Since this young man had no real sense or character, he spent all of his heritance on riotous living. A fool is quickly parted from his or her worldly riches.

A famine came upon the land where the rebellious son had foolishly spent his inheritance. Although the son was impoverished in character, he now had to face his condition as a beggar in the land. The best he could do was join himself to a citizen of that country in the hope of catching the scraps or crumbs that fell from his master's table. However, he found himself competing with an unclean animal, the swine, for even the husks.

The Bible tells us he came to his senses to finally recognize how far he had fallen into the cesspool of his greed and foolishness. This foolish young man had to first taste the bitter vanity of his covetous ways. He had to realize his stiff-necked attitude had brought him to this place of great need. Before he had wanted and demanded what was not rightfully his, but now he was in need of what he failed to possess and maintain in the first place. Because he had lacked character, he failed to be wise by recognizing what was important, as well as possess the necessary integrity to maintain it in an honorable way.

It was at this point that the foolish young man was able to see and come to a state of repentance. For the first time he could actually see the reality of his plight, causing him to come into a place of recognition and agreement. Since he could recognize his real impoverished spiritual state, he could come into agreement about the foolishness that had been his constant companion.

---

[27] Hebrews 9:15-17

The reason that so many people fail to repent is because they maintain their stiff-neck attitude towards what they perceive to be their rightful inheritance in this present world. They insist on holding onto the foolishness of their impoverished spiritual state as they justify their wicked preferences and ways. As they hold onto their stiff-neck attitude they refuse to come into agreement with the God of heaven about their true reprobate state of sin and death. They may hope for or count on the crumbs of the world to only find themselves competing in its pigpen with those who are as impoverished in character and ways as they are.

The son realized he was wayward. He was far from a home that even regarded the servants in an honorable way. Even though he had spent all of his inheritance, he perceived that there still was room for him as a servant in the household of his father. What a change in his attitude! He was willing to return home, humbly concede his sonship since he had treacherously sold it for a temporary inheritance. He reasoned that the best he could hope for was to be a servant in his father's house.

This is the face and attitude of true repentance. Unlike the profane Esau, the young man did not cry tears of self-pity for what he had so foolishly gambled away; rather, he realized he deserved to scramble in the muck with the pigs.[28] However, there is something else he knew. He knew the character of his father. His father was compassionate, kind, and generous. Such virtues pointed to forgiveness. It is true that initially the son took his father's character for granted and greatly used it to abuse his father's generosity. But, he knew how his father would respond toward his state of humility. Since he knew, he risked returning home, a different man, a lost son, who was simply seeking mercy as a servant in his father's household.

There is always room at the table for God's wayward children. Their spot remains empty, silently waiting for their return. He rejoices when they finally return home in a humble position, seeking mercy. For it is from this position that He can once again restore them by His grace to their place at His table. But, such children must first agree with Him about their true state before He can restore each of them as a son or daughter at His table.

---

[28]   Hebrews 12:15-17

For the prodigal son the change began when his attitude changed about what he needed to consider as being important. Such a change points to sanity or reasoning returning. You cannot reason with a fool bent on doing it his or her way. Such people will either insist that their way is the right way or they will insist on having life on their terms. They will see no need to change, and all challenges will be scoffed at and trampled under by arrogance. Such an arrogant attitude can only change when the intent of the heart changes in these individuals.

"Intent" has to do with the spirit behind something. The spirit behind why we do something will determine how we look at a matter. The Holy Spirit will bring conviction in areas of deviation, while a wrong spirit will motivate people to justify or excuse away any deviation. Those who are motivated by a right spirit will always be able to come to a place of humility in order to address sin.

We see the change of intent in the prodigal son. Consider the spirit he left home with and the one he returned with. Meditate on his intent. His initial intent was to live it up, while his latter intent was to seek mercy in order to serve as a servant. True repentance will display a complete change in spirit (disposition), attitude (intent), and approach (purpose).

We can also see this change in attitude and intent in God. Due to the endless wicked imaginations of men, in Genesis 6:6, we are told that the Lord repented that he had made man on the earth, and that it grieved Him at the heart. Clearly, God's attitude totally changed towards man. As a result, His intent and approach also changed. In the end eight souls were saved in the ark, while He poured His wrath out on the rest of the world.

In Number 14:11-23, we once again see where God's attitude changed towards the descendants of Israel. If it were not for Moses' intercession, the Lord would have destroyed them and raised up Moses and his descendants to inherit His promises. Because of their rebellion, we see where God changed His attitude towards Israel, only to repent and change His intention towards them after Moses interceded on behalf of these people. God's attitude still remained the same towards them, but His handling of the matter changed. Instead of destroying all of them, a new generation would enter into the Promised Land, while the wilderness would serve as a grave to the old generation with its idolatrous ways and unbelief.

We see another occasion where the Lord stated in 1 Samuel 15:11 that He actually repented of setting up Saul to be king. It is important to note that God did not need to change His mind about a matter for He is never wrong or caught off guard. However, because of the disobedient actions of people, He does change His attitude towards them, also causing Him to change His intent. In this case God intended Saul to be king of Israel, but because of his blatant sin, he became an enemy of God, causing God to change His attitude towards the rebellious king, taking the kingdom away from him.

Man's main reason for repentance is because of sin. We have to change our attitude towards sin in order to change our intent towards God. Repentance is a complete turning away from the old in order to turn to embrace a complete new way of being and doing. By turning to God to seek His forgiveness, ask for mercy, and hope for grace, people turn from the path or way of death and hell. It is as they humbly tremble before Him in revulsion of the offense and contempt they have blatantly showed Him in their sin and rebellion, can He reach down to lift them up to receive the gift of eternal life and set them in the narrow path that leads to life.[29]

We see this same type of humble attitude in the publican in Luke 18:9-14. A Pharisee and a publican (tax collector) came before the Lord. The Pharisee came before the Lord to present his self-righteousness as a means to impress God with his so-called "goodness" and possibly earn some merits. The publican came humbly before God to possibly seek His goodness in the form of mercy. The Pharisee no doubt eloquently laid his idea of righteousness before the Lord, while the publican laid bare his sin and need before the Lord. One walked away still thinking highly of himself but was walking in a delusion about his doomed state; while the other walked away knowing that he was justified in the Lord because he was forgiven. One showed the attitude of self-sufficiency, while the other one showed the attitude of the repentant, contrite heart.

It is at this time that we must consider that there are two types of repentance. One is the outward show of remorse that Esau displayed when he was feeling sorry for himself after finally paying the consequences for his flippant attitude and action towards his birthright. The other type of repentance involves an inward change that will end

---

[29]   Matthew 7:13-14

in the transformation of the attitude and a complete change in purpose and direction. Without the inward change, a person's mind or attitude will continue to be conformed by the world, while his or her purpose will remain selfish, and his or her direction will continue on the same path of ruin and damnation.[30]

Repentance is a complete change, a turn around from the old way. It is embracing a new way. Paris Reidhead in his book, *Finding God*, refers to repentance as the "perfect tense" of salvation. According to Mr. Reidhead, the "past tense" of salvation is justification, the "present tense" is sanctification, and the "future tense" is glorification. However, the perfect tense that will bring forth the reality and work of salvation in a person's life at all times is repentance. Repentance is all about being ready or prepared to receive what God has done on our behalf.

The Apostle Peter tells us that God is long-suffering towards us for the purpose of giving us time to repent. God has no desire to see any one perish in his or her sins. For this reason repentance is a prelude to salvation. It is the first message that John the Baptist preached when he came out of the barren wilderness to serve as the voice that preceded the Messiah. Clearly, sin must be faced, addressed, and dealt with to ensure salvation. Repentance brings each of us to that place of addressing the sin. It is an about face. Keep in mind that if we are walking in our sin, we will be blinded by its very darkness, unable to see the light.[31] Therefore, in repentance, we will turn from darkness to see the light of heaven. We must truly desire to see the great light of the Gospel that can penetrate into the dark souls of people, as well as seek to let it expose the darkness that has engulfed us.

John the Baptist also made this statement about repentance, "Bring forth, therefore, fruits meet for repentance" (Matthew 3:8). Obviously, if there is a complete transformation in attitude, there will also be a complete change in conduct. Our conduct will confirm whether or not we have truly repented.

John the Baptist was asked what would such fruits accompanying repentance look like. He instructed those who inquired if they have two coats and see one in need give it to the one in need. If there is extra food

---

[30] 2 Corinthians 7:10; Hebrews 12:16-17
[31] Matthew 3:1-3; Hebrews 3:12; 2 Peter 3:9

18

and they saw one who was hungry, feed the person. If they were in some position where they could lord over others in some way, they were not to rob or abuse such a position of power for personal gain. Clearly, fruits of repentance are opposite of the indifferent ways of selfishness, which often freely reigns within our fallen disposition.

Since the new life is compelled by the love of God, the Apostle John summarized a changed life in this way in 1 John 3:16-18,

> By this perceive we the love of God, because he laid down his life for us; and we ought to lay down our lives for the brethren. But whosoever hath to his world's good and seeth his brother have need, and shutteth up his bowels of compassion from him, how dwelleth the love of God in him? My little children, let us not love in word, neither in tongue, but in deed and in truth.

Repentance clearly represents the perfect tense of salvation. It is humble, ready, and willing to turn from what is wrong and deviant to face, embrace, and receive the light of heaven. It will seek forgiveness, truth, and restoration. It will embrace the salvation or deliverance that has been made available to all who will believe the message of heaven, and repent, to walk out the gift of life in the glorious light and power of God.

CONVERSION

True repentance leads to the next stage of Christianity: that of conversion. There is only one reason to repent and that is to be converted to a new way of life. The Apostle Peter's instructions were to repent, therefore, being converted so that the hearer's sins could be blotted out when the times of refreshing came from the presence of the Lord.[32] Repentance clearly turns from the old ways, but conversion establishes an environment where the new can actually take hold of a person's disposition and attitude.

---

[32] Acts 3:19

Most people think you are only converted at salvation. The truth is Christians are being constantly converted to the ways of God. In essence, they are being converted from the error of their old ways when it comes to the truth.[33] If a person is converted to the truth, his or her soul shall be saved from death and his or her sins hidden.

Each of us need to remember that we have been trained in our ways, conditioned in our attitudes, and indoctrinated in our thinking. It is natural for us to prefer the ways of darkness and idolatry, display the rebellious, pagan attitude of the spirit of the world, and think according to the base, humanistic philosophies of the age we live in.[34] This is especially true since almost all of us have been trained by worldly families, cultivated by culture, and indoctrinated by the age we live in. In such a state, we are totally in error. But, who of us in our arrogance are willing to admit that our families could possibly be wrong in what they have taught us, our culture totally pagan and contrary to heaven, and our indoctrination foolish and delusional? If our families, cultures, and philosophy about life are wrong, than we must conclude we are also wrong in how we think. If we are wrong, then we have been deceived by darkness and will prove vain in regard to activities that we have valued as being important and significant.

I have had to acknowledge that in the past I have wasted my time and energy on nothing. Such realities can cause many of us to become more stiff-necked about how we do believe, rather than open to embrace the truth. It is for this reason we each must begin with repentance. We must accept the harsh reality about our present state and turn from it to be converted to that which is true and right.

Although God has provided the way of salvation through Jesus, we must keep in mind as Christians we all start out being positionally saved because of the redemption of Christ. We simply stand in Christ, justified before God due to being ransomed back from our terrible taskmaster of sin. However, the way of salvation has not become a reality. Repentance simply turns and receives the gift of salvation, but conversion is how

---

[33] James 5:19-20

[34] Psalm 106:35-36; Proverbs 22:6; 1 Corinthians 2:12; Ephesians 2:2;
       Colossians 2:8

the seeds of the life that was planted in us upon salvation is worked in, through, and out of us.

The best way to describe it is that we must be retrained in our ways, separated from what we have been conditioned with by casting it off as dung, and unlearn what we have been indoctrinated with. Jesus described this state in Matthew 13:12-16 in relationship to the spiritual heart condition of so many people who are blinded by the present age. They may see, but they remain blind towards spiritual truths. They may hear the matters of heaven, but they will never understand the intent behind them. The reason is because their hearts have become gross by perversion, their eyes are closed due to spiritual blindness, and they are deaf to the things of God. Jesus said this state keeps such individuals from being converted, preventing Him from spiritually healing them. Jesus then put forth this statement, "But blessed are your eyes, for they see; and your ears, for they hear" (Matthew 13:16).

Although in the initial state of being Christians our slate has been wiped clean by justification, our ways still remain fleshly, our attitudes worldly, and our thinking perverted. Such a state can cause us to walk according to the old tendencies, habits, or ways of our former life. It is for these reasons we must be continually converted towards the ways of God. To fail to walk in the ways of God proves that we have not really been converted from the error of our old ways. This conversion can only take place as long as we are seeing the right way. Once the way is clearly illuminated as being truth, we must walk in it in order to properly hear the words of truth that will guide us.

A good example of this is Peter. In one situation, Jesus stated that Peter, the stone, would be instrumental in establishing the Church on the Rock, (Christ). However, in Luke 22:31-32 Jesus made this statement, ". . . Simon, Simon, behold, Satan hath desired to have you, that he may sift you as wheat; But I have prayed for thee, that thy faith fail not. And when thou are converted, strengthen thy brethren." Was Peter not already converted? Clearly, Peter was converted as to who Christ was, but he still maintained much of the world's way of thinking and being. Satan was about to sift him to expose just how wrong his thinking and ways were. In spite of his present devotion to the Lord, he had to recognize those areas in order to be converted to what was true and right.

Granted, we may think some of our old ways are not so bad, but anything attached to the old ways will destroy the purity and purpose of the new life in us. For example, to try to mix the old with the new will defile the new. To try to introduce the new into the old points to compromise, and when tested it will not hold. We cannot live the old life while trying to hide behind the façade of a new life. We cannot serve the dictates of sin and serve the Lord Jesus Christ. Both ways and masters are opposing in nature, character, and fruit. We can only effectively walk in and abide according to one master and one type of life at a time.[35]

We must now consider what it means to be converted. We all assume we know what it means to convert something, but how many of us realize that conversion is a complete transformation of something into a new form, function, or purpose? When one considers that conversion is a complete transformation, it implies that all things must become new or something will not effectively work.

I remember an electrician that rewired a house. He used what he considered of the old wiring to be usable, while revamping the rest with updated materials. Can you guess what happened? There was an electrical fire and the house burned to the ground. Apparently, mixing the old with the new caused a short in the electrical system. The reality is that there is no shortcut when it comes to the Christian life. It is not a mixture of the old and new, it is the new being constantly worked in us to manifest itself in and through our lives.

I often wondered why some people who call themselves Christians never change or experience true victory. Upon studying the concept of conversion, I concluded that they have not yet been converted to God's ways in such matters. When you look behind their lack of conversion, you will not find any real true repentance in such areas. These people are not really convinced that they need to repent by giving up their old way to be saved from it.

In considering the meaning of conversion, the *Strong's Exhaustive Concordance* brings some interesting insight into the Hebrew or Greek meanings or implications of this word.[36] Conversion is a form of repentance because it involves a turning around. However, it is not just about turning around, it also entails turning about to regard or consider what is true or real. It is about withdrawing from that which is hindering,

---

[35] Matthew 6:24; 9:16-17
[36] OT #7725; NT #1994, 1995; 4762

and denying what is wrong in order to recall what is right. It is about recovering what is true as a means of being refreshed. True conversion is stepping back from the darkness of a matter in order to revert or be brought back to center of the light. It definitely points to the concept of being continually converted with the intent of being revolutionized in every area of our lives.

Clearly, conversion is an abrupt change in regard to the matters of God. Therefore, when are God's people going to agree with basic principles governing our spiritual lives? When are they going to agree with God's evaluation about something? His ways and thoughts are higher than ours.[37] Repentance turns around in mental agreement with God about sin with the intent of allowing the inner person to be transformed, while conversion comes into agreement with God in attitude and conduct about what is right. Repentance recognizes that something is wrong, while conversion seeks a proper contrast to come into line with what is true and right.

We often think we can fudge the lines of right and wrong and no one will be any the wiser for it. However, when tested, any system or principle that has been compromised with such a mixture will not stand the test. Compromise will make something vulnerable, causing it to eventually break down. If we are going to live like a sinner because we like the old, we should be the best sinner we can be. But, if we are going to be a Christian we must embrace the excellent ways of the life of Christ. We must be thoroughly converted to every aspect of His life and ways. We must come forth as the new creations that the Bible makes declarations about in 2 Corinthians 5:17.

Conversion will result in salvation. It will revolutionize a person's life. The question is how does true conversion express itself? The Bible is clear as to how conversion occurs. It begins with the right disposition. Jesus stated that to inherit the kingdom of God, a person must become as a child in disposition in order to be converted. Such regression involves ceasing from thinking so highly of what we do know and become open, pure, and teachable like a child.

---

[37] Isaiah 55:8-9

To have a child-like disposition will allow us to face just how wrong we have been. Once again, we must be retrained, unlearned, and be transformed in our way of thinking, being, and doing.[38]

This brings us to what we must be ready to embrace with our childlike disposition. Even though we may be childlike in our disposition, we must be discerning and discrete about what we expose ourselves to. We cannot afford to be converted to the matters of religious man and the world. We are turning around in repentance from such influences in order to be converted to the matters of God's kingdom.

As Christians, we realize we are being converted to the Person of Jesus with the intent of being converted to His ways. Psalm 19:7 provides us with this insight, "The law of the LORD is perfect, converting the soul; the testimony of the LORD is sure, making wise the simple." The Law brings an important contrast between the profane and the holy, as well as reveals the truth as to who our God is, while exposing our spiritual condition in light of His holiness. The Law is what changes our mind about a matter, but His wise testimony or judgments concerning issues of life and death are what will change our attitude and ways.

As we begin to follow the progression of conversion, we can see where we are being converted to the person of Jesus in order to be converted to His righteousness. Isaiah 1:27 makes this statement, "Zion shall be redeemed with judgment, and her converts with righteousness." The opposite of righteousness is wickedness. Repentance turns from the influence and damnation of evil, while conversion converts to the ways of life and righteousness.

The Lord was very critical because the Pharisees were making converts to themselves in their way of thinking and doing. Jesus stated that they went to great lengths to make one individual a proselyte, and when they had accomplished their deed, the person had simply become twofold more the child of hell than they were. He also referred to these religious leaders as being blind and that the best they could assure their followers was that they would both fall together into the same ditch of judgment.[39]

---

[38]   Matthew 18:1-4; Romans 12:3
[39]   Matthew 15:14; 23:15

In my Christian life I have realized that I am being constantly converted to God's ways. Sometimes I have to be totally undone to see the influence and error of my old ways, but once I finally see, I know that I must be quickly converted to the ways of righteousness. It is at this point that I allow the righteous ways of God to bring the necessary instructions to me to be converted to what is pure, true, and right.

The question is simple, what are you being converted to? Check out what is influencing you in your way of thinking. What are you embracing as true and acceptable in relationship to God? How are you conducting yourself toward the matters that pertain to life and godliness? Would honest answers reveal that you indeed have been converted to the ways of righteousness, or would it expose you to be a fake in your Christian claims and walk? Only by examining yourself in light of your real fruit can you answer these thought-provoking questions.

BORN AGAIN

Jesus made it clear to Nicodemus in John 3:3 and 5, that unless a man is born again, he cannot see or enter the kingdom of God. This is not my exhortation and words; they belong to Jesus. He is clear that mankind cannot get into heaven unless his status is changed.

The Apostle Paul explained in 1 Corinthians 15:35-50 that our flesh identifies us as belonging to the earth. Our fleshly bodies are corrupt and will return back to the earth from which they came. However, when a person is born again, he or she is now a spiritual man who will one day receive a spiritual, incorruptible body that will live forever. The apostle's warning is quite clear that flesh and blood cannot inherit the kingdom of God.

It is vital that we grasp what is being said by Jesus and Paul about the matter of our status. As the Apostle Paul brings out in 1 Corinthians 2:1-15, a natural man of the earth will have no attraction to the spiritual. Such a man would see the spiritual as being foolish and silly because it is so contrary to what is considered normal. In the natural there is no way we can get a hold of God, connect to His reality, and be able to interact with Him on the matters of the unseen.

Let me give you an example. What does a farmer know about the world of astronomy? Granted, he may have a handle on aspects of the weather and a certain understanding of how the sun and moon may affect certain changes in the environment, but the working of the universe is completely foreign to him. There is no real premise in which he could truly connect to someone in the field of astronomy. And, what does an astronomer know about growing crops? Both the farmer and the astronomer have their own language to explain their particular fields of expertise. It would be the same as someone who only speaks English, trying to speak to someone who only knows German.

Everyone comes from the premise of what they know and have experienced. The natural man experiences the things of the seen world, but the spiritual man is connected to and has experienced the unseen world. In Hebrews 6:4-5, the writer of Hebrews has described the spiritual man as being enlightened, as tasting of the heavenly gift, the Word of God, and the powers of the world to come, as well as a partaker of the Holy Spirit. What can the natural man know about such matters? Granted, he may be curious, but there is no way he has the means to connect to any of it because everything he knows and experiences stands contrary or foreign to the spiritual.

For the natural man to embrace the unseen world he must be connected to it. There must be a base or foundation from which he is able to connect and interact with the spiritual. But, how can man change his base nature or disposition to connect to that which is opposite and opposing to what he is comfortable and used to? Obviously, there can be no mixture or bringing together of the two because there is no point of agreement. Clearly, the natural man's status has to be changed to connect to the spiritual realm of God.

The only way you can change the status of something is by completely changing the base of it. Since the natural man cannot get into heaven, the person must somehow be translated in disposition by changing his very basis. Consider what the Apostle Paul stated in Colossians 1:12-14,

> Giving thanks unto the Father, who hath made us meet to
> be partakers of the inheritance of the saints in light; Who hath
> delivered us from the power of darkness, and hath translated
> us into the kingdom of the dear Son; In whom we have
> redemption through his blood, even the forgiveness of sins.

According to the Apostle Paul we have been made fit to partake of the heavenly inheritance because we have been delivered (saved) from the power of darkness through redemption. This redemption enables us to be forgiven, and upon receiving forgiveness of sin (through repentance), the Father is able to translate us into the kingdom of His dear Son.

Obviously, being translated from the associations, identifications, and entanglements of the present darkness of this world points to a complete change in status. We are no longer children of darkness but children of the light. Such translation points to a different disposition.

Disposition has to do with natural inclinations and tendencies. Under the power of darkness, the natural inclination or preference would be towards the things of the flesh and the world, while the tendencies would be according to the ways of darkness. However, if we have been translated into the unseen, spiritual, and eternal kingdom of Jesus Christ, our inclination will change towards that which is spiritual and eternal. Once the inclination or natural direction of something is changed, then a person's tendencies will begin to change as well.

In order to translate us, we must be born again with a new disposition. We are told that under the new covenant that we know was established by redemption and secured by the blood of Jesus, God would give us a new heart and a new spirit.[40] For God to give man a new heart and spirit means a man will be given a new disposition. A new heart would change a person's inclination towards God, and a new spirit would allow him or her to connect to Him as a means to interact with Him. Instead of just possessing the breath of spirit of this physical world, such individuals would also possess the very breath and spirit of the Living God. It is the type of breath or spirit that connects people to the plane they are actually living on and are able to interact with. It also identifies them as to the type of breath they are living according to. We each are either living as the natural, fleshly man who is walking according to the spirit of the world, or we are a living spirit who is walking according to the Spirit of God.

---

[40]   Ezekiel 36:26-27

To be born again means to be born from above of the pure water of the Word and the Holy Spirit.[41] We are given a new heart that is responsive towards God and a new spirit that has the capacity of interacting with this unseen realm. It is the Spirit of the Living God who works the new eternal life in us, thereby, changing the tendencies of the old. In essence, we have been given a new lease on life to live according to the spiritual man who is no longer subject, limited, or tormented by the natural man.

The beauty about living this incredible new life is that we have been given the status of children. This status had nothing to do with the will or attempts of man. We are told in John 1:12-13, "But as many as receive him, to them gave he power to become the sons of God, even to them that believe on his name; Who were born, not of blood nor of the will of the flesh, nor of the will of man, but of God." Adopted into God's family by way of redemption, our status has indeed forever been changed.[42]

As we can see, salvation is about translation resulting in believers being miraculously born from above. This new life from above was secured by redemption, received via repentance, and worked in believers through conversion to His righteous ways. It was because of redemption that believers could be brought to the status of a new heavenly family and citizenship. They would be identified to holiness as priests and royalty in relationship to an eternal kingdom.[43]

This brings us to the reality that as born again citizens of the kingdom of God our status lifts us above this present world and identifies us to that which is excellent, unseen, and eternal.[44] Our life or lifestyle, should reflect the excellent ways of the unseen life of righteousness and the eternal kingdom of holiness. As spiritual people, our natural inclination should be towards the light of righteousness, and our tendencies should reflect the ways of the glory of God. For this reason there should be no debate as to what kingdom we belong to.

---

[41]   John 3:5

[42]   Romans 8:14-17

[43]   Philippians 3:20; Revelation 1:6

[44]   Ephesians 2:6

The problem today has to do with mental assent replacing heart revelation.[45] As a result of people saying a sinner's prayer, they mentally perceive that they are saved. The sinner's prayer basically gives God permission to save us, but if we do not realize that we must be saved from the status brought upon us by sin and death, we will not be prepared or ready to be born again from above. If we are not born again from above we are still lost. We might become a religious man because of the mental assent, but we will never become a spiritual man from such a fleshly premise.

Our heart must be receptive to being born of a new disposition that will completely change our status. We must recognize and realize the need to be translated from a fallen fleshly status to a restored spiritual status. Mental assent is not enough; there must be a radical change take place from within to ensure salvation. The new birth experience ensures such a radical change. In the new birth, the old ceases to be as it gives way to the new life that is now present in the spirit of man.

Salvation is accompanied by evidence. It points to being translated because of redemption. Redemption reminds us of a new identity and inheritance. Therefore, if one has been translated by being born again, there is a changed in status, where one has been given a new lease on life because he or she has changed direction and is being converted to what is right, thereby, establishing new purpose according to the status that has been bestowed upon him or her. Such a new life cannot be hidden under some basket, any more than true repentance could ever be faked, and conversion could be simply imitated in such a life. A person either lives as if he or she has been redeemed from the former tyranny of sin or he or she lives like the world.

We are told in 1 John 5:9-15 that there is an inner witness that we are saved.[46] In summation, we can know without a doubt whether we are saved. However, we must be living the life of a repentant, converted believer who knows he or she has indeed been redeemed. Such a person knows that he or she belongs to his or her Lord and Savior Jesus Christ.

---

[45] Romans 10:9-10

[46] If you would like to read more about the subject of salvation, the author's book, *Presentation of the Gospel*, in the 5th volume of her foundational series will add valuable insight.

There is no debate as to who has the final say or what responsibilities belong to those who are redeemed. It is outlined in the Bible, and it is the Holy Spirit who will illuminate the intent and revelation of what each of us as Christians need to understand as a means to maintain the integrity of God's truths.

My question is simple. Do you maintain such an inner witness in regard to your salvation? If not, make sure your conversion was more than a mental assent. You must receive the truths of what Jesus accomplished for you in the heart as being true. You must believe it to the point that you will assimilate it into your inner being as your food, life, and breath. You will not only live what you believe, but you will daily feed upon and take it in as you breathe refreshing truths that will identify you to the heavenly, ongoing life of Jesus Christ.

2

THE CRUX
OF THE MATTER

INTRODUCTION

It is important to understand what it means to be saved. Everything about God's commitment towards each of us had one purpose in mind and that was and is to save us. What would compel a holy God who was separated from man by sin to go to such an extent as to give His only begotten Son as a supreme sacrifice to close the gap between Him and lost man? What would motivate Him to reach into the abyss of such spiritual darkness to try to save those who show nothing but utter contempt toward His words and ways while rejecting His overtures?

Most of us in the Christian realm know the answer to these questions. What compelled or motivated God to send the light of heaven into the dark, barren wilderness of sin and death was His love. The answer of love is simple enough to grasp, but the problem is that God's love has been perverted by the world's influence, adjusted to romantic notions, and twisted to fit an array of worldly, self-serving opinions, ideas, and definitions. In the midst of this foolish conglomeration, the real character or essence of godly love has often been compromised and even lost.

It is vital that we as believers come to terms with God's love. It is the only way we will grow in humility, service, and worship towards Him. The truth is He did not save us because we were lovable, attractive, worthwhile, or desirable. Clearly, there were no selfish or self-serving conditions attached to His love, for we have nothing of value to offer Him in return for it. In our fallen state, we have no real premise or means to know, comprehend, or even describe His love. As a result, in the attempts of many people to claim this love for themselves, they have stripped it of its distinction, downplayed its authority, and negated its purpose.

For this reason I offer this presentation about God's love. Clearly, we need to come back to center concerning the intent, reason, and purpose behind what it means for us to receive, experience, and become an extension of God's incredible love.

THE NATURE OF LOVE

How do you describe the love of God? In the late 1970s, I can remember when some Bible teachers recognized the handwriting on the wall. Many people, including Christians, were buying the Hollywood whimsical notions about love. Other arts such as music either led the way or quickly followed suit. It became clear that with each wave of cultural change, people's concept of love was succumbing to the current presentation. These presentations about love were often nothing more than passing fads of the times. As these changes regarding this subject took center stage, the attitude towards the accepted morality of the country naturally begin to shift in regards to that which was associated with love such as attitudes towards the opposite sex, marriage, and the importance of the role of family. In some cases, Hollywood along with the other arts, were on the front line in changing or reinforcing the moral climate of the times.

These changes could be easily followed by sitting back and observing the different presentations. For example, in the 50s many movies and songs were about what I would refer to as the "romantic love," where there was much ado about the art of romance, but with the change of the 60s, love became a free commodity that could be expressed in any old way. All moral responsibilities were being deemed foolish and obsolete, as everything in the way of love became free-game. The 70s created the era of tension and expectations between the sexes as to who would conquer who in the battle of the sexes, whether the battle was over love or jobs. In the 80s the restraints and responsibilities put in place by morality were all but discarded by some for what I would consider to be nothing more than blatant animal magnetism. This magnetism justified and ended in lustful acts and practices that made terrible inroads into the souls of many. Since all respect, responsibilities, and boundaries were discarded, enlarged, changed, or redefined in the previous decades, the presentation of love could be rewritten in the 90s with the intent of indoctrinating the upcoming generation to embrace the perverted and abominable acts that had at one time been unacceptable to this society.

The attempt to redefine the very nature and purpose of love had been accomplished. Morally, the Church in most cases has been desensitized by its exposure to the various perverted images that have been erected through motion picture, music, and art, while the general public has become more tolerant to that which is indeed dishonorable and offensive to common decency. The casualties have not only been the sanity and soundness that morality often brings to chaotic environments, but the family unit. Without a proper perspective of love, the concept of healthy families has become more foreign. If the family is not healthy, neither will a nation remain strong. Nations are only as great or strong as the moral fiber that defines and holds the family unit together.

This brings us to this decade. As we embark on 2010, the darkness that looms before us is frightening. Without morality and healthy families, many people are beginning to realize that as a people and a nation we have lost our way. The price we are about to pay for being complacent about righteousness and tolerant of wickedness has taken a grave toll on everything that this nation once regarded or held as being precious and necessary for its very survival. A revolution of sorts is brewing. However, people must come back to center, back to their roots to once again get their proper bearings.

The one group that probably needs to get its bearings the most is the Church that Jesus Christ died for. Instead of resisting the flood, many in the Christian realm have allowed it to sweep them into the popular fads and movements of the time, especially in such areas as to what constitutes love. The thinking of some of the individuals is that as long as you adjust or somehow tack Christ onto something, it will become adequate or acceptable no matter how base, profane, or perverted it may be.

The question is, how can anyone who has even a slight inkling as to the character of God and His Word, which I might add clearly refutes such a concept regarding such subjects as God's love, buy such an insipid conclusion? The truth is we can adjust anything we want to our particular way of thinking. For example in the area of love the typical thinking usually runs along this line, "Since God loves me, it is only

33

logical that He would want me to be happy." Where did such a conclusion come from? You will not find it in Scripture, but it can clearly be seen in the world's attitude in regards to life.

At the crux of salvation is the matter of God's love, but at the crux of the problem in much of the Church, is people's perception of what constitutes God's love. Sadly, much of the professing Church's perception of God's love is based on the world's presentation. Either, God's love is considered from a worldly premise as to how it will look or affect something, or it has been adjusted into a worldly understanding that is unrealistic and self-centered. However, God's love clearly stands separate from the base, profane, and lustful appearance that the world has presented in regard to it. In comparison to God's love, there is no real substance or quality in the world's love. It is contrary to the quality of character of God's love. It is self-serving, sentimental, fickle, temporary, and even hateful and cruel if unrequited.

If the Church is going to endure the times it is living in, it better come back to center as to the truths of God. This includes possessing a proper perspective of God's love.

As I have stated, in the 70s I witnessed some pastors and teachers trying to define God's love. You could tell that they wanted it to stand distinct from the various presentations inspired by ignorance and the world. Did they succeed in accomplishing the task? Granted, I walked away from such teachings with the understanding that God's love is not only different from the other types of love a person might experience, but it is far superior. However, I had no idea in what way His love was superior. Granted, I had learned the different Greek words to describe the different types of love such as the love one would have for the brethren, the love a mother has for her children, or agape love which is the type of godly love that we as believers should possess towards God and one another.

It was clear to me there was a difference between the types of love we may have for different individuals and things, but in most cases they were nothing but words that were backed up by a few examples. How do we get a hold of God's love? The examples I had were in regard to how man can love, but how does God's love compare to man's personal understanding or expression of it? How will such love feel, act, or express itself? It is not enough to know something, you must experience it. There must be a point where a matter or subject ceases to be considered from the limited premise of personal understanding, and it becomes revelation to one's spirit that will trump or revolutionize man's best to embrace what is excellent, distinct, and superior.

My study of the concept of love brought some interesting contrast. In the Greek language, you could tell the philosophers of that time were also trying to describe the different types of love that people experienced. As you go through the various words to describe these different types of love man could experience, you get a sense that the translators of the Scriptures wanted to clearly distinguish them as well. Personally, I was a bit amazed at the different takes of love the Greek language distinguished as a means to describe them. When you consider man's love in *Strong's Exhaustive Concordance of the Bible,* the definition of the different Greek words goes from numbers 5360 to 5389. The one word commonly attached to these different types of love was the word "fondness." In the different meanings you could see where love clearly served as a noun to describe an affection. In other such cases, love was presented as a noun in order to serve as the base or source of a response towards something, but it also had other words that served as pronouns. These pronouns also serve as a motivating factor behind how a person will express it. When love turns into active expression, then it becomes a verb.

This full array of love can be clearly seen in God's love. There is a difference between the love _of_ God (noun), the type of love _because_ of God (adjective), and how His love _expresses_ (verb) itself. For example, because of the love _of_ God, He directed it towards love _for_ mankind, and _expressed_ it through sacrifice of His Son. Clearly, whatever the base or premise that serves as our source and understanding of love will determine where we place it and how we respond. We cannot have a love _for_ God until we first possess the love _of_ God. If we do not have the base of God's love, our premise as to how we _express_ our love will come from the world's idea of it and not God.

Since the word "fondness" was a word attached to man's love, it would serve our purpose well to understand it. When I consider a word, I search for intent. I am into terminology when it comes to words. Since I constantly write, I work with them all day. My intent is not to just know a bunch of words, but to understand them in a way where I can effectively express myself in relationship to what I want to effectively communicate to others. Interestingly enough, the Greeks even had a word for my fondness or "love" for words. Since I do not know how to insert the accent marks on the computer, I will simply show you how the Greek word that describes my fondness for words is spelled, "philologos."[1]

This fondness can also be directed towards obtaining something such as wisdom. Therefore, a fondness for wisdom could produce its own "word" to best describe the end results or product of such wisdom. For example, from the Greek word that identifies a "fondness" for wisdom comes the popular word, "philosophy."

This brings us back to the concept concerning my fondness for words. Words will cause some type of association or picture in our minds based on the premise we have of them. For example, what do you think of when you hear the word "hate?" What kind of associations or pictures immediately came to your mind? These associations or pictures are going to determine what kind of frame of reference with which you will regard the word "hate" when you hear it, as well as the conclusion you will end up drawing concerning the text in which it has been attached or associated with. As the saying goes, "A man persuaded against his opinion is of the same opinion still."

Until the premise or intent of a matter is changed, the mind will never be changed. Our understanding of a matter will always start from the same perspective or picture. If you change the premise of a word, you will first have to change the intent of it, thereby, enlarging or changing the picture or image that is in place. Clearly, people can be conditioned or indoctrinated in regard to how they interpret something when they hear a word.

It is important to point out that premise can be quite hard to change. In a way premise serves as our nice, neat little box of knowledge and wisdom. Based on what we think we know, assuming we understand it, and presuming there is no way we can be wrong about a matter, this box is what often serves as our encapsulated premise or source of evaluation. It is from this premise we will always confirm what we think we know to be true, while assuming we cannot be wrong, and presuming that anyone who disagrees with us must be wrong. Proverbs 16:2 best describes this dichotomy, "All the ways of a man are clean in his own eyes, but the LORD weigheth the spirits."

"Intent" has to do with the spirit of something. Spirit is what will ultimately create the environment in which something will operate, as

---

[1]   Strong's Exhaustive Concordance of the Bible, #5378

well as what will motivate or propel individuals in a certain direction. Have you ever heard a person say, "If you can prove me wrong, than I will agree with you?" You get all of your facts lined up and present it to the individual, but for some reason he or she can't see how it would prove personal error or deviation from what is already perceived by him or her as being true. It is because such individuals are often blinded by their premise that they are unable to see any other reality. Jesus referred to such a premise as darkness.[2]

People prefer or insist on their own particular darkness or reality.[3] Obviously, to change a person's perception, the intent or spirit in which he or she regards a matter must first change. Without first changing the intent, everything will pretty much stay intact.

When I think about the word "fondness" I not only perceive it to be fleshly, but, making it inferior or unpredictable in character or substance. Granted, it might begin from the premise of liking someone or something that will invoke some type of affection, causing what is referred to as a "soft spot" in the heart for that which has caught the person's attention. Since there is a "soft spot" in the heart there will be some type of partiality shown to that which now has some emotional attachment being directed at it. At this point one can attach the concept of having "love" for the individual or that which stands at the center of his or her attention and affections.

Another word associated with being fond of someone is the word "weak." It points to having a weak or vulnerable spot for someone. Such a meaning seems harmless or sentimental enough, but the reality is that weakness also points to the aspect that wherever it abides, abuses can also take advantage of a situation. Through the years I have seen people use the concept of love to emotionally and physically abuse someone. With this in mind we must consider if we can regard God's love from the premise of "fondness?" Does it produce the type of presentation that would fairly represent God's love? Is God simply fond of us, or would there have to be more to His type of love for Him to display it in such a powerful way?

---

[2] Matthew 6:22-23

[3] John 3:18-21

Let us now go one step further in the matter of man's love to bring to light the confusion surrounding the world's presentation of it and how it seems to be influencing the Church. Man can become fond of anything. Remember there are various words to describe this fondness. We see where man can be fond of others. In this case he can show himself to be friendly or courteous, which can be translated into brotherly love. Man can become very fond of a spouse, which is not only different from other forms of fondness, but operates in a different environment. There is actually a fondness for mankind that can express itself through benevolence. There is the fondness man attaches to money or silver, which often produces greed and idolatry.

There is also a fondness or love we have for ourselves and for pleasure, as well as God. However, we have been told to deny ourselves of personal adoration. And, as for being both lovers of self and pleasure, these two types of love will be clearly preferred to God in the last days, causing perilous times.[4] When it comes to such fondness, it clearly can become a person's pursuit and obsession that can literally possess his or her will, affections, and desires. Clearly, in this context such love is of the soul, making it fleshly, idolatrous, pagan, and treacherous.

This brings us to the source, influence, or platform from which fleshly love operates. It is the world. The world provides the avenues that will formulate the ideas of love, influences us as to what we might love, and serves as the platform in how such love might be expressed. We know that those who belong to the world will hate Jesus and His servants, and that the spirit of the world works in the children of disobedience.[5]

Believers may be in the world, but they do not belong to it. There will be no agreement that can possibly be found with it. James 4:4 tells us that if those who claim to be Christians, but are friends with the world, will be considered enemies of God. In essence, they are guilty of prostituting themselves with the world, committing spiritual adultery or harlotry.

To come into unholy agreement with anything physically or spiritually is to commit fornication. Fornication is considered an abomination to God. It is a sin that is committed against the sanctity or well-being of the

---

4 2 Timothy 3:1-4
5 John 7:7; 17:14-18; Ephesians 2:2

body that will end in destruction. The Apostle Paul warned that if a man defiles the temple of his body, God will destroy him.[6]

The Apostle John tells us the world is designed in such a way that it is capable of entangling our soul in three ways: through the lusts of the flesh, the pride of life, and the lusts of the eyes. The apostle's exhortation is clear that we are not to love the world or the things of the world. If we possess such love for the world, the love of the Father will be absent.[7] Hence enters this exhortation, "And the world passeth away, and the lust of it; but he that doeth the will of God abideth forever" (1 John 2:17).

We know that God's love does not find its source in the flesh or in the world. It is not soulish, nor is it like the world in its idolatrous or pagan ways. Granted, there can be determination, passion, and unwavering devotion found in His love, but there will be no fleshly, moral deviation or treachery in it.

The Apostle John made this statement in regard to God's love, "Behold, what manner of love the Father hath bestowed upon us, that we should be called the sons of God; therefore, the world knoweth us not because it knew him not" (1 John 3:1). The apostle is telling us to take note of the type of love the Father has clearly shown or displayed towards us. We must ask ourselves, what manner or sort of love could the Father possibly show us beyond what He has already displayed?

"Manner" points to way. The Father's way in which He displayed His love through His Son is beyond description or measure. The mode in which He established His love reaches beyond any fleshly or worldly expression. The method of love which He used to penetrate the darkness of man's indifference, anger, bitterness, and hatred reveals how man's fleshly, self-serving love pales in comparison. God's style of approaching all situations in love is incomprehensible. The way in which our Lord has conducted and behaved Himself because of love deserves an appropriate response on our part. This is why the apostle also made this statement, "We love him, because he first loved us" (1 John 4:19).

What does the love of God say about His character? What makes it different than man's love? The answer is simple: God is love.[8] He is

---

[6]   1 Corinthians 3:16-17; 6:15-20

[7]   1 John 2:15-17

[8]   1 John 4:8

the essence of love, the substance of love, the reality of love, and the example of love. Everything He does is according to, disciplined by His love, and in line to His love. All that He is, is a natural extension or expression of His love. He loves because He can do nothing else. And, it is because He could do nothing else that He sent His Son to die on the cross. However, this love is not of this world and it cannot be found outside of Him.

This brings us to man. Man is not love, rather in his unregenerate state he is a base creature. There is no real source or base of real love in his makeup. For man, the idea of love becomes a choice and preference, as well as a learned behavior. It can be a fleshly, idolatrous pursuit, a fickle emotion, an undisciplined affection, a raging obsession, a consuming jealousy, and an unreasonable notion. It is often based on self-serving ways that can only produce perverted desires and actions. It can be noble about selfishness, such as being forgiving and understandable towards certain things. But, such notions find their base in foolishness, The selfish motives behind the façade makes such nobility nothing more than a mere front to cover up just how wicked, conditional, and unrealistic such love can be.

Let us consider some of the ways that God's love far exceeds man's concept of it. While man must be compelled by real love to do right, God has commended it towards all men so they might be saved.[9] Man must have a reason to love, but God has made His love available to all who will come and receive it by faith. Man must see how his fondness will personally benefit him, while God can only see what He must do to benefit the well-being of mankind. Man becomes angry and bitter when his love is rejected and withdraws behind a wall of suspicion and despondency. However, when people shun, mock, and reject God's love, His heart breaks for them in their darkness, while His Spirit mourns their lost state. In spite of the blatant rejection of His love, His invitation to come and experience it remains standing, ready to embrace every repentant prodigal child with open arms with forgiveness, reconciliation, and restoration.

Clearly, God so loved the world because He could do nothing else but love what He had created. He so loved mankind that He could do

---

[9]   Romans 5:5-8

nothing else but to provide a solution to address man's true spiritual plight. He so loved that He could do nothing else but to give His best on behalf of every man, woman, and child. He did not give His best because mankind had any value or worth in him, for in his present state he was wretched, lost, and undesirable; rather, He gave His best because that is who He is. He is love personified.

For this reason man hides behind God's love, sings about it with enthusiasm, talks about it in glorious ways, takes advantage of it, consoles himself because of it, and uses it to cover up or justify questionable, moral deviate ways. However, the reality is that if man does not possess God's love as his source, it is because it is not in him. The Apostle John confirmed this reality,

> Beloved, let us love one another; for love is of God, and everyone that loveth is born of God, and knowth God. He that loveth not knoweth not God; for God is love . . . No man hath seen God at any time. If we love one another, God dwelleth in us, and his love is perfected in us (1 John 4:7-8, 12)

What manner of love do you possess? Is it a fleshly, worldly love, or is it the love of God? The answer to this question will ultimately reveal your spiritual status.

CHARITY

One of the things that I have noticed through the years is that man does not know how to love. It is really not in him to love in an excellent way. Granted, it is in him to be very fleshly in his ideas, interpretations, and responses of love, but if he is not born again with the Spirit of the Living God, he will lack genuine love. This puts man into a very precarious situation.

Man was created with the capacity to love in a proper way and the means to express it, but when Adam rebelled, it left a terrible spiritual vacuum within man's soul as the Spirit withdrew His very air, breath, or presence from the inner tabernacle of man. Since the breath or Spirit of God removed himself from the premise of man's inner being, man now would have to rediscover what he had truly lost in his rebellion. One of the things he lost was the source, essence, and presence of pure, unfeigned love.

On the other hand, man still had the capacity in his spirit in which God's love could abide, and the means within his soul to express it, but he would have to choose to love God according to His character. This is why we are commanded to love God and others because it is a matter of choice to do so.[10] It must be clearly noted that to love as God loves is contrary to who we are in our wretched state. Fleshly and worldly love is based on conditions, meritorious worth, and often self-serving agendas. Therefore, we must choose what premise we are going to consider and approach the matter of love, and where, as well as how, we are going to direct such love.

Choices bring us to the will, intellect, and emotions of the soul. These three aspects of the soul serve as the necessary means or tools to rediscover what Adam had lost in the garden. These aspects of the soul will also determine how we are going to express a particular virtue, such as love to those around us. For example, man would be considering what manner of love in which he would approach something, choose what form he would embrace of it, and determine how his affections would express it. This reminds us of the free will or choice of man. It is for this reason, man has ended up with a variety of choices as to where, what, or how he would bestow what he ultimately considers love upon that which has caught his attention and affections.

For man to posses God's love is not only a choice but it is a learned behavior. Our idea of love not only determines the creature we become, but the attitude and conduct we develop towards others. Clearly, the ideas we initially develop or have of such affection is based on what we have seen, heard, or experienced. For example, people have labeled romantic notions, emotional games, lusts, and perverted practices as being love. Yet, all of these play off of fleshly sentiment and worldly presentations. It is only as people learn to love that they grow in the ability to properly love others. Obviously, the main reason for the high rate of divorces is due to the fact that most couples never get beyond the idea of love to really learn how to properly love his or her spouse. Such love remains self-serving and surface.

---

[10]   Mark 12:29-30

We know love is a noun. It can serve as a name for a strong affection, feeling, sentiment, or attraction. We know that there are other words that serve as adjectives. In the case of the word "love" I think of each adjective as being a pro-active noun. In other words, the noun can take on action at any time in order to express itself. Love is ultimately meant to express itself in some way. It is not within its nature to remain neutral. It must make itself known. We clearly can see this in God's love when we consider Jesus' sacrifice. Perhaps it is for this very reason we read these strong words from the Apostle John in his first epistle,

> But whosoever hath this world's good, and seeth his brother have need, and shutteth up his bowels of compassion from him, how dwelleth the love of God in him? My little children, let us not love in word, neither in tongue, but in deed and in truth (1 John 3:17-18).

Love will express itself. But, what will determine how it will express itself? This brings us to love being a noun. Love actually identifies the state or character of someone's commitment. What does Jesus' death on the cross tell you about God's commitment towards each of us?

Some people have incorrectly interpreted God's love to be unconditional or unrestricted so that they can hide themselves behind it or console themselves with it. Perhaps they define God's love as being unconditional because man's love is conditional. Due to its lust, selfishness, and worldly influence, man's love proves to be possessive, obsessive, abusive, demanding, manipulative, and unrealistic. In their mind, God's love must be the opposite of man's best attempts to love. Since God loves them He will overlook questionable attitudes and deviant behavior. However, Scripture does not bear this out. God's love does not ignore sin nor can He bestow it on those who spurn Him or His Word.[11] The truth of the matter is that the only place where man can receive God's love in such a wretched state is at the cross of Jesus. God so displayed His love for one purpose and that is to save man. You might witness His love in others, benefit from it some way, or witness its dedication, but none of these encounters mean that His love has saved

---

[11]   1 Corinthians 13:6

or changed a person's spiritual status. People must personally possess this love to be identified with His salvation.

A correct way to describe God's love displayed on the cross is that it has been made *available* to all who will come to Him by faith seeking His salvation. It can only be *bestowed* on those who are open and prepared to receive it. His love can only be *experienced* by those who obey Him, and it will be naturally *extended* towards others for His glory.[12]

What word would describe the character of God's love? As for man, there are many types of love, but when you look at words associated with God's love or the Greek form of it, which is referred to as "agape" in the *Strong's Exhaustive Concordance,* it only takes up two numbers.[13] The idea of God's love is that it points to love in a social or moral sense. The social aspect of love is towards man and the moral sense has to do with the godly disciplines that would identify it to God. It would also point to moral obligation and accountability. The nouns that can be used in place of the word "love" are charity and benevolence, the adjective of it would be affectionate, and the action of it would be best expressed by the actual word "love."

Before we can understand how God's love would be expressed in and through our lives we must understand its origin or state from which it will operate. The word used to describe such a state is "charity".

What does charity say about God's love? It is offered, but not earned. It comes out of a disposition of having good-will towards a matter, not because someone or something has gained the attention or attraction of it. The idea of affection being attached to God's love implies affecting someone's attitude in order to produce the proper behavior. It is also meant to affect us in a beneficial and eternal way as a means to cause an excellent attitude and response from us. The proper attitude would be that of worship and the response on our part would be love itself.

It is important to understand that hard-working Americans hate the idea of being considered charity cases. Yet, spiritually we all start out in need of God's charity. It is not until a person humbles him or herself and acknowledges his or her true spiritual state that God can become charitable towards him or her and give the gift of eternal life. The truth is

---

[12]   John 13:35; 14:15-21; Hebrews 5:8-9
[13]   #25-26

Jesus' great sacrifice on the cross was a matter of God's charity being extended to each of us. Clearly, it was the intention of those who were translating the intent behind God's love to distinguish it from the base, worldly form of man's love to communicate such a reality.

When we think of a state of something, we realize it will affect our attitude about how we receive or view it. For example, what kind of attitude would a person adopt if he or she viewed God's love as being unconditional verses it being a matter of charity? The intent of these two words no doubt are poles apart from each other, and the attitude in which a person would approach God's love would be likewise.

Here lies the crux of the problem in regard to the actual presentation and understanding of God's love. If the intent is wrong, it can strip God's love of its real purpose, water down its authority, and redefine how it expresses itself. Instead of walking in godly love, people would be redefining it according to their attitude towards it. If you redefine the essence of God's character, you will end up erecting another god. Most likely you will like your own god, but such an idol will be lifeless and powerless to save you. Instead of complimenting God's love, man's understanding of it ends up opposing it or using it in a perverted way.

Because of people's erroneous ideas of God's love, they end up stripping Him of His other attributes since they cannot bring them together with their concept of His love. For example, God is holy, and because of His holiness He hates sin, turns His back on iniquity, holds people accountable for transgression, chastises rebellious children, and will judge all unrighteousness. Therefore, how do people who hold to the perception that God's love is unconditional handle the concept of His holiness? Certainly, God is not going to ignore, adjust, or pamper people in rebellion, for it would require Him to cease to be who He is. He cannot, nor will He, cease to be a holy God.

The Bible reveals how love inspires or works with or through His other attributes. Let us consider this in light of His holiness. It tells us in Hebrews 12:6 that the Lord chastens and scourges those whom He loves. It goes on to say this in Hebrews 12:10, "For they verily for a few days chastened us after their own pleasure (earthly father), but he (God) for our profit, that we might be partakers of his holiness." (Parentheses added.) Why is it so important that we partake of that pure, undefiled aspect of our God? Hebrews 12:14 warns us that without holiness, we will not see the Lord.

God will never step down into our pigpens because of some perverted illusion about love. Rather, He will do all He can to provide the means of always bringing us higher to experience the excellence of His love. Genuine love always desires the best for those it cares about, and will never be content to see those it honors accepting less.

This brings us to the character of God's love. When the word "charity" is used to put another face or identity on God's love, it is to reveal the state in which it will operate from. God's love is disciplined by what it is. It is charitable. And, if you are acquainted with the King James Version of the Bible, you will also know where to find the disciplines of godly love that describes this state. It is found in 1 Corinthians 13.

I remember as a new Christian reading 1 Corinthians 13. I could not argue the beauty of it, but the word "charity" confused me. How could God's love be a matter of charity? In light of the powerful presentation of John 3:16, I did not feel that charity expressed the passion or the actual extent or the sacrifice that was displayed on the cross. It was not until years later that I realized that the word "charity" reveals the state of His love that ended in the manifestation of His great sacrifice. Upon understanding this, I realized that this is the state that must be present in my life if I am going to serve as the extension of His love towards others.

Let us now honestly consider this state with the right view or perspective. Keep in mind, godly love cannot remain neutral. We will be able to see how the character or disciplines of it should affect our attitude about it and our responses towards others.

The Apostle Paul talked about showing believers the more excellent way of love. In the first three Scriptures of 1 Corinthians 13, the apostle wants to set up the premise of just how excellent God's love is compared to man's best attempts to pursue, possess, or manifest what is acceptable and good. However, if God's love is not part of the equation in the end, such attempts will not be considered significant, acceptable, or worthy. For example, it is not unusual for man to seek that which is unique or spiritual, but in light of God's love it will be nothing more than sounding brass or a tinkling cymbal. Even though he might pursue after that which brings enlightenment and possess insight into all mysteries, without the excellent disciplines of the love of God it will mean nothing. Man may show tremendous sacrifice on behalf of others in light of his devotion and beliefs, but if godly love is missing, there will be no eternal profit in any of it.

Does this not cause you to pause about your attempts to express your inner character or desires in your religious endeavors? How much of our religious activities, involvements, and pursuits would stand as ashes before our Lord, burned up by the fires of His holy altar because His sustaining love is missing from our service to Him and our attitude towards others?

Is the real state of God's love about doing, or possessing some insight or gift? Is it about doing noble deeds with a deep sense of dedication? Or, is God's love about character, about disciplines that reveals an unseen work in the inner man that will consume anything that would not express His love in an unadulterated way?

In 1 Corinthians 13:4-8, we are told that the state of His love possesses longsuffering or patience towards a matter. It is because of love that God displays longsuffering towards the rebellious, with the intent of giving them time to repent before they perish in their sins. Do we have the same longsuffering when it comes towards those who are immature and struggling in their spiritual lives? Are we patient with those who do not serve our purpose or display traits that are personally embarrassing and irritating to us? Are we considerate of those whose very person just plain rubs us the wrong way? Patience clearly is a discipline of genuine love. It is love that so often restrains us from justifying or giving way to impatience towards that which might inconvenience us and seem too insignificant to trifle with. The Apostle Peter clearly reminded us that genuine love covers a multitude of offenses caused by the selfish, immature, and irritating ways of others.[14]

In the state of charity, kindness is always available to be shown to others. In this text such kindness points to being useful due to benevolence.[15] To make ourselves available to complement and benefit others points to moving past any comfort or convenience zones. Would such kindness express itself in lifting the unbearable burdens of others when we have the means to do so? Perhaps, it even means going the extra mile for someone who could or would never repay us or give us recognition for our deeds.[16]

---

[14] 1 Peter 4:8; 2 Peter 3:9
[15] Strong's Exhaustive Concordance;#5541
[16] Matthew 5:41-42; Galatians 6:2

To have the inner state of charity would mean that a person will not envy the goodness shown others because he or she would rather rejoice with those who are being blessed.[17] In such a state, a person will not exalt him or herself because he or she understands that one must not easily forget his or her own humble beginnings. Likewise, he or she was at one time poor, wretched, lost, and in need of God's charity.

In such a state of charity people will not take pride in what they know or can do. They have discovered that unless it is inspired by the very throne of God, it means nothing. And, since all matters come from the throne, only God deserves the proper recognition and glory for it. As 1 Corinthians 1:29 clearly states that no flesh will glory in His presence.

Love that comes from charity will never behave itself in a way that would be considered unbecoming or a reproach to God, or become bitter to the souls of others. It is pure in its motive and sincerely concerned for others. For this reason the Apostle Paul gave this instruction, "Let love be without dissimulation . . ." (Romans 12:9a). "Being without dissimulation" points to a love that is void of hypocrisy.

Charity is not in the business of being self-serving or always seeking the means to benefit itself. Those who are coming from the premise of being charitable do not respond in such a fashion to feel good about themselves. Charity allows a person to liberally and freely give or serve without conditions attached to his or her action. The Apostle Paul describes the attitude believers should have to such giving, "Every man according as he purposeth in his heart, so let him give, not grudgingly, or of necessity; for God loveth a cheerful giver" (2 Corinthians 9:7).

Another beautiful aspect of the state of charity is that it is not easily provoked by the attitude of others, nor does it harbor suspicion towards others. Charity is not politically motivated. It does not look back to see how impressed others are, nor does it regard whether its kindness is being properly recognized. Its focus is pure in what and why it is involved in a matter. As a result, it does not have to transpose any deviance or evil on others who fail to respond or who may lack it. In many cases such individuals who possess deviance in their character often transpose their wicked motives and ways onto others around them, causing strife, division, and discord.

---

[17]   Romans 12:15

Charity's main desire is to see that others are clearly going to benefit. The Apostle Paul describes how such charity will be expressed towards others in Romans 12:10, "Be kindly affectioned one to another with brotherly love, in honor preferring one another." Those who operate from the premise of true charity are not looking to come out on top for such a state is too busy preferring the well-being of others to its personal welfare. For example, Jesus did not give up the glories of heaven so He could lord His authority, power, and work over others. He came as a servant to those who were servants of sin. He preferred each of our well-being over His own. If He had not, He would have never gone to the cross. It is for this reason that charity will never rejoice in iniquity, but in the truth that sets the captive free from the harsh bondages and darkness of this present age.

Since charity possesses a virtuous character, it will bear much in good faith, it will believe that goodness will ultimately win out, and it will walk in expectation that what comes forth out of such disciplines will endure the test of time. The hope of charity will ensure that all that comes from its godly state will remain standing when the best of man and the world falls in disarray and destruction; for, such love will never fail in its purpose or endeavors.

It is true that for each of us in our present finite state we are a work in progress when it comes to establishing a charitable state within us. We can only know in part about the matters of eternity, and we can only see in a mirror that is shrouded by our various limitations. These limitations remind us that in our present state, we are unable to encompass what is complete. Even though we can only know in part, there is a time coming when all matters of heaven will be made known to us as we are brought to perfection.

When we each come to this place of completeness, we will discover that what remains standing will be a product of genuine faith, a reality of the unending hope of heaven, and the incredible, enduring character and work of God's charity. When we realize that we will be discovering how the grace distributed according to God's charity has truly benefitted our lives, we will come to one distinct conclusion. All that is attached to faith, hope, and charity will forever abide, but the greatest of these three will forever resonate through the corridors of our spirits as we are reminded throughout eternity that "God so loved each of us, He gave His only begotten Son."

Charity indeed offered the best, while faith received the most excellent way in which it was offered, and hope caused our downtrodden spirits to look beyond this present world to see the glory of it all. But, it will be obvious to each of us that if it were not for the fact that love Personified possessed the nature or state of charity to offer His mercy and extend His grace, we would never know the gift of His life, the beauty of His Person, and experience the incredible majesty of His glory. That, my friend, clearly verifies Paul's verdict that charity is the greatest of the three virtues that will remain abiding in the eternal halls of glory. This blessed reality will come to fruition when each of us come face to face with His incredible love in the lovely face of our Lord and Savior Jesus Christ.

BENEVOLENCE

Charity is the spirit and premise we must begin from and the state in which we must operate in to ensure that we express God's love. It is from the spirit, premise, and state of charity that we will develop a proper attitude of love: that of benevolence.

What do you think of when you hear the word "benevolence?" I have thought about this word. Words produce not only pictures but feelings. They can give you a sense of something that far exceeds mental understanding. In a sense they connect the mental understanding to the emotional aspect as to what manner something must be expressed.

For example, I can be charitable without any emotional awareness or sense as to what I am doing. Granted, I might feel good about myself afterwards, but up until the action, charity can be indifferent, lifeless, and without real significance other than the fact that it is the right thing to do or a matter of duty. However, a word like "benevolence" has the capacity to make some type of emotional connection between the state in which something resides and the action in which it might express itself. It will make it a personal matter that will result in something actually being experienced in such a way that it becomes truth, living, and significant to the inner man.

What is the significance for man to experience the spirit of charity? It comes down to disposition. Our disposition is greatly affected through experiencing the reality of something such as charity. It will greatly affect the attitude we adopt about it. Attitude will determine the type of affection or passion we will attach to the action of something.

When I think of benevolence, I think of kindness, temperance, and well-being. Because of the sense of kindness, my actions will be tempered by what I must do to ensure the well-being of someone else. Clearly, we can do various things in the name of charity, but will they be based on sensitivity as to what is truly needed to ensure the best in a situation? The concept of benevolence will ensure the integrity of charity by tempering the correct response.

God so loved that He showed His benevolence. The kindness He extended towards mankind required Him to offer a sacrifice to ensure our redemption. Clearly, God's action was tempered by what it would mean for man to have spiritual well-being. It would be what was needed for man to be saved. It would require the most excellent sacrifice; and, it was for this reason that God could do no less than present such a sacrifice if He was to secure our salvation.

We are told that God counted the cost for our redemption.[18] If you think about it He counted the cost of our redemption in the courts of heaven and paid it on an old rugged cross in the midst of the barren wilderness of mankind. Jesus declared from the cross that "It was finished." In other words, the price for our redemption was paid in full.

When you consider benevolence according to God's action, it is true that He could do no less than pay the sacrificial price, but once He did pay the price, there was nothing more He could do from that point on to add to our salvation. He did what was necessary or reasonable. Because He is love Personified, He took responsibility for us. Due to His charitable state He could do no less than pay the price in full, and because of His benevolent attitude He made it available to all mankind.

What kind of attitude will benevolence develop in us when charity is in place? Benevolence not only will do what is right in a matter, but it will do so knowing that it is its reasonable service to take such action.

People may do grand things to look or feel good, but in the scheme of things action that comes out of the state of true charity has nothing to do with how it will make the one extending it feel or look. Charity keeps the integrity of what we do because it is a matter of benevolence.

---

[18]   Luke 14:28-32

Benevolence recognizes what needs to be done and responds accordingly. It does what is necessary, right, and required to ensure the end results of a matter is sufficient and complete. It is for this reason that genuine charity never becomes an *unbearable burden* to the one who is extending it.

God paid the highest and most excellent price for our salvation. If anyone could act as if charity is the greatest burden of all, instead of a matter of true benevolence, it would be God. He paid the price knowing that many would reject His love. He paid it knowing many would prefer their hatred to His salvation. He knew all of this, but He still commended His love towards each of us in our wretched condition.[19] It was not an unbearable burden to Him, it was the least He could do because of His benevolence.

God's charity is eternal, but it is benevolence that makes His charity exceptional in its conduct. God's love required a sacrifice, the very sacrifice of His only begotten Son. He willingly paid it. We do not see Him lament it. We do not see Him use it as some platform to bring attention to Himself. He simply did it because He could do no less.

As His people we must somehow get this revelation of God's love in our very spirits. How many of us perceive our life and commitment to God as nothing but a burden? Our responsibility to do what is right in regard to others as unbearable, unreasonable, and impossible? How can I love my enemy in word and deed when there is injustice? How can I go the extra distance for someone when there is no desire to do so? The question is, why would I do such things that appear as being foolish and vain? However, Jesus made it quite clear that greeting your brethren does not set your love apart from the heathen who show the same type of regard. Godly love enables us to love our enemies, bless those who curse us, do good to them who hate us, and pray for the people who despitefully use us and persecute us. He goes onto say this, "That ye may be the children of your Father, who is in heaven; for he maketh his sun to rise on the evil and on the good, and sendeth rain on the just and on the unjust" (Matthew 5:45).

The attitude of benevolence can only do right in regard to others. Many times reasonable service ends in sacrifice, but it is never

---

[19]   Romans 5:8

considered in such a light. It does not keep a personal tally with the idea that it must be paid back down the line in some way. The Apostle Paul put it correctly when he beseeched us to present our bodies as a living sacrifice, which would be our reasonable service. He went on to state that such a sacrifice was necessary to prove what is the good (beneficial), acceptable (adequate), and perfect (just right) will of God in regard to our service to Him and others.[20]

In a way, benevolence is the wage or debt we must be prepared to pay at all times. We do not regard what it will cost us because it is the wage that is required to ensure that what we do is adequate to pay the full debt. God's love did not go half way, three-fourths of the way, or even 99% of the way. Rather, it went all the way to a cross and into a grave. It was complete in its commitment and action. Perhaps it is from this premise that the Apostle Paul penned these instructions, "Owe no man any thing, but love one another; for he that loveth another hath fulfilled the law" (Romans 13:8).

God's benevolence is so excellent that it fulfills the Law, ultimately lifting us above its judgment, and bringing us under the auspice of a better law; that of the Spirit of life in Christ Jesus.[21] It is from the premise of charity and the disposition of benevolence that the fruit of the Spirit takes root, thrives, and grows. His fruit proves beneficial to others, acceptable to God, and perfect in its ability to bring about eternal affects. In fact, all virtues of the fruit of the Spirit become the natural expression or extension of the premise of charity and the disposition of benevolence.

Benevolence is what establishes the right attitude in which the fruit of the Spirit will be cultivated and brought forth in our lives. It is the fruit others will taste as God's love is properly expressed. Most of us know what the fruit of the Spirit entails.[22] But, let us consider it from the attitude of benevolence.

The base of the fruit of the Spirit is love. It is the premise (charity), attitude (benevolence), and active expression of love. Without this love, the rest of the virtues of the fruit of the Spirit will never be cultivated or brought forth. It is important to point out that the virtues of the fruit of

---

[20]   Romans 12:1-2

[21]   Romans 8:2

[22]   Galatians 5:22-23

the Spirit speak of the nature, character, and work of the Holy Spirit. He could not produce something in us that was not within His makeup and ways. These virtues not only work the very life of Christ into us, but they become the expression of His life toward others.

It is for this reason that godly, inspired love distinguishes the real disciple of Jesus. Jesus said it best when He stated, "A new commandment I give unto you, that ye love one another; as I have loved you, that ye also love one another. By this shall all men know that ye are my disciples, if ye have love one to another" (John 13:34). We are known or identified by our fruits, not by our religious affiliation or doctrine. If God's love is not the source and base of our life, the right tone and emphasis will be missing in what we do. And, if there is any fruit that has any similarities to the fruit of the Spirit, it will prove substandard or bitter to those who partake of it.

Joy comes out of the satisfaction and contentment that is present in God's love. It is complete and fulfilling. There is no deviation or uncertainty in it. His love took responsibility for our well-being. Out of the action of love came salvation. How many times have the Scriptures made reference to the joy of our salvation?

After the satisfaction of joy comes the state of peace. However, this peace cannot occur unless we are secure in God's love. Benevolence desires to show kindness to ensure the well-being or inner peace of man, but man is often at war with God as he opposes, rebels, and defies His authority. The desired security that so many seek will be missing if they are not following after the ways of righteousness. Hebrews 12:11 makes reference to the peaceable fruit of righteousness. As believers, we are instructed to follow righteousness, faith, charity, and peace with other believers.[23] We have Paul's words in Romans 14:17 that states that the kingdom of God is not meat and drink, but righteousness, peace, and joy in the Holy Spirit.

Long-suffering follows peace in the list of virtues that comprise the fruit of the Spirit. Benevolence is naturally long-suffering. It has no selfish agenda or self-serving reason behind its commitment or actions. Since it is simply doing what is reasonable and required, there is no pretense as to its goal in a matter.

---

[23]   2 Timothy 2:22

It is because of long-suffering or patience that benevolence is able to see a matter through to the end. Such patience is what tempers benevolence as it quietly, and with confidence, diligently works toward the desired results. According to the Apostle Paul, it is patience that ensures a person will experience the hope or end result of the matter.[24]

Gentleness follows patience. "Gentleness" implies kindness, but it will not just be any "old" kindness. Rather, it is a kindness that shows itself to be useful in an excellent way. It clearly will have character, as well as display a certain demeanor.[25] King David stated that it was the very gentleness of God that made him great in his inner character.[26]

Kindness of this type of character is often attached to the attitude we should have towards our brethren in the Lord. It is not unusual to read Scriptural references to, or the words "brotherly kindness" in such Scriptures as Joshua 2:12, Romans 12:10, and 2 Peter 1:7. Such kindness is associated with the word loving kindness and will be followed by that which will bring us to a charitable state of mind towards others.

Next in line in the fruit of the Spirit is goodness. According to *Strong's Concordance,* this goodness points to what is going to be beneficial to others.[27] For something to be beneficial it must be done well.

At the current writing of this presentation, I am in a season of my spiritual life that I find comfort in knowing that our loving God does all things well. There is no underlying treacherous motive in our Lord that will prove to be bitter down the line. There is no moral deviation in what He does that will prove to be destructive in the end. Everything He does in us, and on our behalf, is to benefit our life in Him. In challenging times, we must sometimes cling to this reality. It does not matter if something does not make sense. God's love or benevolence towards each of us will never sway from the commitment He has made because of His great love to save us.

Faith follows goodness in the fruit of the Spirit. When I looked this word up in *Strong's* to ensure the integrity of its intent in this text,

---

[24] Romans 5:3-5
[25] Strong's Exhaustive Concordance#5544
[26] 2 Samuel 22:36; Psalm 18:35
[27] #19

it pointed to the concepts of profession, truth, reliance, and fidelity.[28] In essence, it points to the truth that no matter what comes forth from the benevolence of the work of His Spirit in us and through us to others, it will be faithful in character, purpose, and action to its original profession of godliness. There will be no unholy mixture, selfish motive, or perverted intention, for it will remain pure in what it is and in all that it does.

Such an attitude of benevolence has been instructed to those who are married. The need for faithful, enduring benevolence to ensure well-being in a person and relationship is what is greatly missing in the self-centered and self-serving marriage relationships of today. The Apostle Paul gave this instruction in 1 Corinthians 7:3, "Let the husband render unto the wife due benevolence; and likewise also, the wife unto the husband."

Meditate upon the implication of such benevolence being present in marriages. Could you imagine how it would change the face of this relationship that is now under siege from every direction? There are those who want to pervert its purity by redefining it. We have the government which is now involved in trying to change the moral face of it. We have various forms of selfishness that is willing to sacrifice the sanctity of it to justify fleshly lust, fornication, and adultery. Then, many have the audacity to blame failure of it on the institution of it, rather than the abuse that is taking place in the name of this relationship.

This brings us to the next ingredient of the fruit of the Spirit: that of meekness. Something cannot be tempered unless it is first under control. Meekness in this text points to all matters of strength being under the control of the Spirit. However, if you consider the different ingredients that make up the fruit of the Spirit, you will realize that each virtue tempers the one that follows it in some way. It will determine how the next ingredient will be focused and/or expressed in our lives. For example, the premise of love will greatly determine the type of joy that is experienced. Abiding joy will establish the peace we experience, while peace will produce patience to endure. Patience will manifest itself in gentleness, while gentleness will ensure goodness. Goodness will show itself in faithfulness, and faithfulness will display meekness.

---

[28]   #4102

Jesus was meek in attitude. As believers we are instructed to follow after meekness, and to instruct those who oppose the Lord in such an attitude to give them time to repent and acknowledge the truth.[29] When meekness is missing, harshness is usually present. Harshness will run over people, unmercifully judge them, and strip them of self-respect. However, meekness denotes that benevolence is truly part of the equation. People who are operating in such an attitude do so out of a sober awareness that words and actions will greatly impact a person as to the type of taste it will leave in his or her mouth. Granted, a person may rail against truth, but if he or she has tasted genuine meekness in the challenge, he or she will also be apt to recognize the personal concern, purity, and possible benefits of such a challenge.

If we are under the Spirit then our life, character, virtues, and ways will be tempered. They will be in line with the character and work of the Spirit, while displaying the disposition and attitude of Christ. Ultimately, they will display the life of Christ, bringing glory to the Father. Such a life will not only display the presence of the Spirit, but will produce fruits unto everlasting life.

It is for this reason we are told that there is no law that can possibly be exercised over the fruit of the Spirit. The fruit of the Spirit takes on its own attitude (Jesus) and its own life (Jesus). It is not subject to the natural laws of the world or the holy Law of God that deals with the sins of the flesh. The fruit is spiritual, and can only be associated with the law of the Spirit of life in Christ Jesus.

In order to benefit from the fullness of this spiritual law of Spirit and life, we must reckon that the flesh has been crucified with the affections and lusts. Death to the old ways allows us to live in the Spirit and follow after His Spirit according to the righteous ways of God.[30] If we are walking in the benevolent ways of God, we will not desire the ways of vainglory that provokes or envies others.

It is time to consider if we possess a benevolent attitude. We can speak of and sing about God's love all we want, but if we do not possess it, we will never be able to walk in it. God did not avail His love so that we could make reference to its greatness. Rather, He made it

---

29   Matthew 11:29; 1 Timothy 6:11; 2 Timothy 2:25
30   Galatians 5:23b-26

available so we could personally experience its greatness so that it would revolutionize our lives, and we would walk in its excellent ways in regard to others.

Do you possess and walk in such love? The fruits of your life will tell on you.

SUBMISSION

Love cannot help but be expressed in some way. This is even true for man's different forms of love. If he pursues his form or idea of love, he will try to experience it, take possession of it, or show some type of response or action towards it even if it has been perverted and expressed negativity towards someone or something such as jealousy. Such attempts are meant to gain the attention, the flattery, or control of what he is pursuing in the name of love.

God's love is no exception. It must express itself in some way. However, it will be contrary to how man might express his love. We have been considering the state and attitude of God's love, but now it is time to come to terms with how it will express itself. Clearly, as we can see in the case of man, love will take on some type of form in order to express itself in a certain way. God's love also took on a form in order to properly express itself. To understand the form it took on, we must consider what Philippians 2:6-8 tells us.

Before Jesus went to the cross to express God's love to the world, He first gave up His capacity as God in order to take upon Himself the form of a servant. "Form" implies to be shaped or molded in a certain way. God so loved us, but He also knew that to express it the way that was necessary, He had to take on a whole new form contrary to His present state. He actually had to take on the form of a servant. This required Him to be fashioned as a man.

In His capacity as God He could not pay the price necessary to redeem man; therefore, He had to take on the disposition of a servant and the shape of a man to pay the price for our souls. Even though such action is beyond our complete comprehension, we can catch glimpses of it that will bring us to an understanding as to the means God had to go to in order to secure our salvation.

This brings us to the form we must take on to ensure that we become the avenue in which God's love will be expressed in service to Him and others. Although we all start out as servants to sin, we need to take on the attitude of a servant if we are going to express the essence of God's love in our service to Him and others.

What is the first aspect that will be made evident by the attitude of a servant? It is simple. We are not here to serve ourselves. Most people are serving the idol of self. Everything will become subservient to this self-serving god for the sake or so-called "personal well-being" of the individual. Such a lifeless god has no concern about anyone or anything else. It is quick to justify cruelty, as well as sacrifice everything to maintain its own well-being or purpose.

It is for this reason that love must take on a different form which is contrary to the many selfisms of this world, the flesh, and the self-life. A true servant will present the very essence of self as a sacrifice, which is always ready to be offered up to do service for the benefit of the whole household.

Service of this caliber truly represents service that will prove to be excellent in every way. Again, we must come back to the service that is completely compelled or motivated by the love of God. In 2 Corinthians 5:14, the Apostle Paul speaks of how the love of God constrained him. It served as his motivating force in all he did.

Jesus counted the cost of what it would mean for Him to be benevolent. Love required Him to take on a totally different form to allow Himself to be offered up as the ultimate sacrifice on our behalf. He was constrained to take such measures. Hence enters the active aspect of God's love. It will manifest itself in excellent, sacrificial service in His household.

Genuine service will always be directed to God, but will naturally manifest itself towards others. It may be brought to a place of sacrifice, but in the position of servitude. Those who possess the disposition of a servant of God recognize that they have no personal say over their type of service, rendering any sacrifice that may result as being reasonable service. In the kingdom of God, all reasonable or acceptable service is established according to the Lord Jesus in light of ensuring the function and well-being of his kingdom.[31]

---

[31] Psalm 127:1; Hebrews 3:1-6

The second aspect we see concerning Jesus is that He was fashioned as a man to carry out His responsibility. It is not enough to take on the form of a servant, we must be fashioned in such a way that we can carry out our respective duties. The harsh reality is that man is fiercely independent. Even though he serves the ways of sin and death, he perceives that he is determining the outcome of his own life. In reality he has the freedom to do as he likes, but eventually the harsh taskmaster of sin is going to require his complete loyalty, resulting in him paying the final required wage of spiritual death or separation from God with his very soul.

In what way can we who are already servants to sin, change who we have been fashioned according to? We know we have been conformed to this world's way of thinking; therefore, the first place we have to be refashioned in is how we think or look at something.

Another word for servant is minister. When you consider these two words side by side, what type of attitude do you display towards them? Even though we are called to be servants of Christ, we are also called to minister His life to others. Our loyalties, allegiance, and devotion must be directed towards Christ, but how we minister to others will be according to the leading of His Spirit. It will be His Spirit who determines how His presence, life, leading, instructions, and examples are presented in regard to the benefits and needs of others.

Minister also points to the fact that such a position involves the type of influence that must be present in our lives. We are called to be priests, which points to our responsibility to represent God to man, and man to God. We are to be preachers, responsible to carry forth the good news, truths, and messages of our Lord and Master. "Minister" is also another word for deacon. The qualifications of a deacon include having purity in words, lifestyle, and conscience. There must be sobriety and boldness of faith. As ministers we are also to be ambassadors who have been entrusted with a ministry of reconciliation.[32] Ministry reminds us that it is about administration, or how we are to minister a matter according to our position, responsibility, and purpose.

The third facet of Jesus' act of love is that of submission. Jesus became man in order to come into submission and obedience to the plan

---

[32]   2 Corinthians 5:18-19; 1 Timothy 3:8-13

and purpose of the Father. Jesus' example shows us that there are two ways in which we express God's love, and that is through submission that results in obedience to what is right, and honor that exalts what is right above all personal designs or plans. Do submission and honor ring any kind of bell or association? We know they are both used in regard to the godly responsibilities of wives and husbands towards each other in their marriages.[33]

Most people fail to realize that in Ephesians 5:22-25, the Apostle Paul is explaining how the wife and husband are to express their love to each other in a godly marriage in light of different approaches. Wives are clearly in a position of servitude and must come to a place of *submission* to show forth godly love, while husbands must come from a perspective of what it means to properly *honor* their wives to express godly love.

What can we learn from the examples that Paul clearly outlined in Scripture in regard to marriage? First of all you cannot honor someone unless you first come into submission to what is worthy or honorable. Godly submission will automatically come into a place of servitude in order to properly honor that which is worthy of its dedication and service. Because of love, such service is always ready to offer up the best sacrifice to ensure that its service to the Lord will benefit the whole.

When it comes to the matter of godliness in the kingdom of God, we as servants of God cannot come into submission to something that is not worthy or beneficial. We can only serve well one master at a time.[34] According to Colossians 3:22-25, as Christians we are to do all things as unto the Lord, and not unto men. We are to do what is honorable or right, knowing that we will receive the reward of our spiritual inheritance.

For this reason, the Apostle Paul stipulates that a wife can only come into submission to her husband according to her high calling in the Lord. Clearly, the Lord's lordship or leadership in the marriage is for the protection of the wife, while calling the husband to excellence to ensure that he is worthy and prepared to benefit from such submission by properly honoring his wife.

The fourth aspect of genuine service is the dread of failing to carry out the necessary responsibility that would be considered worthy and

---

[33]   Ephesians 5:22-33; Colossians 3:18-19
[34]   Matthew 6:24

proper by our Lord. Just before his instruction to the wives and husbands in Ephesians 5:21, the Apostle Paul gave this instruction, "Submitting yourselves one to another in the fear of God."

Once again, we are reminded that we cannot honor something unless we first come into a place of submitting to what is right. "Submission" simply means giving way to something that is worthy or greater. We do not give way to mere man for he is not worthy. We do not give way to something that is immoral or destructive for it would be dishonorable to do so. When believers give way in the kingdom of God, they are giving way to what is right in light of what is required of them to ensure that the purpose, plan, and will of God is carried out in the lives of His people. In essence, they are giving way to the headship, Lordship, and leadership of the Lord. This is what ensures the integrity of godly submission in any relationship. Sadly, many Christians, including those who are wives, fail to learn the protection, liberty, and strength that comes from godly submission.

We are to submit out of fear or dread of displeasing our Lord or bringing any reproach on Him or His household. Colossians 3:22-23 goes on to say, "Servants, obey in all things your masters according to the flesh; not with eyeservice, as menpleasers, but in singleness of heart, fearing God. And whatever ye do, do it heartily, as to the Lord, and not unto men."

The fear of the Lord is the beginning of wisdom. Godly love possesses pure wisdom from above.[35] It shows discretion and desires to please the Lord in obedience to His commandments and ways. Such pleasure will bring joy to the servant's heart. It also requires that it does right in each situation because it cannot imagine doing any less, which will result in peace. Such loving service will submit to that which is worthy because it is a natural response of what compels it, showing itself to be long-suffering and gentle. It demands excellence in what it offers, ensuring goodness, and is willing to be true to the end by showing its faithfulness. It is meek because all of its actions are a result of godly submission, and it will reveal that it is tempered in attitude and actions through the willingness to be sacrificial in whatever is required.

---

[35]   Psalm 111:10; James 3:17

Godly love teaches us that it culminates in doing the right and sacrificial service for the sake of others. Sometimes the sacrifice required is not unto death, but choosing life for the sake of others. Consider the Apostle Paul. His desire was to be present with the Lord, but for the sake of others he chose life. He stated that even though he was in a fleshly tabernacle that was groaning and being burdened down by mortality, knowing that sometime in the future it would be swallowed up by physical death, he was content to remain in the body for the sake of others. As a result, the life he was living for the sake of others was being offered up as a perpetual sacrifice for the glory of God. In a sense, the apostle was always walking to his demise as a sacrifice, but ultimately being offered up as a living or ongoing sacrifice for the benefit of others. [36]

How do you express your love to God? Do you declare your love, but express a fierce independence in regard to submission and obedience. Jesus' love caused Him to give up the glories of heaven, put aside His capacity as sovereign ruler, take on a disposition of a servant, and allow Himself to be fashioned as a man so that He could selflessly serve, die on a cross, and be put into an empty grave. In light of His example, how would your present expression of love fair in comparison?

HONOR

As man, Jesus would have to prefer the Father's will and man's well-being over His own personal welfare. In essence, He would have to honor the Father by going to the cross and ensure man's well-being by dying on that self-same cross. Such preference is the result of love that spoke of indescribable excellence.

The Bible makes this important point in Romans 5:7-8, "For scarcely for a righteous man will one die; yet peradventure for a good man some would even dare to die. But God commendeth his love toward us in that, while we were yet sinners, Christ died for us." We would not think of dying for lost causes such as for those who are sinners still lost in their present state. If we were honorable enough, we might die for a righteous man, and just perhaps for a good man we might dare to die. However,

---

[36]   2 Corinthians 4:7-18; 5:5-10; Philippians 3:10-14; 2 Timothy 4:6

God commended his love towards us in our lost, sinful state of darkness, despair, and rebellion by sending forth His Son to die for us.

Jesus' death entailed that He preferred, regarded, considered, and honored sinful man above His own welfare. In essence, sinful man's need for salvation was exalted above the very life of the Son of God. How many parents would allow their beloved child to be offered up for those who very well would reject such an overture in the end? The reality is parents may send their sons and daughters off for the patriotic cause of a nation, but not for the cause of that which would be considered already lost. They would never send their child off to be possibly slaughtered for nothing; yet, God commended His love towards us when we were unable to reciprocate in our doomed state.

According to the *Strong's Concordance,* the word "commend" means to introduce or exhibit His love in a sense of making it stand near for man to see or to constitute it among mankind.[37] Jesus came near to mankind as man, and was exalted on the cross so man could clearly see the manifestation of God's love or commitment towards him to save him from his spiritual plight. He would not only invite each of us to come to partake of the Living Water that would bring life to our very souls, but His love would draw each of us to Him through example.

Jesus stated that He would be lifted upon a cross to draw all men to Himself.[38] Hebrews 12:3 made this statement, "For consider him that endured such contradiction of sinners against himself lest ye be wearied and faint in your minds." "Consider" in this text means to estimate what Jesus had to endure because of the disobedience, strife, and dispute caused by those who He came to die for.[39] How did Jesus respond to such a situation? Did He rage against it, cry foul, or lamented that He would even dare to consider dying for those who would gladly help His demise? No, He asked that they be forgiven in their darkened, ignorant state.

Jesus embraced the cross because of love. He preferred man in his lost state above Himself. We cannot imagine how far the incredible loving arms of God would have to reach. We know they reached from heaven

---

[37]   #4921

[38]   John 12:32

[39]   Strong's Concordance#357 & 485

and embraced a cross for our sake. They reached from the glories of heaven into the very depths of sin-laden souls to establish the way of forgiveness. They reached as far as the grave to embrace mankind in its grave darkness of delusion, disobedience, and death to ensure life.

God's love required Jesus to become the sacrifice. Out of love Jesus willingly submitted to the plan to redeem man. On a rugged cross, He was cherishing those who were even rejecting Him, along with you and me. On the cross His blood was being shed as a means of establishing a covenant that would make Him responsible for the spiritual welfare of others. And, on the cross, God was drawing near to man to give him the opportunity to draw near to Him. He was introducing Himself to man in such a way that if man cared to see what was set before him, he would have no other choice but to reciprocate in like manner. The Apostle John put it well, "We love him, because he first loved us" (1 John 4:19).

According to the instructions found in Ephesians 5:22-33 and Colossians 3:18-19 a godly wife must display a proper disposition of servitude in the marriage, but a godly husband is to serve as a living testimony as to how honor is to work within this sacred institution. He is to express his love to his spouse through properly honoring her. Jesus' example showed how such honor was to translate in the believer's life, and godly husbands are to serve as such an example in the family. If they display the right attitude, their wives will be naturally drawn to them, ready to submit to their example of love. Husbands, are your wives being drawn to you because of the example your love, attitude, and life is exhibiting?

What can we learn from the example of love that is expressed through honor? Before we can properly honor someone we must prefer him or her over ourselves. John 3:19-21 tells us man prefers the ways and works of darkness because he loves it. He loves darkness because it covers his wicked deeds.

We choose our preferences; therefore, love is a choice. For example, I choose to make some type of commitment to the person or the relationship I am in with that person. Sadly, people are often forced to make a commitment to the relationship of marriage instead to their spouses because of dishonorable attitudes and practices going on. The reason we must prefer someone is because we will choose to love him or her.

We must begin by choosing as a means to determine personal preference. But, how do we determine our preference. We have to put value on something or someone before we will prefer it. In marriage man must put value on his wife. This value has to exceed the value he puts on his idea of self and life, or he will fail to properly cherish her.

We cannot prefer, honor, cherish, or properly exalt what we perceive to be inferior. Man is clearly inferior to God, but our Creator put a price on man in order to redeem him. A husband must put a price on his wife and the life he desires for her in order to prefer her welfare to his personal welfare. This price is going to determine the type of investment he is going to make in this relationship to ensure a healthy family.

Once a value has been attached to his wife, then the husband will have the liberty to offer himself as the necessary sacrifice. In other words, he must be willing to offer his right to his life on his terms and begin to regard the welfare of his wife as being far more important. Nothing is too great or small when it comes to investing in her well-being as a means of ensuring joy between them, peace in their relationship, patience to see a matter through to the end, gentleness that allows room for growth, goodness that proves beneficial to their relationship, faithfulness to do right regardless of the challenges, meekness to be wrong in order to be made right, and temperance that keeps all in check to what is honorable, right, good, and acceptable to God.

For the servant of God, he or she is always walking towards his or her demise, but for those who are to honor others, their sacrifice must be offered up front. They are not walking towards their demise; rather, they are walking in light of it. The Apostle Paul put it in this way, "Husbands, love your wives, even as Christ also loved the church, and gave himself for it" (Ephesians 5:25).

You cannot honor others as long as you are honoring or preferring yourself. Hence enters Jesus' words, "Greater love hath no man than this, that a man lay down his life for his friends" (John 15:13). There is no greater love a husband can show his wife than to be willing to lay down or put aside the life he desires for himself in preference to her needs. It is this love that draws us to Christ, and it will be the same type of love that will draw a wife to her husband in a most pleasant way.

Self must be the first casualty when it comes to honoring others. As Christians we are to naturally prefer the well-being of our brethren to ourselves to ensure we do right by them.[40] I have often defined God's love as a commitment to do right before Him and right in regard to others. Doing right is our reasonable service.

When you consider love as a commitment, you will realize it is based on a covenant. In godly marriage, you take a vow of faithfulness, but you make a covenant that embraces spiritual and moral responsibilities toward one another. These moral responsibilities nourish the spouse and nurture the relationship. Sadly, the vow is disregarded and the covenant completely ignored. As a result the spouse or the relationship ceases to be cherished in a godly, honorable way.

Clearly, we cannot cherish what we do not value. Men are instructed to cherish their wives as they would cherish their own flesh. They are to nurture her in the way of encouragement, support, reassurance, and mental, emotional, and spiritual support. If husbands fail to properly honor their wives in such a manner, the Lord will not answer their prayers, rendering the husband totally ineffective from being a spiritual leader in his family.[41]

Today, many unbecoming attitudes have been developed towards marriage. There are practices being thrust upon spouses in the name of marriage that are dishonorable or disrespectful, while the sanctity of the marriage is being compromised and defiled. Such attitudes and practices would not be present if godly love was at the helm of the relationship. Godly love would never think of being unbecoming or dishonorable in attitude or actions. Its natural tendency is to honor and cherish the focus of its commitment and attention.

I realize that there is no way that mere words could begin to capture the love of God. For this reason we must look to Christ on the cross. It is love being manifested in living action. It states, "For God so loved, He gave His best. For the Father so valued and cherished us, He gave the most excellent offering He could. For He so loved that He honored us above Himself and above His Son's life so He could secure life for all who will receive His gift of life. For the Son so loved He gave His all, His very life so we could live forever." Even though these words and actions have echoed down through the corridors of time and eternity, words cannot begin to capture the depth and majesty of God's eternal love.

---

[40]   Romans 12:10

[41]   Ephesians 5:28-39; 1 Peter 3:7

Rayola Kelley

Clearly, we benefit from godly love, experience different aspects of it, and enjoy the fruit of it, but we cannot begin to describe its most excellent ways. As the Apostle Paul declared, we should covet earnestly the best gifts the Spirit has to offer us, and yet even in this he was able to present a more excellent way. We know the way he is referring to is the charitable, benevolent, submissive, and honorable ways of God's love.[42]

The way of God's love is sure; therefore who can separate us from it. It has staying power, thereby, able to withstand tribulation, distress, persecution, famine, nakedness, peril, and sword. Even though it appears that such love requires us to be constantly offered up as sacrificial sheep, always walking towards or in light of our personal demise, we are still more than conquerors through Jesus because He loved us. Because of His benevolence, we are persuaded that all the influence and powers of both the seen and unseen worlds shall not be able to separate us from the love of God which can be personally known and experienced in our precious Lord.[43]

Once again we must ask ourselves do we possess such a love, and does it possess and compel us in our lives before God and towards those we encounter on our journey? Are we walking according to and in the most excellent way of this love, or is our form of love fleshly, worldly, and self-serving? In the end, all façades, cloaks, and imitations of love will be stripped away to expose their base source, while the love of God will remain standing, revealing the excellence of its source, as well as its eternal character and its everlasting fruits.[44]

---

[42] 1 Corinthians 12:31
[43] Romans 8:35-39
[44] If you would like to learn more about submission and honor, see the author's book *Bring Down the Sacred Cows*, in Volume 4 of her foundational series.

3

IT IS A MATTER
OF GRACE

INTRODUCTION

God's grace has always added a comforting aspect to my Christian life. There seems to be so many rules and regulations when it comes to living this life, but the subject of the Lord's grace seems to take away the harshness of such rules. In a way it seems to make the Christian life obtainable and less demanding.

Clearly, the Christian life is an excellent life, but unfeeling religious rules and lifeless regulations often strip it of its excellent qualities, causing it to become a burden too great to bear. However, add God's grace to the equation and there is hope that somehow man can obtain the benefits and rewards of this incredible life.

When the subject of grace comes up it seems so simple, yet it is often shrouded in confusion and controversy. Instead of bringing comfort, it has become a covering that many use to hide their insecurities about their spiritual status. It has been treated like a license in which some of those who want to lay claim to heaven hold up as a means to justify questionable, worldly lifestyles. For others, it has created a struggle in their theology and doctrine as they juggle it along side such subjects as the Law and works. They do not know how to bring what appears to be opposing factors together under one umbrella.

The result of the confusion has produced a perplexing picture of God's grace. As to whether this picture can be untangled and presented in a simple way that is understandable and makes sense, will actually come down to a person understanding the source of it. Obviously, we cannot begin with grace itself if we are to understand its intent or work of it in our lives.

There is one main conclusion I have drawn in my many studies about this subject that is simple and unassuming, and that is everything I have in Christ is a matter of God's grace.

UNDERSTANDING GRACE

Do I believe that we can really understand God's grace? Like all matters that are associated with God, I realize that we are capable of coming to an understanding about such issues, but we will never be able to comprehend them to their fullness as long as we are limited by these fleshly tabernacles. We know in part and see through a glass that is very limited.[1] In our fleshly state, we are unable to see the fullness of matters that are eternal in character and work. To reinforce this concept, consider the Apostle Paul's statement in relationship with the matter of grace, "That in the ages to come he might show the exceeding riches of his grace in his kindness toward us through Christ Jesus" (Ephesians 2:7).

The apostle made it clear that all that is associated with grace will be unfolding before us for ages to come. Although this statement seems simple enough to understand, it also reminds us that there is no way we can possibly know the depths of it. There are exceeding riches attached to grace. When you consider these two words, you realize that what is attached to grace, passes or excels any known or understandable mark. Therefore, the riches that are imbued to us by way of grace are abundant, full, and valuable, and will far exceed anything we can possibly imagine.

Even though grace seems simple enough to understand, problems often occur when man becomes part of the equation. Only the Spirit can unfold the matters of eternity to the spirit of man, while man can only complicate such issues with his limited and perverted understanding. It is not unusual for man to strip the intent of eternal matters with his limited conclusions, concrete doctrines, and arrogant theology. In his high opinion of self, he thinks that he has the proper means to come to

---

[1]   1 Corinthians 13:9, 12

realistic and fair judgments concerning eternal matters. However, the Bible admonishes us against such fallacies. It warns us if we handle truths in unrighteousness, we will experience the wrath of God.[2]

Even though the unfolding of God's truths come from outside of what man can imagine, man forever tries to adjust, compartmentalize, and bring God's truths down to his limited understanding. He puts the matters of God in boxes of theology and doctrines, deeming them as the absolute and complete truth.

The subject of grace has in many ways been rendered perverted or ineffective by the intent or applications of it that man has attached to it. Man's doctrines such as "Easy Believism" have changed the face of "grace" to be considered in improper ways. Legalistic, religious attitudes have actually caused an affront against the real workings of grace, frustrating its very work in people's lives.[3] We could go on and on, but the truth of the matter is the subject of grace has been greatly misunderstood and abused by those in Christendom.

We need to come back to center as to what is true and correct about grace to understand how it works in our life. For believers the most well-known and acceptable work in respect of God's grace is that we are saved by it.[4] We know we are saved by grace, but in what way is grace able to save us? We must come back to the source of grace to understand how it is meant to work in our lives.

When you study grace, you will realize that it was manifested to the world by a person. We also know that it is one of the attributes of God, a truth that is clearly established, and a work that is ongoing. It is vital we see how it was manifested through the person and how it serves as a living expression of God. It is also important to understand the truths it established about an eternal inheritance that has been made available to mankind, as well as a work that is ongoing in the lives of God's people.

The first aspect of grace that we must understand is that it is a description of the person of our Lord Jesus Christ. In essence, our Lord is the fundamental nature of pure, unadulterated grace. When we consider Him we see grace personified. In Christ we have the unfolding reality of

---

2   Romans 1:18; 12:3; 1 Corinthians 2:9-12; Galatians 6:3

3   Galatians 2:21

4   Ephesians 2:8

the incredible character, work, and ways of grace. In a sense, Christ is the faucet. As His work and glory is revealed to us, our understanding of God's grace ceases to be a trickle and becomes a free flowing river that flows in, through, and out of our lives. The Apostle John stated that Jesus was full of grace and truth and went on to say, "And of his fullness have all we received, and grace for grace" (John 1:16).[5]

Let us meditate for a moment on that last part of John 1:16, "grace for grace." Everything we receive from the Lord is a matter of His grace being extended towards us. Our salvation is a matter of grace. All of the riches associated with or attached to our spiritual inheritance are a matter of His grace. Answered prayers, blessings, and kept promises are a matter of God's grace. We can be recipients of His grace in one matter, to only turn around and receive His grace in another situation. Grace for grace, as it is constantly being extended, forever flowing from the abundance of God's eternal riches, which are all found in Christ Jesus.

Grace is associated with Jesus. It has always been available to God's people, but in Jesus, God manifested the fullness and work of grace. In the past man often failed to recognize the grace of God. In some cases he may have assumed that what was bestowed on him was because he was deserving of such regard or consideration, thereby, failing to recognize God's grace. But, in Jesus, God put a face on His grace. He revealed the riches of it when its excellent function came to fruition and was culminated in the work of redemption that occurred on the cross. We know that the death, burial, and resurrection pointed to the main reason God's grace was manifested in Jesus. It was so we could be saved.

My initial introduction in regard to God's grace came by way of salvation. However, there is so much more to discover about this eternal virtue. The Apostle Paul was setting the scene up in Ephesians 2:4-7 in order for us to understand the excellence of God's grace. The apostle reminds us as believers that even though we were once dead in our sins, we have been quickened in the spirit together with Christ for we have been saved by His grace. Because of grace, we have been positionally raised up together, and made to sit together in heavenly places in Christ Jesus. Notice the word "places." Keep in mind that numerous riches will be unfolded to us because of God's incredible grace. We know it is from

---

[5]   John 1:14

72

the heavenly places in Christ that we will be discovering the riches of grace for ages to come.

This brings us to the Scripture that first introduced me to the concept of grace, "For by grace are ye saved through faith; and that not of yourselves, it is the gift of God" (Ephesians 2:8). At the time I had no concept of grace, but I had a sense about it. I realized something called "grace" allotted me something precious and priceless from God. I recognized that it was something that came from outside of me and any personal best as to my actions and attempts. Clearly, grace came from God, and it was because of His great love that He made this gift available to me.

Grace is a gift of God, and gifts are free. They are not earned or deserved. Granted, I do not have to accept, respect, or appreciate a gift, but to benefit, know, or experience it I must receive it as such. James 1:17 tells us that every good and perfect gift is from above and comes down from the Father. It was at this point that I realized that grace comes from above and flows from the throne of God, culminating at and in the person and work of Jesus Christ. Obviously, I cannot experience this gift unless I come to the faucet or fountain of Jesus. Therefore, there is no way that I can miss the reality that all grace, with its numerous riches, solely finds its unlimited source in the Living God of heaven and earth.

Grace is beneficial for my well-being and is complete in all that it is and has accomplished on my behalf. I realized that it possesses the riches of heaven. And, one of the first riches of heaven I encountered because of it was my salvation, the gift of eternal life. For this reason grace became a word of comfort and encouragement to me.

However, my initial understanding of grace lacked much dimension. Sadly, much of the presentation that surrounded it made it sound cheap and flimsy to me. It was as if man's attempt to capture the essence of it, actually took the teeth out of it. It appeared that all he succeeded in doing in light of his limited and often self-serving attempts in regard to understanding or explaining it was simply to exalt some of the obvious qualities of it, while actually robbing it of its excellent substance and purpose. It was as if he made a robe out of grace, rather than receiving and experiencing the actual benefits of it. He could speak of grace in theological terms, but minimized its excellence in the matters of how it established and ensured one's personal well-being.

Granted, grace adorns all that God has done and will do on our behalf. In Proverbs 1:9, Solomon described this virtue as an ornament. "Ornament" in this text implies something that is attached such as a wreath.[6] When you consider the text in which Solomon refers to it as an ornament it is in relationship to wisdom and instruction. He was stating that wisdom, instruction, and the law are like a wreath of grace that will adorn the head or gold chains that will hang about the neck of those who fear the Lord. Once again we gain insight into the riches that are attached to the storehouse of God's grace.

I realized I had to find the fine balance between man's limited understanding and teachings of grace and God's unfolding revelation of it. Where could I look to come to an understanding of its intent to ensure a right attitude towards it?

In the first chapter of the Gospel of John when grace was mentioned, it was mentioned in conjunction with two words: Christ and truth. The Apostle John was setting the premise in which grace had to be regarded in order to establish a correct attitude and response towards it. Jesus was full of grace and truth. Grace came from Jesus, but ultimately it would also ensure the truth about His person and work on our behalf. If grace did not come back to the person of Jesus, while exhuming and highlighting the truth about what He accomplished on our behalf, at best it would be cheapened, perverted, and misused by those who were trying to capture the essence of it. It would be like trying to capture an eagle that is soaring above in the wind current from the tallest mountain. It would not matter how high of a cliff or mountain you are on, you could never capture an eagle that has discovered and experienced the excellence and height of the wind current.

In many cases man is void of the means to capture the spirit or intent of the unfolding revelations of heaven. Such revelations clearly remain far above his limited understanding; therefore, he will simply take what conclusions he arrives at concerning the issue and put any conclusions into a controllable box of understanding, while labeling them as being truths. In such times, the person and work of Jesus will be clearly missing from these scenarios, rendering them lifeless and ineffective, and in some cases becoming heretical.

---

6   Strong's Exhaustive Concordance, # 3880

What is your understanding about God's grace? Are you missing the source of Jesus and the substance of truth? Have you put it in a box that cheapens it, in a doctrine that may be perverting it, or is it part of a lifeless theology that borders on heretical nonsense? Is it time to allow the Word of God to shake your conclusions and assumptions you have towards this important subject, and make sure it has been unfolded to your spirit by the Spirit of the Living God?

GRACE ABOUNDS

Scripture speaks of how God's grace abounds. We know there is no limit as to how far it can reach us in our spiritual plight. As the Apostle Paul stated, it is grace that proves to be sufficient in our times of great need and challenge.[7] In a way the cup of grace overflows with the many riches of God to enable or equip us as His people. As we have discovered it excels in riches, which include salvation, wisdom, and instruction. However, does this mean grace abounds in any old environment? Will it be sufficient in cases where sin reigns? Does it increase to embrace or cover up unholy agreements and practices?

Because it abounds, this is where there is confusion for many as to the part grace plays in each of our lives. This confusion about God's grace has produced two extremes in people's ways of thinking or handling it. In fact, one extreme hides behind the concept of grace, while the other extreme goes to the opposite direction and frustrates its work. Clearly, we need to come back to center to understand it.

The book of Romans deals with the first extreme, while the book of Galatians addresses the other extreme. In Romans the Apostle Paul is addressing the misconception that grace addresses or deals with our sin problem. God does not show us grace in sin. We are told that God commended His love towards us while we were yet sinners.[8] He provided the means in which He could show grace towards us. Clearly, if the provision of Jesus' redemption was missing, God would not be able to allot us the unfolding riches that flow from His grace.

---

[7]   Romans 6:1; 2 Corinthians 8:7; 9:8; 12:9

[8]   Romans 5:8

Grace has no qualities or abilities to address sin. It does not address the fallen state of man; rather it changes his *status* in relationship to the kingdom of God. Jesus' redemption on the cross is what addresses our sin problem. The shedding of His blood provided the means in which we could receive a pardon and be cleansed of our sin.[9] It is from the point of pardon or forgiveness that we receive grace that will change our status from being considered lost and illegitimate to being adopted heirs of the family of God. Jesus' redemption took away the disgrace, claims, and consequences of sin, while His grace enriches each of us with a new and abundant life.

The Apostle Paul clearly stated that grace does not give us a license to sin or remain in our sin, thinking that God will overlook such offense because of His favor. The Apostle John stipulates that if we are truly born again we cannot continue in sin.[10] As I have maintained, Jesus did not come to save us *in* sin; rather, He came to save us *from* sin.

For God's grace to have its way in our life the environment must be present to recognize it and receive it as such. The Apostle Paul confirms this. He stated that where sin once abounded, grace now abounds.[11] In other words, abound is used in the past tense. In this text sin has been addressed and taken care of because of redemption. Where sin once thrived in our lives, grace now abounds.

Grace cannot be abounding in a person's life when he or she is walking and reveling in sin. A person must repent and turn from such sin in order to receive God's forgiveness and salvation. This is when grace becomes apparent and can be received as a gift and appropriated in a person's life. It is at this time when its abounding riches and qualities will be given and made available, revealing there is no limit as to what it can offer our lives or how it can enrich us. It is vital that we as Christians get this truth into our spirits.

This brings us to a very important aspect of God's character. The attitude that God displays towards those who are in sin is that of long-suffering or patience, not grace. He does not ignore sin, for we know that He turns His back on iniquity in rejection and contempt for it. The

---

9   Hebrews 9:22; 1 John 1:7-9
10   Romans 5:20-6:2; 1 John 3:4-9
11   Romans 5:20

Apostle Peter tells us that God is long-suffering towards those who are perishing in their sin in hopes of giving them time to repent.[12] Obviously, God patiently refrains from bringing deserved judgment on man but not because of His grace.

God's grace is His way of showing undeserved man his kindness by favoring him. It will be expressed in graciousness not immunity. Graciousness implies that God bent or stooped down to what is inferior in order to show such favor. His act of graciousness is brought on when one is humbly imploring Him to consider his or her spiritual plight.[13]

God will not show favor by casting the riches or pearls of His grace before those who would simply trample them under their feet.[14] Granted, He will show a form of grace by *blessing* man as far as ensuring his very life or existence, and He will be patient in regards to judging or showing sinful man His wrath, but He will never condone sinful actions by casting His gift of grace, eternal life, before those who have no regard for His provision. God's grace in this light can only be offered to a person at the point of redemption.

This brings us to the other extreme that ends up with people frustrating the grace of God, rather than receiving it. Due to a cheap presentation of grace, many have come into bondage to the Law. They look at people abusing God's grace to hide sin, and hear the preaching and teaching of concepts such as "easy believism" that would have people to believe that they do not have any responsibilities in regard to their Christianity because they are saved by grace. These skeptical individuals see the inconsistencies, weaknesses, and sometimes lunacy that these religious individuals display in their lives, and end up going into the extreme by once again coming under the bondage of the Law of God.

As Christians we have a moral responsibility to live an upright life, but such a life does not require us to come under the letter of the Law. The Law is important to understand what role it is to play in our lives as believers.

The largest Psalm in the Bible gives us some powerful insight into the Law. It is described by various names such as God's Word, law,

---

[12]   2 Peter 3:9

[13]   Strong's Exhaustive Concordance, OT #2580, 2587; NT: #5485, 5543

[14]   Matthew 7:6

testimonies, precepts, judgments, commandments, and statutes. Each one of these addresses the different functions of the Law.

For example, God's word is law, and cannot be changed. Law is not just a rigid code to live by, but it also points to the principles that must be in operation in our lives to honor its intent. For example, if we walk according to the law of sin and death, we will be walking according to the principle of iniquity. We will be fulfilling the intent of iniquity, which will be in compliance to the selfish, fleshly ways of the fallen disposition and the world. The principle in which we are walking will activate the type of law that we will become subject to. In the case of iniquity we are subject to the Law of God that was set forth to reveal transgression with the purpose of righteously judging and condemning not only the action of such ways, but the intent or spirit behind them.[15]

There is also the Law of the Spirit of the life in Christ Jesus that is in operation. In order to be identified to this law, we must be walking according to the principles of godliness. Godliness identifies us to God, which reveals that we have come under the more excellent Law of the Spirit, which is governed and motivated by the life of Christ in us. Because Jesus has fulfilled the Law of God, we have been lifted above any claims of judgment of the rigid Law.[16] Granted, we are still responsible to live according to the moral aspects of the Law which are known as commandments, but we are not subject to every aspect of the Law. We must keep in mind that certain parts of the Law have either been fulfilled and in a sense done away with or replaced by that which is more excellent.

Commandments are never negotiable. They stipulate our moral responsibilities towards God and others in order to ensure the moral integrity or intent of our attitude towards godly requirements. Jesus explained that the only way a person can maintain the intent of the commandments is by loving God and others above self. Without love, people will fail to fulfill this particular aspect of the Law.[17]

The Law was to serve as a testimony of God and His people. The Law is holy and pure and pointed to the character of God. It was to

---

[15]   Romans 8:2
[16]   Matthew 5:17-20; Romans 10:4
[17]   Mark 12:28-31; Romans 8:4; 13:8-10

remind the people of God that they were to live an exemplary life that clearly separated them from the grave darkness of those who succumb to the idolatrous ways of the flesh and the paganism of the age in which they lived. Such separation would cause them to serve as a light to others, which would not only reveal a better way but a way that had the very stamp of heaven on it. In a sense, it would allow them to live above the present age, rather than become victimized or enslaved by it. As Christians we are to serve as living testimonies of this difference. We have been called to be epistles or letters that can be clearly seen and read by all men, as well as being instructed to let our light shine.[18]

Precepts point to doctrines that establish our conduct to ensure a godly lifestyle. Commandments stipulate the do's and don'ts of a matter, while doctrine establishes not only what is unacceptable or acceptable conduct, but it does so in light of spirit or intent. Isaiah talked about precept upon precept, line upon line. Much of the New Testament consists of establishing, as well as explaining the excellent intent and purpose of doctrine. Godly doctrine points to the pure milk of our fundamental responsibilities as believers, but we are told in Hebrews 6:1 to leave the principles of the doctrine of Christ and go on to spiritual maturity. Spiritual maturity enables one to partake of the solid food that leads to righteousness, enabling him or her to properly discern both good and evil. The meat of the New Testament points to actually doing or carrying out the will of God in a situation.[19]

Judgments are best related to the concept of making a judgment call about a matter that is not necessarily black and white. The Law sets up the boundaries in which all matters must be considered, but there are issues that are clouded by unknown factors such as motives, God's personal will for someone, or the actions of others. In such case the Law is to serve as a guide or a counselor that would enable one to make sound judgments as he or she wade through the various issues of a situation. Ultimately, such sound judgments would ensure that one keep not only the intent of the Law intact, but would ultimately end up doing the will of God. We see the Apostle Paul calling for such sound judgment in 1 Corinthians 7 in relationship to being single, married, and divorced.

---

[18]   Matthew 5:14-16; 2 Corinthians 3:2-3

[19]   Isaiah 28:10-13; John 4:34; Hebrews 5:11-6:2

Statutes can be compared to ordinances or outward practices or ceremonies that were established to remind people about their God and who they were in the scheme of things. These practices included dress, the type of food that was acceptable, sanitation practices, circumcision, sacrifices, keeping the Sabbath, etc. In the Church we only have two ordinances, but even these are hotly debated as to how they are to be observed by the different belief systems. They are water baptism and communion.

Statutes were to remind the people of Israel of who Jehovah God was and that they were to be His peculiar or special people by their practices and lifestyle in the midst of grave paganism. However, the Apostle Paul made some very interesting statements about such ordinances in Galatians 4:9-10 and Colossians 2:14-17. He said of them that they were weak and beggarly elements that actually became contrary to the real purpose of the Christian life. As a result, they were taken out of the way by nailing them to the cross of Jesus. He goes on to explain that they simply served as the shadow of the one who was coming, Jesus Christ. Since Christ is the actual fulfillment of them, they were no longer needed. Therefore, why accept the shadow, when you can embrace the real thing?

When we talk about people once again coming under the bondage of the Law, we are talking about those who are running back into the shadow of the Law. This requires them to remove themselves from under the Spirit and bring themselves once again under the flesh in order to practice these ordinances as a means to add to their spiritual status. As the Apostle Paul reminded us in Galatians 6:8, if a person sows to his flesh he will reap corruption, but if he sows to the Spirit, he will reap everlasting life. Keep in mind the holy, unyielding Law addresses the flesh, while the other law has to do with walking in and according to the Spirit of God to secure and experience the very life of Christ. Hence, enters the apostle's exhortation, "Are ye so foolish? Having begun in the Spirit, are ye now made perfect by the flesh" (Galatians 3:3)?

God's Law was put into place to show man that he is a transgressor of His holy ruling. In the workings and attempts of his corruptible flesh, man could only stand condemned in light of His Law. Since the Law could only condemn a transgressor, it was unable to justify or save him or her. It was from this premise that the Law was to serve as a schoolmaster that pointed man to his need for and solution of Jesus Christ. It is the grace of

God that was revealed through Jesus that saves and justifies us. It brings us under the Law of the Spirit. In the Spirit we not only keep the intent of the Law, but we are called to a more excellent life than the existence the people lived according to the Law. The excellence has to do with living the very life of Christ. Living His life allows each of us to serve as living, walking testimonies to those whom we encounter. Such a life can ensure good judgments according to the will of God.[20]

When a person brings him or herself under the Law, he or she must keep the whole Law. This includes every aspect of it from its various statutes and precepts to its judgments. The problem is that since many aspects of the Law have been fulfilled in Christ, much of the Law is not realistic or applicable for today. People cannot pick or choose what laws they are going to keep in their flesh in regard to God's holy Law without negating the presence and work of the Spirit to bring forth the life of Christ according to the riches of God's grace. And, if these individuals fail to keep one part of the Law, they have broken the complete Law, making them transgressors of it.[21]

In Galatians, the Apostle Paul contended with those who would give up the liberty of the Spirit to come under the harsh yoke of the Law. As Peter stated, the yoke that the Law brought unto their fathers was unbearable. For the believers to once again come under the yoke of the Law, is to not only frustrate the real liberating work of God's grace, but it also means they have removed themselves from under it, to place themselves under another gospel that can only bring a curse upon their lives.[22]

Clearly the purpose of the Law was to show man he needed to be saved and the intent of it was to point him to the One who saves. God's grace can only be realized if the Spirit of God is present. If the Spirit is present it is because the environment is conducive for salvation and spiritual growth. In such an environment grace abounds.[23] It is an environment where people have the liberty to discover the life that has been made available, and respond according to the Spirit's conviction and leading in order to receive and partake of the life of Christ.

---

[20] Romans 3:20-25; Galatians 2:16; 3:24

[21] James 2:8-10

[22] Acts 15:10-11; 2 Corinthians 3:17; Galatians 1:6-9; 2:21; 5:1

[23] Acts 4:31-35; 11:19-22;

What law are you under? Are you trying to live the Christian life according to the flesh or the Spirit?

FINDING GRACE

We know two things for sure about grace. We know that grace abounds where sin once abounded. And, when it comes to salvation, grace is God's part. He makes His grace available, but what part does man have in salvation. He must in some way find or avail himself to God's grace to be saved.

To set the stage of what it means for man to find God's grace, I want to relate a dream I had one night. I do not remember many of my dreams; therefore, when a dream makes an impact on me, I meditate on whether there was something that was significant.

The setting of this dream took place in a family room in some unknown house. As to the size of the room, I could not tell you. But, what I can tell you is that it was crowded with people and I was about to preach. This would not be an unusual setting for me due to the fact I have been an overseer of a home church and have spoken at home meetings and conducted seminars in such settings.

There was a large square coffee table in the room in which many people were seated around in expectation. However, to my dismay they were not excited or waiting in expectation to hear the Word of God expounded. What they were sitting in expectation of was the game that was taking place at the coffee table. What I remember are three young men who were actively caught up with this game. I can recall that I had a personal fondest for one of the young men, while I had a recollection of the second young man as to his looks, but the third young man remained vague. He had no face or name. He was just there off to the side waiting for his turn at the game.

At the center of the game was a yellow cup. Apparently there were some dice that was shaken up in that cup and cast upon the coffee table. In the background I was also aware that a storm was raging. As I began to speak, I became aware that the noise of the game was distracting everyone's attention. There was chaos in the environment, causing confusion.

Within the first sentence of my deliverance of the message, I realized that if I did not take control of the matter that everything that would be said would fall to the wayside. I remember stepping into the midst of the crowd and grabbing the yellow cup away from the young man that I was the most acquainted with. I can also remember that the young men that were involved quickly became upset with me.

The one young man that I was personally acquainted with stood up and went to one side of me. He had anger on his face for my intrusion. The young man that had some identity as to how he looked was standing in the same place, but he appeared as if he was shocked that I would do such a thing to their game. Once again, I had no personal knowledge of the third young man's reaction for it was veiled from my eyes, but I sensed he was not pleased.

You might wonder what a dream would have to do with God's grace. It was an answer to prayer. My main request in regard to my writings is that they would be a matter of His inspiration. I do not like to waste people's time in reading that which would represent idle words. The day before this dream occurred I had been asking God for the necessary wisdom to explain His grace. The dream served as part of His answer to my request.

Before I can explain what part God's grace played in this dream, I need to first tell you the meaning of it. There is a storm raging in the world. It represents the great battle for the souls of men. Sadly, people are more interested in playing the game of life, than facing the harsh reality of the next world to come. They are more attracted to that which has no significance than that which will address their eternal well-being.

The worlds that people often create are crowded, but there is no life or substance in what they do in them. They may fit everything into their small square of existences and fill them with nonsensical activities as a means of entertainment, but it simply keeps them blinded and dulled down to the vanity of it all. They are willing to gamble with their souls as they look expectantly towards or into a small cup to see what life holds for them, while ignoring or missing that which serves as the light of the world and the source to the unlimited wells of salvation.

For those who contend for souls, there are those they have a fondness for. Such fondness will stir them up in urgency to battle for their souls, while there are those who they see, and even those who are vague and unknown, but each individual is significant when it comes to the harvest field of humanity. Even though the one that holds our affections is important, the other two are just as important to God. It does not matter how well we know people, in God's sight they are all lost souls for whom He died.

The final part of this dream was the message. Amazingly, I started to preach a sermon in my dream. I cannot tell you the initial part of my message, but I can tell you that I was instructed by the Lord to make it personal. In other words, I was to deliver a personal message to each of these three young men.

One of the problems with some of the preaching today is that it is generic. It is sent forth in the form of pabulum that lacks any ability to bring one to salvation or full age, fluff that may offer a temporary fix or a spiritual high but lacks substance, or regurgitated vomit that has been repackaged by those who have nothing better to offer. However, until a message becomes Holy Spirit inspired and personal, it will have no real affect on anyone. It will never become a sharp sword that exposes, separates, and brings forth life and victory.[24]

There were five parts of the sermon I can remember. The number "five" is the number for grace. Three parts addressed the young men personally, but the last two parts had to do with the significance of God's grace. In fact, the sermon continued even after I finally awoke to the stormy winds that were slamming the rain against the roof and windows of the house. The message I delivered to the one that I had personal connections to was that he was a sinner, who was doomed. Because he was in such a state, he was so inclined to not hear the Word of God, making him deaf towards it. In such a state of rebellion, he would refuse to see the truth about his condition, as well as being quick to show contempt towards God's truth when it intruded into his worldly activities. He needed to repent and cry out for mercy.

When it comes to those who we are fond of, we have a tendency to try to handle them in such a way that we do not insult or offend them in regard to their sinful condition. We hope that they can see their spiritual plight as we try to coddle them for our own sake, shame them into doing right with words and examples, or love them into the kingdom of God. We feel this is our way of showing grace and truth to them, when in reality we

---

[24] Hebrews 4:12

want them to straighten up so we do not have to confront their sin. In all truthfulness we hate possible conflict because of the discomfort it may cause us for we are cowards at heart. These rebellious individuals may sense our real motives, and even in some cases our love for them, but they will perceive that they are deserving of such love. They may know about our personal convictions towards the Lord but they will see no need to be personally saved. As the Apostle Paul stated in Romans 10:14a, "How, then, shall they call on him in whom they have not believed?"

My message to the second young man was that he was lost to the things of God, and God was lost to him. In such a state he would see no need to be saved, for he was not even aware that he was lost. He has never known God, and his present world seemed okay enough that he had no need to know Him. He was blinded by his own state and unable to see the penetrating light of the Gospel. As the Apostle Paul stated that the Gospel is hidden to those who are lost.[25]

Someone once said that it is easy to get a person saved, the problem rests in getting him or her lost in the first place. You cannot save those who do not see that they have any real need to be found. To challenge them in their comfortable state is going to initially shock them. When the shock wears off, you will usually hit insolence.

We may know of such people. We might even be acquainted with them enough to recognize them in the crowd and give some acknowledgment. To some this acknowledgment is a matter of showing such individuals a form of grace. In honesty such regard is to usually make ourselves somewhat known to others for the sake of our own reputation, but in reality we have no regard for their souls. Any recognition we show them is to keep them unaware that at best we are simply tolerating them for selfish reasons, while presenting an outward presentation that hides indifference in regard to their souls. As the Apostle Paul reminds us in Romans 10:14b, "And how shall they believe in him of whom they have not heard?"

The message to the third man was that he was wrong. Who wants to be wrong? We fear being wrong, justify it, qualify it, avoid it, hide from it, flee it, and reject any notion that we are wrong. It takes a big person, or one with character to simply admit he or she is wrong. Granted, people

---

[25]   2 Corinthians 4:3-4

will tout that if you prove them wrong, they will admit it. The reality of it is that they must first choose to love and desire the truth above all else before they will ever allow themselves to see a matter for what it is and admit they are wrong. They must know that before they can be made right, they must come to terms with what is wrong.

The aversion to being wrong causes many people to remain faceless and nameless. Pride sits on the throne of their self-life. They will not expose themselves to any notion that they are wrong. They will avoid any exposure that will reveal differently. They will not be made accountable or responsible for the way their life is. In essence, they will not be made accountable or responsible for their spiritual condition before God. However, it does not change that they are wrong in their being, thinking, and doing. The harsh reality is that without Christ, there will be nothing right in a person's world.

People are forever skirting the issues of their spiritual condition. They are all around us, even in the religious realm. They hide their shame behind fig leaves and construct cloaks of self-righteousness to avoid being discovered. And, when the covering is removed by the light to expose their real condition, they can become fearful and angry. But, as the Apostle Paul stated about such individuals in Romans 10:14c, "And how shall they hear without a preacher?'

The reason people are afraid to face the light of the Gospel, is because they will have to face their real spiritual condition. They are indeed sinners, utterly lost, and completely wrong before God. There is nothing they can do in their own power or under their own volition that will make them acceptable. They cannot come to the Judge of their soul with anything that will change the fact that they are doomed, dead in their sins, and hiding in the darkness of their own wicked preferences.

To such people they cannot imagine they are as bad as God's Word declares them to be. They cannot accept that they are unable to bring anything to the table to prove that they are deserving of His consideration and worthy of His grace. This makes them vulnerable, needy, and undeserving. Hence enters the fear. If they approach God in such a wretched state what would keep Him from totally rejecting them? Clearly, there would be no reason for Him to save them for their own sakes, for they have no personal worth or value for Him to do such a grand deed on their behalf. Obviously, God would be wise, correct, and right in sending them to experience the utter ruin and damnation of hell.

The reality of being wrong brings us to Christians. In Christ we are no longer doomed sinners, but saved saints. In Christ we are no longer lost to God, rather we are found to be identified in, by, and with the very righteousness of Christ. But, when it comes to being wrong, that can prove to be more challenging. Unless Christ is in the equation we will at times find ourselves to be quite wrong in our thinking, being, and way of doing. The reason for this is due to the presence of carnality in us.

Our fleshly ways and the influences of the world still must be identified and rooted out of our lives. These ways have blinded and indoctrinated us. For example, even though we cannot perceive our thoughts to be wrong, the Bible reminds us that God's thoughts are much higher than ours. If such thoughts are not brought into captivity through obedience to Christ, they continue to work on the level of vain imaginations.[26]

Our way of being can prove wrong for it has been perverted. God's ways are higher or more excellent than man's ways. Granted, we perceive all of our ways as being right, but the fruit of them prove differently. They reveal that the death of carnality is still present. If we fail to institute the ways of God in a matter our ways usually lead us to a place of vanity and some kind of ruin.

Our activities or busy works can give us a false impression that we are on the right path, but we have this formidable warning in Matthew 7:21-23 that tells us if such works are not according to God's plan and purpose, they will be discarded. Titus warns us of works that will be considered reprobate. If works are not foreordained by God, the mark of eternity will be missing from them, and they will fall to the wayside when we stand before the Lord at His judgment seat.[27]

The truth is that so much of what we do in our thinking, being, and doing is about ourselves and has nothing to do with the matters of heaven. I once stated that I spent the first seven years of my Christian life being wrong because the spirit and intent behind my motive, attitude, and activities were wrong. Tasting the fruit of such times proved to be quite bitter and humbling to my soul. God spent the next five years trying to line up some of my attitude to the ways of true righteousness, the next

---

[26]   Isaiah 55:8-9; 2 Corinthians 10:3-5

[27]   Isaiah 55:8-9; Ephesians 2:10; Titus 1:15-16

three years trying to right my spirit, and at the present He is constantly working on my activities to reveal my agendas, priorities, and fruits to unveil my present motives and attitudes. At each place or stage I had to face the harsh reality that if the self-life or the world's influences are involved in a matter, they remain and continue to be wrong no matter how right it seems to me. Each stage or level God has brought me to has knocked more stuffing (pride) out of me and has brought me to a place of greater humility before Him.

Obviously, man wants to always bring something to the table so that he does not have to be indebted to anyone, including God. To think that he would be completely beholden to God insults his arrogance, causing insolence in his pride, and fear and anger to his soul. And, if man was so inclined to see his wretched state, face his present status, and know just how wrong he is, it could easily burst his bubble of self-delusion and break him in many pieces at the point of his resolve—a resolve that manages to maintain the delusion of his present way.

The truth is that we all need to be broken by the harsh reality of why Jesus had to die for us. We often view it from a sentimental bubble, but not from the harsh reality that we were drowning in a cesspool of rebellion, insolence, and indifference. It is for this reason Jesus is first presented as the Rock. Granted, we must establish our lives upon who He is and what He has done for us, but our first encounter with Him as the Rock is for the sole purpose of breaking us at our resolve to maintain our present delusion about our status.[28]

From my own personal experience I know that God must sometimes take us through stages when it comes to facing the depth of our depravity. I knew I was a sinner, but I had no idea how lost or wrong I was until I had to face aspects of my character, confront my way of thinking, and take responsibility for my way of being. The Lord was patient to use what I considered different can openers to reveal the wretchedness of the "old man" in me. But, I began to understand that if we as believers fail to experience these stages where God has truly extended His mercy in order to offer His grace, we will not have the attitude to properly receive the various riches of His grace. The more we understand the extent of the grace He has offered us, the more we are able to receive it. Sadly,

---

[28]   Matthew 7:24-27; 21:42-44

most people do not allow the truth of their spiritual condition to totally undo their self-sufficiency and unravel their high opinion of self to allow the deep work of His forgiveness and mercy to prepare the way for them to experience the greater riches of His grace.

This brings us to the harsh reality that man is truly undeserving of God's grace. If He saves anyone it is for the sake of His Son, or even for the sake of those who might be laboring in prayer for such wretched souls, but He will not save them because He is indebted in some way to do so. Outside of His love, He has no reason to save such individuals, nor does He have any obligation to do so.

What is a person to do if God is not indebted or obliged to save him or her? There is only one thing a person in such a state can do. Such individuals must first acknowledge their own personal debt of death that must be paid due to sin, and then they must humbly fling themselves on the mercy of God.

People never approach God seeking His grace for they are undeserving of it. They can only approach God seeking His mercy. When people seek mercy, it is from a state of humility. We see this in the different cases of those who sought God for mercy. The sinners asked for mercy because they knew judgment awaited them, blind men asked for mercy because they could not see the way in which they needed to walk, and the person who was found in the wrong asked for mercy because he or she could not make it right.[29] Such a response required each individual to first humble him or herself in the truest form of repentance or need in order to draw near to God in search of mercy. These examples show us that since God has already commended His love or drawn near to each of us through His Son, we each must draw near to Him by way of His Son's redemption, in humility and repentance. Romans 5:8 and James 4:6-10 bear this out.

The best way to describe mercy and grace is the way the Bible describes it. Mercy is the seat, while grace is the throne. The opposite of mercy is judgment, while the opposite of grace is wrath. Because of God's mercy we will not face deserved judgment and because of His grace, we will be spared from His deserved wrath. Before He can show His mercy, a repentant sinner must first turn and truthfully face the

---

[29]   Mark 10:47-49; Luke 15:17-24; 18:13

judgment that awaits him or her. Once the person turns to face judgment, then he or she can begin to truly seek God's mercy in true humility. Humility will allow God to show His grace, ensuring that such a person will not taste His wrath, for by grace he or she will be saved unto a new life.

Clearly, each of us must first come to the seat of mercy before we can hope to find the grace that freely flows from His throne. Hebrews 4:16 confirms this, "Let us, therefore, come boldly unto the throne of grace, that we may obtain mercy, and find grace to help in time of need." As Christians we have access to the throne of grace, but we must come to it first seeking to obtain mercy before we are assured of finding God's favor in times of need.

This brings us to the significance of mercy. The concept of the mercy seat can be found in the furnishings of the tabernacle. The incredible aspect about this mercy seat is that there was only one such seat and it was located on the Ark of the Covenant. It was for the sake of those God made covenants with that He was quick to show mercy to those who were seeking to obtain it in relationship to His promises. He showed mercy to Isaac and the children of Israel on behalf of Abraham due to the covenant He made with him. Because of the covenant that Jesus established for each of us, God is also quick to show mercy to us when we seek it.[30] It is important to realize we do not do something that is contrary to our personal benefit for the sake of ourselves; rather, we do something for the sake of that which we value outside of ourselves or consider worthy.

We gain insight as to the purpose of this mercy seat in Exodus 25:20-22. We know that the mercy seat was made of pure gold, placed upon the Ark of the Covenant. Covering the mercy seat were two cherubim with outstretched wings. Their faces were looking down towards the mercy seat. The belly of the ark was to hold the testimony that God would later give the children of Israel of Himself. There were three objects that were eventually placed in this compartment, the Law, a jar of manna, and the budding rod of Aaron.

As I considered the significance of the presentation of mercy, in my mind I could see these two angels peering into something that was

---

[30]   Genesis 26:3-5, 24; Ephesians 4:32

incredible. Peter speaks of the things angels desire to look into.[31] They have no need for mercy, grace, or salvation, yet they desire to look into the wondrous face of such matters. Their longing to look into that which we are able to experience should bring awe to us.

When I thought of the wings of these angels touching, I thought of how mercy and judgment met at the point of Jesus' redemption, opening the way for grace to flow down to each of us by way of mercy. Mercy affords grace to lift us above the holy judgment of the Law, ensures us the riches that come from the Bread of heaven (Jesus), and produces everlasting life (the budding rod of Aaron).

The mercy seat also pointed to something else: that of communion. This is what God told Moses in Exodus 25:22, "And there I will meet with thee, and I will commune with thee from above the mercy seat, from between the two cherubim which are upon the ark of the testimony, of all things which I will give thee in commandment unto the children of Israel." Mercy is a place where God can meet man in agreement and communion. It is in such agreement and communion that God is able to show His grace. It is at such a place that man can find and experience God's incredible favor.

As believers we would all like to think that we are experiencing the fullness of God's grace. We are in fact experiencing grace according to the mercy we have sought and embrace. Mercy allows us to understand that we are undeserving, and that what we are receiving from God cannot be earned for it is a matter of His favor or grace. It is from this perspective that His grace is able to enrich our lives with a greater revelation of God's ultimate commitment and intention towards us.

To gain a good comparison to how mercy and grace works, all we have to do is consider the opposite contrast. In man's fallen state he can only unmercifully judge any culprit that might offend, cause insult, disagree with, or cause discomfort to his fragile reality. He has never known the ways of mercy, nor has he tasted the sweetness of grace. He judges from the throne of pride and the heights of arrogance. He judges as a despot who is tyrannical and cruel. He has no compassion because he is void of mercy. He has no means to be just in such judgment because he is blinded by his own darkness. In his treacherous

---

[31]   1 Peter 1:12

reality he can only condemn, curse, and trample under those who dare intrude into, challenge, or disagree with his lifeless standards, unrealistic ideology, and his rigid religious codes. In his mind, such offenders are inferior, insignificant, and must be cast aside as rubble for that which he considers to be worthy of his personal consideration and respect.

Jesus actually spoke of such judgment in Matthew 7:1-6. He stated that the same judgment that is measured out to others will be the same judgment that will be measured out to those who are judging. The reason for this is because we often harshly judge the character, deviation, or flaws evident in others that plague our lives. People with like flaws serve as mirrors who reflect the arrogance and destructive ways that can be present in our personal character, but the beam in our own eyes keep us from seeing and owning such deviate ways. This is why Jesus referred to those who judge in such manner as "hypocrites."

When dealing with the self-righteous religious leaders, Jesus told them to go and learn what it means that He would accept mercy and not sacrifice.[32] He was making reference to Hosea 6:6, "For I desired mercy, and not sacrifice, and the knowledge of God more than burnt offerings."

We often think God will be impressed with our many activities, but what He wants to see is mercy replacing our judgmental ways. The Bible is clear about the necessity for God's people to obtain mercy in order to show mercy. Mercy will accompany salvation. We are told that in salvation, mercy, and truth comes together, while righteousness and peace will kiss each other. Solomon tells us that by mercy and truth iniquity is purged. We know that mercy will manifest itself in forgiveness. Mercy is what will uphold the throne of a leader, and that we need to love it, as well as sow in righteousness in order to reap in mercy. Jesus tells us those who are merciful towards others will obtain mercy. James warns that those who judge without mercy will likewise be shown no mercy because mercy rejoices against judgment.[33]

God delights in mercy, because it will always allow Him to show grace.[34] We must have the same attitude towards His mercy and grace. However, we cannot show what we have never personally acknowledged,

---

[32] Matthew 9:13

[33] Psalm 85:10; Proverbs 16:6; 20:28; Micah 6:8; Matthew 5:7; James 2:13

[34] Micah 7:18

experienced, and possessed for ourselves. We cannot be an extension of God's incredible grace towards others if we do not possess the mercy that serves as the platform or means in which grace can be offered.

A good way to determine if we are recipients of the various riches of God's grace is to discern the depth of our mercy towards those who have offended us. We all can become quite upset with personal offences, but if the love of God is present such offences will give way to mercy. Mercy will turn into forgiveness, forgiveness into compassion, and compassion will enter into service towards those who are hurting and seeking, allowing grace to flow down from the throne of God in, through, and out of our lives.

THE REIGN OF GRACE

We have considered how we receive grace, but how can we be assured that we can continue to receive the benefits of grace? I once heard a pastor explain that when we insist of going our own way, God simply lifts His grace. It is a lot like undoing the ropes of a boat and letting it be carried by the ripples and waves of the water. We know that as the boat floats further away from the shore or pier, that it will become harder to retrieve and in greater danger of destruction.

As believers everything about our life is maintained by the grace of God. Some Christians understand that it is by the grace of God they walk and accomplish anything worthwhile in their lives. They know that without the strong ropes of God's grace securing them to the Rock that they would indeed be doomed. But, there are those who seem to be void of such understanding. They continue to put God's Word to a foolish test by fighting against His advancements to spare them from tasting the fruits of their foolishness. Granted, there is a wrestling match taking place in the spiritual realm, but the Spirit of God will not continue to strive with man.[35] At this time the ropes of grace will be removed to allow rebellious man to taste the consequences and ridiculous folly of his ways. When God lets go of the ropes of His grace, it points to judgment.

---

[35] Genesis 6:3

It is also easy to talk about, sing about, and even debate God's amazing grace, but the truth is we must be actual recipients of it if we are going to benefit from it. This brings us to the active role grace must continually play in our lives. Does grace require any disciplines to ensure that it is present and actively working in our lives? We know it is a gift that we are unworthy to receive, but even valuable gifts carry responsibilities. For example in relationship to salvation, Philippians instructs us to work out our salvation with fear and trembling, while Hebrews warns us that we must not neglect our salvation. We know that we can remove ourselves from under God's grace and actually bring ourselves under another gospel that has no power to save. We have also learned that we can frustrate or cast off His grace and render its work to mean nothing in our lives.[36]

Reasoning about this matter points to the fact that God's grace works according to disciplines that protect its integrity. We know that if the environment is not right, grace will not be recognized or properly received. We must also reason that if the right environment is not maintained, it cannot freely flow. It will either be shut down, hidden, or absent.

The Apostle Paul actually gave us some insight into the main discipline that will always ensure that grace is present. Consider what Romans 5:21 says about this very matter, "That as sin hath reigned unto death, even so might grace reign through righteousness unto eternal life by Jesus Christ, our Lord."

The apostle is clearly bringing a contrast in relationship as to who or what is reigning in our life. In Romans 6, Paul talked about two masters, sin or God. Masters remind us that we are slaves, and as slaves we will serve some type of master, but we can only serve one master at a time.[37] The master we give way to is the one who will reign in our lives. The concept of reigning in this Scripture does not simply embrace some form of directive, it also points to the foundation of power or sovereignty.[38]

In Romans 5:21 we are told that sin is the power that rules in our life, not only in relationship to our physical existence, but it is also going

---

[36] Galatians 1:6-9; 2:21; Philippians 2:12; Hebrews 2:3

[37] Matthew 6:24

[38] Strong's Exhaustive Concordance. # 935 & 936

to follow us as ruler in the life to come. It will reveal itself in our spiritual separation or death where God is concerned.

In light of the sovereign reign of sin upon a person, consider the opposite side of the coin. I must note that the issue of our spiritual existence is not a matter of a flip of a coin; rather, it is a choice as to who or what is going to rule our lives. Death clearly is the fruit that will come forth when sin reigns or serves as the predominate influence in a person's life. On the flip side of the coin is life, but consider what must serve as the base or influence of such a life: God's grace.

Sin is quite attractive to the flesh and ways of man for it has no disciplines, but grace does. It can only reign through righteousness. In summation, grace is sovereign and comes from a base that is powerful, and can only be realized and maintained in our lives when righteousness is present. Righteousness entails three areas of our life. It entails right standing before God, standing upright in Christ, and doing right by those around us. Righteousness is the environment that grace can operate within as a sturdy, immovable base, as well as an avenue in which it can reign through our lives as a powerful influence to ensure salvation.

It is vital to understand how this environment is established so that grace can operate in a sovereign or supreme way in our lives. First, how can we be assured that we have right standing before God? The Apostle John told us that Jesus is full of grace and truth. One of the benefits of being a recipient of God's grace is that we are positionally placed in Jesus. According to the Apostle Paul, Jesus serves as our base or source of righteousness.[39] When the Father considers the believer, He sees the righteousness of His Son, not the filthy rags of his or her best efforts. Since He sees His Son, we as believers are counted as having right standing before Him. Such an environment affords Him the luxury of allowing His grace to flow _to_ us.

This brings us to what it means to stand upright in Christ. People start out bent in all the wrong directions. How do Christians realign their direction towards the matters of God and life? There is only one way to line up to our spiritual cornerstone and that is through obedience to God's Word. However, such obedience is the product of faith.

---

[39] 1 Corinthians 1:30; 2 Corinthians 5:21

The Apostle Paul made this statement in Romans 5:2, "By whom also we have access by faith into this grace in which we stand, and rejoice in hope of the glory of God." When it comes to salvation, God's part is grace, but our part is faith. Genuine faith serves as the access into God's grace in which we stand. Faith chooses to put its reliance in God about what He says or requires and responds accordingly, thereby, opening the door in which grace can flow *into* our lives.

Keep in mind all things that pertain to life and godliness come from God. We are told that God is the one who either gives us the measure of faith to properly respond or the gift of faith to see a matter through to the end. By choosing to believe God, we are relying upon His character and words to be true, which will cause us to align ourselves with Him as our spiritual cornerstone. In such a position we are standing upright in Christ, and as a result we are told that God reckons such faith or reliance as being righteous.[40]

This brings us to doing right in regard to others. God cannot accept works or acts that do not come out of the premise of faith. For example, if we believe God, we will obey Him as far as our responsibilities towards Him and others. We do not obey to bring attention upon personal piousness; rather, we obey because it is a natural response of genuine faith towards God. When obedience is a matter of faith, the Lord actually imputes such works or acts as being righteous, allowing His grace to flow *through* us to others.[41]

It is important to understand how grace reigns through righteousness. It will indeed prove to be superior in all that it does and accomplishes. As we can see, our faith serves as the door or access for which grace can flow through the very corridors established and recognized as righteousness by God. It is also important to note that grace reigns through righteousness unto everlasting life.

The Apostle Paul talked about how sufficient grace is to get us through times of weaknesses and uncertainty.[42] In Romans 5:21 we see grace will reign until we are brought into the fullness of eternal life. Once we are brought into the fullness of eternity, then we will begin to discover

---

[40] Romans 4:9 12:3, 1 Corinthians 12:7-11; 1 Peter 2:6; 2 Peter 1:3-4

[41] Romans 4:18-25; James 2:14-26

[42] 2 Corinthians 12:6-10

in greater measure the riches that we have and will experience because of God's favor.

However, we must note something else. The grace that reigns through righteousness unto eternal life does so because of Jesus Christ. We know we are saved by grace, but grace can only come our way through righteousness unto eternal life by means of Jesus Christ, our Lord.

We must never forget that Jesus is that spiritual faucet or tap from which grace flows from the very throne of God. Grace will come from no other source or by any other means. If the environment is not right, it will not flow. If there is no place for it to freely flow into the souls and hearts of man, the tap will remain close. Grace flows where the Spirit of the Living God is able to freely move upon the hearts, minds, and lives of men with the reality of the Son of God. Grace reaches into the very souls of those who with their whole hearts are seeking to find and experience the source of this magnificent gift of heaven.

What about you? Have you discovered the incredible source of God's grace? Does it reign in your life through righteousness? Or, is grace simply a concept that has no life or meaning to it?

THE PRODUCT OF GRACE

God's incredible grace is something we will be discovering for ages to come. It has been made available in Jesus and it can abound as it freely flows into the various recesses of the wilderness of man's soul. Left barren and desolate by sin, grace can and will revive and restore hopeless, sin-laden souls with the eternal life of Jesus.

The Apostle Paul made this statement in 2 Corinthians 9:8, "And God is able to make all grace abound toward you, that ye, always having all sufficiency in all things, may abound to every good work." We have been talking about how grace benefits our life, but now we must consider how it will manifest itself in the Christian walk. The Apostle Paul is clearly giving us insight into how grace will express itself in the believer's life. It will be made obvious through good works.

God's grace can only express itself as grace. The kindness God displays often comes in the form of good works towards others. The Apostle Paul describes what He does in our life as a good work that will be performed until the day of Jesus Christ.[43] Once again we are reminded of the Apostle John's words in John 1:16, "And of his fullness have all we received, and grace for grace." Therefore, since God expressed grace towards us because of the work Jesus did on the cross on our behalf; it will be natural for us to express grace in good works towards others in relationship to God's kingdom. Grace equips the saint to reciprocate the same type of grace he or she has received. It is available, active, and sufficient in all that it does. It consists of acts of kindness or favor, and since the reservoir will never run dry, it will show itself through gracious manifestations.

There are Christians that perceive that God's grace allows them to sit on their spiritual laurels until they enter the kingdom of God. It is as though it gives them a free ride when it comes to responsibilities, but in reality the opposite is true. God did not sit on His laurels while men were perishing in their sins. Obviously, there are the merciful and compassionate sides of grace that will not turn a deaf ear to the pleading cries of those seeking mercy, as well as those who are downtrodden and in desperate need of pity and compassion. The prophet Jeremiah explained it in this way in Lamentations 3:22-26,

> It is because of the LORD's mercies that we are not consumed, because his compassions fail not. They are new every morning; great is thy faithfulness. The LORD is my portion, saith my soul; therefore will I hope in him. The LORD is good unto those who wait for him, to the soul that seeketh him. It is good that a man should both hope and quietly wait for the salvation of the LORD.

God's grace operates in the present. It has an ear that is sensitive to the plight of others. As His mercy meets each of us in our need and His compassion reaches out to care for us in our humble, poor state, we will begin to feel the benefits of His grace. Such mercy or compassion would never be carried over from the day before because they would not be equipped or sufficient to meet each of us in our present plight. For this reason the riches associated with God's grace will never be outdated or

---

[43]   Philippians 1:6

considered obsolete. Surely, there will never be a time where man will not have need for God's consideration, intervention, or kindness. And, when weary man finds His grace, it will always refresh his parched soul, bringing forth life as he begins to partake of the wells of salvation.[44]

Remember, grace can only operate as grace in and through our lives. This brings us back to Ephesians 2:8-10, "For by grace are ye saved through faith; and that not of yourselves; it is the gift of God—Not of works, lest any man should boast. For we are his workmanship, created in Christ Jesus unto good works, which God hath before ordained that we should walk in them."

Faith and works cause confusion for those who perceive that grace means they are simply going to slide into heaven. What people forget is a slide goes down, not up. Grace is not a matter of sliding into heaven. As we can see from Ephesians it is not a matter of working our way to heaven either, for it is a work and act of God. So how does grace work in relationship to heaven. The beauty of grace is that it is God's way of lifting man above the world to know, experience, and partake of the riches of grace. Scriptures such as James 4:6-10 bears this out. We are told that God gives grace to the humble, and then we are given this insight about humility, "Humble yourselves in the sight of the Lord, and he shall lift you up" (James 4:10).

The Apostle Peter echoed the same words when he warned people that God will resist the proud, but gives grace to the humble. He then gave this exhortation, "Humble yourselves, therefore, under the mighty hand of God, that he may exalt you in due time" (1 Peter 5:6).

Grace allows God to honor, lift up, or exalt the humble to receive or benefit from His merciful, compassionate kindness. He does not show such kindness because a person is worthy of it, rather He shows it because in a humble position the person has great need for it and will be receptive to receive it in a right attitude. Such a person will end up asking for mercy, while hoping to find His grace.

People who are confused about grace, often attach obedience that comes out of faith as being a work, rather than a natural extension or fruit of genuine faith. When you speak of "good works" in relationship to the natural extension and fruit of the Christian life, these confused individuals

---

[44]   Isaiah 12:3

clamor that you are suggesting that they must earn their salvation. They refuse to see that the Christian life is an active walk that will manifest itself according to the life that is being worked in each of us as believers. Such a life is not only responsive to the Spirit and active in expressing itself, but it will be fruitful and productive in good works.

The Apostle Paul gives us insight about good works. He states that we need to walk worthy of our Lord unto all that is pleasing, being fruitful in every good work. In all things we should show a pattern of good works, and that those who belong to the Lord Jesus should be zealous of good works.[45]

It is true that as Christians we are not saved *by* good works, but it is clear that we are saved *unto* good works for the glory of God. In Ephesians 2:10, we are told that in Christ we are being made into workmen that will do works that have already been foreordained by God. For example, God put Adam in the perfect environment of the Garden of Eden to keep and dress the garden. In a sense, God was saying to Adam, you have been given paradise, but it is up to you to keep it as so.[46]

Eternal life is freely given, but it carries responsibilities that I refer to as godly disciplines that ensure it is properly utilized within us, through us, and from us. Life points to the fact that it must be lived or walked out to experience the fullness of it. Since eternal life comes from outside of us, it must be worked into us by faith through obedience to His Word. Such obedience will naturally express itself in good works.

Grace naturally manifests itself in works of mercy, compassion, and kindness. Any grace that is shown through God's people's lives come from Him. I have actually experienced this grace working in, through, and out of my life.

Over the years of ministry the Lord has given me decisive burdens for those He has so graciously entrusted to me. These burdens were accompanied by His grace that enabled me to do incredible works that were clearly beyond any personal commitment or endurance. I recognized it was His grace that sustained me to see such burdens through to the end. However, in many occasions some of the burdens were lifted from me.

---

[45] Colossians 1:10; Titus 2:7, 14
[46] Genesis 2:15

When a burden is lifted it means that you have come to the end of the season as far as ministry in regard to the person's spiritual welfare. There is nothing more you can do to ensure effective growth because the person has come to some type of personal crossroad in his or her own life. It is only a matter of time before God removes you from the equation to test, prove, or bring greater spiritual growth to the parties involved.

What happens when God lifts a burden? Remember, grace for grace. With a burden God's grace is working *in* you to properly minister, but when a burden is lifted, God's grace must work *through* you. It must be constantly extended in the situation to ensure the integrity of what He has done or what He will do. In the first scenario you discover the strength and authority of His grace, but in the latter you actually feel its graciousness flowing through you, showing great restraint as well as kindness. Often times this grace is treated quite badly by those who assume they are worthy of it and do not understand it since Christians are expected to display it regardless of what is transpiring.

In such times, there was no doubt that what I was personally experiencing and displaying towards others was God's grace. However, when the ropes of grace were removed, then the separation or the parting of the ways would follow. It would often happen in an abrupt manner that made it clear that it was time to separate and go different ways.

When God's grace did lift, I would find that I had no more resolve to either contend with someone or show any real diplomacy in matters that required discretion. Each time I found myself in such a state, I was aware that what followed was the sword of truth and separation. In one incident a person pushed me into a corner to get me to agree with her particular delusion. Hitting my human limitation I became obnoxious in my resistance to agree with her false reality. The sword abruptly came down through the last bit of thread that held our relationship together. Although I would have been glad to apologize for my obnoxiousness, I still would have remained at odds with her about her particular take on the situation.

God's love compels His people to pay a debt of obligation to Him when it comes to ministering to others, but it is His grace that affords them the freedom and means to pay such an ongoing debt.[47] This payment is often expressed in the form of respect, kindness, and good works.

---

[47] Romans 13:8-10

Although grace is an incredible subject in which neither the depths nor the heights of it would ever be reached in this lifetime, as believers we can experience various riches along the way. The riches of grace afford us so many spiritual luxuries that can abundantly benefit our life and journey through this world. The greater the depth that grace reaches into our souls to bring forth these riches, the more aware we become of the heights in which it can bring us in our relationship with the Lord.

Admittedly, it has taken me various pages to try to tap into the reality of God's grace.[48] But, to me there is one man who summarized it in a song. A wicked despot who made his money transporting slaves to be sold on the open markets of the world, John Newton seemed like he was too far away for even the grace of God to reach him. However, that all changed when he faced his wicked state in the midst of a storm that threatened to take him down into the watery grave. In his state of need, this wicked man realized his hopeless condition. The result is that he did seek out and find God's grace. Due to Mr. Newton's experience with God's grace, we now have an ageless testimony that has proved to be rich with priceless treasures of truths that best expresses this incredible act and work of God.

How many times have you sung this man's testimony: "Amazing Grace?" Each time I have sung this song, I am reminded that this is my testimony. As I have sung it I realize that God's grace has proven sweet to my ears and that there is no better way to sign off on this subject. It did save me when I was in my wretched state. Even though I was lost, it allowed me to be found. Even though I was blind, it opened my eyes to see another world beyond the one I lived in. It has taught me much along the way, relieving me of the old fears that drove me into dismay, and replacing them with hope. It has brought me safe this far and it will lead me to my final destination. And, when I have been at my destination for ten thousand years, reflecting the brightness of the glory of heaven, I will still be singing praises to the God who was so loving, kind, and gracious in showing such a wretch as me His incredible, undeserved, amazing grace.

---

[48] If you would like to learn more about grace in relationship to such matters as the Law of God, see the author's book, *My Words are Spirit and Life*, in volume 1 of her foundational series.

4

A MATTER
OF FAITH

INTRODUCTION

Faith has become a controversial matter in Christendom. At one time there was a great pursuit to corral faith into some type of working formula for the purpose of controlling God or circumstances. For some, they believed that if they spoke a matter in good faith that they would control the events. For others they concluded that if they could visualize a matter in good faith, that they could make it come true. These methods may have sounded good but the fruits of them eventually proved to the contrary. Many of the individuals that went the way of these formulas or methods either ended up shipwrecked in their faith, deluded, or succumbing to total unbelief.

Faith is not a matter of wishful thinking or strong concentration; rather it is a matter of a sober mind choosing to believe what is true, and receiving such a truth into a receptive heart. It is not declaring a matter to be true; rather, it is being able to say "amen" or "so be it" about what is true and coming into total agreement with it. It is not a way to control reality; rather it is a way of getting a hold of God to ensure that what is true according to His plan and ways becomes a personal reality and experience in a world of ignorance, delusion, and hopelessness.

There is no way that one can exhaust the subject of faith. Faith is only as great as what it has actually embraced in regards to God. Since God is eternal, there is no way to corral this subject into some method or formula in which man could control God or his reality. Faith is about embracing the unseen reality of heaven in order to effectively face the harsh reality of the world we live in. Faith is not about coming out on top of a matter, it is about standing when the world around you does not make sense, withstanding the darkness of a world gone mad, and still standing when everything seems hopeless and disastrous in a world that is falling apart at the seams.

It is my hope in this material to bring sanity back to this subject so that people will possess a faith that is able to stand and endure the days we live in. When all is said and done, it will be a faith that will withstand the fiery trials that are already testing the resolve of God's people. And, when Jesus does come back for His Church, He will find genuine faith in His people who are still clinging to His everlasting promises in abiding confidence in spite of the tumultuous times engulfing the world (Luke 18:8).

GENUINE FAITH

It has been an important goal of mine to understand what constitutes true faith. I have heard other people's explanation of it, but to me it has often revealed their ignorance about it, rather than personal knowledge. It was as if these people had discovered a gold mine, but when their end product was tested in the fires it proved to be fool's gold.

Due to the "quasi" religion that I see operating in many of these worldly churches, I fear that for many the grave tests that are coming in this present age will prove that their type of faith is nothing more than fool's gold. Granted, it may be shining, appealing, and appears as the real thing, but when the fire is put to it, it will end up becoming ashes. It will leave such individuals shipwrecked, vulnerable, and disillusioned.[1] They will not know how to stand as fear takes hold of their minds, nor withstand the onslaught of darkness that will be consuming their souls, and remain standing when all their religious foundations lay in ruin. Such individuals might become angry with God, point an accusing finger at their religious leaders, or deem themselves as faithless and hopeless, while sliding right into a slime pit of self-pity and unbelief.

---

[1]   1 Timothy 1:19; 1 Peter 1:6-7

As I have studied faith there are a couple of aspects of it that as believers we must acknowledge about it up front. The first one being that faith is what enables us to stand in the tough times, withstand in the compromising times, and continue to stand in times that seem hopeless and impossible. It is truly a shield that can cover the whole body when the fiery darts being flung at us begin to consume all that is truly not founded on the true foundation of heaven, Jesus Christ.[2]

The second aspect about faith is that it is active. Most people fail to realize that they do all things according to faith. For example, we turn on a light switch believing that a light will come on. We come into agreement with others believing that whatever is agreed upon will be accomplished. In reality we do something because we have faith that it is going to work. Granted, we do not realize we do things because there is a certain measure of faith to do so, but this is how we all operate.

The flip side to the coin of faith is unbelief. In other words, if we do not believe that by flipping on the light switch that it will produce light, we will have no need to even consider it because there is no expectation that anything will materialize. This clearly shows that we do not have any real belief or confidence that our action will produce any real results. Unbelief is unresponsive because it has no expectation, or in some situations any confidence that something is going to work.

This brings us to an important point about faith, which is that it is not blinded or directed at unfounded activities. Faith is based on something that is known to work. For this reason faith without action is dead.[3] In essence, a person knows without a doubt that a matter will work, and in expectation responds accordingly. Clearly, there is no reason to believe to the contrary that something will not perform in the way it was intended to. This is the essence of simple, childlike faith.

Since the very nature of faith is to act on what it knows or believes to be true, faith always walks in expectation toward a desired result. A good way to think about this is that, *"We do nothing unless we do so in good faith, knowing or expecting the end results."* If you meditate on this for a while, you will see that everything we do is a matter of faith. If we do not have confidence in something, we will not put any faith in it.

---

[2]   1 Corinthians 3:11; Ephesians 6:16

[3]   James 2:14-26

This brings us to another aspect of faith. There are two springboards from which faith operates: they are hope and expectation. Up to this point I have made reference to hope in relationship to faith, but I have been mainly dealing with faith that operates according to expectation. For example, when I flip the light switch on, it is because I expect the light to come on. However, faith that operates from the premise of hope is a bit different. It operates according to unseen factors such as character, intent, or purpose. In such situations, people put their hope in a matter based on the substance or quality of something. For example, every time we make an agreement or contract with a person or an organization, it is because we believe that the person or organization has the character and intent to carry out the purpose of a matter to completion. If we did not have confidence in the character, word, or intent of a person or the organization, any type of hope of ever seeing something accomplished would be missing. Without hope there would be no expectation that a matter would ever come to fruition.

With this in mind, consider what Hebrews 11:1 states, "Now faith is the substance of things hoped for, the evidence of things not seen." What is the difference between hope and expectation? Hope is present when one cannot see the end results up front, while expectation walks in light of actually seeing the end results. Notice how our faith operates according to that which cannot be seen, but we trust that it is true because we have a record and evidence that it is so. Since we can trust the evidence set before us, we can put our hope in what already has been or is being established because of some point of agreement or record. Since we have put our hope in the past reputation of something, we can walk in expectation of seeing some type of agreement, promise, or covenant being fulfilled or kept.

It is for this reason the Apostle Paul tells believers that we walk by faith and not by sight when it comes to our spiritual life.[4] Most religious Christians walk according to their expectations as to how the Christian life will benefit them. However, such expectation may be void of any real substance. What people do not realize is that our hope is based on the character of God, not on what we know, can see, or necessarily expect from Him.

---

[4]   2 Corinthians 5:7

In Hebrews 6:1, we are given this insight, "Therefore, leaving the principles of the doctrine of Christ, let us go on unto perfection, not laying again the foundation of repentance from dead works, and of faith toward God." Faith makes up the six principles of the doctrine of Christ. Take notice of how faith must not be directed at the end result of something but towards God.

Even though we cannot see Jesus, we choose to believe He is who He says He is. The Apostle Peter put it this way in 1 Peter 1:8, "Whom, having not seen, ye love; in whom, though now ye see him not, yet believing, ye rejoice with joy unspeakable and full of glory."

It is because of who God is that we can enter into an agreement or covenant with Him and walk in expectation of seeing His promises fulfilled. It is for this reason that children are associated to the type of disposition that can embrace the simplicity of faith.[5] You tell a child something, and he or she will naturally believe it because the child has no reason not to.

The problem with adults is that the different challenges of life often make skeptics out of them. The reason they develop such skepticism is not because genuine faith does not work, it is because they have their own ideas or expectations as to how something should or must work. For example, if there is no electricity coming to the light switch, it does not matter how much you flip it on, it will remain dark. The truth is the "electricity" is missing from what people often put their faith in.

When we dare peek around our skepticism, we find selfishness and pride. Both selfishness and pride is contrary to a childlike disposition. Selfishness has personal agendas and wants a situation to feed its desire, while pride has personal priorities as to its idea as to what it will deem important. It will also ultimately demand that it be exalted in a situation. When you consider selfishness it will put its confidence in the expectation of something, while pride will rely on personal strengths or abilities to get its desired results. When the wrong source is present, the results are not satisfying. Either way the true environment in which genuine faith operates within is missing from the equation.

These people who possess an unrealistic faith about the matters of God eventually become disillusioned that their expectation did not

---

[5]   Matthew 18:1-4

come forth, or angry because something did not turn out the way they wanted, all the while becoming skeptics or unbelieving towards God's intentions and purpose. This means they become a skeptic because of their personal idea of faith, and will deem genuine faith towards God the culprit.

When these individuals are challenged to have the confident, abiding awe of childlike faith in a matter they cannot see or control, they will often become fearful towards it. The reason for such fear is not that genuine faith is obsolete, rather that it is because such individuals are worried that they will once again become disappointed that they will not get their way in a matter. They will become anxious towards God that He will not see it their way, and unbelieving towards Him because He will not agree with them.

Clearly, the type of faith these individuals develop is misguided, misdirected, and misappropriated. There is nothing genuine, sincere, or child-like about it. It is not directed towards God, and it will never allow God to be God; rather, it will put Him to a foolish test, revealing the folly of these people's pseudo faith.

It is not unusual to walk in unbelief towards God. Unbelief is the basis for idolatry, rebellion, and lawlessness. It will harden the heart towards God's truth, while justifying its particular logic, skepticism, and insistence that it is right in its conclusion.[6]

Once again we are reminded of Jesus' warning in Luke 18:8. The concern remains the same: when Jesus returns, will He find true faith? Man often operates according to some type of faith or reliance in his life as to what he deems trustworthy. That which he constitutes as being trustworthy will serve as some form of truth or evidence that will allow him to walk in expectation towards it. For this reason, we as believers must understand what constitutes real faith.

We know that faith is active. We walk according to the hope it produces in expectation that all that was promised will come to fruition. Since we must put our trust in the unseen, we as believers begin with hope towards God, while walking in expectation of seeing something materialize in light of the future according to His promises.

---

[6]   Hebrews 3:15-19

Walking in the present challenges in light of realizing a matter in the future is the real essence of genuine faith.[7] Since most people walk in expectation of seeing something materialize right away, they have no need of learning what it means to hope according to the unseen substance of heaven. Yet, this is what truth faith is all about. Faith produces the active walk that allows us to develop the necessary character to possess and wait upon what is eternal and lasting. Granted, we may see some promises fulfilled along the way, but such promises represent stepping stones to experience that which is of greater substance and far more excellent. Consider what Hebrews 6:12 states, "That ye be not slothful, but followers of them who through faith and patience inherit the promises."

People who walk in selfish expectation towards this present age will never learn the virtue of patience and endurance that will ensure they possess the promises of God. Yet, it was the genuine faith of those incredible witnesses of Hebrews 11 that enabled believers in each generation to endure their present age as they walked in expectation of the promises of the next world to come.

Consider Abraham. He was promised an earthly inheritance that he would never see come to fruition. However, his hope was not based on seeing that which was attached to earthly blessings come to fruition, but on seeing and experiencing the heavenly. It was obvious that Abraham did not walk in good faith or expectation towards the day he would see all matters materialize for him and his descendants; rather, he walked in expectation of seeing and experiencing the great city of God in the world that was yet to be unveiled to him.[8]

The real crux of genuine faith is that it enables us to walk in light of future expectations. Even though we do not see a matter coming to fruition in our present lifetime, we possessed the faith that is always presently active to respond to God on a daily basis in light of eternity. Such active faith not only reveals our great confidence in Him, but will trust Him to bring about such promises, regardless of whether we see them dashed into a million pieces by the present age we live in. We see this great confidence in Abraham's life.

---

[7]   Hebrews 10:35

[8]   Hebrews 11:8-10

Abraham was willing to sacrifice all future promises when he offered up his son, Isaac on the altar. For Abraham, his son represented the very one who possessed uncultivated seeds of those promises, yet he willingly offered up Isaac knowing that God's promises remained sure. He had such confidence in the character and word of God he believed that He would raise up his son. We are told his action allowed him to see into the glorious future by receiving his son in a figure. Jesus explained what this meant when He told the Jews that Abraham rejoiced to see His day: and he saw it, and was glad.[9] Abraham saw in Isaac the plan of God. Even though God would offer up the Promised Messiah on an altar, He would also raise Him up from the grips of death. Abraham not only wanted to see into the promise of his seed, but he saw it through the example of his own son and was glad.

Genuine faith is directed towards the only real source of hope: God. It does not rest its hope on or in this present world. As a result, it possesses the eyes that are able to see in light of the future hope that awaits the people of God. Such people walk according to this future hope that is more real to them than the wishful thinking or erroneous hype of the present age they live in. They know this present world holds nothing of value, and that the genuine faith they walk according to will sustain and enable them to endure to the end when they will actually possess their true inheritance. Hebrews 10:34-36 brings out this enduring quality of true faith. It is in joy that we wait in expectation for God's promises to be fulfilled.

What are you walking according to? There are religious people like the prodigal son in the parable in Luke 15 that want their inheritance now so they can squander it. Like the foolish young man in the parable, they do not want to wait for it and learn the value of such inheritance so they can properly prize it rather than squander it on useless living. Or, are you like the saints of old in Hebrews 11? They not only valued their inheritance, but they were also willing to wait upon it and endure to the end the challenges and mocking of the present age they lived in to receive it in greater ways. They actually lived in expectation of knowing in the end that their very souls would be saved.[10]

---

[9]   John 8:56; Hebrews 11:17-19

[10]   Hebrews 10:38

BELIEVING

Exploring the virtues of true faith gives insight into its steadfast ability to stand, withstand, and remain standing when all else seems to fall to the wayside. When it comes to the word "faith", *Vine's Expository Dictionary of Biblical Words,* uses such words as persuasion, conviction, trust, confidence, assurance, and belief to describe its qualities. We also see such words being used in Scripture.

It is because of such virtue we can understand why the Apostle Paul clearly tells us that there is only one true faith. We must possess this faith if we are to endure to the end of our journey. At the end of our journey the fullness of our salvation awaits us.[11]

This brings us to another reason our faith towards God must be active. It is our faith towards God that inspires us to take necessary steps of faith and obedience forward through the fearful, challenging times or age we live in. Everything we do as God's people in this age should, and must, be in light of the future world that awaits us. Since we know our hope is not here, we must avoid being tempted like the prophet in 1 Kings 13 to sit awhile under the tree before we complete our mission. It is at such times that temptation will catch up to us and try to cause us to veer away from what we know is right, preventing us from reaching our destination. Nor should we be like the children of Israel who considered the obstacles in front of them to be larger than God. As a result, they rebelled in fear and unbelief, thereby, failing to possess their inheritance.

The question is, how does child-like faith keep us going forward in our life regardless of the obstacles that stand in front of us? When you consider faith, some form of the word "believe" serves as the active aspect that causes some type of response in regards to faith. Since our belief rests in God, we can believe a matter is true, thereby walk confidently according to what we know is necessary and right to acquire a particular promise of God. The key word that is associated with active faith is "believing."

When I first became a Christian, "Easy Believism" was the gospel that was being advocated. Granted, no one referred to what was being presented as being "Easy Believism," but in reality that is what was

---

[11] Ephesians 4:5; 1 Peter 1:9

being promoted. You simply believe that Jesus died for you, while being encouraged to go forward to confess it before others. Sadly, this was the only forward movement many people experienced in their spiritual life. From that point on many went back into the world and never gave their Christian encounter another thought. After all, they were now saved and on their way to heaven. There was no more need to be concerned about their spiritual welfare or destination.

What many of these individuals failed to realize is that to believe a matter is a *process* where a person actually comes out with a belief about something. In the Christian realm, you cannot believe something unless there is a foundation that you can base it on, and you cannot have a foundation unless you choose to believe something.

The Bible talks about faith the size of a mustard seed. This seed is so small, and yet it possesses the means to tap into the power that can move a mountain. It is important to point out that faith is not what moves the mountain; rather, it is God that moves the mountain, but faith creates the environment for Him to do so. Such a grain of mustard seed is a measure of faith that has been given us, and actually points to the initial beginning of the process to develop belief in and towards God. Such faith allows Him to show Himself mighty on our behalf.[12]

Every time we *choose* to believe God about a matter, He is able to *confirm* our faith and belief towards Him, as well as *enlarge* our faith in Him. Notice how there is a progression of believing taking place. Such progression means we are walking according to the measure of faith that is already present, but we are also going to *capitalize* on it.

Most people do not capitalize on the measure of faith given them, let alone establish any real life in Christ. The main reason for this state is because such individuals never develop any substantial belief towards God. They fail to establish a proper environment in which God can show Himself mighty on their behalf.

The reality of faith begins with its approach to believe a matter. Most people approach something to decide as to whether it will fit into what they already know, think, or perceive. For example, due to my faith towards God, I approach the Bible to believe what it says, not debate, judge, or fit it into my way of thinking. The Bible serves as my point of

---

[12]   Matthew 21:21-22

authority, not my personal conclusions. If my personal conclusions collide with the Bible, I usually hit confusion. Rather, than negate the authority of the Bible, I must conclude that the confusion is a matter of my understanding being limited or wrong about a subject; therefore, I must choose to believe what the Bible says to be true, whether it makes sense or not to my way of thinking.

Faith begins with a choice as to what I am going to believe is true. For this reason the Apostle Paul tells us faith comes by hearing, and hearing by the Word of God.[13] I must choose to believe upon something as being true before I am going to progress in my faith towards someone or something.

Once I choose to believe a matter is true, than I can believe what is being said to me. Believing what is being said has to do with authority. It is not just a matter of believing something is true, I must know it is true based on the authority that stands behind it. If I do not have assurance in the authority behind it, it will never become a truth to me. For example, there are many things I agree with as being true in a particular setting, but that does not mean that they necessarily resonate as truth to me in other situations. The test as to whether something becomes truth to me is that no matter what platform it is presented from, it remains true to the end. The Apostle Paul put it best when he stated that you can do nothing against the truth only for it.[14]

For example, a person can tell me something that I can agree with. To my way of thinking I can agree with him or her at that particular point, but if I decide that the individual is not trustworthy, than what has been said along with all other things that the person might say is up for debate because I do not see him or her with the authority or character that can be trusted to see a matter through to the end. Therefore, I will be quick to debate, doubt, and have uncertainty towards what may seem disagreeable with my way of thinking, regardless as to whether it is true or not.

Scripture gives us a good example of how authority must be present for faith to properly function. A centurion came to Jesus seeking healing for his servant. Jesus agreed to come and heal this soldier's servant.

---

[13]   Romans 10:17

[14]   2 Corinthians 13:8

However, this man did not feel worthy that Jesus come to his home. Because he understood authority, and believed that Jesus possessed the authority and the power to carry it out that warranted his faith, he asked Him only to speak the necessary words. He knew upon Jesus' words alone his servant would be healed. Consider Jesus' response, "When He heard it, He marveled, and said to them that followed, Verily I say unto you, I have not found so great faith, no, not in Israel" (Matthew 8:10).

Believing upon and believing are what lies at the crux of many people's struggle with their concept of faith and how it will affect their attitude when it comes to God and His Word. They may agree with aspects of His Word, but that does not mean they are always going to believe the integrity of God's character and authority when it comes to His Word actually challenging what they may perceive to be truth. Such individuals will pick and choose what they believe because they cannot imagine how God could preserve the intent and integrity of His complete Word. These individuals do not trust the all powerful, trustworthy, faithful character of God with what they cannot understand. It is important to point out that in the flesh, we walk according to what we understand, which is considered a form of sight. To paraphrase 2 Corinthians 5:7, "We walk by faith in who we know (to be the truth) based on God's trustworthy character, and not by personal understanding."

In John 8, we see how believing on something, and believing the source can be far apart. We are told in John 8:30, "As he spoke these words many believed *on* him." These Jews could agree with the words Jesus spoke, thereby, they could believe on what He was saying.

However, consider what Jesus said to these very same Jews in John 8:42-43, "Jesus said unto them, If God were your Father, ye would love me; for I proceeded forth and came from God; neither came I of myself, but he sent me. Why do ye not understand my speech? Even because ye cannot hear my word." Some of these Jews could agree with Jesus up to a point, but when they were challenged in their understanding by His words, they became upset with Him. He then went on to tell them that God was not their Father; rather the devil was their true father. He then tells them that He told them the truth, but *they did not believe Him.*[15]

---

[15] John 8:43-45

Genuine faith begins where personal understanding ceases. There is much I do not understand about the things of heaven. Such things will either bring joy to my spirit and/or confusion to my intellect. Confusion is a form of darkness that reveals that the information I just heard cannot be integrated into to my present understanding. It is at this point that I will either choose faith in light of God's character, or the darkness of unbelief towards that which does not make sense. By faith I will choose to trust the character of God rather than words that produce confusion to my intellect. Remember I approach all matters to believe Him, not to understand what He says so I can organize it, adjust it to my understanding, fit it into my way of thinking, or shape it according to my calculated ways. To try to fit what I do not understand concerning the affairs of heaven in my personal box simply means I will ultimately give way to the darkness of unbelief and will remain walking in ignorance and/or skepticism towards God.

If I choose to trust what I know about the immutable, trustworthy character of God, I will do so because I choose to believe in who He is. I may not understand how something fits or works, but I still can believe that it is truth because He spoke it, and trust that in due time He will reveal it to my understanding as I need to know it. Notice the progression of believing.

First I choose to *believe on* a matter as being true, because I *believe* the authority, character, or credibility of the one saying it. If I believe something is true based on trusted authority, I will embrace it wholeheartedly as the truth, regardless of whether it makes sense to me. To embrace something wholeheartedly as the truth, means that I will *believe in* it and personally own it as being part of my belief system. If I perceive something is truth, I will live according to it. Clearly, if I truly believe something, I will live it. If I fail to live it, it is because I do not believe it is true.

In light of the progression of believing something, consider Romans 10:9-10,

> That if thou shalt confess with thy mouth the Lord Jesus, and shalt believe in thine heart that God hath raised him from the dead, thou shalt be saved. For with the heart man believeth unto righteousness; and with the mouth confession is made unto salvation.

We are told to confess with our mouth the Lord Jesus. What do we need to confess in regard to Jesus? The word "Lord" points to the authority of Jesus. If we confess or acknowledge Jesus is Lord, it means He is our owner, master, and God. We are in essence acknowledging the type of authority He is to have in our lives. It is based on His authority that we wholeheartedly believe that what has been said by Him is truth.

It is for this reason Solomon made this observation in Proverbs 23:7a, "For as he thinketh in his heart, so is he." Belief is a heart matter. If believing something is not a revelation of the heart, it will not be consider a truth that has any real merit or base. If there is no merit of base to something, why would any of us believe it and possess it as a truth that will have the power to impact our disposition, attitude, and conduct.

Jesus' declaration was quite clear in John 14:6. He said I am the truth. In other words, He just does not speak what is true, He is the truth. He is the essence and sum of all truth. The problem is people can agree on what He says, but refuse to believe Him in order to believe in who He is. If He is not the essence or sum of all truth, those who doubt can debate, ignore, and reject His sayings that do not fit into their intellectual and theological boxes of understanding. However, if an individual approaches to believe what He says based on the fact that He is truth, he or she will choose to trust His character in spite of those things that do not make sense to him or her.

Peter's response to Jesus in John 6:68-69 reveals such progression of belief in regard to the type of faith that was being developed towards the Lord. Jesus made some hard statements that caused many of His disciples to go back and walk no more with Him. Jesus asked the remaining 12 if they were also going away. Peter's answer reveals that he chose to believe Jesus in spite of whether he understood His sayings. "Then Simon Peter answered him, Lord, to whom shall we go? Thou hast the words of eternal life. And we believe and are sure that thou art that Christ, the Son of the living God."

In Peter's response, we see that he made a choice to believe on Jesus' words because He believed that all He said was true regardless of whether he understood. The reason he believed Him was because he believed in who He was. As a result, there was no turning back for him.

Martha is also another good example in John 11 of believing Jesus in the midst of personal darkness. Her brother, Lazarus, had died four days prior to Jesus entering the scene of the sorrow and mourning taking place. Martha came to Jesus and stated that if only He had been there when her brother was sick, he would have not died. She knew Jesus possessed power and believed His words. It had confirmed her faith towards Him. However, she also believed on Jesus. She stated that she knew that whatever He asked of God that God would give it to Him.

Jesus then asked her if she believed in the resurrection. Martha's reply, in essence, was that she knew for a truth that the resurrection would happen on that last day. Meditate on Jesus' words to her in John 11:25-26, "Jesus said unto her, I am the resurrection, and the life; he that believeth in me, though he were dead, yet shall he live. And whosoever liveth and believeth in me shall never die. Believest thou this?"

At the core of the Gospel is the resurrection. Romans 10:9 confirmed this. We must believe that God rose up Christ on the third day to be saved. Jesus clarified to Martha that He also serves as the essence of resurrection to those who believe Him. It is His life in every believer that possesses the power to raise each of us up on that great day. For Christians, resurrection is one of the principles of the doctrine of Christ.[16] The Apostle Paul reiterated the importance of the doctrine of resurrection in 1 Corinthians 15:14, "And if Christ be not risen, then is our preaching vain, and your faith is also vain."

Martha already had a belief about the promised resurrection. Jesus was standing before her, claiming to be the Resurrection and Life that would raise up each person on that great day. He went on to say that those who *believe in* Him would never die, but they shall live. Then, He asked Martha if she *believed* Him? Notice her declaration in John 11:27, "She said unto him, Yea, Lord; I believe that thou art the Christ, the Son of God, who should come into the world." Like Peter, Martha believed Jesus because she believed in His person and authority as the Christ, the Son of the Living God.

The difference between the Jews in John 8 and Peter and Martha is that the skeptical Jews did not *believe* Jesus when their understanding was being challenged because they did not *believe in* who He was. They did not believe He possessed the authority of the Messiah, or that He was the Son of the Living God; therefore, they walked in unbelief towards Him when it came to sayings that cut across the grain of their personal

---

[16] John 5:17-29; 1 Corinthians 15:1-4; Hebrews 6:1-2

understanding. They refused to agree that all of the words He spoke were true because they refused to see Him as being the essence, authority, and standard to all that was and is truth.

The real problem with most people's faith towards God is that they do not believe what He says because they do not believe in His Person, character, and work. They prefer their ignorance about Him in order to justify walking in unbelief towards Him, especially when it comes to that which might challenge their comfortable perception of Him and life. As a result, these individuals can occasionally agree with Him, as they pick and choose what they are going to believe on, while tacking His name or authority on to the mishmash of their quasi beliefs that have no real substance and power behind them. Jesus referred to such beliefs as mounting to nothing more than shifting sand that will not stand in the real storms of life.[17]

When we consider the examples of the Bible, we can note the progression of people's faith. We can see how the Apostle Paul knew who He believed and was persuaded that his Lord was able to keep that which he had committed to Him. Peter was sure that Jesus was who he knew Him to be, the Messiah, the Son of the Living God, and that He alone possessed the words of eternal life. The writer of Hebrews spoke about drawing near to God with a true heart in full assurance of faith, while the Apostle John talked about the assurance of our heart towards God and the confidence we can have in prayer if we truly love in word and deed.[18]

The Bible is clear that our faith will be tested. All that we have believed, do believe, and will believe will be laid bare before the Judge of our souls. Foundations will be shaken as to what we believe, all religious cloaks stripped away to reveal the credibility of our beliefs, and the blinders cut away from our eyes so that we will see the substance of our faith.[19] Nothing will remain hidden, and what is not of genuine faith will not be left standing. And, at the end of genuine faith is the salvation of our souls

As believers, we must examine to see if we truly are people who believe God. We must connect what we believe upon to what we are

---

[17] Matthew 7:24-27

[18] John 6:68-69; 2 Timothy 1:12; Hebrews 10:22; 1 John 3:18-22

[19] John 15:22; Hebrews 4:12; 12:25-29; 1 Peter 1:5-9

going to believe in. Before we can believe in God, we must decide to believe Him on the basis of what has been said in His Word regarding His person and character. Are you a believer in title only, or are you a believer because you have truly believed all that He has said in His Word to be the truth?

JUSTIFIED

The struggle with coming to terms with faith can be seen in Scripture. It is easy to talk about great faith, but to possess even a tiny speck of faith in a crisis can prove to be overwhelming and seem impossible. Granted, people of great faith make it look or sound easy, but their faith went through various trials before they were able to come to a place of confidence before the Lord.

Let us just consider a few examples in Scripture. One of my favorite examples is found in Mark 9. A father came seeking Jesus on behalf of his possessed son whose demons had often cast him into fire and water to destroy him. Jesus told the father that if he would believe, all things were possible. The father's response often describes the state many people find themselves in when it comes to faith, "And straightway the father of the child cried out, and said with tears, Lord, I believe; help thou mine unbelief" (Mark 9:24).

The father in this incident reveals the dichotomy that can surround faith. In essence, he was saying to Jesus, "I believe what You are saying, but when it comes to my situation, I am struggling with believing it for myself." How can a person believe what Jesus is saying, but is unable to personally receive it?

What a lot of people fail to recognize about faith is that it is not just a matter of believing something can happen, it is also the ability to personally receive it. The problem with this man was that his hope to see his son delivered had already been greatly deferred by past experiences that ended in disappointment and disillusionment. Solomon tells us that hope that has been deferred makes the heart sick.[20]

---

[20]   Proverbs 13:12

You have to wonder to what extent did this father extend himself to seek help for his son to only end up walking away in complete disappointment. Each time this father was hoping that a solution had been found, only to have any expectation dashed to the ground in a miserable heap of frustration and disillusionment. After so many disappointments, hope that something will change may remain, but there is no expectation that it ever will change. Hope may keep the person seeking different avenues, but without expectation, he or she is not ready or prepared to receive the solution. Clearly, this man was hoping Jesus would heal his son, but he was not expecting it.

It is easy to fall into such a state. I know I have been there through the years. You might have waited for a matter to be resolved for so long that after a while you really do not expect it to ever change. You have become weary, which causes you to resolve in your inner man to accept the situation as your "particular lot" in life in order to avoid any more disappointment. You go through the motions of trying to resolve it, but your heart remains unreceptive and sick. What this man failed to realize is that his hope was deferred because it had been placed in the practices of the world and not in the character of God. At least the father in this situation recognized that he was in such a state. He also identified the state as being unbelief, and asked the Lord to help him in his unbelief. He had to put his hope in God and stand in expectation of His intervention.

How would Jesus be able to help this man in his unbelief? Keep in mind the man's heart was most likely sick. Jesus came to heal the broken hearted.[21] This man's heart needed to be revived or healed. How would Jesus revive such a heart? He would deliver the man's son from demonic oppression.

Consider Jesus' disciples. Here were men who witnessed miracle after miracle. It would seem that nothing would cause them concern. However, faith is not something that is carried over from one incident to the next. We see this in the case of the disciples when they were facing the destructive waves of testing. Even though they had witnessed many miracles, the tenacity of the storm found them sliding into unbelief. Even

---

[21]   Luke 4:18

though Jesus was asleep in the boat, they still lacked the measure of faith to trust that everything was still under control.[22]

The Lord is always with His people, but sometimes it appears as if He is asleep. It is at such points we must choose the way of faith in the present tests of life that are confronting us. It can take every bit of resolve to choose to believe in spite of the mounting fear and uncertainty of a matter in order to stand steadfast in the present trial. We must recognize the affairs that truly rest in God's hands. At such time our part is to stand in faith, knowing God is God no matter how great the waves are that are challenging our lives.

The first thing we must do in such trials is recall or remember who God is. He is bigger than any obstacle, as well as being aware of every detail. We also must remember that after every great move or revelation we witness or encounter along the way, it will be followed by some type of test to see whether we got it or not. After all, faith is about inheriting the promise that awaits us at the end of the test. Faith is never revealed or enlarged unless it is being tested. We can say we believe, but do we, or are we still relying on what we think we already know?

You can see Jesus testing His disciples along the way to see if they were connecting to the simple lessons of faith that would enlarge and enable them to face the next trial. Case in point was the feeding of the five thousand in John 6. Jesus asked Philip where they would buy bread to feed all the people. Jesus knew where Philip was in his thinking. The Bread from heaven stood before Him, but Philip failed to realize that the One who provides all of our needs was also present to provide the solution. As a result, Philip only considered the task from a worldly standpoint, making any such attempt in his mind to feed so many people impossible.

In another incident a nobleman came to Jesus to intercede on behalf of his sick son. He asked Him to come down and heal his son. Jesus made this statement to him, "Except ye see signs and wonders, ye will not believe" (John 4:48). We know that Jesus healed this man's son at that very moment. John recorded that this was Jesus second miracle He performed.

When I considered what Jesus said to this man in light of His words in Matthew 12:39, "But he answered and said unto them, An

---

[22]   Matthew 8:23-27

evil and adulterous generation seeketh after a sign and there shall no sign be given to it, but the sign of the prophet Jonah," I became a bit confused. Jesus did not refer to this man seeking signs or wonders as being wicked? What was the difference? After meditating on the two different incidents I realized that this man, along with the desperate father of the demon possessed son, was seeking to believe Jesus, while the adulterous generation seeks signs and wonders for entertainment purpose. Such a generation has no intention of believing on and in Jesus.

We see this in the case of Herod. When Jesus was brought before Herod on the night of His betrayal, the king was not seeking to believe Jesus about who He was, he simply wanted Him to entertain him by showing him some miracle.[23]

The prophecies concerning the coming of the Messiah tells us that signs and wonders would follow Him to confirm His identity. When the disciples of John the Baptist came to Jesus on behalf of their beloved leader to ask Him if He was the promised One, what did Jesus send back as His credentials? He told them to tell John of the things they had heard and seen regarding Him: that the blind received their sight, the lame walked again, the lepers were cleansed, the deaf could hear, the dead were raised up, and the poor have heard the message of the Gospel.[24]

Some see John's desire to know whether Jesus was the Promised One as a matter of unbelief, but there is no indication in Jesus' eulogy of John that followed the incident to confirm such a conclusion. My personal opinion was that John was at the end of his earthly ministry and he was seeking confirmation and assurance that he had completed his mission of preparing others for the Messiah.

Sadly, people do not change as to what they can get caught up with. Signs and wonders were to follow the Messiah as a means to confirm the faith of those who were seeking to believe on and in Him. The Bible tells us signs and wonders will follow those who are preaching His Word so that others could believe the Lord. The signs and wonders would confirm the message of the Gospel.[25] The shift is obvious. In the first situation,

---

[23]   Luke 23:8

[24]   Matthew 11:1-6

[25]   Mark 16:15-18

miracles confirmed the identity of the Messiah, while in the second they are to confirm the message He has entrusted to His followers.

The reason I say this is because there are those who strive to bring attention to themselves by doing miracles. This has nothing to do with confirmation of true faith towards God. If miracles do not confirm the faith of those who seek to believe the true God of heaven, than such signs and wonders must be regarded as counterfeit. Remember, the son of perdition (antichrist) who will be coming on the scene will deceive many because he will perform miracles. But, the source behind those miracles will be Satan.[26]

Miracles are not intended to inspire people to greater faith but to confirm their faith towards God. Since faith comes by hearing what is true, the faith of others will inspire or edify those who may hear about the intervention of God. But, the hearers must choose to walk in the ways of faith before their personal faith can be confirmed and enlarged.

God desires to confirm or justify our unfeigned faith in Him, but we must seek to believe. However, we must realize that miracles are often for those who are new in their search to believe and know God. Jesus had just begun His ministry when the nobleman came to Him seeking a sign of healing for his son. However, as our walk of faith progresses in God, our natural tendency should not be to seek a sign to believe, but to seek the person of Jesus to know or have confirmation about a matter.

A good example of this is Thomas.[27] No doubt the disciple's heart was sick due to the events surrounding Jesus' death on the cross. When the disciples told him that Jesus had risen from the grave; rather than choosing to believe their eye-witness account of such an event, he told them unless he could see Jesus' nail pierced hands and put his finger into the print of those nails and thrust his hand into his side, he would not believe.

We are once again reminded that we choose to believe what we believe. Rather than believe the witness of his companions, Thomas chose the ways of unbelief. In this case we can clearly see where his hope had been deferred by the events surrounding Jesus' crucifixion, causing him to become a skeptic. Such a state will always call for proof

---

[26]   2 Thessalonians 2:3-12

[27]   John 20:25-29

that is not necessary. The disciples all had experienced their hope being deferred on the night Jesus was crucified, why would they lie about what they had personally experienced? When Jesus appeared to Thomas, all the disciple could do was humble himself before the Lord and declare, "My Lord and my God" (John 20:28b).

Jesus than made this statement to Thomas, "Thomas, because thou hast seen me, thou hast believed; blessed are they that have not seen, and yet have believed" (John 20:29b). Faith is not meant to cause believers to blindly believe what has not been backed up, but there must be a decision to believe the witness that has not only been backed up by prophecy, but by what Jesus clearly said about Himself. Jesus prophesied that He would die on a cross, but He would not remain in the grave, He would rise up in three days. Based on Jesus' Words, Thomas had every reason to believe the testimony of the other disciples, but he chose not to.

This is true for Christians as well. We have the prophecies, the promises, and the verification as to Jesus' identity and Words, yet how many truly believe? There are those who deem it all obsolete, while others are seeking signs and wonders, and some are picking and choosing what they believe, but few believe what has been clearly outlined in Scripture.

Faith comes by hearing, not seeing. Some Jews were always seeking a sign, but they had no intention of believing the testimony or witness of others. Jesus made this statement to some of the Jews, "For had ye believed Moses, ye would have believed me; for he wrote of me. But if ye believe not his writings, how shall he believe my words" (John 5:46-47)?

From the premises Jesus set up in John, consider the Scripture in Hebrews 10:36, "For ye have need of patience that, after ye have done the will of God, ye might receive the promise." There are Christians who wonder why their particular faith or actions are not confirmed by God. It becomes obvious that these people were not seeking to please God by doing His will. Sincere faith desires to know what the will of God is so that it can properly respond. It will be justified or confirmed in the end because the person will receive the promise of God. What is the will of God: to believe the words and record regarding Jesus. His words testify of His intent to save us. It is not His desire that any perish in their sins.

Hebrews 10:37 gives us insight into the main promise as Christians that we need to walk in expectation of, "For yet a little while, and he that shall come will come, and will not tarry." As Christians we should be walking in expectation of Jesus' Second Advent. We are not hoping for His coming, for we know He is coming. We do not know exactly when, but we walk and live in expectation of His coming because this event represents the culmination of all that we have hoped for, can hope for, and will ever hope for in regard to our life in Christ coming to perfection or full maturity.

The writer in Hebrews 10:38-39 concludes the thought with this sober warning, "Now the just shall live by faith; but if any man draw back, my soul shall have no pleasure in him. But we are not of them who draw back unto perdition, but of them that believe to the saving of our soul." If we believe we will not draw back from what we know to be true. By faith, we will continue our spiritual journey that will lead us to the full reality of salvation.

Like the woman who suffered from the issue of blood for twelve years, there will be nothing that will hinder us from pressing through the challenges of this present world by faith. Such faith will allow us to grab a hold of our hope for what is true and real, trusting that we will ultimately experience healing and completeness in our life. Like Zacchaeus, we will not let the obstacles in front of us keep us from encountering Jesus. Since He will be faithful to recognize and confirm our faith, we must not only see Him, we must sup with Him, confess our intentions, and if necessary change our lives before Him.[28]

As Scripture tells us, we will never be ashamed for putting our faith in Christ.[29] We will stand justified in believing Him because He meant what He said, and said what He meant. We will withstand in confidence because there is no variance or hidden meaning in what He has said. And in the end, we will be left standing for He is able to carry out what He has promised. It is for this reason faith comes by hearing and hearing by the Word of God.

This brings us to another important aspect of faith. We are not only justified in believing the Lord, but we will stand justified before Him because we did believe His Word. The Apostle Paul made this statement, "Therefore, being justified by faith, we have peace with God through our Lord Jesus Christ" (Romans 5:1).

---

[28] Matthew 9:18-22; Luke 19:1-10

[29] Romans 9:33; 10:11

To be justified before God means to be rendered as just or innocent.[30] We know that the just shall live by faith, but they also stand by faith. "Justified" points to being pardoned from our sin; therefore, we stand justified, or as if we have never sinned. The slate has been wiped clean, making allowance for us to stand before God without fear of rejection, judgment, and damnation.

Paris Reidhead said of justification that it represented the past tense of salvation. In other words, because of what Jesus did on the cross, the shame was taken away; therefore we stand justified by faith. It is from the premise of justification that we can embrace the new life Jesus' redemption has allotted us.

Do you stand justified before the Lord? If you have believed the Gospel of Jesus Christ, your faith not only ensures that you stand justified, but it has opened the door for you to explore the riches of His grace.[31]

RECKONED AS RIGHTEOUSNESS

In my attempt to present a balanced presentation of faith, I continue to realize in greater measure that it is indeed an incredible virtue of the Christian walk. It is so simple, yet it can prove to be illusive to those who cannot accept its simplicity. Sadly, it is so easy to become removed from the faith that was delivered to the saints of the new dispensation of the Church. The Apostle Paul tells us to examine ourselves to see if we really are in the faith, unless we find out too late that we are reprobate or useless in our life and form of belief.[32]

The problem rests with the fact that most people are taught or given the impression that they must some how meritoriously gain God's favor through some type of religious rituals or humanistic works. From such a premise you realize how it would be quite easy to miss the simple faith that actually opens the way for discovering the grace or favor of God. The subject becomes even more shrouded as one develops knowledge, logic, and some type of protocol about how the various aspects of the

---

[30] Strong's Exhaustive Concordance, #1344

[31] Romans 5:1

[32] 2 Corinthians 13:5

religions of the world work around them. Childlike faith is subtly replaced with what seems logical and practical according to the religious fervor of the different age of so-called "religious enlightenments."

This brings us to another aspect of faith. We are told that the just shall live by faith. The word "just" points to righteousness. Because we have been justified by faith we will have "right standing" with God. If our faith is active in the form of obedience it will be visible to others. However, some have argued that to present faith in light of obedience is to imply one must work out his or her salvation. To obey is not really a matter of earning salvation but working the gift of life in, through, and out of our lives. Faith that responds and walks in obedience is nothing more then expectation being expressed in light of obtaining the promises of God.

We are also able to withstand because active faith will be counted or reckoned as righteous by God, and we can remain standing because our conduct based on such faith will be honorable; therefore, also considered righteous. Clearly, the faith walk does away with the doubts, shame, and accusation that come with a life that is plagued by the uncertainty of a person's standing before God.

The truth is those who fear meeting God are often found to be uncertain about their standing before Him. However, faith not only allows a person to seek out God for justification, but to stand before God in assurance of forgiveness and reconciliation. Since such faith chooses to believe what God has said, it can be confident that it will not be surprised or ashamed on that great day when all will be revealed by the powerful, penetrating light of His holiness and judgment.

Most people, even in the Christian realm, can get caught up with the doing because of the Law of God and the many religious rituals that are often established by religious organizations. This is where the confusion comes in as to how faith, obedience, and works play a part in man's salvation. Some advocate that to feel responsible to do "good deeds" is to take away from grace. However, we are saved unto good works for the purpose of expressing the presence and influence of this new life in us. But, there are those who see their works as making them acceptable or holy. Such individuals end up with a mixture of religion and carnality. This mixture reveals that faith has not been properly mixed, applied, or assimilated, into the equation.

This was true for the children of Israel. They had Jehovah God in their midst and had been entrusted with the Law. When it came time for them to enter the Promised Land, the knowledge of God and the Law did not provide them the means with which to enter. It required faith towards God and obedience to His Word for them to enter into the Promised Land to possess it. The truth of the matter is faith existed long before the holy Law of God was ever instituted on Mount Sinai.[33] Righteous men have always walked according to the measure of faith they possessed, in light of their knowledge of God. Their walk was in accordance to some type of leading, conscience, or law that would lead them to the place of promise.

It is important to explain the significance of the Law. The Law was not given to make men holy; rather it was given to show how unholy and untrustworthy men were in light of their holy God. It revealed that they were transgressors before God, and had no personal means or merit to please Him. Men stood perverted, profane, and unacceptable before their Creator. Every attempt on their part to be righteous simply revealed how filthy their best was in light of the righteousness of the Lord. The Law could not save, change the status of mankind, or provide people with a plan of salvation. It simply held a balance up to reveal that man needed intervention: he needed to be saved. As the Apostle Paul stated, it served as a schoolmaster that would point to the Savior of the world.[34]

This brings us back to faith. Just or righteous men do not live by the Law, but by faith. Before Moses and the Law, there was faith. Therefore, those who were considered just lived by faith, not by some moral Law. These people did not have to have a Law to show them what was right or wrong. The inward conscience that has been given to every living soul by the Creator possessed a sense of right or wrong. What they did walk by was a faith that believed that they had a moral obligation towards their holy God to walk according to His righteous character, obey what they knew was right, and to display an excellent conduct that would identify them to their Creator.

We see this in the life of Enoch, Noah, and Abraham. These men lived before the Law but they were reckoned as being righteous. "Reckon" is a word we must consider. It means God counted these men's response as being righteous; therefore, He could impute their standing, attitude, and actions as righteousness. Man in and of himself has no

---

[33]   Romans 3:20; 2:16-21; Galatians 3:6-18 Hebrews 3:15-4:2

[34]   Isaiah 64:6; Hosea 6:7; Galatians 3:6-29

righteousness, and for this reason God must either count or impute certain standing, attitudes, and actions as being righteous to Him or man will stand condemned before Him. God can only count such matters at the point of unfeigned faith.

If faith is missing from a person's attitude or action, neither one cannot be counted as a matter of righteousness. It does not matter how religious or wonderful such actions may have been, what is not of faith is considered sin, reprobate, or a matter of iniquity to God. There are two forms of sin: the sin of commission where man fails to believe what God has already designated as being counted as right, thereby, failing to ensure right standing before Him. This disregard becomes obvious when a person disobeys the moral obligations and responsibilities ordained and establish by the Law and covenants of God. It is said of Moses before the written Law that he chose to suffer with the people of Israel rather than enjoy sin for a season.[35] Moses knew what was right and wrong when it came to God before ever receiving the Law.

Then there is the sin of omission where man fails to believe God as to what is right in attitude and action. This is where a person omits or fails to do right because he or she really does not believe he or she has a moral obligation to do what is honorable. In the sin of commission man is exerting his independence to do as he pleases, while in the sin of omission man is determining what his moral obligation is according to what is comfortable or convenient in light of his own character, thereby, failing to do what is right or honorable in a situation when there is an opportunity to do so.

Enoch walked with God in a time man was clearly progressing in his civilization, but morally digressing away from God. As man fell more and more into a world of independence from God, while becoming more deluded about his self-sufficiency and arrogance to live life on his terms without any regard to his Creator, Enoch was walking with God. During Enoch's time on earth it was evident that man's world was beginning to spin out of control. But, in the midst of this digression, this one man who walked with God revealed what such faith represented. It will always represent the exception rather than the norm. His walk clearly stood out to God for it was recorded in the Bible. Due to his faith, Enoch found

---

[35] Romans 14:23; Hebrews 11:25

favor with God. This righteous man was allowed to see into the future and eventually his walk allowed God the opportunity to translate him into His very glory without him seeing physical death. Clearly, Enoch's walk was the product of his unfeigned faith towards, and in, God.[36]

Noah also walked with God. He walked in an attitude of healthy fear towards his Creator. When he found favor with God in a time that man's imagination was becoming continually evil before God, God instructed him to build an ark. He was ready and prepared to obey. Obedience in building an ark was not a matter of refraining from evil, it was a matter of doing right in the midst of great spiritual darkness. The ark represented expectancy on Noah's part. Its building was in relationship to a time of preparation against the judgment that would come upon the world.[37]

Many people will not be prepared for the darkness that is again coming upon this world because they have failed to do right before God. We are warned that the present darkness that is coming upon the world in this last generation will be like the one that engulfed the generation that Noah lived in. It is said of Noah that his righteousness is what ushered in the judgment that came upon the age in which he lived. Even though there will be those blinded to the real light of the world by their personal darkness, the righteousness of God's people will bring the necessary contrast to usher in judgment on those who insist on such darkness.[38]

Abraham was call out of his land and from his family to go to a place that represented future inheritance for his descendants. By faith he heeded God's call and obeyed His instructions, while believing that he would glory in the unseen. Faith made Abraham a pilgrim, a stranger in the land, but in the end it made him a friend of God. Abraham knew his real portion, reward, or inheritance was Jehovah God. Even though he traveled through the land his descendants would eventually inherit, his vision went beyond the natural to the spiritual. He was clearly a man willing to leave all behind in regard to his present world, and in doing so became rich in faith as to the world that was yet to come.[39]

---

[36]   Genesis 5:16-24; 5:21-24; Hebrews 11:5-6 Jude 14-15

[37]   Genesis 6-7:1; Hebrews 11:7

[38]   Matthew 24:37-39; 2 Peter 2:5

[39]   Genesis 12:1-3; 15:1-6; Hebrews 11:8-10; James 2:5, 21-23

The Christian heritage does not go back to a Law that condemns, but to a man whose faith distinguished him in his age of paganism and idolatry. Such faith makes each of us as believers spiritual Jews or seeds of Abraham.[40] We are not bound by a holy Law, but by faith that expresses itself in an excellent walk before God and man. Our inheritance is not of this world, but of the next one to come. It will not be realized when we walk the length of heaven, but when we embrace the glorious fullness of our redemption that we have in Christ Jesus.

Even though mankind was hopelessly lost in his present state, faith led Enoch, Noah, and Abraham out of what seemed like a helpless state, as well as hopeless situations, towards a loving and forgiving Creator. It allowed them to experience the presence, promises, and reality of their God. It was God who was, and always has been, the real prize to those who walk by faith.

As these men responded in sincere faith they found the real benefit of true faith. The real benefit of faith is not that it is associated with doing the miraculous, but with such faithful souls entering into a place of rest in God.[41] So many people, including Christians, live in a state of self-denial about their present conditions. Some Christians believe that the fruit of faith is a quasi state of worldly happiness and satisfaction. To them such a paradise is their ultimate reward.

Such people often claim or profess such a paradise by thinking their words will conjure up faith to bring a matter about. They logic that if God's very words could bring about the worlds, than their words will justified them in having all they claim or profess. Clearly, such people feel their words will move God to do as they request since they have managed to conjure up what they perceive to be faith. Such people put faith in what God can do without any regard to His character, will, or plan. Of course, they use Scriptures to justify their foolish beliefs. However, such Scriptures have been taken out of context to tickle their ears, allowing them to remain in a place of arrogance and unbelief before God.[42]

It is true that God's words formed the worlds, but He had the power to do so. But, God does not operate according to His power, but according

---

[40]   Galatians 3:13-29

[41]   Hebrews 3:18-19

[42]   Zechariah 4:6; Matthew 12:37; 2 Timothy 4:3-11; Hebrews 1:2-3; 11:3

to the spirit and intent of His character. He will not go against His holy character or His Word to appease those who are trying to conjure up some type of faith by what they say to obtain fleshly and worldly desires. It is also true our words will justify us, but justification in this text means they will confirm or verify our type of character. We must say what we mean, and mean what we say, knowing that every word will eventually expose and judge the real intent of our heart. Our words must be true and realistic in light of what we know we are capable of following through to the end. For this reason Jesus said to avoid perjuring ourselves because of fleshly impulsiveness and motivations that are laced with false intent or pretense about something, our words must be limited to a simple "yes" or "no".[43]

As man we are very limited in controlling anything. We cannot change our present reality by what we say, and we cannot impress God with what we say in order to change the reality around us. Faith enables us to face reality in light of God, not change reality as if we were little gods. Faith towards God gives us authority in our prayer life, but the authority comes from knowing what God's will is.[44] Our faith, displayed in unfeigned faith, can stand confident because we are lining up to His will in a matter. Once again such faith is considered righteous, allowing God the opportunity to honor our prayers by answering them. Such confidence brings us to a place of rest in Him, even in our prayer life in spite of the reality we might be presently facing.

To come to a place of rest in God is to approach a place of quiet confidence and assurance that no matter what giants we are facing, the walled cities that must be conquered, or the chariots that are quickly ascending on us, God is sitting on the throne. He is the one in charge and He will conquer the giants, bring down the walls, and destroy the chariots as He so sees fit. Meanwhile we must step through our fears, wrestle down our doubts, and change our point of focus from maintaining our present life to securing our future life. We must see that our real inheritance is not of this world but of the next.

People of faith have accomplished much in this world, but they also have experienced much in the way of sorrow, loss, and defeat in this

---

[43]   Matthew 5:33-37; 12:36-37

[44]   James 4:2-3; 5:14-18; 1 John 5:14-15

world.[45] However, the greatest place their faith has led them is always to the place of resting in God when the impossible loomed before them, the incredible seemed far from them, and the end results unpredictable, unstoppable, and hopeless. It is during such times that they found their point of consolation, rest, and hope in the unseen and eternal reality of God.

Meanwhile, the question looms in front of each of us; where is our spiritual walk leading us in regard to our relationship with God?

PLEASING GOD

When we consider the benefits of faith, there are three notations we must make about this virtue. First, faith exposes us to the power of God by letting God be God. Many people see faith as a means to control God; rather then to have confidence in the integrity of His character to do what is right in all matters regarding their life.

The second benefit unfeigned faith allots us is that we can trust God with the end results regardless of whether they turn out the way we had hoped. In order to trust Him, we have to accept the way things are that cannot be changed. We cannot change reality; therefore, by accepting what is real, God can meet us as our solution, hope, or truth about something. His truth and perspective about a matter will make us free to accept His solution, while realizing that He not only serves as the essence of our hope, but He is the way in which we can come to rest in such hope until a matter is resolved.

Finally, the third benefit of faith is that if God reckons a matter as being right, we can stand assured that no matter how much circumstances may not make sense to us, how unfair life may appear, or that every godly pursuit and desire appears to fall short of expectations, that it is okay. We often perceive that a matter must end a certain way to assure us that all is okay in our lives. However, if we honestly follow the lives of some of the people of faith, we will see the outcome did not always end in an expected way, but it was okay because God is God. His ways and thoughts are not ours and in the end He will work all things out

---

[45]   Hebrews 11:32-37

according to His purpose and will, ensuring the expected results in light of eternity.

It is for this reason that Hebrews 11:6 makes this statement, "But without faith it is impossible to please him; for he that cometh to God must believe that he is, and that he is a rewarder of them that diligently seek him." People think they please God by doing humanitarian deeds, defending what is proper or living a "good" life. However, the Bible is clear. The only way any of us can please God is by possessing an unfeigned faith toward Him that is responsive to what has been established by Him as being true and right. We, as believers, must be diligent in seeking Him out in all matters. In due time, He will reward each of us for keeping our faith pure, steadfast, and firmly placed in Him.

This brings us to the motivation for pleasing God, which is quite simple. It is because we do believe He is who He is that we walk in faith towards Him. It is because of Him that we are steadfast in our walk of faith, and it is in light of Him that our faith will lead us to our final destination. There is no debate or speculation. We approach His Word to believe what it says about Him, and to respond in obedience to our godly responsibilities in an appropriate way based on His character. To approach Him from any other perspective other than faith is to become confused, lost, skeptical, and unbelieving towards Him.

In my walk of faith, I have encountered what I call crises of faith. Note I referred to *crises*, not *crisis* of faith. The reason for this is that saints of God will experience many crises of faith along the way. Each crisis will shake foundations of belief, expose sources of reliance, and enlarge one's vision. It will refine true faith, while revealing the fallacy of wrong points of confidence.

It is easy to veer away from the true foundation of Christ and put reliance on something that has no real eternal substance. I have unknowingly done it many times. My life begins to go at what I consider a pretty good click, and then I begin to feel some ripples. If I do not stop long enough to examine my point of reliance, then comes the tremors. If the tremors do not cause me enough concern, then comes the shaking. Sadly, before I recognized what was happening in many of these different crises, I realized too late that I had been so dulled down by the world that I had no sense of the ripples. The lack of spiritual sharpness caused me to become clueless about the tremors that followed, ending in a traumatic shaking. The shaking was so tremendous at times that it left some debris and destruction in the wake of it, finally causing me to realize that I needed to come back to what was and is considered simple, important, and eternal.

Sometimes I shake my head at my foolishness. How many times do I have to go through a crisis before I learn how to make sure that my faith is sure and sound in the foundation of heaven at all times?

In each crisis I always had to come back to the center or the source of my faith. I had to once again choose to put my faith in the God of the Bible. This required me to choose to believe Him about the matters concerning my faith, as well as believe in Him regarding the assurance of the life He is calling me to according to the faith He has already given me.

Jude made a very interesting observance in Jude 3 when he made this statement, "Beloved, when I gave all diligence to write unto you of the common salvation, it was needful for me to write unto you, and exhort you that ye should earnestly contend for the faith which was once delivered unto the saints." It was Jude's desire to encourage these people in their salvation, but when he examined their status, he realized that he had to exhort them to earnestly contend for the faith that had been initially delivered unto the saints.

There is only one faith that was delivered to the saints.[46] This faith is the only faith that will please God. Jude warned, admonished, urged, and pressed upon those he was writing to, the urgency to contend for that faith. "Contend" has the same implication as wrestling with or for something. In this case we must wrestle for the one true faith.

When you consider wrestling, it involves wrestling with something or someone down to the ground in which you have the advantage of holding them in a lock position as to where there is no escape. There are so many attacks taking place against the true faith that was clearly delivered to the likes of Abraham, Moses, Peter, and Paul. It is a wrestling match to hold onto the unfeigned faith that requires us to be diligent in doing so and steadfast in keeping the purpose and vision of this eternal virtue ever before us. If we fail to possess and hold onto the one true faith, we will never be able to move mountains, as well as possess eternal promises.

---

[46] Ephesians 4:4-6

I cannot count the wrestling matches I have had before God about the faith I so much wanted to possess in regard to Him. There were those who were trying to steal my affections away from God. There was the world that wanted to entangle my loyalty to its perverted ways. There was the flesh that wanted me to once again commit my devotion to its lustful ways, and the pride of life that wanted me to rely on personal strengths.

At times the wrestling matches seemed endless and unexpected. I would suddenly feel something take hold of my resolve in an attempt to get me to collapse under its weight. I could even feel myself falling to the mat as the grips of whatever was trying to gain my confidence, reliance, or trust was trying to get me into an arm lock of acceptance. Sometimes such wrestling matches would weary me, causing depression and uncertainty.

My heart was to remain faithful to my God, but the weakness of my flesh made it attractive and tempting to give way to something that appeared as an easy way out of the wrestling match. However, I knew that the easy way was a slide downward that would eventually end in an undesirable way. I would cry out in mercy, only to feel the gentle arms of grace lift me above the conflict, and bring me to a place of rest in the mighty fortress of God's loving arms.

The truth is that the only way you can break loose of such destructive grips is by remembering who you love and serve. You often must fall back on the examples that have gone before you such as Job.

Job is probably one of the greatest examples of the wrestling match that can take place when it comes to faith. You can follow the route of his wrestling match in his book. Faith can only be tested in a crisis. Crises can occur in four arenas: the physical, intellectual, emotional, and spiritual areas. For Job the first crisis began with the intellectual, extended into the emotional arena, quickly swallowing him up in the physical aspect, thereby, engulfing him into a spiritual wrestling match for his very soul.

To understand this wrestling match, we first must understand the character of Job. This is important, because inward character is often determined by the faith we possess toward God. The more faith has been developed in us, the more we will be established in the type of character that will ultimately sustain us through each test of our faith. If Job did not possess the right character, he would have never survived the test he had to endure.

James 5:10-11 tells us to behold and count them happy who actually endure suffering affliction in patience. Then we are reminded of the patience of Job. The character of faith produces the patience to endure great testing. However, we must remember such patience is forged in us by the trials of affliction.

Job 1:1 tells us about Job's inward character, "There was a man in the land of Uz, whose name was Job; and that man was perfect and upright, and one that feared God, and eschewed evil." This description reveals a man that had right standing with God. The Lord asked Satan if he had considered Job for he was considered an upright man.[47]

Satan maintained that if Job was tested, he would prove that his faith towards God would not stand. What many people fail to realize about Job is that the real theme in this book is the battle that takes place over the souls of men. It is only faith that enables people to stand, withstand, and remain standing in such battles.

Before this battle was over Job would be brought to the abyss of destruction without any explanation or understanding. He would have to choose to believe in the character of God to withstand the onslaught of tests that would attack any resolve that he had towards God's character and his right standing before Him. He would have to stand on this faith based on what he understood about God's righteousness, as well as remember his commitment towards his Creator.

The first test came against his wealth, the second against his family, the third against his health, and the fourth against his faith. In the first two assaults that happen closely together, he put on sackcloth to seek mercy and to actually worship God. He declared that the Lord is the one who gives; therefore, He is the one who has the right to take it away. The Bible clearly points out that in these two tests, he had not sinned or foolishly charged God.[48]

In the third test that involved his health, his wife asked him if he still retained his integrity or character towards God. He needed to curse God for what He had done, and die. But, he rejected such a temptation by calling her a foolish woman and making this statement, "What? Shall

---

[47]   Job 1:6-12

[48]   Job 1:13-22

we receive good at the hand of God, and shall we not receive evil" (Job 2:10b). The Scripture goes on to say that in all of this Job did not sin.

At this time Job had greatly suffered mentally, emotionally, and physically. However, the greatest assault for Job was about to begin when he was the most vulnerable. It would be against the very faith that had sustained him. He would be accused by close friends of sinning, failing God, and being wrong about what he knew in his heart to be true about his righteous Lord and the relationship he had established with Him.

As Christians we are instructed to sanctify the Lord in our hearts, and always be ready to give an answer of the hope in us.[49] Job was able to answer his accusers, but in each age you will find the friends of Job quick to argue, discredit, or falsely accuse you of possessing such hope when your circumstances become uncomfortable to them.

Job's friends were definitely uncomfortable with his circumstances. If Job is such a righteous man, then what does his circumstances say about God, and what does it say about their own standing with God. If terrible things can happen to a just man, then what will prevent such circumstances from happening to them? Hence, enters the accusation against Job's character. According to Job's friends' theology, God would never be behind such trials if a man is truly righteous; therefore, there must be some hidden sin in Job's life to bring such devastation upon him.

We all want to believe that our faith serves as some type of insurance that will keep us from going through such trying times. Our logic is clear and simple, if we are righteous, surely our righteous, loving God will protect us from such terrible situations. However, faith was not meant to be an insurance against bad things, but the sustaining means of enabling us to walk through them. Jesus stated we would have much tribulation, but do not fear He had overcome the world.[50] If Jesus overcame the world, then He will also help us to walk through such trying times.

The Apostle John brings this into focus even more in 1 John 5:4-5, "For whatever is born of God overcometh the world; and this is the victory that overcometh the world, even our faith. Who is he that overcometh the world, but he that believed that Jesus is the Son of God?" Clearly, our life in Christ does not assure us that we will be spared from tribulation;

---

[49] 1 Peter 3:15-17
[50] John 16:33

rather, it simply has promised us that we have the means to overcome such tribulation because of our faith in who Jesus is.

The spiritual assaults can prove to be the most cruel and inhumane of all attacks. Job no doubt had to wade through the insanity and emotional fallout that had happened in his life. Even though he chose to trust the unwavering, just character of his God, it still would not prevent him from going through the sorrow, despair, and struggle that follows such grave experiences. In a way it is much like travailing. For faith to produce a greater quality of character in the believer, it must, in a sense, be conceived in the darkness of uncertainty, birthed in sorrow, and brought forth in pain, despair, and hopelessness to come to maturity.

We can clearly see this process where Job is concerned. We first see the conception of a greater measure of faith in Job 13:15, "Though he slay me, yet will I trust in him; but I will maintain mine own ways before him." Clearly, Job was making a decision to trust God even if it ended in Him slaying him. He knew that in the end he would be able to maintain or defend his own ways before his God because he knew they were upright. He had nothing to fear or be ashamed of in regard to his life before his Creator. His faith and life in God would ultimately be confirmed and justified in the end.

When it comes to something coming forth through travailing, it always points to the unveiling of a new life. Faith not only has the capacity to bring us to the end of a matter, but also to produce a new, revived direction in which the life being worked in each of us will be expressed. Job makes reference to the ultimate way this life would be unveiled in Job 19:25-27,

> For I know that my redeemer liveth, and that he shall stand at the latter day upon the earth; And though after my skin worms destroy this body, yet in my flesh shall I see God. Whom I shall see for myself, and mine eyes shall behold, and not another; though my reins be consumed with me.

Job knew the end result of his faith would end in his resurrection on that last day that Jesus and even Martha made reference to.[51] He would

---

[51]   John 5:24-29; 11:24

see the One in whom he had always put his confidence and trust in. Even though his very heart was being consumed by the present testing, he would not be disappointed in the end.

Our walk of faith is meant to not only bring us to an expected end, but to sustain us through the many trials that would cause us to lose hope as to whether such an expectation will ever be realized. The expected end of our faith is that of resurrection. Faith and resurrection walk hand in hand. For example, the Apostle Paul stated that if we were not raised from the dead, our faith would be in vain. In Hebrews 11, we are told that there were those of faith that endure greater trials in order to have a better resurrection.[52]

We can only speculate as to what it means to have a better resurrection. However, it should amaze each of us that so many people are earthbound by the type of nonsensical faith they hold onto. They want the things of this world; therefore, they do not live for the time in which the things of this present world will be put aside or put off so that the expected end of true faith can be realized in resurrection power in the next age to come. We humans are so shortsighted and ridiculous in what we value or desired. In his worse crisis, Job kept the expected end of resurrection in sight. He would not let go of it, and as a result found hope and consolation in it.

In the birthing of his faith as to what would come forth through his experience, Job made this statement in Job 23:10, "But he knoweth the way that I take; when he hath tried me, I shall come forth as gold." Job knew his faith towards God would not only survive the fiery test, but it, along with his inner man, would be refined and proven pure and priceless as gold.

Job's statement always reminds me of Peter's declaration in 1 Peter 1:7, "That the trial of your faith, being much more precious than of gold that perisheth, though it be tried with fire, might be found unto praise and honor and glory at the appearing of Jesus Christ." The process is always about refining godly virtues within our character. Such a process can be intense and long, but in the end the results will prove to be priceless.

Faith ensures we inherit the promises of God. Did not Hebrews 11:6 testify that God rewards those who diligently seek Him? What did Job

---

[52]   1 Corinthians 15:17; Hebrews 11:35

come out of his ordeal with? We know that all things were restored to him, but this was not the real reward of his faith.[53] First, his faith was refined. Job had right standing before God, but he did not realize that he also stood righteous in and because of God. Job did all the right things, but he failed to understand that God is the One who provided the means for him to be righteous, and had to reckon such ways as being righteous to acknowledge his upright status.

The second aspect of God rewarding Job was that He acknowledged that Job was right before his accusers in Job 42:7, "And it was, that after the LORD had spoken these words unto Job, the LORD said to Eliphaz, the Temanite, My wrath is kindled against thee, and against thy two friends; for ye have not spoken of me the thing that is right, as my servant Job hath." Job's faith in God was confirmed by his Creator. In the end, Job was not ashamed for standing according to his faith towards God, withstanding with his faith because of God, and remain standing in light of his faith in God.

The final aspect of his faith was that Job in a sense received a special insight into his portion or inheritance. Remember, how Job maintained that on that day of resurrection, he would see the Lord, his Redeemer? Consider what he said in Job 42:5, "I have heard of thee by the hearing of the ear, but now mine eye seeth thee." (Emphasis added.) Job actually saw God in the spirit. His life would be forever changed. Nothing of the present world could compare to the glory that he would encounter and experience in the next.

Job clearly revealed the way of faith. The main purpose of faith is not to see a matter done according to our idea of it, but according to God's eternal plan. The walk of faith brings about character that will become priceless. It is more about what God does in us, than what we do for Him. Faith is about walking according to future expectation, not present wishful thinking. It is about enduring the present trials of this age to inherit the future promises of the next world.

So what do each of us need to take away from this presentation of faith? As believers we need to, by faith, become a Bartimaues who flings the old garment aside to embrace the new that has been prepared for us. We need to be like Peter, who by faith, forgot his present activities

---

[53] Job 42:12-15

and cast himself in the water to reach the Master.[54] We need to do as the writer of Hebrews 12:1b-2 exhorts us to do,

> . . . let us lay aside every weight, and the sin which doeth so easily beset us, and let us run with patience the race that is set before us, Looking unto Jesus, the author and finisher of our faith who for the joy that was set before him endured the cross, despising the shame, and is set down at the right hand of the throne of God.

Genuine faith will result in total abandonment when it comes to reaching the one who is the author and finisher of it. The reward remains the same for each of us. We will receive the expected end of our hope.[55] Who knows, if we run the race, perhaps in the glorious corridors of heaven we will be introduced as a friend of God; and, just maybe what will be said of us in relationship to our faith walk is that, "The world was not even worthy to witness such a faith as ours."[56]

---

[54] Mark 10:46-52; John 21:7

[55] If you would like to learn more about faith, see the author's book, *In Search of Real Faith*, in Volume 2 of her foundational series.

[56] Hebrews 11:38

5

THE ULTIMATE END
TO A MATTER

INTRODUCTION

Everything in this world has a beginning, an in-between, and an end. If we do not start from the beginning of a matter, we will have no means in which to reach the ultimate end of it. However, if we do not understand the end of a matter, we will not understand the journey or the path we must travel in order to arrive at our desired destination. For example, when it comes to man's ultimate end in light of God it is his salvation. In order to experience salvation man must begin from the premise of redemption, which has been clearly unveiled by the cross of Jesus. It is from the premise of redemption that the way of salvation is worked within the very fiber of man's being as he obeys God's Word. Such work simply means that the life of Christ is being worked within him. The ultimate end of salvation will lead man into the unhindered glory of God.

The question is what is God's ultimate end to a matter when it comes to man? In other words, what is God after? What is His intention or desired end when it comes to redemption? Is it simply the salvation of man or is salvation the means in which God uses to bring man to the ultimate end?

The problem is that man often regards everything in light of himself; rather, than realize that what will define him is the intended end of a matter. In fact, his character will be defined by what he perceives to be the ultimate goal or purpose of what he is doing, desires, or is trying to accomplish. However, for man to understand what the very life of Christ will ultimately secure in light of his status, life, and purpose, he must realize God's ultimate purpose for saving him in the first place.

We know that God went to great lengths to save each of us. When we consider the lengths that God went to in securing our salvation, should it not cause us to pause to consider what kind of end was and is He trying to bring about in relationship to those who identify themselves to or with Him. Will His desired end simply cease in our salvation or will it end in something that has far greater significance?

The truth is that salvation may have been secured for us, but for God it was to serve as a means to bring about a greater end. This end would be marked by excellence that would ultimately bring glory to Him.

This brings us to what God's intended end is for each of us. It is something that we often like to ignore or adjust, but few of us want to consider it head on because we just might have to rethink some of our attitudes and ways. However, the Scriptures are quite clear as to what God must accomplish in our lives to bring about and ensure salvation. God's intended end for man has been, is, and will always be that of holiness.

A CALL TO HOLINESS

When you ask people what do they think God wants for their life, many will say He wants them to be happy. Such logic fits nicely in their self-centered worlds. They often back up such logic with the argument that since God loves them so much, it is only reasonable to believe that He naturally wants them to be happy. However, Christ did not die to make man happy; rather, He died because man was far away from God. He came to close the gap between a holy God and profane, perverted, and loss mankind.

The gap between God and man was so great, that the cost of redemption had to not only equally meet but surpass the severity of man's plight to close the wide gap produced by our first parents. The reality of the first fall of man from the grace and fellowship with God was so enormous that it left man in a state that was totally devoid of any real holiness.

Man had not only become totally lost in his state, but he became perverted in his thinking, profane in his ways, and unholy in his alliances and associations. Pointedly, man fell from his former status of innocence into a different state where sin became his master and death freely reigned. However, God's status did not change. In other words, God remained holy, but due to man's fallen state, he is forever trying to demote, perceive logically, or change the status of God in order to justify and maintain his present unholy state. Man in his perverted way of thinking perceives that God should make the necessary adjustments to compliment him in his fallen state, even though it is marked by profane ways and unholy agreements.

However, God did not send forth His Son to adjust to man's unholy state, but to provide a way in which man could once again be made righteous. It is only from the acceptable state of holiness that the holy God can even regard man without displaying His judgment and wrath against the disobedience that is the product of man's rebellion against His authority, truth, and ways.

The Apostle Peter confirmed this harsh reality. He made this statement in 1 Peter 1:15-16, "But, as he who hath called you is holy, so be ye holy in all manner of conversation, Because it is written, Be ye holy; for I am holy." These Scriptures tell us we must be holy in all manner of living. Such conversation should identify us to our holy God.

The Bible describes God's holiness in lieu of the Law. It shows that in His holiness He is just (righteous), undefiled (void of any profane mixture), pure in all of His works, and void of any deviate ways. When you consider that even the seraphim around His throne covered their faces and cried unto each other, "Holy, holy, holy is the LORD of hosts; the whole earth is full of his glory", there is nothing more to do but conclude that God's holiness is unobtainable to man.[1] The Lord summarized His holy state in this manner, "Thou shalt not bow down thyself to them (idols), nor serve them; for I, the LORD thy God, am a jealous God, visiting the iniquity of the fathers upon the children unto the third and fourth generation to them that hate me" (Exodus 20:5)

Clearly, holiness is not an option. As believers we must be holy. However, what does such holiness mean for you and me? How will it manifest in our lives? "Holiness" means to be set apart from that which is unholy in order to be separated unto that which is holy. To be set

---

[1]   Psalm 145:17; Isaiah 6:3; Romans 7:12

apart from that which is unholy entails the act of *consecration,* and to be separated unto holiness involves the work of *sanctification.* Although consecration and sanctification sometimes are interchangeable, they are different in the sense that one is an outward separation, while the other one is the inward preparation. It is not enough to not be entangled with perversion (consecration), one must also be clearly identified to that which is pure and undefiled (sanctification). This holiness will serve as a clear distinction in a person's life and will identify him or her to that which is holy.

The matter of holiness can prove to be controversial to Christians. You actually see people go into extremes about the idea of holiness. Some shun it altogether as being impractical and impossible, while hiding behind the concept of God's love. But, God's love and holiness walk hand in hand. In His holiness God could never accept man in his present perverted state. Out of love, He provided the way in which man could be established in the excellence of true holiness.

Those who shun the concept of holiness are partially correct about their inability to be holy, but what they fail to understand is that God is also the one who reckons what holiness is to look like when it comes to man. God has provided the means to ensure such holiness. For example, God has provided the place of holiness in which man can reside. He also does the work of holiness in man. Granted, man has a responsibility to come to such a state by way of faith and ensure such holiness has its way in him, but he is not the one who makes himself holy.

Undoubtedly, we as believers must be brought to a place or state of holiness before we can be holy. We are told that Jesus is the one who serves as our place of holiness. The Apostle Paul made this statement in 1 Corinthians 1:30, "But of him are ye in Christ Jesus, who of God is made unto us wisdom, and righteousness, and sanctification, and redemption." God must place us in Christ who will serve as the essence of our holiness. However, we must note that wisdom and righteousness precede holiness or sanctification.

There is tremendous discretion in holiness. There is no foolishness in its way. It is aware of the responsibility that is attached to the state and work of being set apart. It is sober about its moral responsibility towards God and others. It is not flippant towards that which has been designated as holy, nor is it casual towards that which is deemed unholy. Such awareness causes the walk before God to be disciplined. It clearly speaks of wisdom from above that is pure, peaceable, gentle, easy to entreat, full of mercy, fruitful, and without partially and hypocrisy.[2]

Holiness also can only be present if there is righteousness. Man cannot end up being holy unless he begins from an upright state before God. Holiness and righteousness are words that are often interchanged. You cannot be holy without being upright, and you cannot be upright without coming from a state of holiness. Righteousness comes down to right standing with God, being right before God, and doing right in the sight of God. Such righteousness is reckoned to us at the point of genuine faith. If a person is doing right in the sight of God, it is considered godliness. Godliness comes from what is considered holy for it will identify such actions as originating with God. Ultimately, godliness will serve as visible fruit that we have indeed been redeemed from the unsavory to be saved unto that which is deemed acceptable.

The other extreme is that religious people have their own idea of what constitutes holiness. You must dress a certain way, act a certain way, and talk a certain way to be holy, but does this constitute holiness to God? Unmistakably, holiness is not measured by man's idea of it, but who God is. He is holy and for man, holiness means that he is manifesting like holiness.

Man is being called to holiness that finds its source and identification in God and not some outward presentation that appeals to man's religious concept or notions of it. God is holy, but man in his unregenerate state is unholy. Therefore, how can unholy man become holy? First of all he must come to terms with how God perceives holiness in order to understand how it must translate in his life.

In studying the concept of holiness it became clear that holiness is an inward state that produces a certain attitude that identifies man by his approach and conduct, and not simply an outward appearance. This was confirmed by Jesus when He said of the pious Pharisees that maybe the outward cup of their lives looked clean, but inwardly they were tombs housing the lifeless bones of their religion. They were defiled by the decay of hypocrisy, damnation, and death.[3]

---

[2] James 3:17

[3] Matthew 23:25-35

Man must, in a sense, come to an upright state before God to ensure a proper attitude and approach that will be clearly expressed in a type of conduct that will truly identify him to his holy God. Keep in mind, God would not call us to such a state or expect it if He did not provide the means in which we could be holy.

This is clearly brought out in Peter's exhortation for believers to be holy in the same way that their God is holy. God always comes from a premise of complete holiness, resides in a state of unadulterated purity, operates according to righteousness, and is godly in all that He does. Man is to operate in the same way.

The Apostle Peter does not simply call man to be holy, but he also provides the necessary insight into how this holiness will manifest itself in our lives. The apostle tells us in 1 Peter 1:17 that the Father is no respecter of persons. His desire towards each of us is the same. However, this impartiality must remind us that we all are being called to the same state and level of holiness. We must remember this when we call upon Him. It is from this foundation that we are given insight into the attitude that ensures holiness: the fear of the Lord.

The fear of the Lord is the beginning of wisdom.[4] Godly wisdom knows how to approach a matter to ensure the integrity of something. We are to approach the matters of God in humility and with reverence. We must ensure that everything we do in our spiritual journey as pilgrims and sojourners is in compliance with the righteous ways of God. Such ways will result in acceptable service and worship. Hebrews 12:28-29 puts it in this perspective, "Wherefore, receiving a kingdom which cannot be moved, let us have grace, by which we may serve God acceptably with reverence and godly fear; For our God is a consuming fire."

The holiness of God should produce a right attitude in us. However, few view God from the basis of His holiness. As a result, many are not prepared to approach Him in a hallow way. They are not sober, but foolish. They do not dread displeasing God in any way; therefore, they have no qualms or trepidation about whether they are prepared to face Him in their present state.

Consider what the Apostle Paul said about holiness and the fear of God in 2 Corinthians 7:1, "Having, therefore, these promises, dearly

---

4   Psalm 111:10

beloved, let us cleanse ourselves from all filthiness of the flesh and spirit, perfecting holiness in the fear of the Lord." When you consider the preceding Scriptures, Paul was making reference to coming out and being separate from the unholy in order to be separated unto God.[5] Such separation would ensure that the Lord would receive the person, and would become a Father to such an individual. In this situation we see where promises are attached to the state of holiness.

As we follow Peter's exhortation of holiness in 1 Peter 1:15-2:3, we are reminded that we were not redeemed by corruptible material such as silver or gold but with the precious blood of Christ, the Lamb of God. As the Lamb of God, Christ was presented without blemish or spot at a time that was foreordained by the Father. By believing the Gospel message of Jesus' resurrection and putting our hope in God, we know that it will be accounted to us as righteousness, but we must also go on to spiritual perfection. Our souls must be purified. Such perfection and purification occurs when we obey the truth through the motivating power and unfeigned love of the Spirit. It is the inspiration and love of the Spirit that enables us to love others, which is the visible evidence of godliness. We are told that we are sanctified by the Spirit. In fact, He is the One who sanctifies the inner man. Once again we are reminded that we cannot make ourselves holy.

In 1 Peter 1:22, we are instructed to love out of a pure heart. The reason we can do this is because we have been born again with a new heart and spirit. Unlike the outer man whose fleshly beauty and unregenerate ways are like the grass and flower that withers away with time, the new inner man will live forever because such a life has come out of the incorruptible seed of His Word. We have the promise that the Word of the Lord will endure forever.[6]

In our new life we need to lay aside, through the act of consecration, all malice, guile, hypocrisies, envies, and evil speaking. We must desire to spiritually grow according to the pure milk of the Word. By properly growing in our spiritual lives, we will taste the graciousness and goodness of our Lord.[7]

---

[5]   2 Corinthians 6:14-18

[6]   1 Peter 1:23-25

[7]   1 Peter 2:1-2

Have you taken the Apostle Peter's instruction seriously? Are you striving to come to some type of understanding or state of holiness? Holiness is not an option, it is a necessity to ensure the quality of our spiritual status, and the right end in regard to our journey on earth.

SAINT'S ALIVE

As Christians we have been called to holiness. As already pointed out, the concept of holiness is not based on our idea of it, but on who God is. He is holy and He has established a way of holiness in which we must walk as believers. Isaiah 35:8 states, "And an highway shall be there, and a way, and it shall be called The way of holiness; the unclean shall not pass over it, but it shall be for those; the wayfaring men, though fools, shall not err therein."

God has established the way of holiness for the Christian. It is called the way, the truth, and the life of Jesus. He is the one leading by way of example, setting us free with truth, while opening the way to embrace the eternal life of heaven. We have His unveiling in the Gospels, His examples and teachings being brought forth through letters, and a greater revelation revealed in the last book of the Bible. One of the main themes of the revelation unfolding in the last book of the Bible, in regard to Jesus, revolves around the fact that He is holy.

In Jesus' holiness He will be judging the world. Because He is holy all who are around the throne of heaven worship Him in awe and adoration. Out of holiness, He will be demanding an account from those who claim they served Him and those who refused to serve Him. There will be no stone left unturned, no deed overlooked, and no fruit untested. It will all be brought forth to the light by the purifying, purging fire of His holiness. And, only those who are holy will be left standing, clothed by the white linen of righteousness, prepared by the fiery tests of faith and persecution, and set apart to be exalted into heavenly places and ordained positions. It is at this time Jesus will take His rightful place as Lord of lords and King of kings on the throne of David.

Meanwhile, Christians must come to terms with holiness in a world that is unclean in every way, defiled by the profane ways of man, and in disarray and decaying under the dark reign of Satan. How can Christians find holiness in the midst of such a world? Where did the people of Israel discover such holiness in their journey through this world?

We know there is no holiness in man. Therefore how can man be made holy in the eyes of God? Like the people of Israel, first of all we must understand as Christians that we are being called to holiness. The Apostle Paul made this statement in 1 Thessalonians 4:7, "For God hath not called us to uncleanness, but unto holiness."

It often amazes me that people think that all God is interested in is delivering them from uncomfortable or tormenting places of bondage. They never think about what God is delivering them to. For this reason so many people quickly run back into the pig pens and mire of their old ways. At first they may feel some freedom, but eventually they begin to lament the tentacles of bondage that begins to grip their souls. In their initial refusal to remember the bitterness of bondage, they are once again entangled into the traps of the world that will eventually prove to be too great to bear.

God was not just delivering the children of Israel out of Egypt; He was also delivering them into a whole new life. However, they had to come to terms with the reality that what He was about to deliver them to was a vocation, a way of life. He was calling them to a place, position, and lifestyle of holiness. They had to recognize the status they were being called to, but first they had to understand the way they needed to travel to be prepared to come to their place of high calling as God's people. God would not compromise His character by becoming identified to the children of Israel; rather, the children of Israel had to be identified to Jehovah God. Identification to Jehovah God is what would bring distinction to them in the midst of idolatry, paganism, and spiritual decay and ruin.

Jehovah God first called the children of Israel out of Egypt to serve Him. We see where the Lord identified the people of Israel as being His first-born son and if the Pharaoh of Egypt refused to let them go, He warned him that He would slay his first born son. We know that the last great judgment upon the people of Egypt in their land was the death of their first born male of every home and their herds.[8]

As Christians we know that Jesus died on the cross so that we could accept our call as God's adopted children to come out from under the

---

[8]   Exodus 4:21-23; 12:29-30

tyrannical rule of sin upon our lives. We have been set free from the rule of sin in order to serve the living God.[9] However, such a call involves taking on a new life or vocation that entails righteousness that would genuinely be a visible product of adhering to a call of holiness and walking according to a godly lifestyle.

The godly lifestyle truly speaks of our identity with the God of heaven. The Apostle Paul put it in this way in Ephesians 4:24, "And that ye put on the new man, which after God is created in righteousness and true holiness." Notice how the new man will be created or formed in righteousness and true holiness. Only God could create such a man

To take on a new vocation, we must choose to put off the old in order to put on the new man or the new way.[10] This new lifestyle or new way was clearly described by the Lord and used in reference to both the people of Israel and Christians. We can read this description in Exodus 19:6, Deuteronomy 7:6-8, 14:2, 26:18, Psalm 135:4, Titus 2:14, 1 Peter 2:9, and Revelation 1:6.

Let me summarize the culmination of these Scriptures in relationship to our vocation as God's people. This description tells us we belong to Him and that we are to be a holy people unto Him for He has chosen us to be a peculiar or special people for His purpose. As His special people, we will also serve as a holy nation, a kingdom of priests, and a special treasure in the midst of the filth of the world. This identity will place us above all the nations of people on this earth.

As we consider this description, we must acknowledge that if we belong to God, then we have been ordained with the vocation of being holy people. This vocation will be made obvious since we have been designated to be clearly set apart by an excellent lifestyle that visibly exemplifies that we do belong to, as well as represent the Lord in this world.

The title that has been given to those who are willing to accept the challenge of being holy is the title of "saint." As Christians we have all been called to be saints of God, living a saintly life that clearly identifies us to the excellent character and ways of our holy God. "Saint" simply means a person who is holy or has been set apart. By being placed in

---

9   Romans 6:14-22

10   Ephesians 4:1, 17-32

Christ upon salvation, our status was changed from being a sinner to being placed in the position of a saint. However, being placed in this position does not mean that we are a saint in our way of thinking, or that we have come to a place that we are living the vocation of a saint.

I recognize how a couple of religions have hijacked the word "saint" for their own promotion. This hijack has caused some confusion among those who have been placed in the position of being true saints. However, the Bible clearly reveals that those who belong to God have been called to be saints of God.[11]

The people of Israel may have been called to a saintly life, but they were as pagan as you could get when they left Egypt. God had to first separate them from the filth and influences of Egypt before He could establish them in their new vocation as a holy people or nation of saints.

God had to bring the people of Israel into the wilderness to produce an environment that would allow Him to establish His holiness among them. The first ingredient to establishing holiness in the midst of His people is that of separation. There must be a separation made between the holy and the profane. This principle was reiterated especially when it came to the priests. The Lord said in Leviticus 10:10, "And that ye may put difference between holy and unholy, and between unclean and clean."

In Haggai 2:11-14, we see the concept of actually being defiled by simply touching that which is unclean. The priests were asked if their holy garments touched anything considered profane, would the unholy object be made clean. The answer was no. Then the priests were asked if anything unclean touched something that was holy, would it be considered unholy. The answer was yes.

As Christians we are told that we have no agreement with the unholy and that we must not only separate ourselves from it, but we are not to even touch it. We are to purge out that which is old and unholy for a little leaven will corrupt what is pure.[12] Such separation encourages the next ingredient that is important in ensuring a proper environment: the presence of God.

God's presence went before the children of Israel, guided them, and abided in their midst. As Christians we know that the presence of God in

---

[11] Romans 1:7; 1 Corinthians 1:2
[12] 1 Corinthians 5:6-8; 2 Corinthians 6:14-18

our midst to be that of the Spirit of God. In fact, as Christians we are born again of the Water of the Word and of His Spirit. This means the Spirit of God resides in our inner man. We are to walk after the Spirit, be led by the Spirit, and to walk or live in the Spirit. If we follow after the Spirit, we will be following after the ways of righteousness. If we walk in the Spirit we will not fulfill the lust of the flesh. And, if we are led by the Spirit towards our status and inheritance as the children of God, we will cease to be under the dictates of the flesh and the condemnation of the Law.[13]

The next aspect of establishing the environment of holiness entails erecting a standard that would bring contrast between that which is holy and unholy. For the children of Israel, that need for contrast gave rise to the giving of the holy Law of God. For us as believers it comes down to both the Word of God and the Holy Spirit. The Word shows us the way of holiness, but the Holy Spirit is the one who reproves us of righteousness by illuminating and exalting the example of the essence of all righteousness, Jesus Christ.[14]

The next step the Lord took to establish holiness among His people was to erect a place of holiness in which He could abide within. We know two such places were the tabernacle in the wilderness and the temple in Jerusalem. There God's presence would abide and it would serve as a place of worship, sacrifice, and celebration for His people.

God ordained the pattern of where His presence would abide among His people in accordance to the pattern of the inner courts of heaven. In a way, the tabernacle or temple was to serve as a bit of heaven in the midst of the barren wasteland of man. We know that what set this place apart was God's abiding presence.[15]

Believers are to serve as the New Testament temple where the presence of God indwells them through the abiding presence of His Spirit. We are referred to as the Temples of God or of the Holy Spirit. Since we are temples of a holy God, we have been given clear warnings.

We are told in 1 Corinthians 3:17-18 that if we defile the temple of God, our bodies, God will destroy them for they are to be holy. In 1 Corinthians 6:16-20 we are instructed to be in agreement or joined to His

---

[13] Exodus 13:21-22; John 3:3, 5 Galatians 5:16, 18
[14] John 16:7-11
[15] Hebrews 8:1-3

Spirit; therefore, we are to flee all spiritual fornication or harlotry. After all, we do not belong to ourselves, but to God.

As believers we have not only been placed in a position of holiness as saints, but we must be holy temples. We house the very life of Jesus through the presence of the Holy Spirit. We cannot be casual or flippant about what we come into agreement with or what we do in these bodies.

Finally, the Lord established a holy priesthood that would represent Him to man. For the Hebrews, the holy Priesthood came out of the lineage of the Levites and the family of Aaron. According to the Apostle Peter, Christians make up lively stones that comprise a spiritual house, a holy priesthood. As priests we are to offer up spiritual sacrifices that are acceptable to God by Jesus Christ.[16]

There are three main sacrifices we must offer up to God that will prove to be acceptable. The Apostle Paul gives us insight into the first sacrifice we must be willing to offer in Romans 12:1, "I beseech you therefore, brethren, by the mercies of God, that ye present your bodies a living sacrifice, holy, acceptable unto God, which is your reasonable service." God desires to use us, but we must first completely present ourselves to Him for such service. Such sacrifice or presentation is the least we can do.

Hebrews 13:15-16 tells us the next acceptable sacrifices we need to offer are that of praise and good works. God inhabits the praises of His people. Remember without His presence, holiness will not be established, and it is good works that are also to serve as sacrifices. Those who are holy or saintly are associated with good works, showing forth a pattern that clearly identifies them to the Lord. As believers, we should richly abound, be zealous about, and fruitful in every good work, as we walk worthy of our holy vocation. Such a walk will allow us to lay up a good foundation in which we may lay hold on eternal life. We must be perfected, prepared, and furnished unto all good works as a means of doing His will.[17]

We are to be holy brethren, partakers of the heavenly calling. "Partaking" means to share or come into agreement. Surely, we must

---

[16]   1 Peter 2:5

[17]   Psalm 22:3; 2 Corinthians 9:8; Colossians 1:10; 1 Timothy 6:18-19; 2 Timothy 3:17; Titus 2:7, 13-14; Hebrews 13:21

assimilate every aspect of our heavenly responsibility and obligation into our way of thinking, being, and living to become saints of the Most High God. We must always consider our profession in light of the way, truth, and conduct of our Apostle and High Priest, Jesus Christ. Jesus is also the Son over the household of the saints. We need to hold fast the confidence we are to have in Him until the end, when we will be rejoicing in His unhindered glory. To maintain the integrity of such a life, we need to hear what His Spirit is saying about the matters of this present age in regard to the type of life we must possess to stand distinct from its influences.[18]

Clearly, saints are made alive by God's Spirit, identified with a heavenly, eternal inheritance, and being brought forth into perfection. Their status as sinners has not only been changed by a higher vocation, but they are being renewed in the inner man by the very breath and life of God. They have been washed by God's Word, cleansed by Jesus' blood, and established as fellow citizens in His kingdom.[19] They are not only considered holy as priests, but part of an eternal royal house that will never cease. They have been translated from the ways of darkness into the ways of light, life, and hope.

As Christians, we all started our spiritual journey with a new status, made alive by the very Spirit of the Living God residing in our inner man. Even though in our infancy as Christians, we were made alive by the Spirit, we still possessed the pagan ways that reminded us that we were fools. However, because of our new status as saints, we would never again have to err if we chose to walk in the ways of our God's holiness. We could come to perfection as the very life of Christ was worked in and out of us by His Spirit. In the end we could be holy temples, a lively priesthood, and a royal household that was clearly set apart by the presence of God, marked by His holiness, and identified by godliness.

Have you been clearly marked as a saint of God or are you identified as a religious person who has some piousness, but no real distinction or identification to the God of heaven? Allow the Holy Spirit to reveal the answer of this question to your heart and soul. If you are not being marked by the holiness of God, you must repent and adhere to His call to holiness.

---

[18]   Hebrews 3:1-7
[19]   Ephesians 1:1-18; 2:19; Colossians 1:13

CONSECRATION

There are two ways in which holiness is brought forth in our life: through separation and cleansing. There must be a separation from the unholy or profane before there can be a cleansing. Once there is a separation from the unholy, then there can be a dedication to the holy. After cleansing, the next step of dedication can occur. Dedication is where someone or something can wholly be committed to the work and purpose of God.

This brings us to the first step of holiness: that of separation. Such initial separation takes place in what is known as the act of *consecration.* Consecration involves the ritual or act or setting something apart in order to separate it unto that which is to be distinguished as being holy or sacred.

We can see such consecration taking place for the priests in the Old Testament. The men from the family of Aaron had to be set apart as priests of God. According to Ruth Specter Lascelle, it entailed various steps which involved the company of Cs: chosen and called by God, committed to the calling, cleansed, clothed, consecrated, Christened or anointed, conformed, and commissioned.[20]

God must chose, call, and cleanse a person according to his or her holy vocation. If the calling is missing, it will not be considered holy. Remember, if something does not find its source in God, it cannot be considered holy. As Christians we have been chosen, called, and cleansed by His Spirit to come into our vocation of being set apart as His holy people in this world.[21]

The Old Testament priests were to serve as our examples and shadows as to the type of distinction that should be prevalent in our lives as the New Testament priests. They were clearly set apart by the garments they wore, along with the responsibilities and burdens they were entrusted with.

The linen of the priest represented righteousness, the breastplate was symbolical of the glory and wisdom of God, and the different parts of the "holy garments" of the priest pointed to complete holiness. For

[20]   A Dwelling Place For God; Ruth Specter Lascelle, pg. 192
[21]   John 15:16; 1 Corinthians 1:2; Titus 3:5

example the broidered coat represented holiness of heart towards the Lord, the linen girdle symbolized holiness of service in all that was done, and the mitre pointed to holiness of thought to ensure purity in obedience, while the undergarment represented holiness of the flesh, which was being separated from that which was profane in order to be separated unto God.[22]

The burdens the priest were entrusted with weighed equally upon his shoulders, as well as were to be displayed and worn close to his heart. These burdens were represented by hidden stones upon the shoulders with the names of the tribes of Israel. However, on the breastplate there were twelve distinct, precious stones that had the individual name of each tribe inscribed upon them. These stones pointed to the priest's responsibility to shoulder the burden of representing the needs of those he was to intercede for before God. The precious stones were also to remind the priest that it is man that is close to God's heart and not all of the rituals or religious requirements. Only love can ensure such burdens will remain light because of how God views such matters. It also served as a reminder that God wants to bring forth the preciousness of His people so they could be distinct in their representation of Him.

As New Testament priests, we have been chosen to represent our Lord in this world. We have been called to an excellent way of love, righteousness, holiness, and godliness in order to be distinguished as His representatives. We have been cleansed by His Word and Spirit, but we must become committed to such a calling by ensuring distinction, clearly notable by what we clothed our inner man in. We must consecrate our lives to ensure that we are anointed from above to effectively be conformed to God's holy ways to carry out our commission of preaching the Gospel and discipling others to be true followers of Jesus.

It is important to point out we cannot cleanse the inner man. Inward cleansing is the work of the Word of God and the Spirit. However, we must clothe the inner man with humility through submission to His Spirit, as we allow our minds to be transformed by the meek attitude of Christ

---

[22]   A Dwelling Place for God, pgs.165-166

through obedience to His Word, while conforming the outer man in godly conduct.[23] We do this through the act of consecration.

Consecration points to a total act of abandonment towards being holy. It begins by presenting our lives completely to the purpose, work and glory of God. We hold nothing back, nor do we reserve any personal rights to do things according to our personal concepts or dictates. In a way, we are flinging all to the wayside, jumping into the currents of the Spirit, and allowing the ways of God to carry us according to the personal workings of His Spirit in us and through us.

In a sense we see this commitment or devotion on the part of the Old Testament priests in regard to abandoning the normal way of life to be totally committed to serving God. After being outwardly cleansed by the water of the laver and clothed in his designated garments, the ear, thumb, and toe of the priest had to be set apart or consecrated by the blood of a sacrifice that had been made on his behalf. The ear had to hear in purity what the Lord was saying and instructing. The thumb of the hand had to be consecrated in regard to the work that had to be done in the tabernacle and service that would be rendered to the Lord. The toe of the foot had to be set apart in relationship to properly walk before the Lord and displaying proper conduct in relationship to the priest's responsibilities to those he was to represent before God.[24]

The reason some Christians suffer such defeat in their spiritual walk is because they will not totally consecrate their lives to God. They will not present their bodies as a living sacrifice. They often want to control matters by choosing their place of consecration, their altar of sacrifice, and the type of sacrifice they are going to offer to the Lord. In their mind they are presenting their best, but Scripture points out that man's best before God is filthy rags, making all such attempts profane and unacceptable to Him.[25]

The priests of God were to be set apart to worship Him in a proper way. In her book about the tabernacle, Ruth Specter Lascelle points out there were three types of service among God's people. They were the

---

[23] Matthew 11:29; Romans 12:1-2; Ephesians 5:26-27; Philippians 2:5; Titus 3:5; 1 Peter 5:5

[24] Exodus 29:19-20; Leviticus 8:22-24

[25] Isaiah 64:6; Romans 12:1-2

warriors made up of the twelve tribes of Israel who were to defend the way of life for God's people, the workers who were comprised of the Levites that were to maintain the religious aspect of God's people, and the priests who were to worship God.[26]

For the kingdom of God, every Christian is instructed to endure the challenges of life as a good soldier. Each of us as believers has been given the armor to withstand the challenges of the enemy. We each are called to be workman created in Christ unto good works that have been ordained by God. We are to worship the Lord in Spirit and truth ensuring the integrity or our relationship with our Creator. The whole of our lives should be a matter of ongoing worship by standing against what is not of God with the sword of truth, while clearly displaying works that glorify Him according to the working and leading of His Spirit. As Mary, the mother of Jesus, in her prayer declared that out of fear and awe, we need to serve God in holiness and righteousness all the days of our life.[27]

As we study the concept of consecration, we can see where it comes down to exposure. We must separate from that which is profane and perverted in order to be established in that which is holy and acceptable. By changing what we expose ourselves to, we change what will influence us.

The Apostle Paul talked about not being conformed to this present world. The greatest influence for most people is the world. The world is an enemy of God. To be a friend of the world is to commit spiritual harlotry or fornication with the world.[28] Harlotry or fornication points to coming into agreement with the unholy.

What most people do not realize is that agreement points to coming into agreement with the spirit or intent of something. The Bible warns us that there is the spirit of the world that influences the children of disobedience. The Apostle Paul reminds us that we have not received the spirit of the world, but the Spirit who is of God, so that we might know the things that are freely given to us by God.[29]

---

[26] A Dwelling Place for God, pg. 191
[27] Luke 1:74-75 John 4:23-24; Ephesians 2:10; 6:12-17; 2 Timothy 2:3-4
[28] Romans 12:2; James 4:4
[29] 1 Corinthians 2:10-12; Ephesians 2:2

It is our natural tendency to regularly expose ourselves to that which we agree with in some way. After all, deep calls to deep. Such exposure points to being influenced by what we come into agreement with. We will be conformed to such influences in our way of thinking, being, and what we will become. For this reason we are called to separate from wrong spirits. It is for this reason we are instructed to test or discern the spirits. As Christians, we are the only ones who can determine who or what will influence the environment of our spiritual lives. We must consecrate ourselves on a continual basis if we are to maintain the spiritual integrity of our lives before God. If we expose ourselves to wrong spirits we will be spiritually dulled down, but if we expose ourselves to the holiness of God, we will gain a greater edge. We are told that we must come to full age by exercising our senses to properly discern both good and evil.[30]

We must consecrate ourselves so that we can properly be partakers of God's holiness.[31] We must not lightly esteem the things of God. To do so will cause us to improperly handle them in some way. We must have a proper environment to partake of this holiness or we will end up defiling it. Such holiness will not only be defiled and made common by us, but it will not be properly presented to others.

As believers we must separate from that which is unholy in order to come to a place of holiness. It is only from the premise of holiness that we can properly assimilate the holy ways of God into our attitudes towards the matters of life we are confronted with, and His righteous ways into our walk and conduct.

Consider your spiritual life. Have you separated yourself in the way of consecration from that which is unholy in order to consecrate yourself to that which is holy? Until you take responsibility for what your expose yourself too, and demand the excellent ways of holiness in your life, it cannot be assimilated into your life. Without holiness to mark your life, God will not be able to regard you as a serious, sober saint of His kingdom.

---

[30] 2 Corinthians 6:14-18; Hebrews 5:14; 1 John 4:1

[31] Hebrews 12:10

SANCTIFICATION

In the Old Testament, there were five sacrifices offered to God. Each sacrifice had some type of significance or symbolism behind it in regard to Christ's sacrifice, and the Christian life that had to be presented to God. For example, the first sacrifice mentioned was the burnt offering. This sacrifice along with the meal offering and peace offering were consumed in the fires of judgment. Jesus served as the sin and trespass offering, but His life was clearly consecrated to do the Father's will. He was the meal or first fruits offering in regard to the kingdom of God, and He was the peace offering that brought forth the fruit of peace through reconciliation. As God's Lamb, Jesus' offering and life was totally utilized or used up to serve as the sustaining and ongoing sacrifice that had long been established by the criteria set forth in Exodus 12:1-28 in regard to the first Passover lamb. However, the significance of the burnt, meal, and peace offerings were symbolized in the smoke or fragrance that was left and emitted from the altar after the sacrifices were consumed by the fire. The smoke or fragrance that floated from the altar represented holiness to God.[32]

In the burnt offering, the complete sacrifice was consumed in the fire, leaving only the smoke to float upon the unseen currents of His Spirit to the altar of God. The burnt offering was also considered the sacrifice that best represented consecration. When one truly consecrates all to God on the altar, he or she was willing for all to be consumed by His fire in order to ensure the type of holiness that would be acceptable to God.

Hence enters the Apostle Paul's instruction to each of us as Christians to present our bodies as a living sacrifice to prove what was good, perfect, and acceptable to God.[33] Every aspect of our life needs to be utilized for one purpose: To glorify God. Clearly, in such a sacrifice, all that would remain would be what would prove to be pleasing, pure, and adequate to God. Such a sacrifice would not be influenced by and conformed to the world ideas, but transformed by the Spirit of the living God into something that God could accept on His behalf and use for His glory.

---

[32] Leviticus 1-6
[33] Romans 12:1-2

When we consider consecration, we can see how it calls for separation through abandonment. However, when we realize that consecration is only one aspect of the work of holiness, we can begin to understand how the fire on the altar pointed to the other part of holiness: that of sanctification.

The act of consecration has to do with separation, but the work of sanctification has to do with cleansing. Whether the fire or the water is applied, all things that are used by God must first be cleansed with the purging of the fire of His Spirit or through some type of purification such as the water of His Word or the uncapped flowing rivers of His Spirit. This is the only way that something can be properly sanctified. Keep in mind that what has not been sanctified by God will never personally belong to Him. Sanctification clearly implies that God's mark of ownership is upon something that has been totally dedicated to Him for His use and glory.

Although there are some incidents in which man cleanses his outside body as a means of sanctification, it is really the work of God. As already alluded to, God has provided the means in which the inward environment of man can be cleansed. If these means are not properly applied or given way to, man remains filthy before God. He will be like the religious leaders of Jesus' day where the outward cup may have been cleaned, but the inner part of it remained dirty and unusable to God and unsafe to others.[34]

The question is, what needs to be cleansed where man is concerned? This leads us to another possible consideration. Is there any aspect of man that can be presented to God without first being cleansed? The only thing man can offer God up front is his body but it will always be for the purpose of sanctification. The reality is that there is nothing of man that can be presented to God without first being cleansed by God.

Granted, man can wash the outside shell of his body in symbolism or good faith as to the cleansing that must be done inwardly. We see God commanding the people of Israel to first clean the outside of their bodies before their encounter with Him at Mount Sinai. This instruction was clearly set up to bring to their attention that they were about to meet a Holy God who required His people to be completely clean before Him.[35]

---

[34] Matthew 23:25-29
[35] Exodus 19:9-15

We also read similar instructions with regard to believers. In James 4:8, we are instructed to clean our hands and purify our hearts. In order to understand how we clean our hands and purify our hearts in a spiritual manner, we must go to other Scriptures. "Cleansing" in this text means we must cease touching or coming into agreement with that which is considered unclean by God, and we must sanctify or set God apart in our hearts. Such sanctification points to setting God apart from all other points that represent idolatrous commitments, profane loyalties, or perverted devotions.[36]

In Hebrews 10:22 we read these words, "Let us draw near with a true heart in full assurance of faith, having our hearts sprinkled from an evil conscience, and our bodies washed with pure water." It is important to point out that we cannot see or properly hear from God if we do not draw near with a true heart. This means a heart that is motivated by sincerity towards seeking out and knowing the truth about a matter.

Those pure in heart will draw near to God in full assurance of faith because the conscience has been made clean through the cleansing blood of Jesus. Most people hide from God due to their sense of shame and guilt that plagues their conscience. However, man cannot address or take away shame and guilt. Only God is capable of forgiving man. He has provided the way in which man can be pardoned. The blood of Jesus points each of us to a new covenant where our sins can be forgiven. Once our sins have been remitted we can be assured that we have been cleansed from all unrighteousness.[37]

Our bodies must be washed with pure water. There are a couple of ways we can wash our bodies. One way was brought out by the example of the Old Testament priests. Before they did any activity within the holy places of the tabernacle, they had to stop at the laver and wash their bodies. The laver represented the Word of God. It was made out of copper that was often used by women as mirrors. They could actually see their reflection in the copper as they prepared themselves for the daily activities of life. Therefore, the copper laver pointed to the Word of God serving as our mirror.[38]

---

[36] 2 Corinthians 6:16-18; 1 Peter 3:15
[37] Hebrews 9:22; Hebrews 10:16-22; 1 John 1:6-7
[38] Exodus 38:8

We know that a mirror reveals and reflects what we really look like so that we can see how far away we are from the best we can present to others. When it comes to the spiritual aspect of our lives, the mirror of God will show us how our disposition is affecting our countenance, what our attitude is doing to our presentation of the Christian Life, and what our conduct of behavior is doing to our testimony. James best explains what kind of reality the Bible brings to not only the inner man, but also the outward presentation of our Christian walk in James 1:21-25-25.

In the Scriptures in James we are reminded that we must put away all filthiness and wickedness in our lives in order to receive with meekness the engrafted Word which will save our souls. Then he goes on to say we must be doers of the Word not simply hearers of it, deceiving ourselves about our spiritual condition. For if all we do is hear the Word, we will be like the person beholding our face in a mirror, but as soon as we walk away from it we will forget what we look like and who we really are. We will be unprepared to spiritually walk out our Christian life. As pointed out in the Scriptures in James, the other aspect of cleansing our bodies has to do with separation from that which would not only defile the outer sanctuary of what we might touch or come into agreement with in relationship to the influences of the world, but in how we conduct ourselves in these bodies.

The Apostle Paul stated how Jesus would sanctify and cleanse His people, the Church, with the washing of water by His Word as a means to present it without spot or wrinkle. The apostle goes on to say that the Church should be holy and without blemish.[39]

In John 17:17, Jesus made this request in regard to His followers the night He was betrayed, "Sanctify them through thy truth; thy word is truth." God's Word is an incredible washing machine, but we must believe it, and assimilate it into our lives with the purpose of obeying it in the right spirit according to its inspired truths.

Jeremiah 23:29 states, "Is not my word like a fire? saith the LORD; and like a hammer that breatketh the rock in pieces?" We see in this Scripture that the word is like a fire that purges, as well as a hammer that is able to break something into pieces. The Word must penetrate our heart to purge, as well as break us at every point of hardness where

---

[39]   Ephesians 5:25-27

sin and unbelief has marred us. Once broken, we can be shaped or conformed into the spiritual man we are ordained to be.

Jesus presented the Holy Spirit as the rivers of Living Water who will not only bring forth life, but will cleanse us. On the day of Pentecost, we see that the Holy Spirit manifested Himself in the form of cloven tongues as of fire that sat upon those waiting in the upper room. We are also reminded of Isaiah who admitted in the light of God's holiness that he was a man of unclean lips. A seraphim took a live coal from the altar, and touched the prophet's lips to take away his iniquity and purge his sin. When it comes to the upper room the lips were being prepared or set apart by the Holy Spirit to take forth the message of God in unadulterated authority and power.[40]

Titus 3:5 tells us, "Not by works of righteousness which we have done, but according to his mercy he saved us, by the washing of regeneration, and renewing of the Holy Ghost." Once again we are reminded that we are not saved or cleansed by personal works, but by the Holy Spirit. He is the one who brings forth the new life of Christ in us as He cleanses us from the old. It is the life of Christ who sets us apart to be about the Father's business

In the Old Testament a particular object or person was set apart when it was properly anointed. Being anointed points to being commissioned for a particular work. In the New Testament the Holy Spirit is the one who spiritually anoints God's people to be set apart for His work and glory.[41]

It is important to note who really cleanses the inner man as a means to set each of us apart as God's people. We see that the blood of Jesus cleanses us from all unrighteousness, His Word is used to cleanse our temples or bodies, and the Holy Spirit is the one who cleanses and revives the inner man in order to bring forth the new life. He is also the one who anoints each of us for our particular mission and work in the kingdom of God.

The need for the cleansing, purifying work of sanctification can be seen throughout the Bible. There is no way to ignore this subject without stripping away a fundamental foundation that could easily make everything collapse from within. Everything in relationship to God had to

---

[40]   Isaiah 6:5-6; Acts 2:2-4

[41]   Leviticus 6:20; 8:10; 10:7; 2 Corinthians 1:21-22; 1 John 2:20

be purged or cleansed before it was dedicated to Him. We see this in the tabernacle. All that was to be used by God and for God had to be cleansed and anointed. This included the vessels and instruments that were used by the priests to do their work in His holy place.[42]

This brings us to the vessels and instruments used by the priests in their service in the tabernacle and temple. Each vessel or instrument had to be anointed, as well as cleansed after being used. In the case of the clay vessel being defiled, it actually had to be broken.[43]

Scriptures make reference to believers being instruments and vessels. In Romans 6:13, as believers we are told to yield the different members of our bodies as instruments of righteousness. In Romans 9:20-24, we are referred to as clay vessels that have been prepared by the great Potter. In 2 Timothy 2:19-22 we are told by the Apostle Paul to depart from iniquity, for in the house of God there are many vessels, but some will bring honor and others will bring dishonor. The apostle goes on to say that let a man purge himself of that which is profane, and he shall become a vessel unto honor, sanctified, made fit for the Master's use, and prepared unto every good work. It is followed up by the exhortation to flee youthful lusts and follow righteousness, faith, charity, and peace with those who call on the Lord out of a pure heart. We see where as Christians we purge ourselves from iniquity by shunning what is profane, fleeing youthful lusts that easily ensnare, and consecrating our lives by following what is righteous, good, and acceptable to God.

Clearly there must be a cleansing that takes place. The Apostle Paul tells us one aspect of such cleansing that comes from consecration, but King David gives us another important insight into what it means to become holy people. Like the clay vessels in the tabernacle, we must become broken to know cleansing, for there cannot be any real restoration unless there is brokenness.

In Psalm 34:18, we are told that the Lord is near to people who have a broken heart and will save those who possess a contrite spirit. In Psalm 51:17 we are told that the sacrifices of God are a broken spirit and a broken and contrite heart.

---

[42] Exodus 30:25-33

[43] Leviticus 11:32-33

As clay vessels, we must be broken for the purpose of complete restoration, purged from iniquity, and dedicated unto God. There is nothing more cleansing to the heart than repentance that flows from a contrite spirit. There is nothing more searing and sanctifying to the soul than brokenness over sin, and nothing more uncomfortable to the body than sack-cloth that is showing its disgust towards personal iniquity. There is nothing more abrasive to a stiffed-neck than submission to God, or proves to be a greater affront to arrogance and pride than bended knees of humility. There is nothing more receptive toward God's conviction of sin and His forgiveness than outstretched arms and hands that are seeking the mercy of God in total abandonment.

Every believer has experienced the cleansing fires and waters of sanctification at one time or the other. The real key is that we continue to know the purifying cleansing ways of God's Word and Spirit. We must not become complacent towards His Word and insensitive towards His Spirit. We must seek that which will separate, cleanse, purify, and anoint our lives to ensure that we serve as righteous instruments in the hands of God, and that we are vessels made and prepared for His use. Obviously, as believers we must be marked by His ownership, clearly set apart as vessels of honor ready to be used for His glory.

Are you such a vessel?

SEEING THE LORD

God often reminded His people that He was holy. He wanted them to know who they were to worship, love, and serve. He wanted them to know in such holiness He not only deserved to be honored and recognized in a hallow way, but He demanded it because He could do no less.

We see how even the angels responded to God in His holiness as they covered their faces and continually declare that He is holy and God almighty. We catch glimpses of His throne as all who surround it recognize His holiness and bow before Him in thankfulness, as they worship and cast their crowns at His feet in humility. In their adoration they are declaring that He was and is worthy to receive power, riches, wisdom, strength, honor, glory, and blessings.[44]

God's holiness was and is to serve as a reality check to His people. It is meant to create a certain environment, attitude, and response from His people. However, for some Christians the concept of holiness pushes them into the extremes. They either see themselves as being worthless worms that live in condemnation because nothing they can do will allow them to live up to any real expectation or standard of holiness. On the other hand, if such people manage to live up to some religious code or perception about holiness, they can become self-righteous and unbearable to those around them. Clearly, the fruit of either extreme reveals that both premises and approaches are incorrect and unproductive.

Man has the responsibility to discern and separate from that which is profane in order to give way to that which is holy and acceptable to God. However, God is the one who does the work of holiness. We are once again reminded that the Father places us in the place of holiness when He places us in Christ. Christ's life serves as the essence of holiness in us, while the Holy Spirit does the work of holiness by working the very life of Christ in us to reflect the glory of God in a dark world. The work of holiness serves as God's mark of distinction and excellence in His people.

God's holiness also has the capacity to change man. For the prophet Isaiah it revolutionized his calling. I have often wondered why Isaiah's vision of heaven did not begin in the first chapter of his book. Clearly, this vision of the Lord in His holiness would have initially defined Isaiah's calling as a prophet. However, what I failed to understand is that Isaiah's encounter with God's holiness was at a time when the spiritual environment of Judah was mediocre. Even though it was not blatantly wicked, the leadership of the kings at the time of Judah was spiritually lukewarm. There was no real clarity or passion towards Jehovah God, but that was about to change as the world around the people of Israel would unravel.

There was no doubt that Judah had experienced great prosperity under the reign of King Uzziah. According to Isaiah's prophetical

---

[44]   [44] Revelation 4:8:10-11; 5:11-14

warnings in the first five chapters of his writings, the prosperity was being taken for granted as the people became more self-sufficient, worldly, idolatrous, and indifferent to their high calling as Jehovah God's peculiar people or holy nation. In their prosperity they had strayed away from their high calling and were quickly losing their way. The harsh reality is that judgment was following. Due to its idolatrous way, the northern kingdom would fall within a couple of decades of Isaiah's encounter with the heavenly. In Judah, its spiritual decline as a kingdom during the prophet's lifetime would be marked by the wicked reign of King Ahaz. His reign brought to the light any hidden idolatry, while the doors of the temple were closed, as the people faced imminent defeat by their enemies.[45]

A mediocre spiritual environment is unacceptable to God. In His holiness Isaiah had no doubt as to how He viewed such a lukewarm environment when he personally cried out that he was a man of unclean lips who dwelled among a people of unclean lips. There is nothing like the holiness of God to bring the sober reality of just how unclean each of us are in our fallen, arrogant state. There is nothing that will cause us to become totally undone in brokenness and repentance as standing in the holiness of God. There is nothing that will cause us to dread, tremble, or want to hide our shame as knowing that we are about to face a holy God in a lukewarm or complacent state.

This response can clearly be seen in the lives of others who also encountered the holiness of God. Moses and Joshua had to take off their shoes in the presence of God's holiness, the children of Israel trembled at the holiness of God, and the Apostle John fell as dead when he encountered the holiness of his righteous Lord.[46]

Consider the righteous Job. A great theological debate occurred because of Job's situation. At the core of the debate was the question that since God was not unfair or unjust towards the righteous, Job had to be in sin for such unexplainable and unbearable events to unfold in his life. It was as if God's reputation was on trial because of Job's situation and He had to be defended. However, God's reputation was not on trial; rather man's theology was being tested while Job's faith was being refined.

---

[45]   2 Chronicles 26-29:9

[46]   Exodus 3:5; 20:18-21; Joshua 5:14-15; Revelation 1:17

At the end of the great debate that took place in regard to Job's plight, God answered Job out of the whirlwind by asking Him to explain the beginnings and workings of the different aspects of creation. Even though Job stood righteous before the Lord, he became aware of just how vile and insignificant he was in light of God's incredible majesty. It did not matter how right he had done things, inwardly God's holiness and majesty would still completely undo him even in his present state of being counted or considered righteous before his Creator. Job knew God was holy, but it was only when the stark contrast of his insignificance in light of God's character and power that he understood just how abhorrent he was. It caused him to repent in dust and ashes even though he had not sinned with his lips. In spite of being deemed right by God, Job was even more attuned to the great gap between the holiness of God and the spiritual state of man that had to be reckoned by God as being righteous. As Job declared, he had known these things about God, but now he had seen God and there was nothing more he could do but repent.[47]

I maintain the Church that Jesus died for does not need a revelation of God's love, for that has been made clear and defined by Jesus' redemption on the cross. However, I do believe the Church needs to be revolutionized in its thinking of God, and that will only come when those who Jesus died for are completely undone by the revelation of His holiness. It is only from this premise that the Church will gain a vision of its true calling, as well as come back to center as to what is true and what its real vocation and high calling is in this present age.

Holiness is clearly not an option; it is a necessity for every true saint of God. When I think about the different attributes of God's character, I see how they uniquely stand out, but also how they influence and interact with each other. For example, God's love is the attribute that most attracts us to Him; His mercy shows His willingness to forgive; His grace reveals His intention towards us; and His faithfulness shows His enduring quality that gives us assurance. But, what does His holiness reveal about His character? To me it reveals His integrity in all that He does. It is what ensures that all of His attributes can be trusted for they are pure and will never change when it comes to His people or circumstance.

---

[47]   Job 40:3-7; 42:5-7

When you study the composition of things, there is that glue or one element that combines or brings everything together into one substance and holds all the other factors together. Without this glue there would be no consistency or trustworthy character or quality in the final product. When it comes to God, it is His holiness that clearly serves as the glue that brings into focus the sustaining and caliber of His attributes. His holiness will define how each of His attributes will be expressed to us, as well as how they will affect our lives. God is clearly who He is because He is holy in every way, means, and act. There is nothing insincere, profane, inconsistent, or compromising about His character or ways.

When it comes to man, this is the one aspect of God that he often struggles with the most. While some individuals try to hide their sin behind God's love, God's holiness takes away their coverings to reveal the iniquity behind their real motives. While other individuals try to console themselves with their religious best, God's holiness reveals their depravity. While people try to justify their sin, God's holiness holds them accountable. While some people try to make themselves holy, God's holiness reveals how far away from the mark they are. While others try to find ways to let themselves off the hook from living an upright, godly life before God, God's holiness will ultimately demand that they give an account of their godless deeds and ways wrought by unbelief and rebellion.

The truth is we, as believers, must insist on holiness in our lives to maintain the integrity of our own lives and walk before the Lord. We must cease to hide behind religious masks and cloaks, and sanctify the Lord in our hearts, while we separate ourselves from the pagan, perverted influences of the world. We must give way to the cleansing, purifying ways and works of God's Word and Spirit. We must maintain an unsullied life by becoming spiritual pilgrims and strangers in this godless world, while we daily put on the life of Jesus. We must neglect the reign of self, while being made alive by the presence and power of the Spirit to walk in this incredible life as priests and kings. We must become holy because if we fail to, we will not see the Lord.

The writer of Hebrews 12:14 made this statement, "Follow peace with all men, and holiness, without which no man shall see the Lord." Jesus said in Matthew 5:8 that the pure in heart shall see God. Do not forget, Job confessed that he had heard about the great things of God, but after his encounter with Him, he actually saw God in light of His greatness.

The ultimate end of our journey as Christians should be to see the Lord. Our purpose in seeing Him is to worship, serve, and love Him in a manner He is worthy of. However, as we have been shown, there is only one manner in which He can be properly considered, honored, and approach and that is in and according to true holiness.[48]

---

[48] If you would like to learn more about the subject of holiness, see the author's book, *Follow the Pattern*, in Volume 2 of her foundational series.

THE
CHALLENGE
OF IT

Book II

1
KNOWING GOD

INTRODUCTION

One of the greatest challenges, we as Christians, must confront is coming to terms with whether or not we truly know God. There is so much in this world we can know about God, but such knowledge does not mean we personally know Him. I have knowledge of many people. I know of some because of historical presentations and I know about others because of the limelight the world has shed on them, but I do not know them on a personal level.

Knowing of or about someone simply proves that we do not personally know him or her. Granted, we may have some sense of people's character and opinions about their way of doing something, but the reality is we still do not personally know them. It is the personal knowledge of someone that implies we have more than a knowledge of the person; rather, there are personal, intimate revelations we possess in regard to that particular individual that others are not privy too.

If believers are going to survive the test of the age they are in, they better know who their God is. The prophet, Daniel even confirmed this in his exhortation surrounding the end days in Daniel 11:32b, ". . . but the people that do know their God shall be strong, and do exploits."

From the promise of the prophet Daniel, let me be the first to extend the following introduction to our wondrous God. If my introduction to God causes you to seek Him out for yourself to know Him in a personal, intimate way then I will know this particular presentation has been successful in accomplishing its purpose.

PERCEPTION OF GOD

Over the years I have realized that what determines what I know concerning God comes down to my perception of Him. Perception has to do with how I perceive something according to my own understanding.

One of Jesus' warnings in Scripture was to take heed how we hear something. As Christians we can know in part and see through our frame of reference in a limited, perverted, or distorted way when it comes to spiritual matters.[1] We assume we are hearing or seeing clearly, but the harsh reality is that such assumptions are based on presumptions. For example, I might presume that what I am hearing or seeing is correct; therefore, I assume that my understanding of a matter is also conclusive.

However, the Bible warns about the folly of such conclusions. We are only able to hear or see through a distorted frame of reference. Even though our way seems right it can lead to destruction and death. Even though we think we are standing, we could be very close to falling. Although we think highly of our conclusions, our thoughts fall short of God's ways of thinking. Even though we think we know something, in reality we have a very limited knowledge or understanding of it.[2]

We are even faced with a greater challenge when we insist we are right about a matter. Due to our pride, we often are not open to be challenged in our present perception. Such unwillingness to be challenged means we are not willing to be found to be wrong, limited, or foolish in our understanding or thinking. If we are wrong, it means we have to take responsibility for how it might be affecting our life as well as others. This can be hard on our pride, which is quick to justify such wrong. If we are limited, we have to concede that we do not know all things; therefore, we are not often qualified to judge matters in a fair way. If we are foolish in our thinking or conclusions it means we lack wisdom and discretion, revealing our real state.

It is for these reasons people often bluff their way through situations. They want others to think they know about a matter when in reality they have no clue about any of it. Such people figure they will learn as they

---

[1]   Luke 8:18; 1 Corinthians 13:9-12

[2]   Proverbs 14:12; 16:25; Isaiah 55:8-9; Romans 12:3; 1 Corinthians 10:12; Galatians 6:3

go, while pushing their way through a situation. However, those who do know about a matter, will discern if these individuals possess the goods or whether they are pretending to know.

When it comes to knowing God you see four diverse camps. There are the "great pretenders". These are the religious people who pretend they have a corner on God. Granted, they may know of God, but they do not know Him. They bluff their way through by quoting the Law or Scripture. They hide behind religious cloaks that cover up tombs of dead men's bones. There is no life in what they claim. These people have a mixture of truth and traditions, but the Spirit is missing, making their religion dead letter. Since the right Spirit is missing, these people are wrong about God. They may have certain things right about God, but they have created a god according to their traditions.[3]

The second group is comprised of those who have been limited in their understanding about God. These people have had some experiences with God but they have never graduated from the milk stage of doctrine to develop a taste for the meat of God's Word. The milk stage means these people have settled for being told what to do. They are still at the stage of the Christian life being a matter of dos and don'ts. They have not gone on to partake of the meat that enables them to walk in the Spirit.[4]

When we speak of walking in the Spirit, we are reminded as to what the Apostle Paul stated, "For the kingdom of God is not meat and drink, but righteousness, and peace, and joy in the Holy Ghost" (Romans 14:17). As Christians, we walk after the Spirit in order to walk in the ways of righteousness. We are led by the Spirit into the ways of peace with God, and we walk in the Spirit to possess the abiding joy as we do the will of God according to His Word and the leading of His Spirit.[5]

At the core of those who remain immature in their Christian life is carnality. These individuals may have a correct understanding about God but their ways remain fleshly. They may conduct some of their life and activities according to pure doctrine but they still walk according to the ways of the flesh. For example, their doctrine may be right, but they

---

[3] Matthew 15:3-9; 23:26-28

[4] John 4:34; 1 Corinthians 3:1-3; Hebrews 5:11-14; 1 Peter 2:1-2

[5] John 15:11; 16:24; Romans 8:1, 13-15; Galatians 5:15-18, 25

worship God according to their fleshly ways and not in the Spirit. This mixture points to an unholy agreement that will greatly limit or inhibit these individuals from coming to any real spiritual maturity.

The third type of people you encounter along the way are those who are foolish towards God. The people who fall into this category varies, but they all have one thing in common; they are ignorant of God. These individuals do not believe God, do not care to know God, and/or have erected their own god. This group is comprised of those who say in their heart there is no god. Granted, some of these individuals may claim they believe in God, but in their heart they do not believe Him.[6]

These people have no fear of God or His Word. They mock the concept of sin for they are amoral in their philosophies, and they shun the idea of righteousness because they hold to their own personal humanistic code of love, as well as right and wrong. These individuals can tout enlightenment but scorn the wisdom of God. They can also rage against the idea of hell because they fear a judgment seat, as well as refuse to foresee a future world yet to come. And, although some of them can prove to be spiritual, their connection with the unseen world comes through the spirit guides and demonic forces of the New Age, the humanistic darkness of the present age we live in.

As you consider such individuals, you realize they have a false sense of who God is. They are actually blinded by a false light, created by the environment that has greatly influenced or indoctrinated them. Although the light makes perfect sense to them, it simply blinds them to the destructive path they are on. This path of darkness gives them a false hope about what they perceive to be true. It possesses a false gospel that has no power to save, is influenced and inspired by the antichrist spirit of the age, and is often created by the false religion of humanism. Humanism is man centered and points to some aspect of man actually being worshipped rather than God.

The Apostle Paul explained that this false light finds its source in one who can present himself as an angel of light, Satan. Even though he is a murderer, Satan has no qualms about promoting a façade of love that really disguises hate. He has no problem promoting truths that are laced with the poison of lies. He is not in short supply of those who will promote

---

[6]   Psalm 53:1

some form of righteousness, while sowing the seeds of death and destruction into the equation. However, it is all a lie that blinds people to the darkness and destruction that lurks behind such masks and cloaks. People are attracted and prone to buy such presentations because as Jesus commended, such people love darkness rather than light, lest their deeds should be reproved. Such individuals hate the light and have no intention of ever letting it penetrate their dark souls.[7]

If you are a child of the light, you may even stand amazed that people prefer darkness, but it is important to point out that we choose what we love. These people have chosen to love darkness. It serves their purpose. The crux of the matter is that to know someone we must first of all choose to love him or her. Obviously, these people love their particular darkness, and in doing so they have chosen what or who they will ignore, reject, despise, and ultimately hate.

The Holy Spirit cannot convict such individuals of sin because they will reject His sweet overtures. He cannot lift Jesus up as the solution because such individuals have no desire to see the light. He cannot warn them of judgment to come because they have already judged Him and His truths as being foolish and deceptive. In the end, such people will be turned over to their preferences as they lose all sense of the true God of heaven. They will become reprobates, castaways, or useless in their knowledge and pursuits of life and truth.[8] No doubt they will erect some god, but it will not be the God who can save them.

Jesus stated that all the commandments could be summarized in two commandments Mark 12:29-31,

> And Jesus answered him, The first of all the commandments is: Hear, O Israel: The Lord our God is one Lord: And thou shalt love the Lord thy God with all thy heart, and with all thy soul, and with all thy mind, and with all thy strength: this is the first commandment. And the second is this: Thou shalt love thy neighbor as thyself. There is no other commandment greater than these.

---

[7] John 3:19-20; 8:44; 2 Corinthians 11:3-4,13-15

[8] John 16:7-13; Romans 1:24-32

It is clear there is only one true God. He not only commands our love but He deserves it. He could not command love unless love is a matter of personal choice, and He could not expect such love unless He deserved it. As the Apostle John reminds each of us that since God first loved us our natural response and responsibility should be to love Him back in like manner.[9]

How did God love us? He loved us in a manner that was so far reaching that the most we can do is point to a rugged cross where His only begotten Son was offered as a supreme sacrifice on our behalf.[10] There are no words to describe such love. It is pure, consecrated, and excellent in every way. It stands above the world's presentation of love, as it reaches into eternity, through the very corridors of heaven, and touches the very throne of God as it freely pulsates back to those who have received it and allows it to abound in their hearts.

We must choose to love God in the same abandoning way. Such love will not only prove loyal and steadfast to Him, but it will be the motivating factor to follow after and find God in the midst of the deceptive darkness of the world. The Bible is clear that we must seek out the true God of heaven in order to find Him. Being the true light of the world, as well as all-knowing and powerful in His ways, He knows where we are, but He must be found by us in the midst of darkness.[11]

Due to our fallen condition, God has become lost to us. We must not only know how to find Him in the midst of all the false presentations and lies of Satan, we must be able to discern Him when we do find Him. This will require us to know His voice, discern His presence, and not be content to settle for anything that is not of Him, regardless of how comfortable it may be to our flesh, stimulating to our carnal mind, and acceptable to our preferences. It is obvious that we must choose to love, find, and know the one true God for ourselves.

The question is do you know the one true God of heaven or have you erected a counterfeit in His place? Do you know the voice of your Savior or are you following a hireling shepherd who will leave you as prey, vulnerable to a predator who will ultimately destroy you?

---

[9]   1 John 4:19
[10]   John 3:16; 1 John 3:1
[11]   Jeremiah 29:13

APPROACHING GOD

What does it take to know God? How we come to know someone often comes down to how we approach him or her. As Christians we must know how to properly approach God to ensure an environment in which we can freely discover and know who He is. The first epistle of John is clear that we must know our God. If we fail to know Him, we will not be able to discern spirit, establish right doctrine, or ultimately display the fruits that will identify us to Him.

When you consider knowing someone, you must first consider how to properly approach him or her. Approach is often determined by the person's position, the type of relationship you may desire with that individual, and the type of investment you are willing to make if a relationship is established with him or her.

In many cases people initially will give up on the idea of having any association with someone because there is no familiar ground in which to approach the person. I may respect or want to know someone, but if there is no familiar ground in which to approach that individual, I will reason out that since I do not "run in the same circles" as the person there is no way I am ever going to have such a relationship with him or her.

There must be some kind of common ground before I can approach anyone in establishing a relationship in which I can know him or her. It might mean having mutual friends, interests, or careers that cross paths before there can be such a ground in which I can meet or approach a person. The truth is, in my limited sphere of relationship with others, I cannot know everybody; therefore, I can only know those who I somehow find common ground with.

Scripture is clear, due to sin we have been separated from God. You cannot know someone from a distance. Intimate knowledge requires you to come to a place of familiarity in order to personally know a person. Obviously, we cannot approach God from our fallen state unless we find some common ground. Praise God, He provided the common ground in which each of us can approach Him. However, like King Saul, we need to learn a valuable lesson when approaching God.

The king took matters into his own hands when the prophet Samuel did not show up to offer the sacrifice at the appointed time. It was from this premise the king discovered the harsh reality about what it meant to have a common ground in relationship to God. If we try to approach God in any other way than what has been established, our overtures to meet with Him or know Him will be rejected and all attempts cast aside into the utter judgment of damnation.[12]

The sole common ground in which each of us can approach God is at the point of Christ's redemption. In spite of the world's rhetoric and propaganda about tolerance towards other beliefs and religious ways, Christ is the only way to a life with God, as well as serving as the truth about what it means to be reconciled back into a relationship with the Father. There is no other way to God and there is no other ground in which you can meet Him. In spite of the world denouncing, raging against, and persecuting those who refuse to compromise such ground, God will not recognize any other position except the place of redemption. He will never cease to be who He is, regardless of the world's attempts to redefine Him, mocking His ways, adjusting His truths, and replacing His life.

Another aspect of knowing someone comes down to the manner in which we must approach that person. In what way or with what kind of style do we approach God? Clearly, God is not going to accept just any old way. In the past we see man trying to approach Him in ignorance, and Him calling for repentance because such superstitious individuals have no clue as to how to approach Him. Jesus told the Samaritan woman that she did not know how to worship God. The reason she had no concept of how to worship God is because she did not personally know Him.[13]

Like the religious leaders of Jesus' day many people in the different religious arenas approach God from the point of rituals and self-righteous piousness. We see how God rejected such attempts. Such religious people hid the fact that not only did they not love God, but they did not really know Him. They covered up their indifferent hearts toward God and others with their elaborate robes. They hid their lifeless religion behind rituals and judgments that simply enslaved others into their petty religious codes that had no real eternal significance to them.[14]

This brings us to the manner in which to approach God. We can only approach Him in good faith. Genuine faith approaches God's Word to believe what He says is true in order to come to terms with His

---

[12]   1 Samuel 13:8-14; Matthew 22:9-14; Luke 13:24-28; John 10:1-3
[13]   Acts 17:27-31; John 4:22
[14]   Matthew 6:1-8; 15:3-9

identity and plan. Such an approach allows God to reckon it as a point of righteousness. God is therefore, able to meet a person at the point of his or her faith, and unveil Himself to him or her through His Spirit.

Since faith approaches to believe, it is also prepared to receive what God has already established as truth. Faith will embrace a matter as being trustworthy with child-like confidence. There is no need for debate. This is why the Bible speaks of faith that comes by hearing the Word of God. Faith chooses to believe that the words are from God, thereby, trustworthy and pure in intent.[15]

We see that we are to approach God's Word in good faith to know God, but we must possess a right attitude to approach God in prayer. "Prayer" is communication with God. However, if we do not possess the proper attitude, we will not be able to even address Him in a way that gives Him the opportunity or the grounds to meet with us.

In the model prayer Jesus taught His disciples about prayer. He sets up the attitude in which we are to approach the Father. "Hallowed be thy name."[16] "Hallow" has to do with making something sacred and holy. It is the means in which to deify God in your heart and be able to create a proper attitude in approaching Him

The right attitude to have towards God is that of fearing or dreading meeting Him in a way that will not properly honor or regard Him. Sadly, there are those who have become too casual towards approaching God and others who act like whipped dogs when they come near to Him. The key to approaching God in a right attitude has to do with not fearing what He will do to you if you do not regard Him, but fearing you will not honor Him in a way that is worthy of Him. The first attitude comes from fear that is void of perfect love, while the latter attitude is a product of perfect love that desires to please and regard the Lord in a proper way since He is the focus of sincere adoration and worship.[17]

God deserves to be regarded and treated in a certain way. In fact, He is the only One who has the honor of being regarded and treated as divine or deity. No other entity or person is worthy to be placed in such a position.

---

[15]   Romans 10:17.

[16]   Matthew 6:9

[17]   1 John 4:16-18

A right attitude will ensure that you receive the matters of God in a right way. It is important to receive the things of God in a correct way to be assured of the proper impact. Like others, in the past I have been unprepared to respond properly to God's overtures. As a result, I missed opportunities of establishing a ground in which I could not only meet with Him, but ensure a greater opportunity of knowing Him. I sometimes shudder at the missed opportunities I had in the past because I did not understand or recognize that it was His time of visitation in which He intruded into my life as a means to meet with me. Such times may only last a moment, but when He steps on the scene, everything must take a back seat as each of us take time to meet with Him.

Meeting with God requires us to "take our shoes off" by stepping aside from normal activities and humbling ourselves before Him. Both Moses and Joshua had to take their shoes off before approaching God. The shoes represented involvement in the world, for each of us, we must walk in and through this world. Our walk often makes us earthbound to the limitations and perversions of the age we live in. We are often dulled down as the world chokes out the sharpness of the Word of God.[18] God must first get our attention before He can meet with us in a way that would maintain His sacredness and become beneficial to us.

When was the last time you actually met with God? Perhaps you have never had the freedom or understanding to approach God. Moses boldly approached God in intercession for the people of Israel because He understood the heart of God. When presented by Joshua the potential need to defend God's reputation among the pagans due to the army of Israel's defeat at Ai, Joshua was told to get up from a humble and repentant state and root out the sin that was in the camp. After Hannah lamented in total despair before the Lord, and was misunderstood by the priest, Eli, she was then told to go in peace and the God of Israel would grant her, her petition. She walked away in complete confidence that the Lord would give her a child she could completely dedicate back to Him.[19]

These people knew how to approach God because they had a personal knowledge of Him. They did not have to wonder about His

---

[18] Exodus 3:5; Joshua 5:14-15

[19] Numbers 14:10-24; Joshua 7:7-13; 1 Samuel 1:11-18

response for they knew who they were encountering when His instruction or promise was passed down to them.

As God's people we must know Him if we are going to have any credibility with Him and make any real impact on behalf of others. Instead of majoring in the doctrines, rituals, and deeds of religion, we must seek to know God for Himself. Such knowledge should be our heart's desire and relentless pursuit.

ENCOUNTERING GOD

As Christians our desire to approach God has to do with encountering Him. It is not unusual that many people may approach God, such as in prayer, but they do not expect to encounter Him. Yet, Jesus clearly instructed people to ask with expectation, seek with the desire to find, and knock with the intent of knowing something would be open to them.[20]

When you couple Jesus' instruction in regard to how we are to approach God with the summary of His ministry as being the way, the truth, and the life which leads back into a relationship with the Father, it is obvious that each point was to serve as a means in which to encounter God.[21] Granted, it would be wise for us to ask in light of the way that has been provided through Jesus. We should seek to find the truth that will unveil the reality of who He is, and knock on all doors until we come to a place of partaking of His bread and meat in communion with Him. If the way has been provided, the truth prepared to be revealed, and the right door constructed for us to knock on, clearly we must travel that way, find the truth, and come to the right door to encounter God in a personal way. Keep in mind the way, the truth, and the life culminates in the person and work of Christ Jesus.

One of the statements I would make to those at our fellowship services is that every time we come together, we need to be prepared to do business with God. If we have no intention of doing business with God, or meeting with Him, why bother entering the doors. Jesus' ministry is one of reconciliation, not one that majors in religious knowledge,

---

[20]   Matthew 7:7-11

[21]   John 14:6

activities, or experiences. We must encounter God on a personal level if we are to experience the change and impact that is so necessary for our lives.

Sadly, most people are quick to accept a casual or distant encounter with God through some type of mediator. Whether it be that of a religious leader such as a pastor, religious rituals, or activities, people are content to accept long distance encounters with God as being an indication that all is well on their spiritual front. However, you cannot effectively know someone as long as you keep it at the level of being long-distance. Granted, you can think the best, live in some type of fantasy, and maintain unrealistic notions about someone as long as you do business with them from long distance, but you will never really know him or her.

We see this same scenario with the people of Israel. They came as far as Mount Sinai to encounter God, but when they began to see the sobering reality of what it might mean for them to have an intimate encounter with Him, they quickly called for an intercessor. This allowed them to stand afar off from God, while letting one man pay the necessary price to intimately know Him.[22]

The problem with long distance relationships is that since you do not really know the person, you will not only err in your heart about who he or she is, but there will be no sense of faithfulness or loyalty to that person. Granted, you can be in love with your notion about the person, but if someone comes along that is able to catch your fancy, you will emotionally swing toward the one who has presently caught your affection. The Bible is clear that you cannot serve two masters.[23]

We see this lack of loyalty towards God on the part of the children of Israel. Since they had no personal investment in a relationship with God, they had no real loyalty toward Him. Regardless of His miraculous provision, these people did not really understand the dynamics of it because as slaves everything was naturally provided for them to a certain degree. Therefore, why should they understand a loving, caring God who would chose to not only deliver them from slavery, but chose to love them and set them apart as a great nation that He would reveal Himself to, pour out His blessings upon, and establish as His people.

---

[22]   Exodus 20:18-21

[23]   Matthew 6:24; Hebrews 3:10

This is true for some in the Church that Jesus died for and has redeemed. We each have been slaves to sin, the world, and Satan. In our arrogance, we can presume God has an obligation to take care of us even in rebellion. However, a rebellious slave was beaten and a runaway slave was killed. The truth is we often hold a different standard for God than we do the world. We assume God has to put up with our rebellious, obnoxious ways and indifferent service. We would not tolerate such behavior in those who serve us, but apparently God is desperate for people to serve Him; therefore, He will accept any type of crumb or tainted service that people just happen to throw His way. Such individuals will discover how wrong they are in their thinking!

God did not tolerate the idolatry that the children of Israel succumbed to when Moses did not come down from the mountain. His reaction towards the people of Israel and their lack of love and fickle devotion towards Him was decisive, the judgment clear, and the bitterness that was left in the wake unmistakable. He will not accept crumbs, leftovers, or tainted, compromising worship or service. He is God, and He is the one who determines the truth as to what He will accept from mere man.

The God of heaven who created man desires to have each of us personally encounter Him, but not because He is desperate. He loves us, but we are the ones who need to encounter Him to be saved. The truth is that He has provided the way for us to encounter and know Him, but the reality is that few will accept His terms.

Most people want to meet God on their terms, they want to erect a god to their liking, and they want to control how much God intrudes into their particular reality. However, God is God and not subject to man's mere whims, fickle devotions, and self-serving ways. While man tries to adjust God to his small world, God, out of love, is always calling man higher in order to know Him.

Man needs to personally encounter God in order to sense who He is. Man will never know how and when God might intrude into his present reality to reveal Himself, but he must be aware that God in His sovereignty reserves the prerogative as to how and in what environment He will manifest Himself.

For Jacob, God met him during a time of transition when he was on his way to his uncle's home. In the case of Moses, it was in the midst of normalcy that He made Himself known. To Joshua, He met him just before he was about to lead the children of Israel into their first victorious battle in the Promised Land. For Gideon, He met him during an oppressive time, Hannah in the bitterness of her despairing soul, young Samuel in the night, and a young shepherd boy named David while he was tending sheep.[24]

The truth is we will never know when God will intrude into our particular reality. The key is we must be prepared to encounter Him in a personal way. We must be willing to turn aside from normalcy, and meet Him before we make any attempts to make any advancement to possess what He has promised us. We must know that He is our only hope when it comes to oppression and our despairing soul, and that He will often meet us in the night, or while we are faithfully tending to the business of life.

In the New Testament we have the record of many who encountered God, only they encountered Him in human form. Jesus Christ, God in the flesh, became a neighbor to mankind. As the "good Samaritan" He went beyond the extra mile and the call of duty to meet the downtrodden such as the lepers. He entered in with those who were spiritually wounded such as those rejected by society. He met the outcast such as the Samaritan woman at the well, and sat among those who were considered insignificant such as the shepherds, fishermen, and the publicans. As a result, He forever changed the lives and course of many who were on the road to hopeless destruction and spiritual ruin.

We also can see those who sought out Jesus. Consider Jarius, a religious leader who was willing to sacrifice his position in the religious community to encounter Jesus on behalf of his sick, dying daughter. There is the woman with the issue of blood. Considered unclean, she sought Jesus out to grab a hold of the promise that in Him was the power to heal. Even though touching Him would cause Him to be deemed unclean by the religious community, and her action regarded as unethical and wrong, she risked it all. Her faith not only was confirmed by Jesus, but she walked away whole. There was the Roman officer who understood the authority Jesus had. He knew he was not worthy to even receive Jesus in his home, but He also understood that Jesus possessed

---

[24]   Exodus 3:1-2; Joshua 5:13-15; Judges 6:1-12; 1 Samuel 1:9-18; 3:1-10; 17:31-37

the authority and power of heaven to change the circumstances of the plight of others by His mere words.[25]

For our lives to change, we must encounter God. The only way we can is through the person of Jesus. We must pursue Him in a reckless way, risking reputation, position, and honor that are attached to this present world. We see in the case of one man he would count all associations with the world as being dung in light of gaining Christ.[26]

The man I am referring to had a decisive encounter with God in the New Testament that was recorded in Acts 9. The man's name was Saul. Saul was on the road to Damascus to persecute Christians. He was determined to put a stop to what was being referred to as the Way. However, on the road, he encountered the Way, the Lord Jesus Christ. There he was blinded by the light of the world as Jesus revealed the darkness of his soul and the error of his ways.

The man who learned from the best in regard to the Law of Moses found himself facing the one who not only was the Lawgiver, but fulfilled the requirements of the complete Law and the prophecies concerning the hope of Israel. Saul actually met the Promised One, the Messiah who he, along with the Jewish nation, had been waiting for. He was brought low when he realized his response to Jesus was not much different than those who crucified Him. He had walked in ignorance and unbelief towards the Promised One. He had been a fool.

Saul became a believer, changing his name to Paul. He became a man made small in order to walk in the authority and power of a great God to carry out an incredible mission. In light of his past activities of persecuting the Church, the Apostle Paul recorded his evaluation of his encounter with Jesus in 1 Timothy 1:15-16 when he stated that Jesus Christ came into the world to save sinners, of whom he was the chief of all. However, Paul went on to say, "Nevertheless, for this cause I obtained mercy, that in me first Jesus Christ might show forth all long-suffering, for a pattern to them who should hereafter believe on him to life everlasting."

We must initially encounter the Lord if we are going to know Him. Clearly, our lives will never be the same. Moses received his marching orders to lead the people out of bondage through the wilderness, Joshua

---

[25]   Matthew 8:1-13; 9:18-26

[26]   Philippians 3:7-9

came away understanding who the real Commander and Chief was, Gideon realized his potential as a man of valor, Hannah walked away knowing her prayers would be answered, Samuel became a prophet and judge, and David a victorious king.

The question is, have you encountered God? Do you have a sense or awareness of who He is? Or, are you going the wrong way, emphasizing the wrong agenda, and missing the opportunities of knowing God? Only you can honestly answer these questions as you examine your knowledge and understanding of God.

DISCOVERING GOD

One of the main reasons we need to encounter God is so that we can discover who He is. Moses encountered God in the wilderness but discovered Him in a greater way on Mount Sinai. As a child, Samuel encountered God in the night, but was brought to maturity as he discovered God in his daily walk.

God wants to meet with each of us on a personal level. Hence, enter the calling, "Adam where are you?" Here comes the invitation from Jesus, "If any man thirst, let him come to me and drink." Then comes the knocking on the door for fellowshipping, "I stand at the door and knock."[27] Whether it comes in the form of a calling, an invitation, or a knock, God wants to establish a common ground in which fellowship can take place. He wants to meet with us to contend, instruct, encourage, and commune with us. He wants us to know Him so we can grow in our spiritual lives and reach our heavenly destination.

At this time it is important to point out that all great people of God had a history with Him. In other words, they discovered who He was. They were not content to settle for a few encounters with their Creator, they wanted to know Him in greater ways. They were willing to risk it all to discover the unfolding depths of His character, the incredible heights of His ways, the endless width of His love, the unfolding riches of His grace, and the beauty of His glory. Each depth they attained in their spiritual life signified how much higher they would be brought in regard to seeing,

---

[27]   Genesis 3:9; John 7:37b; Revelation 3:20

hearing, and knowing God. Clearly, man must first be enlarged in order to receive the deep things of God to discover the heights that can be found in Him.

It is from the perspective of discovering God that we realize we must find Him in the midst of the confusing, pagan, idolatrous ways of self, the world, and Satan. He is the great treasure hidden by the darkness of the world, the garden that has yet to be discovered behind unseen walls, the refreshing spring that must be uncapped, and the bread from heaven that must be gathered in faith, prepared in obedience, and partaken of to ensure life. He is in all that pertains to life and godliness, and must fill all to overflowing.

We must ask ourselves what we must do to discover God. Clearly, He is hidden, but is there a desire to find Him? He can be found, but are we looking in the right places? We can encounter Him, but will we recognize Him when we do? We can discover Him, but do we possess the character and the diligence to wade through the religious muck of man's traditions, the endless counterfeits erected by deception, and the deluge of foolishness that mark our vain, empty ways to find Him for ourselves?

The woman at the well was looking for the Messiah, and even recognized Jesus as a prophet, but it was not until He introduced Himself as the Messiah that she knew who stood before her. The crowds could not keep blind Bartimaeus from calling out to Jesus in desperation. When Jesus bid him to come, his blindness could not keep him from flinging all aside to find Him and discover His healing power.[28] The woman with the issue of blood had to press through the crowd to even touch the fringes of Jesus' garment. She would not let anything deter her from her mission. She had to grab hold of Him only to discover how her faith caused Him to take note that someone had tapped into His very power. The centurion officer knew he had to seek Jesus out on behalf of his sick servant, and recognized His heavenly authority to accomplish the impossible without even touching the servant.

Another interesting person who discovered Jesus was a man named Zachaeus.[29] The Word of God tells us that Zaccheus was a Jewish tax

---

[28]   Mark 10:46-49

[29]   Luke 19:1-10

collector. In the eyes of many of his brethren, this made him a traitor. It was also said of this man that not only was he considered small in the eyes of others, but he was also small in stature. An outcast who probably did not command much respect physically, Zachaeus had some major strikes against him. Whether this man's character and practices were questionable would be mere speculation on our part, but the one thing we know about him is that he desired to see Jesus.

His physical stature proved to be a hindrance for him in the crowd, but that did not stop him from showing some type of initiative and innovation. He would not be prevented from seeing this man whose fame preceded Him. Calculating, as to the route Jesus would travel, this man ran ahead of the crowd and climbed up into a sycamore tree in order to see the One who had done the miraculous and incredible.

No doubt the crowd ignored this man, but there was one who would take note of Him, the Lord of lords and the King of kings. That day, Jesus stopped in the midst of the crowd, looked up and saw Zachaeus. He instructed the man to come down and make haste for that day He would sit at his table.

Jesus knew all about Zachaeus, and Zachaeus was about to discover the reality of Jesus. From that day forth the insignificant man with an unsavory profession and of small stature discovered the incredible impact of supping with the One sent from the very throne of heaven, Jesus. He made this statement to the Lord in Luke 19:8, "Behold, Lord the half of my goods I give to the poor; and if I have taken anything from any man by false accusation, I restore him fourfold." Jesus' reply was that salvation had truly come to this man's household. As the Son of man He had come to seek and to save those who were and are lost.

Even though Zachaeus had climbed the tree to see Jesus, Jesus was the one who found Zachaeus. The truth is we cannot find Jesus until He finds us in the midst of the crowds. The one attraction that will always catch our Lord's attention is a seeking heart that desires to see, touch, or hear Him in some way. We must somehow touch Him to benefit from our meeting or encounter with Him, but we must come to a place of communion if we are going to discover Him.

It is hard to comprehend how we can find God until we are found by Him. The truth is all we can do is come back to center as to what we know is true and right. Like Joseph and Mary in Luke 2 it may require us to go back to where we last left Jesus, due to the activities of religion and the world. Like Bartimaeus we might have to cast aside the rags of the old self-life to discover what God has for us. Perhaps like the woman enslaved to an issue of blood, we may have to press through all that stands before us to discover how God can move the mountains of traditions that may loom in front of us. And, maybe like Zachaeus, we may have to climb above all the obstacles that beset us to discover what it means to be saved by the One who is always seeking out His lost sheep.

Each of these individuals discovered Jesus in a personal way. Whether it was His compassion, authority, or power, they recognized that Jesus was not just any ordinary man. He was who He said He was, and as a result He touched each of their lives, allowing them to experience a bit of heaven on earth.

This brings us to the key of personally discovering God. It will require a very special connection to the throne of God with the intent of discovering Him on a personal level. Such a discovery will ultimately lead a person to the place of knowing Him. The Apostle Paul tells us the connection that will result in us knowing the deep things of God is His Spirit.[30]

The Holy Spirit is the One who unveils and reveals the deep things of God to the very spirit of man. Man cannot know such things in his natural, unregenerate state. He can only know them if the Spirit brings forth the proper revelation and teaching to his spirit, thereby, enlarging his mind to receive it in a right way. In such revelation the necessary contrast is produced, allowing a person to compare spiritual matters with spiritual truths and teachings. It is from such a premise that saints not only discover the deeper things of God, but they begin to establish a personal history. Each new discovery allows each truth seeker to experience God. Experiencing God affords us as believers, the opportunity of knowing Him.

Have you come to that place of discovering God? Do you have a history that speaks of experiencing God in a personal way, implying you have first hand knowledge of Him? Or, is He simply a concept that has been place in a nice doctrinal box or theological package as a means to soothe the religious conscience?

---

[30]   1 Corinthians 2:9-14

EXPERIENCING GOD

There are many people who desire some type of spiritual experience, but such experience does not mean they are pursuing the reality of experiencing God. Such desires can lead to experiences defining people's perception of God; rather than people discovering God and knowing who He is.

Sadly, Satan is capable and quick to present counterfeit experiences that seem more real than the actual reality around us. These spiritual experiences not only serve as a counterfeit as to what it means to know God, but they are also mistaken for the salvation experience and spiritual enlightenment that will often be exalted in the mind of the person. Such exaltation points to the experience even superseding the validity of the Word of God.

It is not unusual to meet people who have had tremendous spiritual experiences, but they fail to bear any life or likeness that can be identified as belonging to Christ. Spiritual experience alone does not denote salvation or revelation. It is the presence of the Spirit in us that bears witness to a matter and it is the life of Christ that serves as the fruit that clearly identifies the source or inspiration behind our experiences. Granted, we receive the life of Christ by faith, but God gives us the Spirit to work His life in us. Such work is not a matter of having a spiritual experience; rather, it allows us to experience God in a personal way.

For this reason we must ensure that the saving, eternal life of Christ is worked in us by the Spirit of God. It is the evidence of Jesus' disposition and attitude that will distinguish us as being indeed citizens of the heavenly, unseen kingdom of God. It is the Spirit of God who connects us to the throne of God in communion, and it is the life of Christ in us that reveals that God has been able to show us grace as His life becomes a point of identification and agreement with that which is heavenly and eternal. It is from the place of communion and the point of agreement that we are able to learn about and know God in an intimate way.[31]

I had to learn these lessons first hand. There have been two ways that I have approached God. The first way came in the form of knowing

---

[31]   2 Corinthians 13:14

196

about God. I strived to gain as much information about God as I could. It was my way of convincing myself the more I knew about God, the more that I would know Him. However, my attempts to know about God kept me from seeking to know Him on a personal level. Instead of tasting of the sweet manna of heaven, I was sucking on, and from, the lifeless carnal reserves of religious knowledge that has no real life to it.[32] You cannot know someone unless you experience the reality of tasting, hearing, seeing, touching, and smelling the essence of the person.

It was only after I came to a place of crisis in my spiritual life that I realized that I had to experience God in a personal way. I had to taste of His goodness, hear His longing invitation to come aside and actually come away with Him, see Him in His holiness, touch Him in His compassion, and smell His sweetness that I would begin to experience the essence of His countenance, character, and ways.

It was only after I had experienced Him in a personal way that I had the desire for others to know Him. However, I encountered a tremendous gulf that prevented me from accomplishing my desire. I could not know God for others. Every person had to experience God for him or herself. Granted, I could provide people with tools or even valuable insights about the reality of God, but I could not know God personally for them. I could lead them to the water of His Word, but I could never cause them to partake of the waters in a personal way. I could try to stir them up to love Him in greater measures, but I could never cause them to love Him. I could create a bit of hunger, but I could never cause them to hunger and thirst after God's righteousness in a relentless way.

For years I struggled under the burden of knowing there was an urgency to know God, but I could never communicate such urgency to others. The urgency at times pushed me to provide the tools as I contended for souls, but eventually I was brought to places of despair as I watched people remain content to stay in their pigpens, become stagnant in their amoral realities, and often run back to the empty or poisonous cisterns of man-made religion.

Eventually, my urgency brought me to a place of complete depression. I wrestled before God in my attempt to understand how I could come to such a place of despondency at such a time. I could not

---

[32]   1 Corinthians 8:1-3

see how I could afford to be at a place that left me without the edge of urgency that had so often stirred me up to run with intensity the race before me.

In reality, I had come to a dead end. I could not take these unwilling souls any further than they were willing to come in their spiritual lives. My urgency in itself had not brought me to such a despairing place, but the actuality that there was nothing more I could do for those who I had been laboring amongst in the harvest field. It was obvious that I had discovered the vanity of the dead ends erected by spiritual indifference. The dead ends did not represent my state, but the end of the trail regarding my work with those I had been laboring among.

This place reminded me of Moses. He was journeying up into Mount Sinai to receive the Law and instructions for the building of the tabernacle. The people of Israel were being provided with the means of becoming holy people and fulfilling their true calling and vocation in the Promised Land. The leadership had even sat at a table of communion and was allowed to see God before Moses separated himself. It was clear that Moses would not simply witness the Lord in his midst and benefit from His presence; rather, he would eventually experienced Him in a greater way.[33]

Forty days later Moses was called down from the mountain to face the harsh reality that the people had gone into blatant idolatry. Even those who had supped in the presence of the Lord were involved in the erecting and worshipping of idols. Can you imagine how Moses must have felt? We know how he reacted, but to be faced with the continual dripping of man's fickleness towards God is tiresome. Clearly, man can do lip service to God while his heart is fickle and remains unstable and often far away from God in love and devotion.

Most of the time all we can see are the Demas' who run back to the world, while failing to see the Joshua's that have come as far as they dare as a means to personally experience God. We see the Aarons of religion erecting the golden calves of idolatry in the sanctuaries of churches, and not the Noahs who are hidden in the ark of Christ. We see the children of Israel dancing around the altars of idols but do not see the seven thousand who have never bowed their knees to the idols

---

[33]   Exodus 24:9-13

of the present age. Like Jonah who was asleep in the hull of indifference while the storm raged above, we see those who are asleep in the pews of churches as the darkness of the present age slams against the doors of indifference, but we do not see the ones who are hidden in the secret chambers of communion or the caves of God's abiding protection.[34]

It was at this time that I realized that all I had left to give those I had labored among was my oil. Like the wise virgins in the parable in Matthew 25, I had to recognize that my oil represented the measure of His Spirit that I had acquired by the type of investment that had been made in my relationship with God along the way. In other words, I could not know God for other people, and they could not possess such personal knowledge without paying the price to possess a greater quantity of the presence of His Spirit for themselves.[35]

The truth is, most people do not want to pay the price to know God. They want you to pay it for them. They do not realize that what they refuse to pay to know God, ultimately they will end up losing. No one can come into the secret chambers of fellowship with God for you. No one can press towards the high calling in God but you. No one can scale the heights of excellence or taste the depths of identification with God to come out with a greater awareness of His character and ways but you.

It costs to know God, to experience Him in deep ways so that He can bring a person higher in his or her life in Him. Even in my present state of despondency I was aware that God was going deeper with me. The urgency was being tempered by the knowledge that this was my personal time with God and could not be shared with others. I was being taken deeper into the abyss of my own personal need for Him to become my all in all in order to be brought higher in my walk with Him. He was being faithful to create a greater dependency upon Him in order to bring forth a greater inward preparation to face the times I could sense were looming before me.

I was also aware that to walk through such an abyss would take time. In the hyped up religious environment of the visible church, few leaders would dare take such time out to experience the ominous impact such a

---

[34] Exodus 24:13,18; 32:1-10; 33:11; 1 Kings 19:18; Jonah 1:5-6; 2 Timothy 4:10; Hebrews 11:7

[35] Luke 11:13

journey would require. They have been conditioned to keep up the façade, as well as keep the pot stirred up to ensure the money continues to flow into the coffers. Sadly, such people will become burned out or unprepared to lead the people through the darkness that is encroaching in this age.

The spiritual journey to seek, find, and know God will not end with each encounter, discovery, or experience with Him, for He is eternal. However, each encounter with Him will whet your appetite to know Him more, and each discovery should cause your senses to become wings that lift you into greater heights in order to know Him. Personally experiencing Him should cause your vision to enlarge to see beyond this present age to embrace the heavenly and eternal aspects of the life that is being gained.

As I studied the lives of those who possessed the promises of God with unfeigned faith, I realized this was the secret behind their incredible journey. Their faith led them to places where they did encounter, discover, and experience God. As a result, this world held no attraction. In these people's hearts they were not earthbound by the forces around them nor were they interested in enticement offered by the terrain of their present age. Their hearts were in another place, their vision was focused on an unseen world, and their path led them beyond the normalcy of this present life to see and know the existence of the glory of the world to come.

What about you? Where is your life and walk leading you when it comes to God? Are you encountering, discovering, and experiencing God? Do you possess the unseen life that will prepare you to embrace the unseen world that will be unveiled in glory? Do not accept the status quo of today's religious environment, but always know that there is so much more. It is up to each of us to individually seek out more of the kingdom of God as we strive to find our Lord and know Him for ourselves.[36]

---

[36] If you would like to know more about this subject, see the authors' books, *Prayer and Worship and Don't Touch That Dial (Hearing the Voice of God)*, in the 3rd volume of her foundational Series.

2

IT COMES DOWN
TO RELATIONSHIP

INTRODUCTION

When we think of God, we often see a benevolent entity or a fearful force that cannot help but unmercifully discipline or judge us whenever we make a wrong decision or move. The truth regarding most people's perspective of God is that it is lopsided, vague, or just ridiculous. The ultimate conclusion is that people's perspective or understanding of God is that in most cases they are just plain wrong.

In Acts 17:30, we are warned that God will not wink at those who are ignorant of Him, but that He is calling for repentance on their part. The reason He is calling for repentance is because there is no excuse for man not knowing who his Creator is. Granted, people have various reasons why they do not know the true God of the Bible. For some they are content to have their own take on Him, while for others they have gone the way of religion where they have allowed religious personalities to define Him. For others they remain confused for they have allowed the unknown spiritual aspects of Him to be humanized, spiritualized, or demoralized into an arena of rituals and superstition. Each perception or approach to God simply proves that man has failed to recognize that what has been clearly verified by the witnesses God has put in place reveals not only the foolishness of man, but his unwillingness to step past the comfort zones of his ignorance and unbelief to know God.

There is only one way that man can intimately know God, and that is by having a relationship with Him. God not only has established the means to have a relationship with each of us, but He has made it clear that He deserves such a bond.

This presentation is about having a relationship with our Creator. As Christians, we can talk about the matters of salvation, debate doctrinal understanding, and lament knowing God in greater ways, but our understanding and knowledge of God will come down to whether we have a relationship with Him and the type of personal investment we make in it.

It is time for those who consider themselves God's people to soberly approach the matter of what it means to have a relationship with their Creator by laying aside all preconceived notions about God and the life He provides. As believers, we need to come to terms with what was lost in the Garden of Eden so many years ago. The first man, Adam, became separated from God when he rebelled against His authority. In essence, his relationship was broken and lost with God. As a result, man became lost to all that had substance and life.

It is time we each understand what we must regain to once again find our way back to what became lost to us in Eden. We must rediscover how to enter into the place with God where a relationship with Him can be established, developed, and nurtured.

THE PROBLEM
WITH RELATIONSHIPS

What does it mean to develop and live the Christian life? In reality it means to have total dependency on God. We do nothing but what is ordained by the Father. We do nothing outside of the will of our Lord Jesus. We do nothing that is not in line with His righteous ways. We do nothing unless we are being directed to do so by His Spirit.

The Christian life is nothing more than the life of Christ being established in believers by faith, walked out in simple obedience to His Word, and serving as the sole means that enables each saint to walk in the narrow path of righteousness.

There are many challenges that can hinder the Christian life from coming to fruition. Due to the influence of the world, the biggest challenge has to do with how this life is often perverted by man's additions to it with religion, or subtraction from it in regard to moral irresponsibility. Much of this life has been perverted by those who simply do not approach the Word to believe and obey it. Rather, many such individuals approach the Word to confirm their own point of view or adjust it to their religious personal agendas. Such people not only adjust the Word, but they often lightly esteem it when it does not fit their notions and agendas.

Such individuals will mock God's Word, while hiding behind a set pattern of Scriptures that lack correct intent. In other words if you follow these people's presentation of Scriptures they do not end in truth being upheld; rather, they lead to personal religious views that can prove to be seductive, deceptive, ignorant, and heretical. Such views are empty for they have no life or real power in them and will ultimately lead to spiritual ruin.

It is important to point out that if life is missing in Scripture, it is because the right spirit is absent. Without the right spirit, the intent behind such Scripture will be self-serving rather than liberating. The Holy Spirit is the One who takes Scriptures and makes them living, powerful, and liberating. It is the Holy Spirit who empowers the sword of the Word with revelation to cut through spiritual dullness in order to bring life by quickening our spirits.[1] It not only cuts through spiritual dullness, but it reveals sin, while transforming and renewing the inner man to embrace a new way of thinking and walking.

We must consider how this new life is developed in us and the new way it will be cultivated. It can only occur if we develop an active, growing relationship with the Lord. Christianity was never meant to be compressed into a religion. The idea of Christianity pointed to a way of walking and living that was inspired by heaven and empowered by the Spirit of God.

This brings us to a very important point of consideration. What does it mean to have a relationship with God? In the beginning of my spiritual odyssey to discover the spiritual truth about the Christian life, God was, at best, a vague notion. I had no concept that God had a desire to have a personal relationship with me. I often viewed God either from a sentimental notion inspired by a story of a baby born in a manger or a far away force that in the end would balance out my bad in light of my good.

---

[1]   John 3:18-21; 6:63; 2 Corinthians 3:17; Hebrews 4:12

My deceptive hope was that my good would outweigh my bad, and God would accept me.

However, I encountered a harsh reality in my life. The harsh reality was that of sin. I could not get around the fact that regardless of how well I played the outward game of piety, I was very much aware of my inward struggle with spiritual depravity I could not explain away nor overcome. I had a sense that even if I could display some type of "goodness" to the world, I knew what was going on in my thought process, my feelings, and my lifestyle. It was as though this feeling of utter failure would descend on me like a thick blanket.

Each time I faced my inward depravity, I also came to the awareness of how empty my life was. There was a vacuum present that could not be explained. Everything I attempted to do seem empty and vain in the end. Every small goal I set and managed to accomplish left a temporary mark of satisfaction that would end in disillusionment and despair. Ultimately, life did not make sense.

Even though I somehow knew God was the answer, I was at a loss as to how to connect with Him. I prayed, but there was no life or power in it. I had a religious conscience but it only condemned me, making God further away and more impersonal. My personal inward examination of my hidden life taunted me that there was no way God would ever accept my religious best. At each point of examination or consideration, I found the distance between any concept of connecting with God widening, rather than bringing me closer to some type of connection or way in which I could find common ground in which to meet Him.

The more I struggled with my dilemma, the more depression swallowed me into an abyss of hopelessness. In my mind, I was an utter failure. There was no real resolution except resolving that the utter darkness that was beginning to enslave my soul was my inevitable reality. There appeared to be no hope for me. Either I would continue to fake my religious veneer that clearly had become tarnished or I would accept the reality of my terrible lot and allow the formidable darkness that clung to my very being to claim my soul.

Clearly, I was at some incredible crossroad with no option or hope. I had to make some decision, but what were my options? It was during this time a light began to penetrate my soul. It started out small because I had already considered it to be a possible answer, but could not see any way to bridge the great gulf that not only was present, but had become wider with each personal examination.

This small beam of hope was that God was the answer to my plight. The answer somehow rested with Jesus. In all honestly the small beam of light seemed to be illusive as it appeared to dance around the edges of the darkness of my soul. Since I had a vague concept about God, I could not quite grasp the light as understanding eluded me, but I knew that somehow He was the answer to my miserable plight.

As the light of God's truth was beginning to dawn in my soul, I became aware that I could have some kind of interaction with God. Granted, I did not comprehend the ground in which I could connect with Him to interact, but I knew it was possible. Such an understanding began to take hold of me.

However, the challenge was obvious. How can I interact with someone who I could not see? What would it mean to find a common ground with a God who was not earthbound? In a way, it seemed an impossibility to ever find any real common ground, but there was something about the light that was beginning to penetrate the recesses of my mind that brought a glimmer of hope.

Even though at the time I did not realize it, the concept of finding a common ground with God in order to connect to Him and interact with Him pointed to establishing some type of relationship with Him. At the time of my spiritual plight I was not thinking in terms of having a relationship with God, just simply connecting with Him so that I could resolve the tormenting inward struggle of my soul.

In many ways my approach to God revealed my understanding about so much of my life. Even though I had relationships with others, I really did not understand the dynamics of what it really meant to have a healthy, lasting relationship. Much of my understanding and notions about relationships operated in the realm of fantasy. I had friendships, but through the years they often proved to be temporary. Friends seemed to move in and out of my life like the changing tides that were intruding onto the ever-changing landscape of my existence.

When it came to lasting relationships, I saw them already established by family ties and bonds that one could take for granted, or assume that no one had a say over whether or not there had to be any real connection or interaction. In such relationships the common ground was already established. The key to such relationships was often not based on what it would take to establish healthy or vibrant interaction, but how to play the game to keep the peace in such associations. For people in such relationships they know their place and have already learned if they play their cards right they can keep a semblance of peace. The game was often to keep others at bay to prevent them from discovering how faulty, hypocritical, inept, or dysfunctional such relationships can prove to be in the end.

The truth is that I really did not know how to interact with God. My understanding came down to some religious associations, rituals, and activities. However, such dealings proved to be empty. When one is in a crisis of identity and purpose, he or she needs to encounter that which is living, real, and personal.

When you consider earthly relationships you can't help but see that there are many different challenges that confront such associations. When it comes to the many different types of relationships, it appears as if the concept of having a healthy relationship with others is also impossible. The divorce rate is 50%, children seem at war with parents, friendships often prove fickle, and healthy relationships almost extinct.

Healthy relationships are possible, but because of man's imperfection relationships become an obvious casualty. Since such associations require all parties to be realistically engaged, ready to make the necessary commitment, and prepared to make the investment and sacrifice to create a vibrant place of union and agreement, relationships find themselves vulnerable and often a target.

Selfishness and pride are the biggest enemies of healthy relationships. Man's concept that relationships are to serve his purpose and bow down to his whims, causes such associations to serve as platforms for tyranny, torment, misery, and oppression. People find themselves entangled in relationships that are abusive, hateful, and dishonorable. There are no grounds in which to have a healthy relationship with those who see such an association as one-sided. There are no real emotional connections or interactions to nurture such an association. It is all give on the part of one of the partners, while it is all take on the part of those who prove tyrannical in their demands. These individuals will dole out bread crumbs here and there to pacify any conscience that they might be unfair or unrealistic towards those they have a relationship with.

If the relationships we have on a horizontal plane of this present age poses real challenges, what makes each of us think that we know how to have an effective relationship on a vertical scale with an unseen God? Perhaps the fact that we lack such a vertical relationship with our Creator causes our horizontal relationships to be out of order or unrealistic.

As I struggled with the lack of connection with the unseen God, I had to face the harsh reality that I did not know what it would mean to have a connection with a God who seemed so far away from me. There was no way I could draw near to Him, and it seemed that He had no real reason to draw near to me. I had a sense that the gap had to be closed by something outside of my miserable attempts. I became aware that I was lost to ever making any real connection to God. However, the light that was beginning to penetrate my soul gave me hope that somehow God had or would make a connection to me. Even though the problem of relationships clearly rested with man, God had the means to solve such a problem.

It also dawned on me that until the problem could be remedied, life would not make sense. Granted, I could look to other relationships, but my miserable plight would follow me into such associations. I knew that I could not trust myself in any earthly relationships because I carried around with me a heavy load that was becoming more unbearable each day. Something had to give. Before I could offer anything of value and worth to others, I had to resolve the darkness that had enfolded my soul.

Somehow I had to come to terms with the matter of my spiritual plight. One way or another I had to find the common ground with God in order to make the necessary connection with the intent of resolving the matters of the soul. I determined that come what may, life needed to make some type of sense before my relationship with others would ever make any sense. In some way I had to come to the end of my misery to even begin to have any type of hope of securing a life that would possess any real measure of meaning or purpose. This life would have to lift me out of my present pit of hopelessness for me to have any direction. Somehow I had to find the means to meet with the only one who could answer my questions and set me at rest about the darkness that was encroaching in every area of my life.

MEETING GOD

When I think about my journey to discover the answers to the questions regarding my soul, they sometimes took on the intensity of silent screams. As I recalled the struggle in my soul, I could best relate it to the Samaritan woman at the well in John 4.

Due to the Samaritan woman's unsavory lifestyle, she appeared to be alone, an outcast in society. She had been married five times and was presently living with a man. Yet, her heart harbored unseen gems. From all religious calculations God would have not given her the time of day, let alone draw near to her. However, God knew something about her that no earthy person would ever be able to imagine. He knew she had viable questions about eternal and unseen spiritual matters that silently were waiting to be brought to the light. Perhaps unanswered questions drove her to seek her consolation in the wrong places? Maybe, if someone had rightly answered her questions, she might have been a different woman whose vision was straight and lifestyle was honorable. On the other hand, who could she trust with such questions? Who would know the answers, or even take her seriously? Most religious people were probably too busy judging or gossiping about her to even consider that God would even bother drawing near to her, let alone unveil and answer the silent questions of her heart.

Through the years the imperfection of man that is often hid behind religious garbs, self-righteous piousness, and judgmental attitudes has often come to the forefront. Like the poor woman caught in adultery in John 8, instead of caring for miserable souls such as her, the religious people were ready to offer such a soul up on the altar to be sacrificed in utter disgrace and humiliation for their own personal self-exaltation and glorification. So many times such judgmental individuals have taken the knife of accusation, gossip, and slander to the disgraced soul being held up as an example as they offer him or her on the indifferent and cruel altars established by self-righteousness. They console themselves by telling others, "If you only knew about his or her sins;" or, "Have you heard what so and so has done?"

As these self-righteous judges relish the thought that they hold the key that would certainly confirmed their sinister, judgmental attitude towards such a wretched soul, they fail to remember that Jesus drew near to the woman at the well, while admitting at a different time that the Spirit was present to heal the religious people of His day, but they were not open to receive.[2] The same Jesus that drew near to the outcast Samaritan woman was the same Jesus who stayed the judgment that was aimed at the adulteress woman by stripping the Pharisees of their self-righteous façade by stating, "He that is without sin among you, let him first cast a stone at her" (John 8:7).

It is true that sin has broken fellowship with God. It is true that man is separated from his Creator. It is true that the best of man is considered filthy rags before a holy God.[3] It is true that man has no means to reach God or draw near to Him in His holiness in his present, lost state. It is true we all deserve to die in our sins no matter how much religious garb we wear over our wretched stench. It is true that without God's intervention, there is no hope for any of us.

Until we recognize our wretched condition we will have a tendency to downplay our own miserable condition while harshly judging others in their wretched plight. I have discovered those who are the most critical are the ones who think they have cleverly hid their sins or are trying to hide them at the expense of others who are being judged as being inferior or unacceptable by the religious environment.

It is vital that God meets us. But, we must prepare to meet with Him. How will God meet us? There is only one place in which God will step outside of the eternal dimension in order to meet us in our spiritual plight. We need to understand this place to meet with Him, and that is at the place of redemption.

It was my awareness of my sin that not only liberated me to consider the place of redemption, but it allowed me to be brought there by the example and testimonies of others who had come to the same place to seek God's mercy. I was acutely aware that my spiritual condition separated me from God, but I had no understanding that He had provided a place as to where I could seek His mercy, thereby, obtaining His grace in the form of eternal life.

God can only connect with us at the point of His Son. Jesus came to redeem us from our miserable plight. It is Jesus who is able to reconcile

---

[2]   Luke 5:17

[3]   Isaiah 64:6; Romans 3:23; 6:23

man back to God.[4] He is that incredible bridge that closed the great gulf between the finite and the eternal. He became the one who stepped out of the unseen realm of glory into a material world to bring the opposing and diverse dimensions of the impossible in regard to man's salvation and the work of redemption together at one point. He is the place where man can draw close to God, knowing that God can draw near to him.

Reconciliation is an important aspect of the Christian life that must not be casually brushed over. Since people are separated from God, they have no idea of what that separation entails. They do not know what value or worth such reconciliation implies, that is until they are separated from something they truly have come to treasure. In man's lost state he has no conception as to what another man lost in the Garden of Eden. It is only when he becomes aware of the wretched depravity of his hopeless condition does he begin to sense the preciousness of what it means to be reconciled back to God.

In the Old Testament, man had to settle for atonement. "Atonement" simply covered his sins allowing him the freedom to benefit from the blessings and promises of God. However, redemption shows us that our sins have been taken away and now we can partake of the blessings and promises of God. Benefitting from something and partaking of something differ in the fact that we can experience certain aspects of God that benefits us, but partaking implies we can actually be identified with Him. Benefits serve as an extension of God that somewhat connects us to His heart, intention, and purpose, but identification takes us beyond simply connecting to God. It points to becoming an extension of God so that the life we are living in Christ becomes real and beneficial to others.

The Apostle Paul tells us that Jesus had the ministry of reconciliation.[5] He was that connection extended from God to each of us. He was a point of identification with man on a personal level in order for man to become identified with God on a spiritual level.

Obviously, it is vital to understand how Jesus serves as that incredible common ground in which God can meet with man. Jesus is fully God and fully man. As God, He stands righteous, an ark in which man can hide in, knowing that when the Father considers a person, He

---

4   Colossians 1:20-21
5   2 Corinthians 5:18-20

will see His Son. When He sees His Son, He will see the essence of pure wisdom, acceptable righteousness, the mark of sanctification, and the fullness of redemption.[6] As a result, our holy God is able to meet with those who draw near to Him through His Son.

On the other hand, Jesus is fully man. He allowed His glory as God to be veiled by humanity so that we could approach deity without the fear of being consumed by His holiness. He made God personal, reachable, and real to seeking hearts. When those with a seeking heart encountered Him, they were truly meeting with the fullness of God in bodily form. In His humanity Jesus experienced the reality and challenges that comes with being human. In the flesh, He overcame the sins that beset man, and now in His new glorified body He sits in light of the finished work of redemption as a High Priest in the courts of heaven. As High Priest, He represents us to God and represents God to us.[7]

Because of Christ, God no longer needs to remain a vague concept or notion. He can become living, personal, and accessible. In His humanity Jesus clearly made God approachable. He truly serves as the revelation of God's love to all mankind. He reveals the intentions of God towards each of us. It is because of Him that the Father bestows on us gifts from heaven. It is because of Jesus' life in us that we are made alive and anointed by His Spirit and empowered by His Word. We can know peace because we have finally found the place of reconciliation with God. We can know satisfaction because the spiritual life is being restored back into our being. We can know contentment because the real answers to life are found in Christ. We can end the identity crisis that plagues us because the life of Jesus will allow us to find our position, know our purpose, become an extension of the eternal, and come to a place of rest in our souls.

The greatest challenge of any relationship occurs when it has been broken in some way, is presently being broken, or appears that it will become broken because there is no substance to hold it together. So many relationships lie in ruin and need to be restored. However, to restore such bonds there must be reconciliation between the parties

---

6   John 14:6; 1 Corinthians 1:30; Colossians 3:1-3

7   John 1:1, 14; Philippians 2:5-8; Colossians 2:9, 1 Timothy 2:5; Hebrews 4:16; 7:24-8:1

involved. In most cases people do not know how to benefit others, let alone be an extension of that which would be honorable. To understand how reconciliation occurs, people need to understand why so many relationships become shipwrecked.

Most of the time relationships are broken because of the foundation on which they have been established. Foundation serves as the common ground on which a bond was initially established. The problem with most of the foundations relationships are built upon is that they lack real sustaining substance. They were founded on fleshly attractions and lust. Most of the time people enter such relationships based on fanciful notions of how such associations will best serve their purpose. In such situations the premise of such a relationship is selfishness.

Selfishness sees the relationship revolving around it to serve its purpose or whims without any real regard for the other party involved. It is conditional and feels that it has rights to expect, demand, or manipulate the other party to accept its standards and verdict about the ways things should be and must be. Since selfishness can only value what serves it, it is unable to value any real relationship that will not be molded to its way of thinking.

If the relationship is not valued, people will fail to put the necessary investment in it. Instead of possessing the necessary attitude to ensure the integrity of a relationship, they will sacrifice the relationship to justify or maintain their selfish ways. Instead of being willing to be reasoned with, they become unreasonable.

At this point where the relationship has become broken, there is no common ground to be found to bring about reconciliation. What is present is tyranny. Tyranny declares that there is only one ground in which a relationship will even be considered, and the ground is based on that which is dishonorable and wicked. In a sense the relationship has already been sacrificed on the altar, and all that is left is an appearance or image of what could have been and what might have been. The image or idea of a relationship may keep the other parties together, but eventually the ways of death will cause such relationships to crumble, leaving the parties involved disillusioned and angry.

Since the place we meet God is at redemption, the Bible declares that Jesus is the only foundation when it comes to our spiritual lives with

God.[8] As the foundation, Jesus ensures the integrity of a relationship with God. He reminds us that man was unable to bring about reconciliation in his own power. It was out of love that God went the extra mile to provide the means in which man would able to meet with His Creator. It is on the foundation of Jesus' character and work of redemption that a relationship is established and built up in an honorable way.

However, to establish our relationship with God, He must be able to reason with us about our sin.[9] It cost God His best and Jesus His all to enable us to have this relationship with Him. Out of love, God made the commitment to pay the necessary price. But, the key is will we put any real value on having a relationship with our Creator by accepting the payment made on our behalf, or will we lightly esteem or disregard it altogether? There cannot be reconciliation without the means to reason with the other party as to what it will mean to have a viable relationship with the one that has been offended by dishonorable attitudes and behavior.

Man has clearly been dishonorable towards God. He has been divisive towards His Law, derisive towards His righteousness, and disrespectful towards His ways. Man has clearly made his intention known to God. He does not desire an honorable relationship with Him. If God refuses to bow down to man's perverted way, he will deem it unnecessary to even regard God in a way that is worthy of His character and ways.

God has done all He can to meet with man. He has provided a common ground that man can meet Him upon. It is up to man to come to this place by faith in order to establish a right foundation that will ensure the integrity of an honorable and acceptable relationship with his Creator. Outside of the place of redemption there is no hope of reconciliation. There will be no place of reason in which man can draw near to God, and God can draw near to man.

The question is, have you come to the place of redemption to ensure a common ground has been established with your Creator? Have you been clearly established on the right foundation to ensure a viable relationship with God? Only you can properly answer these questions.

---

[8]   1 Corinthians 3:11

[9]   Isaiah 1:18

However, you need to make sure these questions are answered. Your spiritual well-being and destination depends on you coming to this place with God.

ENVIRONMENT

The place of Christ's redemption serves as the only real common ground with God. We know that Jesus serves as the sole foundation as to the relationship we must establish with God. As our foundation, Jesus will ensure the integrity of the relationship.

The other aspect of our relationship with God or people is the proper surroundings. In the right environment we will be able to nurture and ensure that the relationships in our lives are able to grow and develop into healthy and vibrant bonds that are beneficial to each of us. People are not meant to be islands unto themselves. They have been formed in such a way that they must have relationships to come to maturity. It is much like the seeds that are planted in the ground. They must be nurtured to ensure that they come to maturity and produce the proper fruit.

As we consider a relationship with God we have to come to terms with what will nurture such a relationship. We have already established that there first must be a common ground in which to establish a relationship. However, the other aspect of relationship is that there must be some knowledge with regard to the person we seek a relationship with as to what kind of environment would he or she be drawn or attracted to. For example, you would not meet a saint in a bar. You would not find people who are pure steeped in some form of perversion. You would not find a decent person in the midst of lawlessness.

Environment points to spirit or intent. This means environment clearly defines intent, purpose, and point of influence and reason. We must reason that if we desire a relationship with God, we must first of all draw near to Him, realizing that He will only meet us in an environment that is conducive to His Spirit and character. We know that the only environment that would be conducive to nurture a relationship with God is that of holiness.

We are told to draw near to God and He will draw near to us. Notice He will not meet us in our sin, transgression, or iniquity. We must turn away from such lawlessness and moral deviation, separate from all worldly influence, and flee such perverted, fleshly environments, and draw near to God in repentance, sincerity, and honesty. Otherwise, we will never meet God. He is unable to draw near to us for His holiness separates Him from us. If He drew near to us in a sinful, perverted state, His holiness would require judgment on His part and produce a cleansing fire that would purify or destroy that which was contrary to His righteousness. It is because of His longsuffering towards us that He will not draw near to us when we are in such a spiritual state of disarray and defilement.[10] When in such a state, there is no common ground in which He can meet us, and no means in which He could truly interact with us.

It is because of His desire to interact with us that God provided the common ground of redemption. Christ serves as the essence of wisdom, righteousness, sanctification, and redemption for those who by faith are hid in His death, burial, and resurrection.[11] When God sees believers, He sees the purity of His Son's wisdom, His disposition of righteousness, His state of holiness, and the complete work of redemption. It is from this premise that He can draw near to us in His holiness, knowing that He is able to meet with us.

However, it is not enough for God to draw near to us and us to draw near to Him. There must be a means that enables God to interact with each of us. God is Spirit and truth. This tells us that God can only interact with us on a spiritual level. The earthly man cannot relate to that which is not physical, the natural man cannot interact with that which is spiritual, and the fleshly aspect of man has no agreement with the spiritual aspect of God. To try to bring together the fleshly and the spiritual amounts to the same thing as trying to successfully mix water and oil.

As believers we have been told that we have not received the spirit of the world, but the Spirit of God. The spirit of the world works within the sons of disobedience. Such a spirit is inspired and influenced by the world we live in. It is contrary to the Spirit of God who has been given to us as a gift upon our salvation experience. In fact, we must be born again with the Spirit of God and the pure water of the His Word. The gift of the

---

[10]   James 4:6-10; 2 Peter 3:9

[11]   1 Corinthians 1:30

Spirit was promised in the Old Testament and serves as the seal of the New Testament or place of covenant upon our lives.[12]

In our natural state of sin and death we have no means in which to connect, understand, relate, or interact with God. There is no way that the deep things of God could enter into our dead, lifeless souls without the breath of the Spirit bringing forth life and revealing it to our hearts. The Holy Spirit is the One who reveals and searches all things out in relationship to God. He is the One who connects us to the throne, heart, mind, and will of God. He is the only way in which we can spiritually interact with our unseen, eternal God.[13]

Man in his natural state can only know and interact with the natural environment that has been established by the world he lives in.[14] As you follow the trend of our society, it must be noted that many neighbors are separated by walls and fences, families have been separated by entertainment whether it be that of television or games. These separate realities allow individuals to hide in their own worlds of fantasy, delusion, and destruction. In such realities man can erect walls of silence and indifference where he can hide in his personal perverted conclusion without any interaction.

Today, much of our society is nothing more than a plastic environment where man relates to unrealistic images or words on a screen, small or big, rather than face-to-face. Instead of even being challenged by some semblance of the natural world that exists around each of us, much of the present environment is so far removed that many people do not have to interact in a personal, human way with those around them. The emotional detachment that is occurring in the arena of homes and societies is not only unnatural, but it is dangerous and deadly.

The truth is so many in the present generation no longer know how to interact in a natural or personal way. The common ground for many in our society is established by lifeless technology. Blackberries, cell phones, or computers are the main means of communication. In such an environment people are far removed from personally interacting

---

[12]   Ezekiel 36:26-27; John 3:3, 5; 1 Corinthians 2:12-14; Ephesians 1:13-14; 2:2; 1 Peter 1:22-23

[13]   1 Corinthians 2:9-10

[14]   1 Corinthians 2:11-14

with others. They can create a reality among themselves that has no real substance. They can operate behind an image that has no real responsibility. Such an environment creates an unfeeling generation that can be left unchallenged in their selfish, small, insipid, morbid, and immature worlds. Such individuals will be left unprepared to meet the realities of life. Many are vulnerable to be taken prey by predators that have no conscience as to the lives they destroy or use up. Once they have used up such lives they cast their prey aside as rubbish. Because of the lack of relationship, we are creating a frightening society that is not prepared to address, face, or recognize the insane world that is beginning to intrude into every aspect of life.

Sadly, the generation that is emerging is a generation that is selfish, self-centered, and unrealistic. They have no consensus of responsibility, moral character, and sacrifice. They have been clearly taken captive by the spirit of the world, and are ready to revolt against that which will not cater to their indoctrination, moral irresponsibility, and godless attitudes. Since they have no real connection to those around them, they will have no qualms in sacrificing anyone who does not serve their purpose. In reality many in this generation for the most part do not care about the plight of others. In their selfishness and arrogance they do not possess any real concern or compassion for others because there is no real personal connection since they have never learned to interact with others. They have no real relationship that has meaning or purpose; therefore, they have no sense of responsibility. They are incompetent to have healthy relationships that do not bow down to the one-sided, tyrannical, and unrealistic concepts of their particular realities.

Since many people do not know how to interact with those around them, they have no idea or concept as to how to interact with God. Sadly, the professing Church has fed this plastic environment by providing entertainment that is also removed from the seriousness and sobriety of the reality of God. In some ways the visible Church that is greatly influenced by images on TV and messages that inundate radio waves has become another club with its creeds and civic duties that often serve as a center for socializing rather than doing business with God. Such an environment is about providing a religion that will make man feel good about self and God, while avoiding the cutting edge of the sword of truth that will often tear down, rip apart, and expose the harsh realities of man's spiritual plight and condition in light of a holy God.

God is real and cannot meet us in a plastic environment. He will not adjust His character to have some indifferent type of interaction with man. He will not give way to popular pressure and demand so that man can maintain his personal world. Granted, God will meet each of us in our need, but never in our sin. He will meet us in our brokenness, but never at the point of our arrogance. He will meet us at the point of our desperation, but never in our self-sufficiency. He will meet us in Spirit, but never in our comfort zone. He will meet us in truth, but never in our plastic environments of make-believe fantasy, self-serving entertainment, and indifferent blackberries.

The reality is that we need God, He does not need us. God has drawn as near to us as He can in Christ, but now it is up to us to draw near to Him in our need, out of brokenness, in humility and repentance. The challenge for most people rests in the fact that they can become delusional in regard to their spiritual condition. This delusion often finds its source in their pride. Because of pride most people are unwilling to see their need for God. They deceive themselves about their spiritual condition. Since God resists all pride, the Spirit of God is absent.[15] There is no conviction or awareness of the broad path such individuals are on, or the abyss of spiritual destruction and ruin that they are blindly walking towards.

This brings us to another aspect in regard to relationships. Much of our relationship with others is influenced or determined by the position they are to hold in regard to our lives. For example, you would not have the same type of relationship with your spouse as you would your children.

The Bible speaks of God becoming our all in all.[16] When it comes to having a relationship, the position He would take in our lives would initially be based on our need. If we need to be delivered, we would approach Him as our Savior. If we need to be set free from the entanglements of slavery, we would approach Him as our Redeemer. The reality of it is that God can be approached as an honorable Master, a caring and fair Lord, a loving Father, and a committed husband.

---

[15]   James 4:6

[16]   1 Corinthians 15:28

However, there must be a point where our need takes a black seat as we grow in a relationship with our God. Our need should begin to give way more and more to the sincere desire of pleasing our God because of love that is being developed in a growing vibrant relationship with Him. From this premise, our main desire would be to know Him in order to please Him. This means we must commune with Him. At this point He becomes our bread that sustains, the giver of water who refreshes, and the lover of our souls who holds us close to His heart, as well as become our place of satisfaction and rest.

Our desire to know Him must graduate to our pursuit to possess all we can of His life to ensure that His Spirit possesses us. We need to be consumed by the reality of God. It is a matter of ensuring that He is in all that we do so that in all matters He ultimately becomes our starting point. He will become our place in maintaining what is right in regard to our relationship with Him to ensure that we will end up possessing the fullness of His Spirit and the abundant life of His Son.

Even though the Christian life is lived out in the physical realm, it is clearly established in the spiritual. The "spiritual" points to the obscurity of secret chambers, the shadows of that which is often hidden from the physical eye, and the veil of separation that has been created by His holiness. However, the Spirit is able to bring us into the chambers of partaking of His life, under the shadows of His abiding presence, and through the veil of sanctification to truly commune with Him.

Relationships are meant to be personal. Healthy relationships have the potential to grow, while the majority of worldly, self-serving relationships will become stagnant from neglect, selfishness, and abuse. Such relationships will wither away as drudgery replaces the inspiration, desire, and commitment to develop, nurture, grow, and reach great heights of discovering the extent in which a relationship can be brought forth.

The inability to discover such heights in a relationship would especially be true in the case of a relationship with God. He is eternal. The heights that can be reached in a relationship with Him would far exceed our understanding of the heavenly. The depths it can take on will take us into places that few have ever reached. The width that we will travel will embrace impassable gulfs of the spiritual, the unbearable barren places of the soul, the deep ravines of the self-life, and the walled up gardens of the heart. It is only as we give way to being consumed by all that God is that we will find God in all we become, think, and do.

What kind of relationship do you have with God? To answer such a question, you will have to consider the inward environment that you have prepared in relationship to your life before, with, and in Him. Make sure you are not accepting what is familiar, while avoiding discovering what is excellent, incredible, and heavenly.

POINT OF REALITY

The greatest challenge for most Christians is to not accept what is substandard or nominal when it comes to their relationship with God. Everything associated or attached to a relationship with God points to that which is not only excellent but is eternal, satisfying, and worthy of all consideration.

This brings us to another challenge or problem that can easily beset God's people, and it has to do with them coming to terms with what must be truly regarded as being important to them. So many people hold to that which is insignificant while allowing what is important to slip by them. For example, we see that people are so busy supporting their lifestyles that they have failed to support their relationships. Relationships involve personal investment, and should be a priority. It is relationships that will add substance and purpose to our otherwise meaningless life and vain activities.

This becomes more of a reality as you consider the quality of relationships. For years I have heard how men have been busy working to provide for their families, when in reality many men are busy working towards ensuring a certain lifestyle that serves their selfish desires. It is easy to hide personal selfishness behind what appears to be noble causes, but the reality is that spouses and children need their partners and parents' personal nurturing, instead of inanimate things to fill their empty lives. When you consider the discontent in many families it is often due to the sense of loneliness that comes from disconnection to those around them and feelings of not belonging. Such individuals lack purpose, which is equated to an empty life. Granted, they may have things, but there is no life in any of them. They may have various activities, but there is no lasting substance that will add to the quality of their existence.

When we consider what relationships bring to our life, we must remember that people are not just physical creatures, they also possess a spirit and soul. Spirit becomes a connection to that which is spiritual, while soul connects people to that which is unseen and emotional. The spirit discerns, while the soul senses and interprets its environment. The spirit will determine what a person will come into agreement with, while the soul will determine how one will interact with his or her environment. Much of what determines the environment that is influencing or dictating the impact that our reality is presently rendering upon us comes down to what is happening in our relationships, especially our relationship with God.

We already know that only God's Spirit can connect us to Him in a relationship. But, we must also be able to relate and respond to God on an emotional level. It is in the soul area we gain an intimate knowledge of God. We must be able to recognize Him in our environment, be able to discern and affectionately respond to His overtures to commune with Him, smell the essence of His character, be cognizant of His presence in our midst, and taste His sweetness in fellowship. In essence, we must be able to sense God. The problem with relating to God in an emotional arena is that we must understand the premise in which we must always relate and interact with God. There is only one premise from which God will interact with us, and that is truth.

John 4:24 tells us that God is Spirit and truth. Since He is spirit He can only relate to us on a spiritual level, and since He is truth He can only interact with us when truth is present. We are told that the Spirit of God is the One who leads us into all truth about a matter.[17] You may know the truth about something, but when it comes to God, you must be able to discern, recognize, and properly respond to the truth if there is going to be any relationship or fellowship with Him.

Hence enters another challenge for most people. Truth proves to be contrary to the natural man's way of thinking and doing. It can be down-right insulting to pride, repulsive to the flesh, and maddening to the world. It is not something that is easy to embrace, partake of, swallow,

---

[17]   John 16:13

and apply. Even though it may display wisdom to the intellect, it will cause the carnal mind to harshly judge it because it has no tolerance towards that which is not in agreement with its spirit or intent. Even though it proves to be righteous and honorable, man's pride will resist it because it will not smooth out its decisive sharp ways of exposing something down to its real motives and intents. Even though it is liberating to the soul, it will not adjust to what is considered nominal or acceptable by the fleshly ways of the soul, causing a person to become uncomfortable, unreceptive, and angry towards it. Truth will constantly challenge any deceptive reality that may be in operation. It will expose any real compromise when it has been laced with lies, false presentations, or innuendos, as well as what has been shrouded by that which would pervert the intent or purpose of it.

Sadly, the environment of America has allowed many to believe that they can control or determine truth. The Bible is clear that truth is summarized in one person and not religious beliefs, philosophies, or preferences. Jesus stated that He was and is the essence of all truth when it comes to the ways of the heavenly, the accuracy about God's character, the spiritual plight of man, and the life that has been ordained by the Father. Therefore, if wisdom does not find its source in Jesus' example and teachings, it will be void of any authority. If the ways in which we are walking are not in line with His righteousness, they will prove to be the ways of sin and death. If truth concerning Jesus' Person and work is not serving as the test as to what is true, real, and acceptable in regard to reality, people's lives will never be sanctified and set apart by the Spirit. If these people's lives are not marked by the truth of redemption, they can be assured that they do not belong to Him and that they remain condemned, already judged by His work on the cross.[18]

One of my favorite ways of challenging people's reality is to remind them that their reality may not be truth, but truth is always reality. I never tell people that their particular take on something is wrong, but I do challenge them to consider whether their reasoning about a matter is marked by the excellent ways and eternal perspective of God. People will never find agreement based on compromising their different perspectives in order to somehow fit them together; rather, they can only come into

---

[18]   John 14:6; 16:7-13; 1 Corinthians 1:30

agreement when they embrace the truth of that which is absolute, higher, worthy, and eternal.

When I have counseled with married couples, I encourage them to quit insisting on their particular realities about something, and together embrace God's truth about it. Such agreement would defuse all conflict and bring unity and harmony in the midst of contention. Harmony of this nature would allow for the warring parties to come together and actually reason a matter out according to the excellent ways of truth that would be acceptable to everyone who has been involved in the conflict. This would be true for all disagreements among God's people. Most of the time people are not disagreeing about what is right in regard to a matter that is proving to be contentious, rather they are disagreeing about how to arrive at or approach it to get the desired results. Simply put, people are demanding their own way instead of insisting on God's righteous way.

People will not reason with what they perceive to be inferior or unacceptable. They will not concede to a way that appears to be substandard in quality. After all, in their minds the end results will prove to be inferior and substandard. For this reason people will maintain that their approach or way is clean, right, and obvious to any sane person who has the intelligence to see it. However, to every person his or her way of doing and thinking seems clean and right to his or her way of thinking.[19]

Scripture is clear that God's thoughts and ways are higher than our thoughts and ways.[20] Until we step outside of our earthbound ways from under the influence of the world, and rise up to embrace the excellent ways of God, we will find ourselves consumed by petty, unprofitable disagreements that eventually turn into battles of the wills. Such battles end in division and ruin. Instead of soaring according to a heavenly perspective that proves liberating and realistic, we will be constantly brought low by perspectives that create ongoing cycles or ruts of despair and hopelessness in our relationships with others. Even though we cleverly try to seduce or manipulate people to see it our way, the end result will always prove to be unfruitful.

---

[19] Proverbs 14:12; 16:2

[20] Isaiah 55:8-9

We need to honestly realize that our ways fall short of God's excellent ways, and our thoughts or conclusions to a matter lacks a heavenly perspective. I often wonder what it will take for God's people to finally concede that when God states a matter in His Word, it is truth, absolute, unchangeable, and always applicable. As the Apostle Paul made clear, we can do nothing against the truth, only for it; therefore, we each need to come into agreement that in light of truth a matter is "amen" or "so be it for it is so."[21] There should be no debate, adjustment, or justification as to why we would insist that any personal thoughts or conclusions on our part possesses the wisdom of unadulterated truth, nor do our ways exemplify that of a righteousness that would prove acceptable to God.

As Christians we must also concede that unless we are operating from the premise of truth we cannot properly sense, interpret, or interact with our environment. Most people cannot stand their individual realities. For this reason people operate from points of fantasy, manipulation, intimidation, and control to ensure their desired reality. In doing so these individuals will ignore, reject, mock, and try to adjust their environments to fit their idea of reality. However, each reality represents a false way that has no basis or premise of truth. In such cases, man is not only failing to operate from the premise of truth, but he is attempting to be God by trying to change, create, or manipulate what is true to fit his particular view of a matter.

It is interesting to note that in the case where man is trying to interpret what is going on according to his own perception of truth or reality, that it is strictly from a soulish or carnal perspective. This means the soul is determining reality from the premise of how it wills something should be, judges how something must be according to its personal standards, or adjusts something according to how it makes it feel about a matter. Much of the calculation arrived at was a matter of intellectual logic that was influenced by worldly understanding and fleshly preferences.

In such cases, there is no connection to spirit. In such a state man is not open to relate to God, and God is unable to interact with man. In such incidents reality is coming into subjection to carnal, undisciplined senses of the soul; rather than the senses of the soul coming into submission of the Holy Spirit to be tempered so that it can rightly discern

---

[21]   2 Corinthians 13:8

and interact with its environment. When the senses are judging the truth rather than discerning the spirit, people become judgmental bigots about their particular way of doing something. They become pigheaded, bullheaded, mule-headed, or hardheaded. They are not about to move or be moved in their conclusions. The Bible refers to such a condition as being "stiff-necked."

The result of man trying to determine or control his own reality serves as the framework in which he will consider his environment. Needless to say, man will consider everything through the tinted glasses he has constructed, perverting what he does see or understand. Because man's perception has no basis of truth, God has no other choice but to leave him to taste the bitter defeat and consequences of his own ignorant and wicked devices. Granted, God's Spirit will try to convict or warn him as to his deluded state, but if man is unwilling to heed the waves of truth that often challenge the headways of the bow of his life, he will become more indifferent against the truth. Like Pharaoh of old, the ways of deception that find their basis in unbelief will harden his heart and cause his resolve to become obstinate against receiving the truth as being so.

I have often warned people that if they have concluded that they cannot be deceived they already are. It is so easy for man to become swayed or deceived because of his affront against the truth of the unpleasant or uncontrollable reality that often confronts his fragile sense of balance and worth.

It is also easy for us in our fallen state to establish our idea of truth or reality. All we have to do is change the intent of a word or a matter, and we can change the spirit and frame of reference in which we perceive something. For example, when we try to silence the truth we often attempt to demote or outlaw it by calling it unloving, obsolete, wicked, and unjust, when we adjust truth it becomes propaganda, when we pervert the truth it becomes indoctrination, when we change the truth it becomes a concrete viewpoint, and when we deny the truth it becomes a point of debate. However, since we can do nothing against the truth we must never forget that in the end the truth we may hold lightly, change according to selfish agendas, or reject to maintain personal reality, will ultimately judge us. It will remain standing when all else collapses in utter ruin.

Even though people perceive that they can comfortably live with their preferred reality, they remain unprepared to face the reality around them.

They become enslaved to their perception as they try to manipulate their environment and control those in their world to submit to their particular view. They become tormented as they watch their chaotic worlds enclose around them, and they become miserable as they realize life is slipping by them without any resolution about the life that is eluding them.

Jesus stated that if we know the ways of truth, the righteousness it maintains, and the life it possesses, we will be set free by it. Granted, it is unpleasant to every aspect of the carnal man, but it possesses the means to set us free from all selfish and worldly entanglements and gives us the means to honestly face the reality around us. But, for it to have the right affect on our souls we must chose to love it regardless of how unpleasant or negative it might prove to be to our self-life and worldly philosophies. It must become our preferred reality as a means to meet and interact with God on a spiritual level. This truth also provides the means in which we are prepared to go forward in our life in Christ. Truth will give us the space to discover what it means to soar in the liberty of the Spirit, as we discover and experience such life.

If we do not love the truth, we will go the way of lies. We know that Satan is the father of lies, and that these lies rob people of their ability to realistically interact with their environment, kill what is true, and destroy what is liberating. We also know that Satan's lies become a tidal wave that will take those captive, who refuse to love the truth, on a ride to destruction and damnation.[22] The ride may initially seem exciting, but eventually it will crash against the shores of reality with such intensity that it will result in complete spiritual ruin.

Clearly, in our fragile spiritual condition, we can easily appear quite noble and receptive of truth, but if we fail to choose to love it and prefer it, we will eventually resent, abuse, or reject it as our personal reality. If truth fails to be our reality, we will never be able to interact with God. He will never relate or meet us at the point of lies, reason with us when our souls are undisciplined by selfish, worldly and demonic agendas, or interact with us when our spirits prove to be contrary. He can only meet us in Spirit and interact with us at the point of truth. The question is, what is your attitude towards the truth?

---

[22]   John 8:44; 10:10; 2 Thessalonians 2:10-12

THE PLACE OF SATISFACTION

Most people spend a lifetime searching for that which is satisfying and fulfilling. Sadly, for many of them their search ends in vanity. What is man searching for? The problem rests with the fact that he really does not know what he is searching for. The flesh entices him to feed it to find satisfaction. To a point it is true that there is some satisfaction once the flesh is fed, but it is temporary. It simply leaves a greater vacuum where something else will come in like a flood such as emptiness, loneliness, guilt, and despair.

The world also promises satisfaction, but each pursuit leads to a certain pinnacle or measure of what is considered exciting, rewarding, or successful. However, each pinnacle with its up side is also shaped by the same angle of decline on the other side. Each decline causes a person to slide down into vanity and hopelessness. When all is said and done, there doesn't appear to be any real permanent place of satisfaction when it comes to the flesh or the world.

Since satisfaction eludes people, they must constantly struggle with the real matters and questions of life. Is this all life has to offer? If so, it appears as if life is nothing more than a bad joke. From such angles of disparity the matters of life can become unbearable, as it proves bitter to the soul and empty to the spirit.

It has taken me some time to discover what is satisfying to my inner being. It is not material possessions, for they can prove empty. It is not having the right appearance for it is nothing more than an image that proves vain and useless. It is not having an adoring public that will recognize you because when the new wears off, such notoriety can become old quickly as it proves to be temporary, taxing, foolish, and empty.

What I have discovered that brings the most satisfaction to my soul has been good, vibrant relationships. The one relationship that is able to satisfy my spirit is my relationship with God and the ones that prove to be satisfying to my soul are with those who have the same love and intensity towards God. Otherwise relationships often leave each of us feeling dissatisfied and empty. Granted, we may see relationships as a means to avoid loneliness, but the reality is some of the loneliest people are those who are married or are busily caught up in the different relationships around them.

The one thing I have discovered about our earthly and worldly relationships is that if God is missing from the center of such associations, there will be no real source of lasting satisfaction. God is the one who brings meaning to our lives, substance to our relationships, and purpose to our walk.

As I meditated on my journey to discover God, I remember how overwhelmed I was when my spirit was able to grasp the simple reality that the Creator of the great universe wanted a relationship with me. Realizing that I was a simple speck at best in light of even the world I lived in, I was consumed by the awe that God wanted to not only benefit my life, but I also saw a means in which I could benefit Him. After all, a viable relationship is beneficial for the parties involved.

At the beginning of my spiritual journey, my understanding of relationship was still operating in a limited plane of serving God to discover His fullness in the next world. However, God' wants a vibrant relationship with me here and now. But, what would it mean to have such a relationship? What would such a relationship look like and what would it mean to maintain it? Personally, I was aware that as His people we do not determine the standards or quality of such matters.

Since everything is perverted when it comes to our perception, as believers we cannot assume we understand what something such as a relationship will look like. Judging from our perception of what something should look like is based on how it will personally affect our world, attitude, and feelings. From the fleshly and worldly perspective, such a relationship will make us feel good about ourselves, right in our particular worlds, and deserving of having life on our terms. It will feel comfortable, prove convenient, and will flow with what seems natural and acceptable to us. As we have already discussed such reality speaks of selfishness, immaturity, and unrealistic notions.

As believers we cannot presume our understanding of a matter is correct. We must understand that if it has not been challenged by a heavenly perspective along with the realities of others, sharpened by the contrary winds of conflict and adversity, and confirmed by the approval and presence of God, we must honestly conclude that we still only know according to a limited, perverted plane.

This brings us back to what kind of relationship will actually benefit and please our Creator. We must consider what God is after in a relationship with us that will prove satisfying to both of us. When God invited Moses to meet with Him at the mercy seat between the cherubim on the Ark of the Covenant, it was for the sole purpose of communing with Him.[23]

What type of communion would be beneficial to God? After all, there are two types of communion. The first entails partaking of the things of God, while the second one has to do with coming into agreement with God for the purpose of fellowshipping with Him. We need to first learn to partake before we can come into agreement or fellowship. Clearly, God desires agreement with us, but due to our fallen condition, we are out of sorts with Him. There must be a point at which we are able to partake of that which would identify us to God before we could actually fellowship with Him. The problem is that man wants God to partake of that which is contrary to His very character in order to fellowship with him.

God will not cease being who He is; therefore, we must be reasoned with at the place where there is common ground in order for us to come into agreement with Him. Once we come into agreement with our Creator, we can freely partake of the things of God. Like the elders of Israel we can commune before Him in agreement. It is for this reason we are not to forsake the assembling of ourselves together. We must come together to reason about the matters of God, and partake together in agreement as to how we must live and conduct the affairs of our lives as Jesus' living Body, His Church. Such understanding will enable us to become walking, living epistles and witnesses to others.[24]

Sadly, many religious people have used the exhortation of not forsaking the assembly together in an improper way. They have used it as a hammer to cause people to think it is about going to some building where they are conditioned or sedated into a spiritual sleep or seduced into some emotional, soulish realm that creates a state of utopia or ecstasy that allows the person to operate on a religious, emotional high. It is much like a drug fix, but in the end people come crashing down as reality once again sets in. However, it causes them to have to go back to "church" to get their religious fix for another week. In such environments there is no communion because the Spirit of God is missing.

---

[23]   Exodus 25:22

[24]   Exodus 24:9-12; Hebrews 10:24-25

In order for individuals to partake of the things of God, His Spirit must be present to bring agreement. This was obvious in the case of the elders of Israel when they supped in the presence of God.[25] Clearly, when the Spirit was and is present everyone is on the same page, partaking of the same eternal food from heaven to ensure the integrity of their calling or vision that God is trying to bring forth for His glory through them as a Body, as well as on an individual level. The truth is that when God is glorified, His Body will be edified. Edification speaks of contentment and satisfaction.

Agreement among the many members of the Body of Christ is beneficial for the soul, but it is agreement with God that will prove beneficial to our spirits. Moses went up to the mountain into the midst of God without the elders to personally partake of the matters of God. When it comes to communing with God, it is an individual matter. We cannot take everyone with us into the midst of God's holiness. For the High Priest, he alone went into the Most Holy Place once a year to come face-to-face with the Shekinah glory of God. Sadly, the priest's entrance into the Holy of Holies had nothing to do with communion, but making atonement for the children of Israel.[26] Clearly, Scriptural examples show us that we must individually find our way to the place of communion or agreement with Him.

It is easy to speak of communion when we consider that we can sit together in the presence of God with others, but the idea of traveling into the midst of God to seek Him out to individually commune with Him can prove to be intimidating for those who have never personally tread into such unknown territory. How does one find God in the midst of the darkness created by His holiness, a darkness that hides Him from the naked eyes of pagan, idolatrous man while shrouding Him in mystery and uncertainty to those who desire to know Him? Is it no wonder that many are content to consider God from a distance? Is it surprising that people's natural tendency is to accept a religious experience since the soul feels satisfied by such an encounter without going any further in one's spiritual walk?

Once again we are reminded that the problem with accepting such religious encounters is that one cannot have a relationship with God from

---

[25] Exodus 24:9-12

[26] Leviticus 16

a distance. It must also be pointed out that communion before Him is not the same as communion with Him. Jesus' invitation was that He stood at the door and knocked. His heart cry and desire is to have the door of the heart opened to Him so He can come and fellowship or personally commune with us.[27]

The difference between communion before God and communion with Him has to do with intimacy. Intimacy is a foreign concept for many. Most people perceive it from the premise of a physical, sexual nature. However, real intimacy can only truly happen when the spirit comes into agreement with the same spirit, the soul finds agreement upon that which is worthy and honorable, and the body comes into complete submission or surrender to partake of such agreement in consecration or total abandonment. Granted, the body may come into some type of surrender, but if the soul is not coming into agreement in light of that which is worthy, and there is no agreement in the spirit, real, satisfying intimacy will be missing or lacking.

Intimacy is what is lacking in many marriages. As a result, marriages lack substance and fall short of being satisfying. There are many that will submit their bodies in hopes of experiencing some type of intimacy with another, but the satisfaction will prove to be temporary and empty. There are couples that have found some agreement on an emotional level where they agree as to the purpose and goal of their relationship, bringing some satisfaction to their soul. However, they find themselves enslaved to the prospect of always having to stir up the soul in order to maintain a semblance of intimacy that lacks the mark of excellence. Excellence that comes out of intimacy in a relationship is what takes the relationship out of the soulish, fleshly realm and makes it exceptional and worthy of consecrating and abandoning all to discover the heights and potential in which such a bond can be established.

The truth is, most relationships hit the ceiling of selfishness or drudgery that often comes with familiarity with someone where he or she is taken for granted. This ceiling can also be experienced when discontentment or disillusionment takes center stage. These fruits come when dissatisfaction, conflict, and adversity begin to envelope a relationship. Such ceilings in relationships end with emptiness. It is

---

[27]   Revelation 3:20

from the premise of emptiness that people can begin to perceive that there is more to discover, and that present relationships are stopping them from discovering the potential of what can be. In some cases such relationships are actually sucking the very life and resolve out of them.

No relationship can reach its potential unless there is intimacy. But, it takes the unseen aspect of spiritual agreement to begin to reach beyond the familiarity that often occurs at the soul level to discover the potential or heights of a relationship. There cannot be true spiritual agreement unless the Spirit of God is present to bring about a common ground between the spirits of the parties involved.

This brings us to the type of relationship with God that will prove satisfying to us and beneficial to Him. When He is calling us into communion with Him, He is calling us to a place of real intimacy, where we enjoy Him, and He enjoys us. Such intimacy was alluded to by the Apostle Paul when he revealed that marriage was a shadow or type of relationship Jesus would establish with the Church.[28]

When we think of communing with God, we have to conclude that being in the position such as a servant would not afford such communion. A servant must be faithful to the master in terms of loyalty and obedience, but there does not have to be intimacy to be a good servant. Granted, a servant must understand the position of servitude to carry out the wishes or will of the owner, but it puts such a person at a subservient level rather than an equal level. To have intimacy, one would have to possess an equal playing ground to have such closeness.

Being a child of God does not result in such intimacy. Granted, a parent may enjoy the purity of a child, but such a position is not conducive for one who is in a parent position to share that which requires a level of maturity and equality.

This brings us to the matter of what constitutes real intimacy? We are given an insight into this matter by the Apostle Paul in 1 Corinthians 2:9-10, "But as it is written, Eye hath not seen, nor ear heard, neither have entered into the heart of man, the things which God hath prepared for them that love him. But God hath revealed them unto us by his Spirit; for the Spirit searcheth all things, yea, the deep things of God."

---

[28]   Ephesians 5:22-32

Intimacy involves being able to entrust a person with the deep things that concern your inner person. You must know that those with whom you share your inner most being and thoughts will not abuse them, use them against you, or pervert them for personal gain, agendas, or manipulation.

In John 2:54, we are told that Jesus did not commit himself unto those around Him because he knew all men. We know that the disciples started out with Him as His followers. Eventually they graduated to the status of being servants that could be entrusted with carrying out certain duties as co-laborers in the great harvest field of humanity. However, there came a point when Jesus stated they could have even a more intimate relationship with Him. It would be a relationship in which He would make known to them the deep things He actually shared with the Father. That relationship entailed a friendship.[29]

Can you imagine being a close, trustworthy friend of God? It was said of the Lord that He talked face-to-face with Moses as a friend. We know because of His faith that Abraham was called a friend of God.[30]

I have had different relationships, but there is nothing as valuable as a trustworthy friend. True friends will allow you to be yourself. You can trust them with the matters of the heart for they will not betray you. You can entrust them with your deepest thoughts because they will not mock you. You can share your dreams and aspirations and they will not chide you. Such friends will encourage you to become all you can be, and to explore every possibility to ensure you do not accept less. They will also challenge you to climb the necessary heights to discover what you can achieve. Due to the equal standing that is present in healthy friendships, real friends do not put limitations, demands, or standards on you to meet some personal need, unrealistic demands, or bow down to their personal realities. Friendship is an equal playing ground for both parties involved to meet upon and establish a viable relationship without pretense and formalities.

What type of friendship does God desire with us? Jesus actually gives us insight into the answer to the question. First He implies that real friendship is sacrificial because it is compelled or inspired by godly love that is pure. He stated in John 15:13, "Greater love hath no man

---

[29]   John 15:12-15
[30]   Exodus 33:11; James 2:23

than this, that a man lay down his life for his friends." It is interesting to note that in John 13:35 Jesus told His disciples that all men would know that they were His disciples if they love one another. In John 15:13 He is distinguishing the love that will identify His followers from the type of love that will establish those who would be identified as His friends.

Jesus clearly laid down His life for us, but are we willing to lay our life down for Him in the same manner? Do we value our relationship with Him enough that we are so compelled to abandon all to have a more intimate relationship with Him that has no religious pretense attached to it? In such an intimate bond, unadulterated, and honorable conduct would mark all activities that were or are being done in relationship to the other party? We can easily speak of great love, but unless it is sacrificial, godly, and honorable it will never point to that which will make it an excellent ground in which an intimate friendship can truly be established with God.

God deserves the best from us. This is equally true when it comes to being a friend of God. Abraham was willing to offer his own son on the altar to prove his faith and confidence in God. Moses did not want to accept his present relationship with God, he wanted more. He wanted to see His glory. Every saint that ever desired a greater relationship with God was forever coming into deep places with God so he or she could obtain greater heights of intimacy in his or her relationship with Him.

There was an incident where a person was praying over me. The Lord gave her a word of knowledge about my relationship with Him. The gist of what she said was that God was aware of my desire to be known as His "faithful servant," but He wanted to call me "friend." I remember how overwhelmed I became at such a thought. I was no Abraham in my faith and far from being a Moses in my spiritual feats, yet God desired to call me His friend. This was a humbling reality. I was willing to accept being a servant, but God wanted so much more for our relationship. It was up to me to move into the relationship of being a friend to God. Would I accept the challenge of raising the bar of my present relationship and commitment to God to a more excellent level? Did I possess a sacrificial love for Him that would not allow me to settle for anything that would dishonor my relationship with Him and my life in Him?

It was from the premise of being a friend of God that I realized the importance of intimacy in a viable friendship. In such a friendship it is a matter of choosing to not only draw near to God, but become close to God. The closeness was not something I simply wished or talked about, I had to make it happen. I had to show myself friendly to God as I ensured an environment that would allow me to stand before God and allow God to freely reveal Himself to me.[31] It had to be an environment that showed regard for Him. After all, He already made His overtures towards me through Christ, now I had to accept His overtures by ensuring an environment that not only recognized who He was but would properly honor Him.

It is clear that we determine the type of relationship we have with God by what we pursue. We establish the quality of relationship we have with God based on what we value, and we set the tone of our relationship with God by the environment we create. Our relationship with God will, in turn, determine who we become and who we ultimately allow ourselves to become in light of our potential in His kingdom.

As we come to the end of this presentation, each of us must examine our relationship with God. We must allow it to reveal our heart and intentions towards Him. No viable relationship is one sided. It takes both parties to have similar commitment and intention towards one another to ensure that a relationship has what it takes to stand, withstand, and endure through the various challenges that affront it. God has proven His level of commitment towards each of us, but have you or I established the same level of commitment towards Him? The only way to honestly answer such a question is to examine our present relationship with Him. What would your relationship with God say about you? What would it say about me? Our fruits would clearly reveal the type of relationship we have with our Lord.

---

[31]   Proverbs 18:24

3

THE
INVITATION

INTRODUCTION

I am sure that through the years you have received some type of invitation to an important event. Perhaps someone was getting married, having a baby, graduating, or being recognized for some accomplishment. In studying invitations we would all have to agree that when you receive one, it is meant to attract your attention. It is as though the invitation beckons, urges, or demands that you open it to see what event is about to take place that will greatly affect or impact someone's life.

As I have studied the Word of God, I have been aware that God has sent forth invitations. We can read about these different invitations in different places of Scripture including the parables. If I were to ask you what God was inviting you to, if you are like me, you would most likely have asked me in what context was the Lord giving the invitation. After all, an invitation is not simply marking and going to an event, but preparing for it as well. Perhaps the event requires you to dress a certain way, bring a gift, or be prepared in some way to join in the celebration.

When I have studied the invitations put forth in the Bible, they are quite simple. In fact, there is only one that requires you to be prepared and ready to participate in the event. Otherwise, it appears as if God's invitations are pretty straight forward. The main requirement is that you accept them in good faith.

Although I am going to consider the different invitations in Scripture, I will mainly focus on one invitation. It is found in John 7:37. However, this invitation must be cross referenced with another invitation found in John 4:10-14.

My goal is to show you how God's invitation has gone out to each of us in various ways. Like any invitation we can ignore, disregard, discard, or accept it. We may even consider it, but prioritize it according to other events that are self-serving, but in light of eternity the invitation may hold no real importance. However, our response to His invitations will reveal what is really important to us.

The question is, as believers, are we ready to face the harsh challenges and reality as to how we regard the matters of God and life?

DIFFERENT INVITATIONS

Have you ever studied how God and His servants invited His people? It is also important to consider what He invites them to. In my desire to understand how God interacts with His people, I have noted that He is very clear in His invitation. Granted, it is not in some formal envelope or greeting that would cause it to stand out. However, you do not have to guess if He is inviting you, nor do you need to figure out some means of manipulating Him to invite you. In fact, His invitation has gone out to all of us. The first word He uses to signal that an invitation of some type is following, is the word, "come."

"Come" is an interesting word. It is a word that requires action on a person's part. It points to bringing something. Whether you bring yourself, as well as others, or a gift, you are still essentially coming in response to an invitation.

In a sense the word, "come" is a call. God's call goes forth. It is much like a command. If it comes from God, we must approach His bidding with the intent of adhering to His call, and responding accordingly. We must move towards the desired point or results.

The word "come" implies that someone is granting some type of permission to participate in a matter of the utmost importance. The only response required is to follow the rules or guidelines set forth in the invitation. After all, it will have the event, day, and time it is to occur. To not comply with the information given, means that a person will miss the event.

Finally, to "come" implies one has the intent of entering into the activity or place. To enter into something points to drawing close or coming near in order to share or be part of a situation. In a way, it points to identification and communion.

As I considered the invitations to "come" in Scripture, I noted how practical they were. The first obvious invitation from God came to Noah.[1] He told him and his family to come into the ark. We know this invitation was to save Noah and his family from the wrath that was about to be poured out upon the world. No doubt, for as long as Noah was building the ark, the warning of future judgment, as well as the invitation to be saved, was going out to the people. However, in their wickedness, the people either would not respond or they chose not to hear the invitation. Their wickedness of unbelief and rebellion could have made their ears dull and their eyes dim to the impending judgment.

The Bible tells us that Noah did everything the Lord commanded him to do. After all of his family members, along with the creatures, were inside of the ark, the Lord shut them in the ark. Most likely, He sealed them in.[2]

The example Noah leaves with us is that God prepares a place of safety for His people, and then He invites them in to experience Him as a place of refuge. For those of the New Testament, the ark is Jesus and we are sealed into an eternal inheritance by the Holy Spirit. Jesus has gone before us to prepare a place. During the preparation, the invitation of inviting those who clearly hear it and respond to it will continue to go forth. However, if people fail to respond, the time will come when God will shut His people in the place of safety, while shutting or sealing out those who failed to respond or refused His invitation, leaving them to taste His wrath.

In the life of Jacob's sons you will find a contrast as to the type of invitations that can be sent forth. The first invitation was to do wrong, but the second invitation resulted in reconciliation of a life and a family.

It is hard to believe that there are evil invitations being sent forth, as well as invitations to partake of or share life. In the life of Joseph he knew about the bitterness of the first type of invitation all too well. In fact, he tasted the bitterness of the wrong invitation twice.

[1] Genesis 7:1
[2] Genesis 7:6

His older brothers were jealous of Joseph's relationship with their father. In a sense each of his brothers were accepting an invitation when they came together in agreement to do something about what they considered to be their younger arrogant brother. It is important to point out that invitations are about people coming together in some way for some reason. Such invitations may not be formal, but nevertheless, they are there to partake of some type of event in unison with others. The brothers came together in agreement as to what they would do to Joseph. They would kill him, but thanks to the intercession of Reuben Joseph was spared. However, in Reuben's absence, the brothers sold Joseph into slavery.[3]

For Joseph the second invitation came directly to him. Potiphar's wife invited him to taste of her forbidden fruit.[4] The first temptation resulted in his brothers coming into agreement at the point of their jealousy towards him, thereby, justifying their wicked way of dealing with him. The second invitation came along the lines of blatant temptation.

Sadly, most men would have accepted the invitation to taste of the forbidden fruit of a pretty, seducing woman, but Joseph was a godly man and fled from the temptation. Even though Joseph paid dearly for his unwillingness to accept a wicked woman's invitation, God gave him favor in his trials. Eventually he was exalted into a high position in Egypt. As a result, he was able to send forth an invitation to his father to come to Egypt to avoid the results of the destructive famine that was upon the land.[5]

The wicked invitations that put Joseph into slavery and prison were used to exalt him in a position in which he had the power to send forth a very important invitation to his father. It was an invitation to live.

For the Christian, one of the greatest invitations in the New Testament begins with the word "if". This word would not imply that an invitation was following; rather, it points to a conjunction that is being used to signal a prerequisite or circumstance that must happen before an event can occur.

---

[3]   Genesis 37:21-29

[4]   Genesis 39:10-12

[5]   Genesis 45:9

However, the invitation was present, and it had to do with being Jesus' disciple. Jesus invites all who call upon Him to follow Him to the type of life that He desires for each of us. However, this life requires us to become His disciple or follower. This indirect invitation along with its various versions are found in the Gospels. Let us consider one of them, "And he said to them all, If any man will come after me, let him deny himself, and take up his cross daily, and follow me. For whosoever would save his life shall lose it; but whosoever will lose his life for my sake, the same shall save it" (Luke 9:23-24).

Jesus invited Peter to come and follow Him in order to be a fisher of men, which would carry eternal dividends.[6] However, Peter had to first follow Him to discover how to fish for the souls of men. He had to become a disciple, who would live according to the godly disciplines exemplified by Jesus. These disciplines included denying self to any right to live according to personal dictates, as well as picking up a cross that pointed to death to the works of the flesh and the influences of the world.

Once again we are reminded that invitations may not carry prerequisites, but they do carry some type of protocol. The type of occasion that people are being invited to, determines the protocol that is to be practiced on such an occasion. In the kingdom of God, the protocol is clearly being established so that His people will properly conduct themselves in the right way.

As we consider the disciplines for people to be Jesus' disciples, we must come to terms with the intent behind them. Clearly, if we do not lose our present life, we will never find our promised life. If we insist on saving our present life, we will lose it because it possesses the seeds of death. There is no life to be found in any of it.

This brings us to an important aspect of the Christian life. Why would we want to maintain the reign of self? The answer can be found in Luke 9:25, "For what is a man advantaged, if he gain the whole world, and lose himself, or be cast away?" The reason we want to hold onto self is because we want to partake of the world. We want to gain the advantages of the world, and we can't if we let go of our old selfish life.

We know the world represents the tree of knowledge of good and evil. Granted, it allows us to partake of whatever serves our flesh, but

---

6   Matthew 4:19

there are no seeds of life in it. Knowledge may allow us to experience both good and evil to have contrast, but the combination results in death. There is no life in what was formerly considered good that has not been contaminated or corrupted by evil, and there is no life in evil that has some goodness mixed in the equation. It is the root of the tree that determines the fruit that will be produced in the final product. Jesus put it best when He said, "Even so, every good tree bringeth forth good fruit, but a corrupt tree bringeth forth evil fruit. A good tree cannot bring forth evil fruit, neither can a corrupt tree bring forth good fruit" (Matthew 7:17-19).

God invites us to partake of the tree of life by inviting us to follow Jesus to that life. Granted, the tree begins with a dead tree, the cross, but what has been lifted up on the cross (Jesus) possesses life. The more we walk in the righteous ways of God, as we become identified to the tree (work of redemption) in order to partake of its life (Christ), the more goodness will be imparted into us and then in turn emitted from our lives.

As we consider God's invitations in the Bible, they have to do with life and death matters. Perhaps there will be various evil invitations with the fruits of death going forth that will threaten life, but God sends forth invitations with the intent to bring life or add to the quality of it, as well as preserve it.

COME AND DRINK

God's invitation to us has to do with life. We have a choice: to choose the enticement of this world or our Lord's invitation to partake of life. Recently, I was thinking about these two choices. When we choose the enticement of the world, we choose death, but when we choose God's invitation, we choose life.

Reason would tell us what choice is obviously right, but in reality most people do not see these two choices as a matter of death or life. In their mind, when they choose the world, they are choosing their own destination. In fact, they believe that they have the means to determine their destiny. As a result, they feel clever, rational, and wise in choosing the world.

One might ask what makes any of us think the world can offer us the means to choose the quality and direction of our lives. The answer is knowledge. Remember, the tree of knowledge of good and evil in the Garden of Eden? Man believes through knowledge or some type of enlightenment that he can become the master of his own destination. This means that he feels he can solve the problems of his world through knowledge. On this basis he goes and drinks from the stagnant, tainted, broken cisterns of the world. Such water will cause spiritual dullness and despondence, perverted perspectives, as well as spiritual emptiness, ultimately resulting in spiritual death.

God's invitation is to come and drink of the Living Water that will bring eternal life. This was made obvious when Jesus encountered the Samaritan woman at the well in John 4. She was seeking physical water, but encountered the One who could give her lasting, eternal water.

Even though she did not fully understand what it meant to receive this water, the Samaritan woman was ready to accept His invitation to drink of it. Before she could drink of the water, the truth of her life had to be brought to the light. After all, there were some moral issues in her life that had to be acknowledged, but underneath the deviation of her character was a seeking heart.

Before God can offer us life, He first invites us to come and reason with Him about our sin.[7] He knows that the guilty conscience must be addressed and cleansed before a person can accept the invitation to drink of the pure water of His Spirit. The writer of Hebrews brought this reality out in Hebrews 10:22, "Let us draw near with a true heart in full assurance of faith, having our hearts sprinkled from an evil conscience, and our bodies washed with pure water." Notice, the writer begins with the invitation to draw near to the Lord with a true heart.

The Samaritan woman at the well not only had a seeking heart, but a true heart. She desired to know what was real when it came to worship. This brings us to the openness of her heart. Even though there was moral deviation, she had a sincere heart towards the matters of God. She had faith that when the Messiah came, He would answer her questions. And, from all accounts, He did not disappoint her.

When Jesus invited the Samaritan woman to partake of His water, it was a personal invitation. It met her at the point of her personal spiritual

---

[7]   Isaiah 1:18

thirst. However, Jesus also has sent forth a general invitation to all to come and drink of His water. We find this invitation in John 7:37-39.

The truth is that many people are spiritually thirsty, but few ever recognize that the listlessness in their soul is due to a lack of lasting, sustaining water. In fact, most people take water for granted because it makes up the majority of the earth's surface. However, not all water sources possess life. In fact, there are water sources that would rob a person of well-being, kill him or her, and possibly destroy certain functions of a person's body. And, not all water sources will prove to be refreshing. Granted, they may maintain some semblance of life, but they can prove to be bitter tasting, dirty in color, and full of bacteria that can cause physical problems and possible death.

Today people have substituted much for actual drinking water. As a result, they are dehydrated, weak, and ineffective. For example, they might have substituted soda drinks, coffee, tea, and etc. for water. Even though these substances may contain water, the water has been compromised or tainted in some way. Therefore, the body does not process such drinks as water. This is why many people are dehydrated.

We can see this same development in the Church. Instead of offering the water from the wells of salvation, people are being given a mixture of man's worldly religion and God's truth. Instead of drinking from cisterns that have preserved the water for lean times, they are drinking from cisterns that are leaking, allowing dirt to work its way through the cracks to create muddy waters.

It is not unusual to see people go from one well to another, as well as from one cistern to another cistern. However, the wells prove to be contaminated or dry, and the cisterns leaking, allowing for the water to become dirty or stagnant. Once again, these wells or cisterns represent various sources that man often turns to such as government, leaders, religion, and works. However, there is no life in any of these waters. It might bring some fulfillment, but it will prove to be temporary.

This brings us back to Jesus' general invitation to come and partake of the Living Water. It was done during a time that the Jewish people would have some semblance of understanding as to what He was inviting them to.

It is important to set up the occasion that Jesus was using to send forth the invitation to come and drink of the Living Water. In John 7:37, it explains the last day of that great day of the feast. The first question is, what feast is Jesus talking about? The Jews celebrated various feasts, which all pointed to the Person and work of Jesus, the Messiah.

The answer to this question can be found in John 7:2. It was the last day of the Feast of the Tabernacles. The Feast of the Tabernacles reminded the Jews that they were once strangers in that land where they served as slaves; however, God gave them an identity and an inheritance, the Promised Land. It also pointed to the future reign of the Messiah in Jerusalem, where once again the people of Israel will possess all of the land promised to them through the covenants God made with such individuals as Abraham and King David.

This brings us to the significance of this feast. Part of the Feast of the Tabernacles involved a water-pouring ceremony that took place over a period of six days. It would climax with a ceremony on the seventh day, which is known as the day of the "great Hosanna."

The mention of the exclamation of "Hosanna" should remind us that this pointed to the Messiah coming as a King. We know this ceremony as "Palm Sunday." In some churches they get out their palm branches as they sing songs commemorating the countdown leading up to Resurrection Sunday. However, the significance of this Sunday is also recognizing that Jesus was acknowledged as the Messiah, the Promised One, and the King of Jews while riding on the back of a donkey. The Jews even gave Him a red carpet treatment by laying palm branches and their clothes before Him as He passed through their midst. Jesus clearly fulfilled the prophecy found in Zechariah 9:9 that pointed to Him being the Messiah.

On the seventh and last day of the Feast of the Tabernacles, the highlight of the water ceremony, was when the priest dramatically poured the water over the Altar of the Temple, also known as the Altar of Burnt Offering. As we are about to see, there are some very important symbols in the practices that were observed. To understand the significance of this action, we must understand what or who represents the altar, the temple, and the water.

Jesus said of His body in John 2:19-21 that it was the temple that would be destroyed. We know according to John 7:39 that the water was symbolic of the Holy Spirit, and according to Hebrews 13:10-13 that the Christian's altar is the cross. When you bring these types or representations together in one picture, you have Jesus (the temple) being anointed by the Holy Spirit so that He could be designated as the offering that would be sacrificed upon the altar, the cross.

It was at this precise part of the ceremony that the people would respond with immense joy. Their joy was in relationship to the promise found in Isaiah 12:3, "Therefore, with joy shall ye draw water out of the wells of salvation."

Part of the ceremony required the priest to offer sacrifices. Again we are reminded of how God offered His Son on the altar of the cross. The priest than took the ashes of the sacrifice out of the east gate to dump the ashes. Remember, Jesus had to suffer outside of the city on the cross, and then his body was put in the tomb.

The people would cut down willows measuring 24 feet in length. The number "24" has to do with heavenly government and worship. We can clearly see glimpses of this type of government and worship in Revelation 4-5. According to the prophet Isaiah, the increase of the government would be on Jesus' shoulders. He would not only establish an earthly government as far as Israel, but a heavenly kingdom. He would rule with a perfect, heavenly order according to justice and righteousness. However, like the willows He would be cut off in the prime of His life and raised again in order to bring about this incredible work.[8]

The people would then line up shoulder to shoulder along the road back to the temple holding these willows. They would wave the palm branches, while chanting Psalms 113-118. It would truly be a day of rejoicing because it pointed to their future when the Messiah would come as King and reign. They would end their chanting with Psalm 118: 25-26: "Save now, I beseech thee, O LORD! O LORD, I beseech thee, send now prosperity! Blessed is he that cometh in the name of the LORD; we have blessed you out of the house of the LORD." We can see Jesus being a fulfillment of this prayer in Matthew 21:2-11.

Eventually the High Priest would exit out of the Water Gate to the pool known as the "Pool of Siloam" or the "Pool of Gently Flowing Water." There the High Priest drew the water known as "Living Water" into a golden vase. The priest's assistant had a silver vase containing wine. As the priest marched with the people, the willows would make a swishing sound.

---

[8]   Isaiah 9:7; Daniel 9:25-26

There are various representations in this exercise. The pool points to the Holy Spirit gently flowing through those who are vessels of God. The High Priest points to Jesus as our High Priest. The golden vase reminds us that He is also deity that came down in the flesh so He could stand in the gap. The silver vase reminds us that He secured redemption for us by becoming our sacrifice (the wine). The swishing sound points to the Day of Pentecost when the Holy Spirit came upon believers in the upper room like a wind.

Jesus was inviting those who would hear Him to drink freely of His Spirit in order to come into that place of spirit and life. We know the Father sent the Spirit as a gift, and the Son baptizes us with the Spirit to fulfill the promise of power from above, but we must receive the gift and be immersed in the Spirit to know the powerful affects of the Water of heaven, the water that never ceases to flow from the throne of God.

Hence enters the invitation from the High Priest of heaven, Jesus, on that last day of the great feast inviting people to come and drink of the Living Waters, which brings us to another interesting fact about the Feasts of the Tabernacles. It is also known as the Wedding Feast. Jesus' millennium reign will be preceded by the wedding feast or the wedding supper of the Lamb.[9] He is clearly inviting us to this feast where completeness and oneness will be consummated in blessed fellowship with Him. It will be a joyful time indeed for all of those who are at the wedding supper of the Lamb.

Here is the example of the complete work of God. Jesus is inviting us to come and experience the many facets of the wells of salvation, but our hearts must be uncapped for the water to flow. After all, some hearts are hard and need to be broken, other hearts are stony and will need the powerful force of the water to wash away the stones, and yet other hearts are worldly, and will need to be cultivated. Clearly, such hearts need to be circumcised, plowed up, and transformed by the power of the free flowing rivers of the Living Water that finds its source in the heavenly springs that supplies the wells of salvation.

Have you accepted Jesus' invitation? Have you receive the Living Waters from the wells of salvation? If you have not, consider this invitation found in Revelation 22:1, "And the Spirit and the bride say,

---

9   Revelation 19:6-10

Come, And let him that heareth say, Come. And let him that is athirst come. And whosoever will, let him take the water of life freely."

COME AND PARTAKE

God's invitation to us is to come and partake of that which is able to give us life. He wants us to understand what it means to live according to His Spirit, walk according to His ways, and recognize that our well-being is established in Him. Even though Jesus' invitation is clear for us to come, we must come to partake of what is being offered us.

People want to pick and choose what they receive from God. However, the concept of drinking water is not a matter of picking and choosing, but of one that entails a life and death decision. People might come to the water, but they may fail to partake of it.

There are various reasons people fail to partake of the spiritual water of heaven. Some come to consider whether it will benefit them as far as the flesh, but find no real attraction. Others come because they were invited to find some type of relief to their trying situation. However, when they come to the water, they do not see a lasting solution. It all looks temporary. There are those who come to the water to get what they can, but they fail to receive it because they lacked the necessary faith to properly partake of it.

"To partake" of something means to associate with, share in order to fellowship, become identified to, to relate to something, and/or to assimilate something into our way of thinking, doing, and being. Jesus is not just inviting us to the wells of salvation, but He is inviting us to partake of such wells so that we can live.

To partake in this manner means to believe what He is saying in regard to the invitation. He is inviting us to come and live. In the second aspect of the invitation, He is inviting us to believe Him based on His person, character, and reputation. Such belief will allow us to freely partake of His Water so that we can walk according to His life. Therefore, in the initial invitation to come, Jesus is inviting us to take *on* His life, but in the second aspect of the invitation, He is inviting us to *experience* His life. In the first incident, we will be walking *towards* life, but in the second aspect of it we will be walking *in* His life.

When we consider the two distinct aspects of this invitation, we must recognize that to initially come to the water, requires the presence and intercession of His Spirit. And, in order to partake of it, we must see what is being offered to us as the truth. Without the right Spirit, we cannot properly receive and assimilate the truth that is available in the life that is being offered to us. This is why Jesus said of His words that they are Spirit and life.[10] It is His Spirit that brings the truth of His life to His invitations, instructions, examples, and ways.

The Bible outlines what it entails to partake of the life God has for each of us. In fact, He invites us to come to partake of every facet of this life in order to receive the fullness of it. Even though there is no way I could do justice to this matter, I will try to summarize His various invitations.

Place: God sends forth an invitation to come to the place where man can meet with Him. In the case of some of the patriarchs in the Old Testament, God met them, but when the tabernacle and temple were established for the presence of God to dwell among His people, His people were often invited to come up to the place where God dwelled to observe His name, celebrate the feasts, offer sacrifices, and honor Him.[11]

For the Christian, the place is Jesus. It is at this place where man can celebrate the greatness of His God, as well as the type of life God has given him. It is a place for fellowship and rest, where man can find rest for his spirit and peace for his soul. However, to come to this place, man must come out and be separate from the world and its activities. God's people are always being called to come out and be separate in order to come to this special place of communion.[12]

Presence: The reason we are called to come to the place of God is so we can experience His presence. Moses was called up into Mount Sinai to encounter the presence of God. There he received the Law and the instructions for the tabernacle. God is always calling His people to come aside to the place of His abiding presence. It is in His presence that we can worship and serve Him, hear His voice, witness His works, praise His Name, express our thankfulness, and offer sacrifices. It is in

---

[10]   John 6:63

[11]   Deuteronomy 12:5; Matthew 11:28-29

[12]   2 Corinthians 6:14-18

the place of His presence that we can erect a memorial as a reminder of His greatness and glory.[13]

Communion: The Lord is calling us into His presence so we can commune with Him. He invited Moses to commune with Him between the cherubim on the mercy seat located on the Ark of the Covenant. It is difficult to comprehend that the Lord so wants to commune individually with us. He created the universe, but He wants to individually commune with each of us. He orders the function of creation, but He wants to individually sit with you and me. He oversees the details of the world around each of us, but He wants to enjoy our company. He not only wants to fellowship with you and me, He wants each of us to partake of His life. Ultimately, He wants to be able to call you and me "friend."[14]

Communion is about partaking of Jesus' life, becoming identified in His work of redemption on the cross, sharing in His sufferings, being part of His work, and being associated with His glory. In John 6, we are invited to partake of His body (bread from heaven) and of His blood (the covenant) in order to live. To partake of Him in this text means to *believe on* Him as to the words He spoke, to *believe* Him because of who He is, and to *believe in* Him because of what He did on the cross for us. Such belief points to totally assimilating every aspect of His word, person, and work as being truth that must be applied to our walk to ensure life.[15]

Inherit His Promises: In the second epistle of Peter, the apostle explained how according to Jesus' divine power, we have been given all things that pertain unto life and godliness. He goes on to say, "By which are given unto us exceedingly great and precious promises, that by these ye might be partakers of the divine nature, having escaped the corruption that is in the world through lust" (2 Peter 1:4).

The Apostle Peter clearly explained that we have been given exceedingly great and precious promises that enable us to partake of our Lord's divine nature. Once again, we see that point of sharing in the blessings of His promises as we become identified to the righteous character of His nature. To have such identification points to escaping the corruption of this present world or age.

---

[13]   Deuteronomy 10:1-5; Psalms 46:1-8; 66:13-16; 95:1-3, 6; 96:6-9; 100:2

[14]   Exodus 25:20-22; John 15:11-14

[15]   Luke 22:14-20; John 6:35, 53-58; Romans 8:13-17

Hebrew 6:12 instructs that we cannot be slothful about inheriting God's promises; rather, we must be followers of those who through faith and patience inherited them. There are various aspects to the wells of salvation. Each well possesses the different elements of life that flows through and from the wells of heaven. These wells possess both the promise and fullness of life. However, each of us must partake of the Water to possess the life that God has ordained for each of us.

COME AWAY MY BELOVED

There is a reason that the Lord invites us to come to the Living Water. It is only by partaking of the heavenly water of life that we can come into a sweet abiding fellowship with God.

When we talk about the Christian life, most refer to it in light of salvation. It is true that the Lord came to bring us deliverance and life. However, the Apostle Paul is quite clear that Jesus' ministry was one of reconciliation. In other words, He came to close the gap created by sin. He became the way to the place of fellowship with God, the truth about where such communion will lead to, and the life that comes out of such oneness with God.[16]

God gave us an example of this oneness when He established marriage. He stated that man and woman would become one or complete in this union (Genesis 2:21-24). Solomon talked about the protection and strength that can be produced when two become one in purpose and function. He stated, "Two are better than one, because they have a good reward for their labor; For if they fall, the one will lift up his fellow. But woe to him that is alone when he falleth; for he hath not another to help him up" (Ecclesiastes 4:9-10).

The prophet Amos talked about the necessity of this oneness. He stated, "Can two walk together, except they be agreed" (Amos 3:3)?

Jesus talked about the necessity and power that there is in real agreement. In Matthew 18:20, He assured His followers that where two or three are gathered together in His name, He will be in their midst. In John 10:30, He said that He and the Father were one. He gave us a

---

[16]   John 14:6; 17:21-28; 2 Corinthians 5:18-19

picture of oneness in relationship to abiding in John 15. We must abide in Him for His life to flow through us. If we are abiding in Him, we are one with Him in function, purpose, and in the type of fruits that will be produced. We will be the extension of His life. But, if we are severed from Him in any way, we stand alone. There will be no source of life. We will have no purpose, and the future we have before us is one of judgment.

In His prayer in John 17:21, Jesus made known His heart towards believers in this way, "That they all may be one, as thou, Father, art in me, and I in thee, that they also may be one in us; that the world may believe that thou hast sent me." Jesus heart was to see His followers becoming one as He and His Father. He did nothing outside of the will, plan, and purpose of the Father. Likewise, His followers cannot be one unless they submit their wills to the same heavenly plan and purpose Jesus did when He was on earth. If His followers come into such agreement, they would become one with Him and the Father. In fact, such oneness would testify to the world that Jesus was and is who He said He was.

Jesus continues this theme in John 17:22-23,

> And the glory which thou gavest me I have given them, that they may be one, even as we are one: I in them, and thou in me, that they may be made perfect in one; and that the world may know that thou hast sent me, and has loved them, as thou hast loved me.

Consider what this oneness means for those who follow Jesus. First, they share in His glory. His "glory" is what makes Jesus distinct, and it will also make His followers stand out in this present world. Once again Jesus reiterates the need for His followers to be one as He is one with His Father. We can only reason that if we are one with Him that He is in us. Since the Father is in Him, we are one with the Father as well.

This brings us to how the oneness we have with Jesus is necessary. There are three ways in which such agreement will affect our lives. The first is that in such agreement, we will be made perfect in our relationship and communion with our Lord and with each other. "Perfection" points to maturity. Obviously, spiritual maturity will not happen unless there is such oneness.

The second reason has already been established. "Oneness" of this nature will verify that Jesus has been sent into the world by the Father.

Such verification points to His identity, credibility, and authority. Like Noah, our established witness concerning Jesus will ultimately bring judgment on those who refuse to believe. The Apostle Peter put it in this way, "And spared not the old world, but saved Noah, the eighth person, a preacher of righteousness, bringing in the flood upon the world of the ungodly" (2 Peter 2:5).

The third way oneness affects our lives as believers is that it also proves to the world that the Father loves both us and Jesus. Love identifies each of us to the kingdom of heaven and each other. Jesus put it another way when He stated, "A new commandment I give unto you, that ye love one another; as I have loved you, that ye also love one another. By this shall all men know that ye are my disciples, if ye have love one to another" (John 13:34-35).

The Apostle Paul brings this oneness together in light of the Church being the Body of Christ. In fact, the oneness that God ordained for marriage was to serve as an example or type as to the relationship Jesus would desire and establish with His Church. Each believer would be fitted into Jesus body, the Church, to function with the other members of His Body according to His direction as the head.[17]

It seems so simple, but the truth is unless each member is ready to give away their individual identity to take on a heavenly one as a member of His Body, the Church, will not be able to function as one fine-tuned Body. This is the reason there are so many challenges in the Church. Different members have diverse agendas and purposes. They have not yet submitted to the leading of the Holy Spirit to ensure that they are of the same will, heart, and mind as their Lord.

Jesus clearly invites us to take of the Living Waters to receive eternal life, but the Living Water wants to bring us to a place of intimate communion. This can be best described by the invitation that is found in Song of Solomon. This small book of the Bible gives us insight into the struggles and challenges that can be found in our relationship with the Lord.

The invitation that goes out to His Church reveals the sweetness behind all true fellowship with the Lord. This sweetness is the result of unadulterated love. It is a love that is so caught up with the commitment

---

[17] Ephesians 4:11-16; 5:25-30; Colossians 1:15-22

and devotion of the One who has come to us to claim us for Himself. Granted, there is the introduction (thirsty), the attraction (Living Water), the courting (invitation), the acknowledgment (our Redeemer), the openness to receive (salvation), and the joyful marriage (born again of the Spirit and Water [Bible]), but there is so much more. There is the consummation of that marriage at the marriage supper of the Lamb. This is where two come into complete intimate communion and fellowship. They will actually become one in Spirit, heart, and mind, allowing them to walk together as they share their life with one another.

We see the invitation that goes out to such a loved one in the Song of Solomon. Let us consider the extent of this invitation. In Song of Solomon 2:8 it begins with the joy that comes from hearing the voice of the beloved one. Jesus' voice should make our hearts skip with joy. After all, He desires to come to us to establish a close relationship. Then, the beloved one speaks, "My beloved spoke, and said unto me, Rise up, my love, my fair one, and come away" (Song of Solomon 2:10).

Intimate fellowship can only occur when two people come apart from the outside influences to spend time together. In a way it is a point of consecration as far as the relationship. This is where the relationship is set apart from all other interests. But, a person must first rise up from his or her daily, normal activities in order to separate him or herself to a time of fellowship.

In Song of Solomon 2:11-12, we see reference to the springtime. Sweet love that results in fellowship is like a breath of fresh air. It implies shedding the old in order to embrace the new. True love is new every day in its commitment, benevolence, and compassions. It was in the setting of springtime that the invitation goes out again: ". . . Arise, my love, my fair one, and come away" (Song of Solomon 2:13c).

When you consider the terms of endearment that is describing the sentiment and devotion of the bridegroom, you can see how much he prizes the one he is bestowing his love on. This is true for our Lord. We are so dear and close to His heart. He wants us to hear His invitation to realize how precious we are to Him. After all, it was His love that put a value on us.

When we consider the next invitation in Song of Solomon 4:9 to his beloved, we see him actually inviting her to come away to share or experience life with him. Jesus wants us to come away with Him to experience His life. He wants to share His world with us in a new life.

In Song of Solomon 4:16, we see where the beloved wanted his bride to come into the garden. But, first he requested that the north wind awakes and that the south wind blows upon the garden to ensure a fruitful garden that can be shared and enjoyed by the two lovers.

Jesus wants us to come into His garden and discover the abundance that has been made available to partake of. In fact, we will never be dissatisfied with such a garden; therefore, we do not need to look elsewhere. There is sweetness, communion, and fruit in the garden of fellowship.

We have the final invitation in Song of Solomon 7:10-13. In this love song, we are told in verse 10 that the beloved and his prized bride are one. After all, she belongs to him and his desire is towards her.

As Christians we know that Jesus purchased us; therefore, we belong to Him. His desire is also towards us, making us aware that He does prize us. It is this attitude that brings us to the invitation, "Come, my beloved, let us go forth into the field; let us lodge in the villages. Let us get up early to the vineyards; let us see if the vine flourish, whether the tender grape appear, and the pomegranates bud forth. There will I give thee my love" (Song of Solomon 7:11-12).

We see how the relationship between the bridegroom and his beloved has developed. His invitation to her is to come and go forth into a new life, a new adventure, a new beginning. Clearly, the couple has come to the place in their relationship where the groom's invitation is to come to that place of intimacy where he can show her love, as well as give love to her. Clearly, the bridegroom's love has been restrained or put aside until he could bestow it on his bride at a time in which she would indeed be ready to receive it in a proper way. At such time she would also be receptive to come away with him to share his life by becoming one with him.

God has revealed His love to all of humanity on the cross. He has availed it to each of us through Jesus' redemption, but many refuse to receive His love. Those who receive the love made available on the cross enter through a door that allows them to discover the strength or steadfastness behind such love that is described by the Apostle Paul in Galatians 5:6, as faith that is brought forth through love.

As a person discovers the strength of God's love, he or she begins to grow in love towards the Lord. This growth is what causes the person to accept His invitation to come away to higher ground where his or her perception could be enlarged, allowing a deeper relationship to develop that will lead to greater intimacy. Finally, comes the invitation "to come" in order to go forth into a new life, as well as the harvest field, in oneness of heart, mind, and purpose. Clearly, these invitations give us insight into the type of relationship the Lord wants with each of us.

Another example of an invitation to "come away" that was clearly orchestrated by the Lord can be found in the life of Rebekah in Genesis 24. In fact, there are two distinct invitations. One comes from Abraham's servant. It is a wedding invitation, where Rebekah is asked to be Isaac's bride. The other invitation comes from Rebekah to the servant. In Genesis 24:31, she asks Abraham's servant to come for she has prepared the house and room for the camels. One presented a dowry to bring credibility to the invitation, while the other one prepared a place for a weary messenger, revealing her character and intention.

God sent forth His Son to pay a dowry for a bride, while the Holy Spirit serves as a messenger to secure the bride, the Church, for the Son. The Church will serve as the abiding place for the Holy Spirit to reside; therefore, it must prepare itself in a proper way. This means it must prepare itself to serve as a temple of the Spirit of God.

We know in the future that Jesus will come for His bride. Meanwhile the invitation continues to go forth to those who will truly hear what the Spirit is saying in regard to the Lord's invitation. Revelation 22:17 gives us insight into this invitation, "And the Spirit and the bride say, Come. And let him that heareth say, Come. And let him that is athirst come. And whosoever will, let him take the water of life freely."

HAVE YOU RECEIVED HIS INVITATIONS?

It is hard to put into words the importance of hearing and receiving the Lord's invitation to come and partake of His life. We do not always understand the complete implications behind such an invitation, because we do not understand the type of life that our Lord wants to lead us to.

There are those who have received the invitation, but they have failed to accept the request to come into a place of greater relationship with our Lord. As a result, these individuals experience leanness to their souls because there has been no spiritual growth. You have those who have ventured somewhat into a relationship with the Lord, but they possess a mixture as far as their loyalty to Jesus. As a result, they display much inconsistency in their lives. You have those who play outside the fringes of a relationship with the Lord, while giving an impression they have it altogether. However, there is no substance or steadfastness behind their façade.

Some people think that since the Lord loves them He must be desperate for them to receive His invitation. The truth is He is not desperate for us; rather He is desperate on our behalf. He knows if we do not accept His invitation to partake of His life, we will experience the separation of death. He wants to spare each of us of this death by sharing His life with us.

Other people perceive that they have time to determine when they will accept such an invitation. However, we know that the Lord will not always contend with foolishness. We can never know what tomorrow will bring. Each of us need to seek the Lord while He can be found, otherwise, we might find that the messenger can no longer be found who will lead us to the water, or that time has personally ran out for us. This is why today is the day of salvation.[18]

Finally, you have those who could care less about the things of God. They have no inclination or desire to know about the spiritual things of life. They are content to stay in their foolishness and delusion about spiritual matters. Yet, the Lord's heart broke over such people. After all, life has been offered to them, but they prefer the ways of death.

My prayer and hope is that you have received every invitation that our Lord has put forth. I pray that you have not just drunk from the wells of salvation, but my sincere desire is that you have gone on to accept His invitation to partake of His life. It is for this reason He stands at the door of people's hearts, knocking to be invited in to sup with them.[19]

It is also my desire to see that communion at His table will lead to communion in His garden. He so desires us to consecrate our lives to Him and come away to discover what it means to be intimate with Him. He desires that oneness with each of us that will bring Him glory and benefit our lives. He wants us to taste the sweetness of His love,

---

[18]   2 Corinthians 6:2
[19]   Revelation 3:20

know the satisfaction of His commitment, and enjoy His doting devotion towards our well-being.

The Song of Solomon best describes that desire. It also revealed that such communion will result in a composition of a song. This song will be played according to the rhythm of the tenderness of our heart towards Him. It will not only be based on the One we have come to know, love, and desire, but it will be dedicated and sung to Him as we commemorate our love and devotion to Him. As the writer of the Song of Solomon noted in 2:4, "He brought me to the banqueting house, and his banner over me was love."

4

A MATTER
OF ATTRACTIONS

INTRODUCTION

My co-laborer in the Gospel asked me to write this presentation after discussing the confusion people have when it comes to their attractions, preferences, and lifestyles. In people's attempts to explain the different attractions they have adopted through their lives, various terms have been attached to them to justify or explain questionable preferences. Ultimately, people have complicated these attractions, causing them to be set up in lifestyle patterns that have proved to be anything but satisfying. However, if you bring them back to the original source, most preferences started out as attractions.

These attractions became points of identification. In other words, they were used to define the person; rather than the person discerning the attraction and determining how he or she was going to define, discipline, or handle it.

This information is designed to clear away confusion and call people back to center, a place of being ethically accountable for personal preferences and taking the necessary responsibility for coming back to moral integrity in their conduct. Although people could take issue with what I have observed and discovered about this matter, they would eventually have to agree that there is definitely some merit to the following presentation.

WHAT IS AN ATTRACTION

A simple question is what is an attraction? Attractions are often assumed. In other words, most people do not consider the dynamics behind them. They are simply attracted to something, which seems natural, exciting, or desirable. However, to understand what an attraction is, we must come to terms with how such a drawing occurs.

Attraction occurs when something exerts some type of power or influence upon one of our senses. For example, one of the five senses is stirred up to consider how something will make us feel once we partake of it. Case in point, eating a certain food is going to prove pleasurable and satisfying. Being able to have certain experiences with a person or an activity will bring the desired happiness and satisfaction. In fact, this is how advertisement works. It must appeal to one of our senses in order to exert the power to stir up our imagination to consider the possibilities of how something will bring satisfaction to our lives. Notice how the lure of attraction to most things is to experience some type of happiness or satisfaction. Once those possibilities of finding personal satisfaction takes center stage, it becomes desirable, ending in the pursuit of it.

This brings us to the first aspect of attraction: it is often very carnal or fleshly. Such an attraction has to do with stirring up what we refer to as fleshly lusts. When it comes to fleshly lust or appetites, there are always expectations or fantasies attached to each one of them that will eventually leave the person dissatisfied or pursuing it more to have the "imagined" or "supposed" expectation or fantasy fulfilled. This is why the Apostle Paul tells us to flee all youthful lusts and follow after righteousness, faith, charity, and peace.[1]

The second way people are attracted is by some type of quality or feature of something. Why am I attracted to this person, this place, or this product? It is important to realize most of us are caught off guard as to what is going to attract us to someone or something. For example, there was something about that person, place, or product that catches our eye. Perhaps that person has a winning smile or personality, the place gives us a certain sense of fulfillment, and the product is what would add some type of value to our lives.

---

[1]   2 Timothy 2:22

In the first scenario we see where attraction attaches an expectation to something, while in another situation it will actually attach a bias to something. People do not realize that a bias or prejudice is attached to someone or something based on what we recognize to be worthy (quality) of our attention. Such worth is going to be determined by some type of feature. By attaching some type of bias or prejudice, I am determining what I will give my attention to up front based upon what I consider superior. Such a judgment will determine some type of evaluation chart that will also allow me to regard someone or something as significant of consideration or not creditable to be regarded in any way.

For example, in my younger years I discovered that I was attracted to men who had blond hair and blue eyes. When I was in a crowd of men, guess who would catch my eye first? Granted, perhaps there would be another feature of some other man that might catch my eye later on, but my initial attraction would be based on the bias I had placed on all men according to outward features. However, such prejudices can change or be done away altogether because people are not generic. A man may have blond hair and blue eyes, but such surface features will not determine his character. The more you lay aside the immature, romantic notions that find their origins in the images of the world, the more a person's character becomes a major consideration.

It is also in this arena that I might attach a need for something to make my life better or more fulfilling. I need to be around this person to add meaning to my life, I need to experience this place to feel happy, or I need this product to make my life easy or more fulfilling. However, whether it is a need or prejudice being attached to an attraction, it shows how our eyes can exalt something to an unrealistic, idolatrous position. This is why the Apostle John gave this exhortation in 1 John 2:15-17,

> Love not the world, neither the things that are in the world.
> If any man love the world, the love of the Father is not in him.
> For all that is in the world, the lust of the flesh, and the lust of
> the eyes, and the pride of life, is not of the Father, but is of the
> world. And the world passeth away, and the lust of it; but he
> that doeth the will of God abideth forever.

Clearly, attractions are based on fleshly appetites and worldly images. This brings us to a very important consideration. Why do attractions vary with people? After all, people often consider their attractions as a point of reality, truth, or normalcy. If you do not share their attraction in a particular area, you might be considered stupid, abnormal, and foolish. If you do not attach the same bias to their attraction as they do, you could be considered a misguided fool.

Since attractions vary with people, they cannot serve as a point of present reality, truth, or what is normal. After all, reality comes down to the way something really is, while truth never will change no matter the circumstances. And, in the case of what is considered normalcy such judgments can always be debated by others who have a different take on what is "normal". This is why attractions must be properly discerned in order to discipline them in a constructive way. However, before we can properly discern something, we must understand those things that might influence such attractions.

THE ENVIRONMENT

We need to come to terms with how environment affects the attractions we adopt. We know that family, friends, cultural, religion, and education will greatly affect our preferences. It is hard for us to accept that our tastes and pursuits are indicative as to just how easily we are influenced by what we have been exposed to.

The truth is, our choices or predilections are not only influenced by our environment, but when it comes to the philosophies of the world, we often have been indoctrinated as to what we end up preferring. It is the influences around us, along with the indoctrination we are exposed to, that will determine our attitudes towards the issues of life, such as God and morality. In other words, these influences will determine our worldview as to how we view social and moral matters.

This brings us to what constitutes environment. There are different types of environments. There is the environment of our nation and society, the environment of our homes, and there is an inward environment in regard to our souls. Each environment is affected in different ways, but will ultimately affect each other. For example, the environment of the nation will be determined by the quality of leadership, society will be affected by the moral climate that is being upheld, homes will be affected by the standard of authority (responsibility and accountability) that has been established by the parents, and the inward environment is going to be determined by the spiritual condition of the person. If the person does not possess a right inward environment, the home will find itself in chaos. If the family is in chaos, than society will be affected by the lawlessness that will spill out of the chaos. Since society is trying to combat lawlessness, the courts and financial stability of the nation will be affected.

As Christians we know that the real culprit behind the breakdown in our different environments is sin. However, when sin runs rampant, every aspect of society will be affected. Sin always eats away at the foundation, eventually causing the structure to fall into utter ruin. Many times people do not recognize what is happening until the destruction takes center stage on a national level. For example, a nation that does not maintain justice is a result of societies that have become ill equipped to address lawlessness. Societies that are being overrun by lawlessness revealed that families have become broken because sin has been allowed to destroy their moral compass. Without moral compasses, individuals will not see any real need to take personal accountability for deviant attitudes and ways.

When sin is running rampant, it is not hard to find philosophies or ideologies that have redefined or have done away with the moral absolutes that God has put in place to ensure constructive environments. In today's world everything is relative. The philosophy behind it is amoral. Since there is no real moral standard, man can define his own morality according to his personal take on it. All lines of truth and moral accountability are being fudged, blurred, or done away with altogether. As a result, nothing is considered wrong or right; that is unless you maintain that there is a definite moral standard that everyone will one day be held accountable to by a holy God.

This brings us back to environment. Environment points to status, condition, or the disposition of something. Status will come down to how one will operate or respond in a situation. In fact, status will determine how a person will perceive or interpret a matter. This is where natural inclinations and bias exist.

Condition points to the state of something. It will influence the prevailing mood that will take center stage about what is going on. The prevailing mood can prove to be touchy and unpredictable as it swings with personal fickleness, fancies, or dislikes. Or, on the other hand it proves to be stable and reasonable because it is grounded by personal character and resolve. Ultimately, it will determine how a person will receive something.

Disposition represents the state of something, but it speaks of the nature, character, and temperament or attitude of something. This actually points to the spirit that is active or prevalent in the environment. The spirit will determine how a person will process what is going on. For example, a person can have a very judgmental attitude towards something, or he or she can be cautious but open to consider, test, or discern what is really going on in a situation.

Now with this in mind, let us now consider how the environment can affect our attractions. Let us first consider the temperature of this nation. Nation defines a person on the basis of status or worth. It is going to influence the ideology that people will be attracted to. This will determine not only people's attitude towards government, but it will also affect the political favor of a nation.

For example, the generation that is emerging in America is attracted to what is called a "Nanny State." A "Nanny State" is where big government does away with the middle class and makes everyone a slave to governmental dictates and whims. Those considered to be part of the "elite" will get richer off the backs of those who are considered stupid and peons. Any opposition will be put down or done away with altogether. It will require people to sell their very souls to receive the "bread" of bitterness from the government's unmerciful tables of tyranny. Sadly, this last generation might end up partaking of this bitter cup down to its very dregs. Many of them have gleefully bought its presentation because they have been indoctrinated into it, but they have done so to their own destruction.

If you peer behind the philosophy that this generation has been indoctrinated with, you will see the ideology of Marxism. Since the younger generation is interpreting all matters according to their indoctrination, Marxism is serving as their premise or light in which they are regarding all issues that would personally affect their lives. Therefore, they would be attracted to politicians that would agree with their type of attitude that is best described as the "Me Generation."

Needless to say, Jesus would consider these people's light to be darkness, but to these individuals who have begun from the Marxist or Communistic premise, it is considered to be the true light.[2] They see those who disagree with them as being inept, stupid, or just plain wrong.

For the sake of comparison, let us consider the perspective of those who comprised what is considered to be the last, great generation of this nation. These are the people from the WWII era. It is important to realize these people were living history. They knew the destruction of Marxism (Fascism), the insanity and senselessness behind the holocaust, and the sacrifice to maintain what was honorable, true, and right.

The generation of WWII's premise was freedom, their banner was patriotism, and they were willing to sacrifice all so that future generations would have the freedom to pursue a certain lifestyle. They were opportunists. They believed if they worked hard they could make a decent life for their family. They also believed in the simplicity of the American way that was best portrayed in Norman Rockwell's paintings. In their mind, there was no separating God, country, and decency. To them, it all ran together because without God, there would be no country or decency.

This is not to say that America did not have its issues, but the foundation that made this country great stood as a shining theme in the darkness that was engulfing much of the world in the late 1930s and 1940s. This darkness was created by a few men who saw themselves as the world's dictators.

The madness that caused world wars of the past is now taking center stage in this nation. As people struggle with what is happening, they realize that the environment of this nation has caused many to become apathetic. They have been lulled to sleep with the idea of "business as usual in the government." This has allowed people with a progressive (Socialist, Marxist) ideology to infiltrate our colleges with their insanity. Instead of teaching our young people to explore beyond the acceptable, they have been indoctrinated into a narrow box of hatred and skepticism by those who mock all that America stands for. Indoctrination changes

---

[2]   Matthew 6:22-23

the worldview of people. Keep in mind the worldview determines how people perceive their moral obligation to others.

As we consider how we approach or regard a matter, we must realize that we have been indoctrinated with or have adopted a particular worldview. This worldview will not only determine how we perceive our moral obligation, but it will determine the intent or spirit in which we approach situations. In other words, the spirit that is prevailing in the environment will determine the condition of that environment. The environment will in turn determine what a person is attracted to in regard to the ideology that he or she will embrace. Such ideology will become the underlying agenda that the person will pursue.

The Bible warns us not to let the philosophy and vain deceit of the world spoil us against the truth. It is important to point out that truth stands on its own merit; therefore, there is no need for indoctrination. People will either love the truth and desire it above all else, or they reject it in lieu of worldly attractions that serve their desired realities.[3]

Let us now consider how this attraction works in regard to worldview in the following illustration.

---

[3] Colossians 2:8; 2 Thessalonians 2:10-12

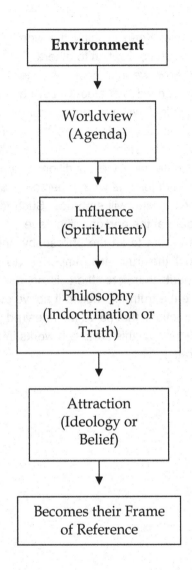

What ideology or belief are you attracted to? Have you been indoctrinated or do you have a real love for the truth? Your worldview will determine how you perceive the issues of God and life.

EMPHASIS

The next area that determines what we will be attracted to is the emphasis we put on something. Granted, emphasis can start with an attraction, or it can also end with us being attracted to something because we have put some type of significance in someone or on something.

Most of us understand the significance of emphasis. We actually are putting a special importance or personal value on something. Ultimately, we will end up stressing such importance in our pursuits. As a result, emphasis can become a powerful motivation in which we seek to express the impression that someone or something has left on us, or the importance that someone or something is having on our inner being. In fact, such attractions will say something about our integrity, as well as how we view our moral obligation towards that which we put emphasis on.

This brings us to a very important aspect of attraction in regard to our emphasis. There are three different aspects to emphasis that we must understand. They are affection, estimation, and obsession.

Often the driving force behind emphasis is affections. To make something important we must emotionally become attached to it. In fact, we determine where we are going to direct our affections. This is why the Apostle Paul gave this instruction Colossians 3:1-2, "If ye, then, be risen with Christ, seek those things which are above, where Christ sitteth on the right hand of God. Set your affection on things above, not on things on the earth."

Depending on the intensity of our affections towards something, they will determine what kind of value we put on it. Once again we are reminded that we determine the type of attractions we possess. We may not understand the dynamics behind such attractions, but we do determine the attitude we adopt towards them, as well as how we are going to perceive, approach, and pursue them.

We know that environment is determined by our worldview. Clearly, our worldview entails our mind. Our mental attractions entail the influence of spirit and philosophies. The problem is that when attractions remain on an intellectual level, they will prove to be indifferent towards the present reality. Most people actually live in an unrealistic reality due to their worldview. However, in the case of emphasis, it has to do with the heart. Where your treasure is there is where your heart will be also.[4]

Once again such a connection or attraction comes down to affections. Affections cause some type of emotional stirring or attraction that is being directed towards something. The mental attractions will bring people into agreement on an intellectual level, but the emotional attractions will bring people into agreement on an emotional level.

Since affections cause us to have emotional attachments to an attraction, such attractions become our emphasis. These attractions often find their origin in the images of the world. We will pursue the images or ideal of something to have some type of personal interaction in order to gain an inroad or possession of it. This brings us to a very important aspect of affections or emotional attachments. If they are not kept in the right perspective, they can turn into lusts.

Lusts often cause people to attempt to possess that which they are lusting or coveting after. In fact, their focus, determination, and desires are completely caught up with what they are pursuing. The harsh reality behind such pursuits is that they are being done for fleshly purposes.

Attractions that become lusts prove to be tormenting and controlling. This brings us to another important contrast. People can be indoctrinated into some mental reality. However, if lusts are involved, people can be controlled or manipulated to comply or adjust to the pressure that is being exerted by the intensity of affections, thereby, tormenting or driving the lust.

A good example of this type of attraction can be found in the lives of those who are entangled in pornography. Lusts consume these individuals as they pursue the possibilities of experiencing or possessing the particular ecstasy or fantasy that has captured their vain imaginations. They are often being pushed to capture the sensation that they perceive the experience will bring them. It becomes a tormenting drive as they struggle to control it. However, such lusts usually end up winning as they, in due course, take control of the individual. Eventually, these lusts can become obsessions. "Obsessions" mean they will possess the individual; rather, than the individual controlling them. Obsession clearly results in possession.

People who are indoctrinated will gnash their teeth towards truth, but those who are bound by wrong emphasis will show contempt

---

4   Matthew 6:21

towards that which will not agree or adjust to their pursuits. Clearly, we see this contempt being shown towards righteousness. People who are giving way to wicked emphases show disdain towards the contrast that righteousness will clearly bring to their wickedness.

Let us now consider where attraction fits into our emphasis.

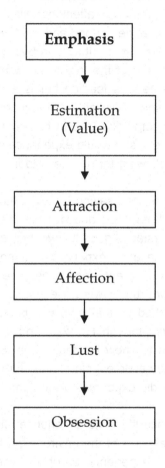

According to what you value and pursue, what do you treasure? Do you treasure the Pearl of Great Price, Jesus, thereby; you are so gripped by the glorious obsession of possessing Him that all other pursuits pale in comparison. Or, do you covet or obsess after worldly attractions? It is clear that something will possess your affections, but the object of your focus will be determined by you.

EXPERIENCE

Experiences will also determine what we become attracted to. We are meant to experience life. However, not all experiences represent the life that God has designed for us. They can taint our understanding of life, as well as define the person we become.

To explain how experiences affect our life, all we have to do is consider the tree of knowledge of good and evil found in Genesis 2:9 and 3:1-6. The real temptation Satan put forth to Eve was that she needed to actually experience the fruit of the tree to know the difference between good and evil. The lie he was feeding her is that by experiencing the good taste of the tree she would also experience the evil aspect of the tree, causing her to become like God in her understanding. Sadly, she did not realize that the evil she would experience would come by way of separation from God, allowing for darkness to invade the soul, resulting in spiritual death.

Consider what Satan was saying to Eve. His lie to Eve was that if she could experience both good and evil together it would put her on the same level of understanding, or knowledge, as God. We know that experience does not make us experts or all-knowing about a matter. Granted, it may serve as a great teacher, produce some common sense in us, or end in wisdom, but it will never make us all-knowing. Jesus became man, experienced all that man was/is subject to in this world, except for sinning. Even though He was God in humanity He did not have to experience sin to know its destruction. Since He kept Himself from sin He was able to become a sin offering for us. Although Jesus did not experience sin, He did experienced the consequences of sin on our behalf, that of death.

We are to experience life. This experience often entails our senses taking in the different aspects of the environment that surrounds us. We perceive that if we can experience all of the different elements of the environment around us, we will understand or know what constitutes life. This brings us to another important point about personal experiences, and that is that our senses will interpret the meaning, significance, or importance of an experience.

For example, when Eve considered the tree she saw that the fruit was good. Notice the sense of sight was being enticed by the outward beauty of the tree. Satan tempted her to eat it. In this case the sense of hearing came into play. As she considered the possibilities as to how this fruit would taste, her imagination was being stirred to pursue the satisfaction the fruit of this tree would bring to her flesh. At this point all reason was subdued by Satan's lie as her senses became heightened, causing her to pursue the so-called "satisfaction" and "enlightenment".

I do not know what the fruit of the tree tasted like. Apparently, it must have brought some type of satisfaction because she also gave it to Adam. Sadly, they would experience the fruits of death. Granted, they would personally know the difference between good and evil by experiencing the harsh consequences of evil. Instead of just knowing joy, they would also experience sorrow. Instead of only knowing peace, they would know inner conflict. Instead of walking in innocence, they would fall into darkness and hide in shame. Instead of being able to embrace all that was good, they would contaminate all goodness with some type of perversion.

Clearly, experience will usually define who we become in our life. It colors our perspective about what constitutes life. In such cases, the senses will be determining our reality. These senses will create impressions in our life about who we are and what we are attracted to as far as obtaining some type of life through fleshly pursuits.

However, due to the fallen condition of mankind, people may experience a particular lifestyle, but rarely do they experience real life. Real life eludes them because they are unable to receive it. As a result, they pursue the different presentations of life put forth by families, education, society, and the age they live in. Each pursuit proves to be empty and disappointing.

In people's attempt to experience life, they often find themselves in an identity crisis. Nothing makes sense in their world or in their lives. They have tried to fill the vacuums of their souls with the things of the world, only to discover it all turns into vanity. They try to fill the vanity of their lives with religion or good deeds, only to discover that any sensation that may come with it lasts for a short time, making everything in life seem insignificant and useless. When the worldly and fleshly fails to add to or satisfy people, they look to others or relationships to bring meaning and purpose to their lives, only to become disillusioned and depressed.

It is in such crises that people prove to be the most vulnerable. Where or what do they look to, to come to terms with who they are and what truly constitutes life? At such uncertain times, everything seems fragile, temporary, and untrustworthy. For many to try to get their bearings they look at past experiences. Their reason is that it was during such experiences they at least were feeling alive. Even though the situation might not have been right and even confusing to their tender conscience, such experiences often become defining moments as to who they now perceive they are. Sensations of this nature not only can become defining moments in how people see themselves and life, but they often serve as a source of attraction to the flesh and tormenting confusion to people's souls.

A young woman confessed that her defining moment happened when she lost her virginity at a very young age. From that moment she felt the shame of her action, which began to define her as a tarnished, unworthy person. She struggled with the shame, but at the same time the door had been open to a fleshly attraction that had blatantly taken center stage. In her logic she perceived that since she was already "spoiled or damaged goods" she might as well go with her fleshly attractions, regardless of how such actions left her feeling. At least her flesh was temporarily satisfied, and just maybe something would come out of such fleshly relationships and experiences that would prove to be lasting and satisfying.

Scripture and example is clear, we do not need to experience something to know whether it is right or wrong. There are three witnesses that will testify to the moral status of an attitude or action. These three witnesses are our conscience, the Word of God, and the Holy Spirit. Our conscience will prick us against betraying our moral code, the Word of God will instruct us as to how to respond, and the Holy Spirit will warn us to flee and convict us if we give way to any form of wickedness.

As Christians we need to remember that our conduct will say much about our character. The Apostle Peter tells us in 2 Peter 1:4 that we have been given everything that pertains unto life and godliness. Clearly, we have the means to bring our senses under the control of the Spirit, as well as experiencing victory over the flesh, thereby, possessing and experiencing Jesus' life.

This brings us to the attitude that experiences often create in people when they are being challenged by what they have experienced. When it comes to environment people can gnash against opposition, while in the case of emphasis, any opposition will cause contempt. When challenged about their experiences, people often become insulted. After all, personal experiences have made them elite; therefore, making anyone who does not respect the validity of such happenings as being stupid.

Let us now consider how experiences influence our attractions.

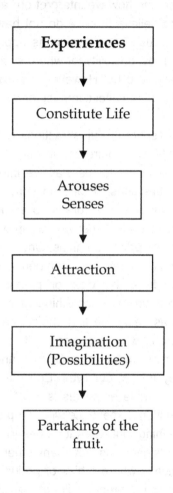

As you can see, attraction connects the senses to the imagination. Imagination clearly allows for all the possibilities in relationship to happiness and satisfaction to take hold, resulting in the person partaking of the fruit to experience life in some way.

What is your take on life? Are you experiencing it or is it deluding you as you partake of the fruits of death to feed the flesh in an attempt to find some semblance of life? Real and lasting life only comes from God through Jesus Christ.

PREFERENCE

It is important to see how attraction works in each aspect of our lives. It is clear that we determine how we interpret our attractions. Due to our fallen state we want to believe that we do not have any say or control over that which attracts us. Since attractions appear natural to us, we have a hard time taking responsibility for where such attractions mentally, emotionally, and morally lead us. However, the truth is we will be held responsible for how attractions affect, impact, or influence our disposition, attitude, and conduct.

Another important aspect of our attractions is that the environment determines what attitude we acquire about that which attracts us. Since the environment primes us as to the way we interpret our attractions, it is natural for such attractions to take on some type of emphasis or importance in our life. Since we are drawn to an attraction, it is easy to attach some type of affection to it that will stir up our senses to consider how such an attraction will add to our lives. Once our senses take center stage after experiencing an attraction, it can become our preference.

Preference begins from the view or premise that something or someone is more desirable than something or someone else. Such a preference is marked as being the first choice, causing a person to be naturally inclined towards it when a choice has to be made.

When we consider environment, emphasis, and experience we can begin to see how they impact our lives. Environment determines what will seem normal to us, while emphasis is what we will consider to be necessary for us to function. Experience will set up the tendencies we will develop towards something, but when it comes to preference we will be naturally inclined towards choosing it over any other thing, person, or way.

In a way, preference is where a bias or prejudice is attached to that which is desired. Such a preference will not tolerate any substitution or be swayed from that which is preferred.

Jesus made reference to the power and influence of preference in John 3:19-21. The one word associated with such an inclination is the word "love." Most people are naturally inclined towards their preference because they have directed some type of loyal attachment such as love towards it.

Let us consider what Jesus said about this matter in John 3:19, "And this is the condemnation, that light is come into the world, and men loved darkness rather than light, because their deeds were evil." Due to man's fallen condition, he is naturally inclined toward darkness rather than the light of God. The reason he harbors this preference is because his deeds are evil.

In John 3:20, Jesus goes on to say, "For everyone that doeth evil hateth the light, neither cometh to the light, lest his deeds should be reproved." We see where man is inclined to attach a bias when it comes to his particular darkness, and a prejudice towards the light. He desires darkness because he can hide his sin, while he hates the intrusion of any light that would reveal such matters to be foolish, rebellious, and destructive. Clearly, his inclination causes an attraction towards what he prefers.

Jesus concluded this presentation in this manner, "But he that doeth truth cometh to the light, that his deeds may be made manifest, that they are wrought in God" (John 3:21). Clearly there are two preferences or inclinations that can be seen operating in man: the preference for darkness and wickedness or the preference for light and truth. In one case the works are hidden by the darkness of wickedness in order to cover up their evil origins, and in the other case the light is embraced to ensure that all works have been inspired and brought forth by God.

The wicked inspiration behind the wrong preference is the self-life. The self-life is naturally attracted to what it perceives as its right to pursue what it is inclined towards, regardless of the moral indications or the consequences. Wicked preferences often hide behind thin veneers of "goodness" in the name of religion or philanthropy. However, these veneers are outward games and masks that are designed to keep people from seeing the darkness that will prove to be ruthless towards anyone who does not serve their purpose. The games are directed at the emotions in order to manipulate them, while the masks are meant to mentally seduce people into a different reality.

When it comes to worldview, people will gnash their teeth against that which would oppose their ideology. When emphasis is challenged, people can show contempt towards opposition, and in the case of experience, people will become easily upset or insulted when challenged in their reality. When it comes to preference, people will hate the light that exposes the darkness that is lurking in the background. Jesus explained it in this way, "If I had not come and spoken unto them, they had not had sin; but now they have no cloak for their sin. He that hateth me hateth my Father also" (John 15:22-23).

A couple of years ago the word "preference" was being used in relationship to sexual inclinations. Sexual preference outside of the moral boundaries clearly set up by God, became a means to cover up the fact that these individuals desire a particular lifestyle that Scripture would clearly rebuke and declare as being abominable. In order to justify such preferences, claims were put forth that such preferences were a matter of birth, and not a preferred lifestyle that has been chosen along the way.

Through the years I have dealt with people that have confusion as to their sexual preference. Due to the influence of environment or some type of experience in their life, they discovered that for some unknown reason they have an attraction towards that which is not considered proper to God. Instead of discerning the point of attraction such as spirit, experience, personality, abilities etc. the attraction can easily become perverted in the person's understanding.

For example, attractions and affections do not distinguish gender. However, if people do not properly discern what they are attracted to concerning an individual, their feelings or affections can become perverted, thereby, they end up attaching an unfounded bias onto it. The bias could be based on gender, race, or culture. This bias would determine the type of emphasis a person would put on the attraction. For example, I am attracted to this person because of gender and not because of spirit, personality, abilities, etc. Often times if an attraction is not properly discerned, the perversion that is present in our fallen condition can turn the attraction into a lust, leading to obsession.

If the bias is not accepted as being normal, acceptable, or religious enough by an individual's way of thinking, it will cause an identity crisis for the person. Ultimately, the chaotic experience can cause the person to define his or her person according to the attraction. For example, each of us are told by culture how we are to feel towards the opposite sex. Let's say a person finds he or she is attracted to someone who would not be considered acceptable by family, culture, or society. Perhaps the individual is attracted to the spirit of the person. Maybe, the person is attracted to the individual's outgoing personality. However, certain youthful lusts have also become stirred up, causing confusion for the person as to what or why he or she is feeling a certain way that may be considered abnormal or unacceptable.

Since the feeling does not line up to what is considered the normal order of things, confusion takes center stage. It is important to point out that to begin with, most people in their teen years enter uncharted territories when it comes to feelings, youthful lusts, and affections. These feelings or lusts take center stage when such individuals are not mature enough to recognize them in a proper way, let alone understand how they work or affect their lives. It is important to realize that without these feelings along with emotional or sexual drives, we would not be here because our world would have never been populated.

People's immature or unrealistic ideas of how they should feel about something are often based on images or overrated and inflated presentations produced by television, books, the media, and peer pressure. When they encounter feelings they do not understand, they resort to considering what they have seen, heard, or have been told about such matters. Since maturity or experience is missing from the equation, these individuals will often draw erroneous conclusions, which will end up defining them in a destructive way. For example, since I feel this way about this person, this must be my preference based on the person's gender, race, or culture. By erroneously attaching a pleasurable bias to one area, a person can turn around and attached a prejudice in the opposite direction as a means to explain the confusion and indifference he or she may feel. This indifference or lack of attraction towards what would be considered normal, morally right, or acceptable can be deceptively used to confirm in the mind of such a person that his or her present preference clearly labels and defines who he or she is in the scheme of things. These conclusions are based on nothing more than vain imaginations and unrealistic, worldly, false images.

It is important to point out that all behavior is learned. Attitude will follow behavior, and behavior will be reinforced by attitude. How we interact with others or respond to attractions is learned and reinforced. What we learn will be determined by what we are exposed to in our environment. What we become exposed to will establish what we will come into agreement with, as well as emphasize. Emphasis will bring us to a place where we will pursue the means to experience what we desire. Experience opens us up to coming into agreement with what we now have personal knowledge of. Agreement implies preference. After all, we naturally are inclined towards and will surround ourselves with what we agree with. Such a preference points to the lifestyle a person will naturally adopt.

Note that preference may lead to a lifestyle, but it does not mean it will lead to life. Bear in mind, people must be indoctrinated into darkness.

After all, the main reason people are inclined towards any darkness is because they think that they are deluded by or hiding their wicked deeds and evil ways under such a covering. Even though these individuals have been indoctrinated into believing a lie, they naturally prefer the lie to the light of truth. Additionally, they now have been indoctrinated into liking a certain lifestyle. Their natural inclination is to give way to it regardless of how perverted it might be.

Let us now consider how attractions work in light of preferences.

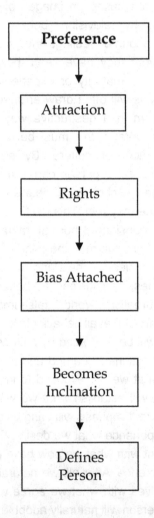

So much of what we pursue today is because we have bought some type of presentation that has indoctrinated us enough to produce a wrong premise. As we walk according to the erroneous premise through the different attractive doors of this world, darkness engulfs us as we struggle with conflicting messages, confusing feelings, and what often seems like insanity. At such times we question our own sanity because nothing makes sense. In such thinking all values are often called into question and examination. To justify the intensity behind wrong preferences, all sanity towards that which would challenge such preferences is called into questioning. Perhaps those who believe in God, morality, and decency are the abnormal ones after all. At this point good can be considered evil and evil, good.

Isaiah 5:18-23 calls perverting what is considered good by God as being evil as a time of woe. However, we can see in the days we are living that preferences are being perverted to adjust to the wickedness that is engulfing the world. We live in times that the Apostle Paul labeled as being precarious.[5] Darkness has taken center stage, and for some it is not only revealing the darkness of certain people's souls and ways, but it is causing them to go mad with power to control, obsession for a way of life that will ultimately elude them, and greed to have life on their terms.

These people will gnash against righteousness, they will show contempt towards purity, be insulted by truth, and will hate the true light of this world. They will falsely accuse those who stand for righteousness, show disdain and disrespect toward those who dare stand for what is pure, will crucify the truth, and rage against the light that will reveal their true self-serving motives. As Jesus stated, they love their own particular darkness because it allows them to pursue their wicked ways.

What is defining you as a person? Is it the dark preferences of your heart or is it the love for the true light of the world? Your attitude and fruits will ultimately tell on you.

ORIENTATION

Have you heard the latest when it comes to sexual preference? It is now called "sexual orientation." "Orientation" means to determine the tendency or direction in which a person will end up going about a

---

[5]   2 Timothy 3:1-7

matter. However, to be politically correct, the source in which I receive the meaning of "orientation" from declared that the meaning of the word does not apply to sexual orientation. If it is not applicable in this particular case, then why use this word?

As I watch the changes, finagling, and manipulations that are going on in regard to sexual orientation, I would have to conclude that the meaning and intent of the word "orientation" is clearly applicable as far as this subject. The radical people who proudly wear this handle attempt to shove what is considered as unacceptable or abominable down other people's throat to force them to accept it as being acceptable or normal.

These aggressive individuals clearly have an agenda to push their way of thinking on everyone who disagrees with them. Although such orientation is based on the darkness of delusion, these individuals present it as truth and want those who oppose them to not only agree with their darkness but to also partake of it, either in support or behavior. They want everyone to become attracted to their lifestyle as well as embrace it for themselves.

These individuals are very active and aggressive in selling this package to our society. They have infiltrated the government and education systems in order to pass bias laws, as well as indoctrinate and train our children in this behavior so that it will become their tendency or point of attraction. All of these attempts are to dull down or do away with the moral grain of any morally responsible society. These individuals are bent on and aggressive in forcing their particular lifestyle on everyone, regardless of the measure or length they have to go. For them, there is no room for disagreeing with them or having an opposite opinion. Everyone must and will agree with them or each person will be considered a hate mongrel, and prosecuted with injustice, persecuted with slander and false accusations, and silenced with hubris.

In these people's mind the freedom they have enjoyed in America to pursue and live their particular lifestyle is their platform to hypocritically deny others of the same freedom. It does not matter that what they are advocating goes against the personal moral and religious beliefs of those who do not agree with them, for in their minds, these "misinformed", "stupid" individuals must see it their way or else! In their book, if these individuals do not agree with them, they do not deserve to even breathe the same air. However, a person who is being forced against his or her will is of the same opinion still.

These people may get verbal agreements from those they intimidate, but they will never own the heart and minds of those who live according to a holy standard. They may silence those who oppose their lifestyle by being mean spirited, bullish, and hateful, but they will never do away with the holy standard that was clearly established in the Garden of Eden. They may gnash against God's Word, but in the end it will remain standing in judgment against them. They may try to wipe out every bit of opposition, but in the end they will unmercifully judge themselves.

The problem is not that these people are being denied their right to live any way they choose; rather, the problem that they are having is that there is a mirror that has existed from the very beginning that reveals that their particular way is that of darkness. Regardless of what is being said or done to redefine their way as being good, their particular lifestyle stands in complete opposition to the standard clearly established by the Creator of heaven and earth.

This standard has been made obvious. A mirror has been erected in the midst of darkness as to what is considered morally right and wrong according to the just Law and judgments of the Judge of the universe. This mirror will clearly reflect the light or darkness that minds, hearts, and lifestyles are emitting. These individuals hate this mirror because it will not adjust to their preferred lifestyle. This mirror causes resentment because it will not justify or tolerate their practices so they can merrily go down into the abyss of damnation in total delusion and denial. It will not be clouded by their rhetoric or their attempts to wipe out the immovable standard established by their Maker, along with those who dare advocate it.

This mirror not only challenges these people, but it causes them to know the truth about their preference. Their only hope is that the God who erected the mirror does not exist. However, if He does exist, in the end they will personally own such preferences. They will be held accountable as all matters are judged by the righteous standard of His Law. The delusion and justifications these individuals have hidden behind to condone and promote their particular lifestyle as being normal and acceptable will be stripped away, revealing that their preference for this particular lifestyle was a matter of personal choice. Granted, their environment may have influenced them, but they still chose the attitude or way in which they would live. No one forced them to adopt the way; rather, they chose to make it a personal preference.

Even though these individuals advocate and insist that their way is light (truth, right, and acceptable), they must question why they must force it down others throats? Why must they insist it becomes everyone's light if such a lifestyle can stand on its own merits? And, why would it matter if someone agrees or disagrees with it? If these people want to change the laws of this nation, that is their right to do so; but if they want to change the Law of God by changing the definition of marriage, that is another story. Marriage is based on the definition and Law of God, and it will remain so regardless of these people's aggressive attempts to change it in the courts of the land and in the courts of public opinion. It does not matter if these individuals have the backing of immoral Hollywood, the liberal leadership of this nation, and the insane, immoral judges of this court system, God's Law and Word remains unchanged.

This is true for all matters concerning the kingdom of God. The Law and principles of God are set in the annals of eternity. They are moral, just, right, and eternal. They are not debatable, negotiable, or subject to any adjustment or change. People can set out to orientate according to personal preferences, the world, and even religion to determine what we become attracted to, but the Rock of Ages, along with His Word, remains unchanged in it views, stands, and judgments.

When we consider orientation we can see where a person will take on a tendency. They can see the change of lifestyle as becoming the essence of what constitutes life. When opposed, they can respond by rejecting the concerns of any opposition, and if their spirit is hateful they can also set out to destroy any disagreement or opposition.

Let us now consider how orientation works.

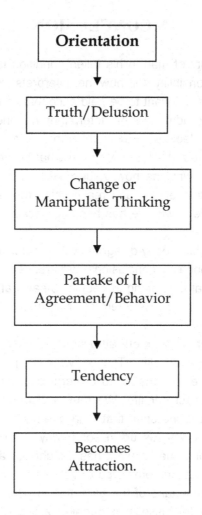

Notice how orientation in spiritual matters is often based on a delusion that will cause a person to live in denial about his or her thinking. Its goal is to manipulate a person's thinking so that he or she will partake of something that is contrary to his or her will or moral fiber. Once there is agreement, the behavior can be changed to embrace the tendency of being attracted towards the lifestyle that is being promoted.

IN CONCLUSION

The harsh reality of man in his fallen condition is that he does not want to take responsibility for how he interprets or responds to his attractions. He does not want to be held accountable for his preferences nor does he want to admit that he determines his orientation. He wants to believe that his ideology is the right frame of reference in which to judge morality, and that he had no part in what he ended up putting an estimation on as to what he now values. He wants to believe that his experiences constitute elitism and reality, his preferences are right for him, and his lifestyle is who he has become because of factors beyond his control.

However, the Bible clearly disagrees with the above conclusions. The wrong ideology, emphasis, conclusions, preferences, and lifestyles are a matter of the sin that is reigning in people. Clearly, attractions come out at different points, but how we interpret or let them influence us rests at our door.

The truth is that we think our attractions will add, determine, qualify, clarify, and influence our life. That is why we pursue them without realizing that we are responsible to discern, determine, discipline, and control how they affect our life. We must recognize that what initially attracts us up front is the spirit that is in operation in the environment. Since the spirit is stirring us up in some way, we often see the need to put some type of value on what has caught our attention instead of discerning it. After putting some type of value on it, we often decide we must experience or partake of the attraction in some way. Often times, we see our pursuit to possess or partake of the attraction as a right, attaching some type of bias to it. From there we can become entrapped into a lifestyle pattern that will orientate us into delusion and destruction.

As Christians, we have been born again with the Spirit of God and by the powerful impact of His Word. Since we have His Spirit in us we will be attracted to the spiritual matters of the Lord's kingdom.[6] We should be desirous in knowing, pleasing, worshipping, and serving Him according to His truth. In fact, nothing else will make sense, and all matters outside

---

[6]   1 Corinthians 2:9-14

of this realm will seem vain and useless. We can only accomplish this if we begin to own and discipline our attractions at every level of our life.[7]

I have discovered that there is a tremendous liberty in taking one's life back from the lies, entanglements, and pursuits of selfish and worldly attractions. There is such victory to be found over the flesh, the world, and Satan if we would only choose to embrace, know, and love the truth about the matters of heaven.

Let us now consider the complete picture of how the different influences in our life determine our attractions and how our attractions will determine how we regard God and life. Consider where you might fit in the following table. Do you need to repent and take back your life, or do you need to recognize a troubled area that with the help of the Lord can be easily overcome as you take responsibility for how the different attractions of life have been affecting you?

---

[7]   If you would like to learn more about this subject, along with other matters that are associated with it, see the author's books, *The Manuel for the Single Christian Life*, located in Volume 4 of her foundational series, and *The Issues of Life*, in the 5th volume of her foundational series.

Environment	Emphasis	Experience	Preference	Orientation
Worldview	Estimation (Value)	What Constitutes Life	Attraction	Truth or Delusion
Influence	Attraction	Senses	Rights	Change or Manipulate Thinking
Philosophy	Affection	Attraction	Bias Attached	Partake of it
Attraction	Lust	Imagination	Inclination	Take on Tendency
Determines Frame of Reference	Becomes An Obsession	Partaking Of the Fruit	Defines Person	Point of Attraction
(Gnash against Truth)	(Shows contempt towards Truth)	(Will be insulted by Truth)	(Will hate Truth)	(Will try to destroy Truth)
Affects Mind (Necessary for life)	Affects Emotions (Must possess to have life)	Affects the Flesh (Natural for life)	Affects the Self-Life (Normalcy of life)	Affects Lifestyle (Serves as the essence of life)

5

LETTING GO OF THE PAST

INTRODUCTION

One of the issues I wrestled with was why, after putting their shoulders to the plow, Christians end up looking back to their old life. Being human I understand some of the dynamics of people looking back to their old ways. After all, I have occasionally been guilty of cranking my head back in that direction. However, Jesus takes such an action as being a very serious offence when it comes to His kingdom.

In this small presentation, my goal is to address some of the major reasons why God's people would commit such an offence and what it will take to make peace with our past. After all, we have examples in God's Word that reveal the reasons people fail to maintain a forward momentum in their Christian walk, as well as how they can be healed and equipped to go forward in their lives.

THE CHALLENGE TO LET GO

In order to understand why people look back to their old life, we must consider why people would see their old existence as offering some measure of importance in relationship to their present situation. One of the reasons people keep looking back to their old life is because they have not really let go of it. There are various reasons why people have failed to let go of the past, but one of the reasons has to do with *unresolved issues*.

There is much conflict in some people's minds about their past. There are those who feel that they have greatly missed something in their past that continues to define their dysfunctional present. They reason that if they had all the right elements working together in their past that they would not be the unhappy, unfulfilled, or miserable person they are in the present.

Such individuals try to resolve the inner conflict by seeking out the missing link to close what they consider to be the gaping hole left in their lives. For some it is a relationship and for others it might be material things or recognition. However, the hard reality is that it would not really matter if these people had all the right elements working together in their past because they are still making the decisions as to how life will affect them in the present. For some of these individuals, the past is an excuse for their wrong attitude or conduct. In such cases people in this category end up divorcing themselves from present reality to avoid taking accountability for the type of person they are currently becoming.

What each of us must realize is that the past will affect us in some way, but we will individually determine if we are going to let it define who we become. For most people the past often proves disappointing. In fact, these people can always mark some great loss or a point where a determination was made to somehow control the affects life might have on them in the future. However, people find themselves bogged down in the mire of disillusionment as matters never really seemed to change for them.

When people are bogged down emotionally by the past, they will not have the fortitude to go forward. Hence, these individuals find themselves in a state of limbo. As they hold onto the past in order to seek out the missing link, they fail to grow emotionally. Emotional immaturity prevents them from realistically facing the present in order to influence the direction of their future.

Since these individuals are bogged down, they are unable to go forward in their lives. After all, you cannot hold onto the past and expect to go forward in the present. The reason for this is because the past is opposite of the present. The present stands as a crossroad between the past and the future. Decisions must be made about how we interpret the past. Such interpretations will influence our present attitudes. Will we live in a state of perpetual pity or will we learn the lessons of our past to ensure integrity and wisdom in our present to walk forward in our lives?

Why is it so hard for people to let go of a past that enslaves, wounds, or hinders them from discovering their potential? The truth is that the past is what we are used to, the present is uncertain, and the future is unknown. Even though the past is uncomfortable, it is familiar. Although it may have been hurtful, it can serve as an excuse for those who do not want to face the present in light of coming to maturity in their lives and taking the necessary responsibilities to properly handle the matters of life.

When we examine these elements, as believers, we must recognize that the past does not require us to have any faith. Faith enables us to walk in the present in light of the future. It is active; therefore, able to possess what has been promised. The writer of Hebrews 6:12 confirms this, "That ye be not slothful, but followers of them who through faith and patience inherit the promises."

In considering this Scripture, we can begin to see that those who live in the past are slothful towards the present, and inactive about walking out a matter according to the saints of the past who now serve as our examples. Clearly, we may regard the past in light of examples, but we must not longingly look back or regard the past as that which now defines our present life and the future hope. We cannot place our past in front of us if we are planning to follow the examples of those who left all behind to follow God into a new life.

It is through faith and patience that we inherit the promises of God. However, when people are in limbo it is due to a lack of faith. Since a person is not waiting in faith according to God's plan, there will be no need for patience to be established. Obviously, these individuals have no need to inherit promises because they never have left go of their fantasies of the past. They are not looking to inherit such promises, but their desire is to do the impossible by changing their past, thereby, changing the type of person they have become or are allowing themselves to become. Sadly, such people will never possess any promises or realize their potential in the kingdom of God.

In order to understand why people longingly look back at the old, we must scripturally consider those who did look back. Keep in mind, these people would not let go of their past in order to walk towards their future inheritance in order to possess it.

The first people we are going to consider are the children of Israel. There were various times that they looked back to Egypt. Even though they had been slaves in Egypt, they would often imply that slavery was far better than following Jehovah God. The first time they looked back to Egypt was due to fear. They were afraid of dying in the wilderness.[1]

Life is precious, but it cannot be discovered or lived if there is bondage and slavery. The Lord wanted His people to understand the essence of real life by knowing Him so they would love, worship, and follow Him. He wanted them to have the liberty to inherit the Promised Land.

God shows so much mercy when He is delivering His people from the old. He allows circumstances to bring them to a state of desperation to make them aware and receptive of their need for Him to deliver them. Upon deliverance He baptizes them. In other words, He separates them from the influences of the old in order to shut them in with Him.

I can recall when the Lord was calling me into full time service. I had been deeply rooted into the community where I had spent almost 25 years of my life. He used some trying circumstances to bring me to a place of desperation where I cried out for His deliverance from what seemed to be my baptism of fire. I could see where the adversity was consuming all attachments to this place I had known as my home.

As I was leaving this community for the last time as one of its official residents, I felt as if a steel door had closed behind me. There was no turning back; I could only go forward. I realized that in His mercy God had used circumstances to change how I regarded my hometown. It was no longer a safe haven that served as my home and point of identification. It had become a strange, uncomfortable place. Clearly, it became obvious that it was time to move on.

Through the years I have looked back at what was, but not in a longing way. I do not see my former residence as a home, but a place in which I had visited for a season. There, I had some learning experiences and even times of personal growth. However, it proved to not be the home that I was searching for. My home is a city made with the hands of God. In spite of the promises of God in regard to my journey here, nothing will outweigh the eternal glory that is awaiting me at my real residence.

---

[1]   Exodus 16:2-4

Every Christian should perceive that the present world is not the home he or she is searching for. Granted, as believers we may be visitors passing through, but as we grow in our relationship with God, the world will become strange to us, causing us to become pilgrims in search of our real home.

The children of Israel had cried out for deliverance in desperation. God had heard and began the process of cutting and consuming all of their ties with Egypt through judgment. He then called them out of Egypt, parted the Red Sea, and they passed through it on dry ground. The Apostle Paul stated in 1 Corinthians 10:1-2 that the Red Sea experience was a type of baptism for the children of Israel. However, once their baptism was finished, the sea closed in on the pursuing Egyptians, clearly shutting the door to the children of Israel's old life.

Even though the door was closed, the children of Israel had no vision beyond their old bondage. In the wilderness their new beginning appeared as if it would mark their demise rather than a new life. They seemed to forget that they were simply passing through the barren wasteland to their real home, which was into the land God had promised Abraham 400 years earlier.

In a way they were coming to a place of demise. However, it was not a death to the promise of God, but death to the old way of thinking and being. These people may have come out of Egypt, but the ways of Egypt were very much entrenched in their thinking. They still thought and acted as slaves. Obviously, slaves would never be able to possess and maintain the land. In order to embrace the new that was yet before them, they had to be prepared to be a nation of people who understood that they were to be a peculiar people set apart by the One they were to worship, follow, and serve. This peculiarity would serve as the secret behind these people's power and success as a nation.

When the Red Sea closed in behind the children of Israel, they did not realize that they were being shut in with God. Granted, it was a barren wilderness, but they were still shut in with God. He would teach them to depend on Him for leadership, spiritual inspiration, and needs.

When the children of Israel faced the wilderness without any obvious provision, they felt God had played a terrible joke on them. They claimed that they would rather die as slaves in Egypt than die in the presence of their God. After all, they at least had some form of life as slaves, while in the wilderness there was no apparent hope for life.

Sadly, people become comfortable in their old way even though it has no real life, purpose, or hope in it. This is true for those who are slaves to sin. Even though the darkness of it is tormenting and unfulfilling, at least they know what to expect. Even though they may eat in their slavery that which is mingled with the gall of bitterness, they still have to be maintained in such a life by their master. Although they may desire freedom from slavery, they become fearful about the unknown elements that freedom might bring.

Clearly, responsibilities change when status changes. Even though freedom from the bitterness of slavery is desired, the changes that come with it are frightening to those who have become quite accustomed to their present state.

Much of our attitude is influenced by our fallen, perverted view of God and life. Our conclusions reveal that we have everything backwards. There is no life in spiritual slavery, but there is life wherever God is present. Granted, such life might not be obvious in such places as the wilderness, but it is available to those who by faith are willing to search it out.

The children of Israel kept their former life in Egypt as an option in case it did not work out with God. Clearly, they had not let go of their old life. It was still serving as some type of security blanket that could be brought out of moth balls when times proved overwhelming or frightening.

When we consider the "old life" we must recognize that it is an extension of the self-life. The children of Israel were emphasizing their self-life; rather than their deliverance and future hope of the Promised Land. In other words, they were trying to maintain a right to life according to what they were used to. Even though it was bitter slavery, they still had their self-life.

Self-life will take center stage when people long for the old ways. It is at this stage that people begin to complain, cry, pout, or fall into self-pity and despair. They will claim that their present life is unfair or that they have been betrayed. This is when people will sit down in the middle of their journey and protest about their situation.

Jesus' first command to His disciples was to deny self of its right to have life on its terms. Without denying the right of self, people will fail to disown their old life, preventing them from completely walking away from it. Unless people deny self by disowning their present life of bondage and vanity, they will never be able to follow their Lord into the life He has secured for them.

The children of Israel did not have to worry about surviving their journey; they needed to worry about whether they had what it would take to finish the course. This is true for every disciple of Jesus. The spiritual journey will mean nothing unless he or she finishes the course to truly possess the promises of God.

SELECT MEMORY

It is interesting to follow the children of Israel through the wilderness. Their old life was always on the back burner as an option if their situation with God did not work out for them. This pointed to the harsh reality that they had not let go of the past in order to follow God into their future.

Their big downfall did not come from their departure from Egypt or because the Promised Land rested in the future. The real challenge for the children of Israel proved to be all those steps in between Egypt and the Promised Land.

It is amazing what the daily walk will produce along the way for those who have not let go of their past. It will develop what we know as a select memory. In the first situation the Jewish people forgot the bitter taste of slavery. When challenged, they actually preferred its taste to possessing the eternal God. They forgot because their self-life with its so-called "right" and "instinct" to live, took front stage, drowning out the real reality of Egypt.

This is a challenge for all of us. We tend to forget those things that would bring the proper perspective to a matter. After all, we want our own way, and somehow we logically deduce that we have the right to have our way. In such times, we tend to forget why we are in the wilderness. The wilderness for each of us as believers is to serve as a place of escape from the old in order to be established in the new. However, when we become uncomfortable in our unusual situation, we can only see our present plight in light of what was comfortable, while forgetting the bitterness or nightmare of it. At such times we choose to forget the details in order to focus in on what we consider to be our present giant of adversity.

God sent the bread to the children of Israel to reveal that He was their provider, no matter where they may be. Obviously, if He does not bless man's attempts or provide for him in the barren wilderness, he will die.

In the second incident it was not the matter of forgetting what Egypt was like; rather it was about remembering what they liked about their former place of bondage. The children of Israel had their needs provided. Every day, except the Sabbath, the bread of heaven was waiting for them to gather it for their daily sustenance. It was satisfying, but to the children of Israel it became boring.

We all can relate with these individuals. Who likes eating the same thing every day? Such drudgery can be hard to bear when a person has tasted the things of the world. When we desire the things of the world it is because we have partaken of the fruits of the world: that knowledge of what we would consider to be good or not acceptable. The different tastes present a contrast, but they are designed to appeal to the flesh, not the spirit. They contain the seeds of death.

We would all like to taste something that reminds us of the good "old" times that are associated to the pleasant aspects of the past. However such memories are based on the flesh. As Christians, we know the things associated with the flesh are corrupt.[2] Since the flesh looks to the world to feed its appetites, these things also prove to be temporary.

It tells us in Numbers 11:5-10 that the children of Israel fell to lusting after the old tastes of their former life. They remembered the fish, the cucumbers, melons, leeks, onions, and garlic. Now notice they did not remember their former tastes until they fell into lusting. Obviously, something stirred their memory, causing discontentment and ingratitude in them towards God's provision. In this discontentment, they showed contempt towards what God had provided.

These people's attitude caused the Lord to become angry and Moses to be displeased. Moses even asked the Lord to kill him because the discontentment of the people was too much to bear.

Consider how the children of Israel forgot their former life in the first situation, but remembered some of it in their second incident. In the first

---

[2]   Galatians 6:7-8

situation, they did not have food, but in the second incident they had sufficient and satisfying food, but it did not cater to their fleshly desires.

Let us just consider for a moment what the children of Israel forgot to remember, and what they should have recalled to keep their present situation in the right perspective. In the first situation they were afraid of dying, but they forgot that Pharaoh was determined to wipe them out as a people. After leaving Egypt after the judgment of the first born, most likely if Pharaoh had caught up with them in his state, he would have probably had them slaughtered, especially the leadership. Remember, he also had ordered the killing of every male Jewish baby that was born to ensure population control. If he had been successful, the women would have been integrated into the Egyptian society to wipe out their identity as a separate people. In a sense, these people were selfish enough to value the vanity of their present life to the survival of future generations.

In the second situation they remembered the food of Egypt, but forgot that they ate such food in the bitterness of slavery. They had sufficient and satisfying food in the wilderness, but they preferred the temporary tastes of the world. The bread was provided by God in abundance in the desert, while in Egypt as slaves they provided the bread for their masters to maintain a certain lifestyle.

Clearly, we forget our bondage, while remembering what brought temporary pleasure to our flesh. However, this is select memory. We forget so we can emphasize our right to life on our terms, in order to remember what will serve our fleshly appetites. Such justification will allow us to pursue the old life.

In the second situation the children of Israel were focusing on the flesh. When we focus on something we put importance on it. In other words, it becomes important to us; therefore, we must pursue it regardless of the cost.

God sent the quail but in the end they became a source of judgment and not a blessing. The meat would become loathsome to the children of Israel because they despised the Lord for what He had provided. Instead of satisfying their soul, the meat brought leanness to them.

"Leanness" of this nature points to a soul that has been left with very little in the end. It is like gorging yourself on something you really like, then in the end you are not only sick because of your indulgence, but you feel more miserable and empty. However, what can you fill the misery and emptiness with because what you thought would satisfy the longing or appetite turned out to be disappointing?

This is the harsh reality of the flesh. Pursuing it will not only leave your soul lean, but it will eventually lead to death. This is why Jesus' second command to His disciples was to pick up their cross. The cross points to mortifying the flesh in order to become crucified to the world's influence upon it. It will also discipline one's focus so that the Lord can determine what should be important to those who follow Him.

Are you carrying your cross so that it is ready to offer up the flesh and ensure unresponsiveness towards the world's attractions?

CONSIDER LOT'S WIFE

Jesus often used examples to reinforce a point. In Luke 17:26-36, He is talking about His second coming. He relates that the spiritual condition of people would be like those in Noah's day before the great flood came and destroyed all of them except for Noah and his family.

After mentioning Noah, He goes on to use the days of Lot as another example. Lot lived in the wicked city of Sodom. Much like the days of Noah, the people of Sodom were busy giving into their fleshly appetites. There seemed no boundaries to the people's evil except for the day that fire and brimstone rained down on the city and destroyed all the people, except for Lot and his family.

Jesus was clarifying that when He comes for the second time, wickedness will abound in the same way. People will be partying instead of repenting. They will be justifying grave wickedness, instead of wearing sackcloth to express the shame and disgrace for such ways. They will pursue every type of wicked imagination instead of being vexed over it and separating from it.

Jesus is assuring the hearers that just like in the days of Noah and Lot, judgment will also fall. The challenge is the same as it was for Noah and Lot. When God instructs His people to leave all behind and seek the ark of His safety, they must not hesitate to flee the judgment that is coming. Then he makes this simple statement in Luke 17:32, "Remember Lot's wife."

We do not know the name of Lot's wife, but her example is ever before us to soberly consider. And, what is her example? She looked back to the judgment falling on Sodom and turned into a pillar of salt. Granted, as believers we are called to be the salt of the earth, but not a pillar of salt that stands judged for future generations to consider the actual folly of our action.[3]

Why did Lot's wife look back? After all, the angels had delivered her out of the doomed city. You would think that she would be grateful to be alive and would obey the angels' instruction to not look back at the wickedness being judged by our holy God. But, she did look back and became an example of what not to do when judgment has been pronounced on that which is doomed and is actually being carried out.

Let us consider Lot's example to understand why his wife looking back would serve as such an offence against God. We know that Lot's spirit was vexed over the sin of Sodom.[4] If the wickedness was so offensive to Lot, how great was Sodom's wickedness? Granted, it had been the home for Lot's family, but he was not comfortable in the midst of such wickedness. It caused distress and anguish for him. Obviously, he did not see it as home, but simply a place where he lived.

The truth is that like Lot's wife, people look back at what is being judged or will be judged because they are at home with sin. Granted, there is implication that family members remained behind. Once again, we must love God more than our family. We cannot afford to be judged with family members that refuse to leave the cesspools of the world. Surely, there will be sorrow for lost souls, but not for that which already lays in spiritual ruin.

It was clear that sin does not bother people who are comfortable with it. They are not hot or cold towards sin. It simply is what it is, and it is no big deal in the scheme of things. Clearly, Lot's wife was desensitized about sin. She most likely loved the wicked lifestyle provided by Sodom and longed for it, even though it was being judged. Sodom was her home; therefore, it was where her heart belonged.[5]

Heart points to our affections as to what we treasure. Hence enters Jesus' stern warning in Luke 9:62, "And Jesus said unto him, No man,

---

[3] Matthew 5:13

[4] 2 Peter 2:6-8

[5] Matthew 6:19-21

having put his hand to the plough, and looking back is fit for the kingdom of God."

Lot's wife had set her affections on Sodom; therefore, she was judged along with her wicked city. The fact that she turned back revealed that she preferred the wickedness of Sodom, no matter what a stench it had become to God. She was given a chance for pardon and deliverance, but she chose Sodom's fate when she looked back.

This is a problem for some Christians as well. They hold onto their old life because their affections are loyal to their past life in some way, whether it be because of family members, a lifestyle, or the tastes and sounds that made impressions in their memories. However, the world has already been judged. It stands doomed, and it is only a matter of time before judgment is poured out on it. If these individuals do not take the measures to flee the judgment coming on that which is associated with the world, they will partake of its judgment.

We need to remember we are living in days like Noah, and in a civilization like Sodom. Various judgments are clearly gathering from all corners of the world. Like Lot's wife, when challenged or instructed to leave behind that which is going to be judged, how many of us will end up looking back at our Sodom because for whatever reason, we were at home in it's cesspool of wickedness?

It is vital that as believers we make our decision about whether we are going to look back. If we do look back, we could very well become locked in the judgment. Such judgment implies that people have not really let go of the wickedness, and that it still holds them captive in some way. Judgment will end with such individuals becoming pillars who might mark the folly of the foolish, but they will never make any eternal difference.

For this reason the Apostle Paul instructed believers to set their affections on things above and not on the things of this earth.[6] The purpose for setting our affections in such a way is because the heart will naturally follow our affections.

What does your heart say about what you treasure?

---

[6]   Colossians 3:2

I WANT TO FOLLOW YOU

It is easy to tell the Lord we want to follow Him. However, the Lord revealed three very powerful worldly influences that prevent His followers from totally consecrating themselves to Him. It is true it is easy to look at these examples and become critical of these individuals who show some form of unbelief, but the truth is that there is a cost in following Jesus.

"Cost" implies that there is a personal price tag that is going to affect a person in such a way that he or she will not easily forget what it did cost to possess the prize. In fact, most of us start off with a sentimental notion about following Jesus. We relate this notion with how it is going to make us feel or look in the end. However, such a notion is fickle and will not withstand adversity when it is challenged with the harshness of reality of the discipline Christian life.

Some people understood this cost and had no desire to pay it. One of the most obvious individuals who had no desire to pay the price was the rich young ruler in Matthew 19:16-26. He sought out Jesus to find out what it would cost him to inherit eternal life. Jesus basically told Him that to inherit eternal life he would have to keep the commandments. Note, Jesus did not say obey the law, but keep the commandments. According to *Strong's Exhaustive Concordance,* "keep" in this text implies to guard (the predominate place they are to have in a person's life), watch (they must be a person's focus to ensure he or she does not leave the path), and serve as the person's strict boundaries.

When Jesus instructed him to keep the commandments, the rich young ruler asked him which commandments should he keep. Most people, especially a Jewish man in that day, would know that the Law required them to keep all of the commandments. Perhaps such individuals do not understand the intent or spirit behind the commandments, but they do know what the ten major commandments are in the Torah. Jesus actual quoted five of the commandments, and ended with summarizing them in the commandment to love one's neighbor as him or herself.

One could debate as to why Jesus quoted the commandments He did, however, I believe it was to set the young man up in order to expose his real spiritual condition. The reason I say this is because the young man was able to claim that he had kept those particular commandments from his youth.

However, there were other commandments I feel this young man had failed to keep. Jesus knew his life and was about to put His finger on the commandments he had broken. In fact, I believe he was breaking the first two commandments up front, and possibly was guilty of breaking the last commandment. The first two had to do with idolatry, having no other gods before Jehovah God and erecting an image to be worshipped. The last one had to do with coveting. This young man was worshipping his wealth and had erected the image of a particular lifestyle that was not only attached to such wealth, but would demand devotion and worship that produced the environment of coveting in his heart.

Jesus put His finger on what held this young's man heart, and it was not God. We can criticize the children of Israel and Lot's wife, but many times we do not know what really holds our heart. But, our Lord does, and He will require us to let go of our points of worldly, idolatrous reliance that we covet in order to follow Him into eternal life. It will be at this time that we will discover how much we covet that particular part of our life. Even though letting go of such a covetous way or part of our life would be our reasonable service in order to follow Jesus, it would be regarded as a supreme sacrifice on our part. Such a sacrifice could easily be considered as something too great to offer up, even if it meant finding and possessing eternal life. Like Lot's wife it all comes down to what we truly value.

In most cases the Lord will ask us to give up the worldly or self-serving ways or parts of our lifestyle. We can see this in similar examples of people in Scripture who would not let go of their old lifestyle to partake of a heavenly inheritance. These examples can be found in the parable of the great supper in Luke 14:15-24.

We know at the end of this age the Lord will throw a great supper known as the Wedding Supper of the Lamb.[7] Up until this supper takes place in the future, the invitation has been going out to all who will hear and respond to Jesus' invitations. If they hunger or thirst for that which is living, righteous, and eternal, they will accept His invitation and they will come to Him. If they need forgiveness, rest, or peace, they will come to Him and partake of His life, receive His salvation, and know His leadership and protection.

---

[7]   Revelation 19:7-10

We see individuals being invited to this supper, but they claimed that they had more important matters to take care of. To one, he had to check out a piece of ground he purchased. I don't know about you, but I would not purchase ground I had not first checked out.

The next one refused the invitation because he had failed to prove five oxen he had purchased. Again, we see the same lame excuse as the first man, only it had to do with the beast of the field, rather than land.

Let us consider the third excuse. He had married a wife and could not come. Did this mean he just married? If so, why was he not with her in the first place? Being married, for most people, does not prevent them from accepting an invitation to come to other events, but it can serve as an excuse for why some never get real about their life in Christ. These individuals were covering up the lack of honorable character with worldly excuses that ultimately exposed their real preference towards the matters of the world. Clearly, there was no preference towards the one who sent forth the invitation.

According to the parable, the master of the house that sent forth the invitation became angry, and instructed his servants to go to the poor, maimed, lame, and blind and invite them to the supper. He also stated that those who refused His invitation would not taste of his supper. We see Jesus went to those who were poor in spirit. He knew they would be open and receptive to hear His invitation to come and receive. James 2:5 summarized it the best, "Hearken, my beloved brethren, Hath not God chosen the poor of this world rich in faith, and heirs of the kingdom which he hath promised to them that love him?"

It is important that as Christians we understand what our real responsibility is towards the world. We must expose our personal priorities in order to ensure that we are prepared to accept Jesus' invitation to come, or His call to follow Him. People's excuses for failing to accept His invitation or putting off following Him are the same. Granted, they have different scenarios set up, but it comes down to investments (oxen), inheritance (land), and identity (wife). For instance, in Luke 9:57-61, there are three individuals who desired to adhere to Jesus' call to follow Him. The possible obstacles and reasons for failing to follow are clearly brought out in these examples.

In the first incident, the man tells Jesus that he will go wherever Jesus goes. Such a declaration is commendable, but Jesus' statement would cause any "wannabe follower" to consider the cost he or she would have to pay. A person would have to leave the normal life behind. The normal life represents a lifestyle with all of its possible investments. Jesus' reality check is clear. A person could possibly be required to leave the normal life behind with all of his or her worldly investments in order to follow Him.

In the second situation, Jesus actually calls a person to follow Him. Notice the first one volunteered to follow Jesus, but in this second case Jesus calls this person to follow Him. People will follow Jesus for three reasons: 1) out of ignorant zeal, 2) Jesus calls the person to follow, and/ or 3) a person follows out of obedience because he or she loves Him.

In the first case, zeal without real knowledge proves to be like a flash in the pan.[8] As long as the zeal is present the person will be enthusiastic. As soon as the zeal wears off so does the passion, revealing that such a person possesses a fickle commitment. In the second case Jesus' call becomes a test that will expose the real person's point of reliance or misguided loyalty. The final scenario is what produces a true disciple of Jesus; when a person follows out of love and obedience.

When Jesus called the second person, he was willing to go, but first he had to bury his father. This seems rational enough, but Jesus stated that he needed to let the dead bury the dead; and that his real responsibility was to go and preach the kingdom of God. The real issue is that the father was not yet dead and waiting around for the event represented wasted opportunities when it came to the kingdom of God. There are always those around who would take care of the matters of this present world.

The second incident also points to inheritance. All that is attached to the world is dead. There is no reason or purpose in the world or in the activities associated with it. Even though some type of inheritance may be attached to the world, it also will prove to be vain in light of the life that will be realized in relationship to the heavenly inheritance. Jesus was asking this man to choose that which is living, worthy, and greater and let the world carry out its own activities.

In the final example the man told the Lord he would follow him, but first let him go home and bid his family farewell. Family represents worldly identity. Such family can cause the greatest temptation or hindrance

---

[8]   Romans 10:2

when it comes to following Jesus. Family members will usually use any means to become a person's reason for not selling out to Jesus. Jesus made reference to the possible entanglements families can have on us when He made this statement in Luke 9:62, ". . . No man, having put his hand to the plough, and looking back, is fit for the kingdom of God."

The truth is that any of these three issues can be used as excuses and/or hindrances from following Jesus. As Christians, we must consecrate our life completely to Christ. In order to do this we must flee worldly involvement, attachments, and claims that would pull us back into the world's web, and consecrate all to follow Jesus into a new life.

In order to consecrate our lives, we must not look back. To look back allows us to be tempted, become confused as to our responsibilities, and be hindered from fulfilling our purpose in the kingdom of God. It again points to what or who holds the affections of our hearts.

This is why Jesus stated that we have to deny ourselves from looking back at the old, crucify the old in order to prevent it from serving as a platform for the world or giving it any audience, and follow Jesus into a new life that will appear strange and foreign to those who belong to the present age.

How have you responded to Jesus' invitation and call? Did you excuse yourself away, put some type of condition on it before you respond, or did you respond by consecrating yourself?

If you are following Him, are you proving to be fickle because you have zeal without knowledge, or are you trying to tie up some lose ends before you consecrate yourself? Perhaps you are trying to prepare your family so you won't lose their support, but such attempts have the capacity of entangling you back into the world.

MAKING PEACE
WITH THE PAST

A friend commented on the fact that she had a terrible time understanding how God could forget past sins, and reckon them as if they never existed. We have a tendency to consider God in light of how we struggle with our past sins. It is not easy to forget sin when it leaves scars behind, whether they are mental (guilty conscience), emotional (broken heart), or spiritual (wounded spirit).

As my friend and I discussed the matter, we came to two important conclusions. The first one is that God *chooses* to forget our past offences.[9] However, for people, we must choose to not remember such matters of the past. We cannot give such memories audience because they will irritate raw places that have not been healed by God, and reopen those areas where accusations from the enemy have hit effectively, making us targets at vulnerable times. We cannot change the past, but we can change how we allow it to impact us. If there are past sins, failures, or tormenting memories, we need to lay them at the cross in a humble spirit, with a repentant heart to receive healing and restitution. We need to choose to believe that we have received a full pardon from the Judge of heaven and earth, and have been restored.

The second aspect of God's character is that He does all things well. In other words, unresolved issues of the past never cling to Him for His ways are perfect. He has no regrets for He does all things in the framework of what is honorable and eternal. There is no guilt or lamentation over missed opportunities for He keeps His words and promises. He does not look back and speculate about the "if only's" or the "what ifs" in life. He does not seek to open doors that have been closed by time and change.

It is because of these two reasons so many people will not let go of the past. The writer of Hebrews speaks of those things that easily beset us in our spiritual race.[10] We need to lay such hindering aspects of our lives aside and become intense in focusing on the finish line. We must learn to let go of the past in order to live in the present.

To let go of the past, we have to let go of those tormenting regrets of the past. Regrets can prove unbearable. I know of individuals who make present decisions based on avoiding any possible regrets. They fail to see that they are still living in the present in light of potential regrets.

In our humanity we cannot forget the offences of the past. Granted, we may choose to forgive such offences, but there are times when present challenges or situations can drudge up former offences from the recesses of our mind to be brought to the forefront to be once again played on the screens of our minds. The impact such offences can

---

9   Psalm 103:12; Micah 7:18-20; 1 John 1:9
10   Hebrews 12:1-2

have on us can vary as to how fresh the wound is or how deep or raw it remains.

God may choose to forget offences, but for man it points to the reality that he fails to do all things right. He often fails to heed warnings, do right in uncomfortable situations, or recognize the opportunities that are before him. Therefore, what follows man into his present reality are those tormenting regrets that turn into unresolved issues that constantly mock the present and threatens to haunt the future. Regrets can cause people to rage at the present reality, deny the future reality, and miss the present opportunity. As the fear, anger, and torment of past regrets seize people in light of their present reality the cloud of despair can cause matters to become unpleasant.

The truth is that for such individuals the present will often represent failures and be tarnished by missed opportunities. The reality of it is that so many miss the opportunity afforded them in the present moments. The real opportunities people miss occur when they fail to live or experience the life God has given them. They fail to see such opportunities and moments as a gift. When they look back at the missed opportunities they simply acquire more regrets that they end up carrying with them into the next day or situation.

People need to quit living in light of the past as they live from one situation to another. Such people miss the moments and opportunities to embrace the small gifts that life will allot to each of us. I have watched so many people rage against what is, try to manipulate what is not, and totally miss what could be that I have come to realize why so many end up regretting the missed opportunities that will not pass their way again.

You would think we would learn our lessons, but we rarely do because we are so busy trying to manipulate circumstances to bow to our way of thinking that we fail to accept the way things are. Such acceptance would allow us to properly embrace the moment and opportunity that is before us.

The only way we can avoid present regrets is to realistically face life for what it is. We must learn to do what is honorable before God to do away with both the regrets and shame that often occur because we have or are selfishly demanding our own way. At such times of selfishness we will become indifferent toward our present responsibilities. In such responses we will also avoid missed opportunities that turn into regrets in the future. Clearly regrets are not always based on what we do, but they can also be founded in the missed opportunities that occur when we are caught up with that which is insignificant and destructive in the scheme of things.

Failure and regrets will always be part of the equation in our lives to some extent. But, such equations can serve as mirrors that produce personal growth, or as hindrances that become an excuse for living in the constant shadow of regret and guilt. Due to our inability to deal with failures and regrets, our past can serve as the grave clothes that cling to us in the present. These grave clothes are rotting and decaying, emitting a stench that is not pleasing or attractive. In some situations it is hard to know if these clothes are clinging to us, or if we are clinging to them. We need to let such clothes fall to the way side so we can walk in newness of life.

Jesus commanded that others loosed Lazarus from his grave clothes after being in the grave for four days.[11] The grave clothes represent that a death has occurred. For Christians, a death blow has been leveled at the old life. We must leave the tendencies of the old life in the barren grave. We must come forth to live a new life. If there are grave clothes identifying us to the tendencies of the old still clinging to us, we must seek whatever means available to put them aside to follow Jesus into a new way of life. We must seek complete healing from the old and restitution of the new. We must rest in the future promise of Revelation 21:4 that all such memories will be wiped away, to be remembered no more, as we experienced the eternal bliss of our heavenly home.

Obviously, our Christian life is before us, not behind us. We also know the life ordained for us is satisfying; therefore, why do we insist on holding onto the vanity and regrets of our past life? We know His life in us is eternal, why are we tempted to look back at that which is temporary and has already been judged?

Our reasons for looking back or returning to the old seem justifiable and logical, but yet the results end up costing that which is heavenly and priceless. In fact, it points to backsliding once again into the old way of doing, thinking, and being. We discover that it is so easy to be like the children of Israel. We begin to cry and whine because we choose

---

[11]   John 11:44

to remember what we considered was the "good" part of our old life. Such select memory also allows us to conveniently forget that the old represented the darkness of bondage and death.

It is also true that we may not like certain parts of the old life, but there are those parts that we are at home with. Regardless of whether such areas are carnal and void of life or purpose, we will cling to them like barnacles to a ship that is ready to be taken to dry dock. As soon as the barnacles are out of their environment, exposed to the sun, death will overtake them. All that will be left is the repugnant smell of their demise.

The old life is dead and the only smell that can come out of it is the smell of death and decay. Needless to say, people who are spiritually dead are incapable of smelling the death that is working in them, and they are unable to recognize that there is no life in them or their activities. But, what about Christians? The problem with something dying is that if a person is around the smell of it long enough, he or she can become quite comfortable in an environment where death will be victorious.

In my life I became aware of the fact that certain areas of my life were not beneficial to me. However, I would justify the smell and vacuum they left in my soul. Eventually the stench of my sin became so great that I could do nothing but face it. At that time I realized that I not only needed to be cleansed where the ruin and decay of death were operating through my sin, but I needed to be raised out of the grave of indifference that it created in me.

The old life represents that which is dark, dying, and already judged. It has no part in a heavenly life or inheritance. This is why Jesus in Luke 9:62 was clear about putting our shoulder to the consecrated plow of service, and beginning to follow Him into a new life. Subsequently, we must never allow ourselves to long for the old life. If we long for it we will look back, making us unfit for the kingdom of heaven.

When I come to this Scripture in Luke, I am reminded of Elisha in 1 Kings 19:19-21. Elijah came upon Elisha plowing in the field. The great prophet cast his mantle upon him. Elisha stopped his plowing, kissed his parents goodbye, slew his oxen, boiled their flesh, gave the meat to the people to eat, and then rose up to follow Elijah to minister unto him. Elisha's actions clearly show us what real consecration is by burning all the bridges associated to his old life.

Jesus clearly laid out this same radical example of separation in Scripture. Today, His cross casts the great shadow upon us. As believers, it reminds us that we do not belong to ourselves. After all, Jesus has passed our way, called us to follow Him in a radical new way, and now we have the opportunity of possessing this new life ever before us. We have been entrusted with a mantle to share the Gospel with the world and to tread where few dare to venture. However, we must cut all ties with the old if we are going to discover and embrace the new.

As Jesus' true disciples, we must leave the matters of the world to others when He calls us, say our final goodbye to all that we have held dear in this present age, burn all bridges that would lead back to the old way, and give what is left to others. This is the only way we can be assured that we will not look back or return to the cesspool and stench of judgment and death. After all, there will be nothing left to go back to, and there will be no unresolved issues to tempt us to return to the place of our initial deliverance to resolve an unsettled matter. There will be no regrets that will remain clinging to us as we allow the grave clothes of the old man to fall to the way side.

As we come to the end of this presentation, we must conclude that if we turn back to our old life, we are not worthy of the kingdom of God. The question is why? If you go back to the old life, it is the sin of commission. You are not only being disobedient by trespassing back into the things that have been judged, but you are coming into an unholy agreement with them.

If you look back to the old life, you will be committing the sin of omission. In other words you will be omitting the ways of righteousness in a matter by failing to go forward by faith in your life with God. Both responses show a lack of love for God, His truth, and righteousness. Therefore, to be associated or identified with either sin does not designate you as belonging to the kingdom of God, but to this present age and the god of this world, Satan.

God has set his people free from their past, but if they fail to consecrate their lives totally to Him, they will keep the world as a possible option. When times get challenging, the temptation and tendency to longingly look back at the old way will take center stage. Not only will such individuals lose sight of their real hope, but they will once again become identified with the death, judgment, and destruction of the old.

What about you? Have you burned all bridges leading back to the past or are you maintaining the right to keep them as an option just in case our Lord fails you? Remember, if you look back, you are not fit for the kingdom of God. It could cost you not only the heavenly life you will end up improperly valuing, but it could easily cost you your own soul.

THE REALITY OF IT

Book 999

1

THE SPIRITUAL MAN

INTRODUCTION

One of the realities of the Christian life is the premise that it operates from. Granted, the Christian life has to be worked within the soul in submission to the Spirit and worked out in the physical arena through obedience to the Word of God, but its premise is strictly spiritual.

God is Spirit and truth. The obstruction is that man is subject to and identified to the workings and laws of this earth and is influenced by a physical, fleshly world. Such identification and influence caters to the reality that we all begin from the base premise of being fleshly or carnal. The natural inclination and tendencies of such a state makes man an earthly man that has no real inclination towards the unseen, spiritual reality of God. The tendencies of the fleshly man are soulish, which is nothing more than selfishness that is influenced by lustful appetites that often become perverted, obsessive, and tormenting.

The Bible tells us that the earthly man whose disposition remains unchanged by the transforming power of God will not enter His kingdom. Scripture is clear that the earthly man must become a spiritual man.

The following presentation you are about to embark upon will attempt to explain how the earthly man can become a spiritual man. The reality of the earthly becoming the spiritual is that it entails a miracle, an actual intervention of God. He is the only one who can change the disposition of something which represents the inherent state, to a new creation that is radically different and unrecognizable.

The question we must personally ask ourselves is, are we ready to experience such a radical change? Even though it entails a miracle, it also calls for a willingness on our part to submit to the process and change that will and must occur.

It is unmistakable, that we cannot partake of the spiritual if we are bound by this earth, influenced by the world, and catering to the carnal, fleshly preference of an unregenerate state with its lustful, undisciplined appetites. It is a decision we are individually responsible to make. It is a decision that must be made if we are to see the glory of the unseen world to come.

STATE OF AFFAIRS

In 1 Corinthians 15:45-50, the Apostle Paul makes reference to the reality of the Christian life. We all start out being earthly people. In other words we are bound to the earth. The only thing that stipulates that there is any type of life is the unseen air that we breathe. Since we are of the earth, we belong to this present world. The earth reminds us we are but dust when it comes to the makeup of our bodies, but the carnality in which we walk in identifies us as belonging to this world or present age. Granted, we may have a soul that is able to interact on an intellectual and emotional level with the world around us according to our will, desires, and pursuits. However, we also possess a spirit that was meant to interact on a spiritual level. The soul may connect our present reality around us with our spirit, but it must not define who we are and who we are becoming. We each must decide who or what will influence our thinking, and in what way are we going to express such influences in the environment we live in.

Due to the first man giving into the soulish arena of the intellect, will, and emotion, he ceased to be able to interact on a spiritual level. Although he is considered a living soul because his premise originated from the arena of the soul, it does not mean he is a spiritual man. It all comes down to what arena a person is regarding a matter from, and what he or she will ultimately interact with that will determine an individual's real state of affairs. Granted, a person may be a living soul, but if his or her spirit is not alive with the reality of God, he or she will never reach his or her real potential. Ultimately, such a person will remain an earthly man who will function according to the fleshly ways of the soul and not the godly ways of the Spirit of God.

The Apostle Paul was quite clear that we are meant to be spiritual people. Our premise must be from the perspective of spirit, our inspiration must come from the heavenly, and our very life from God. If we are not relating to the world around us in light of Spirit and truth, we will be considered an earthly man who is not only bound by the earth that firmly holds our feet to the laws of the world, but our lifestyle will be greatly influenced by the age we live in.

When I think of an earthly man becoming a spiritual man, I am reminded of the incident where the blind Bartimaeus came up to Jesus, and the Lord asked him, "What wilt thou that I should do unto thee" (Mark 10:51)? For any sound thinking person, he or she would automatically assume or conclude that this man would want to be healed of his physical blindness. However, the reality is that such healing would radically change Bartimaeus' state of affairs. He was used to begging in the streets, and healing would mean that his very profession and way of life would radically change. We assume that such changes would be positive, but in reality any revolutionary change of such nature can cause a whole different state of problems and challenges to occur. Clearly, Bartimaeus would be taken out of the familiar and put into unfamiliar territory to function in a way that would be quite contrary to his old way of life.

We see this in a case where people have lived in extreme bondage. They see the fruits of liberty, but they do not understand the challenges and responsibilities that liberty carries with it. They have only tasted the bondage, but they have no understanding or real contrast as to how liberty is an actual state that will revolutionize one's thinking and lifestyle.

When people lack the proper contrast or understanding of the state they live in, ignorance will prove to be bliss, but the reality of it can end up becoming a bitter pill that is not easily swallowed without grave repercussions. For this reason, ignorance allows people to maintain a wonderfully fanciful concept or superstition of a contrary state that promises the opposite. However, when faced with the dramatic changes such a new state would require and produce in their lives, these individuals often find themselves becoming overwhelmed and frightened by it. After all, it is one thing to dream of how something will manifest itself in one's life, but to actually understand the challenges and responsibilities such a change would require and produce is a different matter altogether.

When Jesus asked Bartimaeus the question as to what could He do for him, it most likely had a two-fold purpose. The first reason was that of faith. Did Bartimaeus believe that Jesus could heal him? Bartimaeus had no doubt that Jesus could do the impossible. After all, the testimonies of many had preceded Him. The declarations as to His identity had long ceased to be something that was quietly being murmured among the crowds who seemed to seek Him out. In many ways it was being joyously shouted and proclaimed.

As previously pointed out, the second possible purpose behind Jesus' questioning could have done with the revolutionary change that was about to occur in his life. Was Bartimaeus sure he wanted such a drastic change? After all, was he prepared to change his complete lifestyle from a beggar on the streets to a responsible, productive citizen in society where extreme competition could take center stage? In such a state, he would no longer have any excuse for being a beggar; therefore, he would lose his source of bread and butter? Obviously, the beggar was about to lose his present lifestyle, flinging him into a new complete life.

This scenario is true for the Christian life. As believers we are given the measure of faith to believe that God wants to save us because we have the declarations of His Word. But on the other hand, are we ready for the drastic changes that will fling us into a life that is completely foreign to us? We can cry out for deliverance from that which enslaves us, but are we prepared to come face-to-face with the changes that will require us to give way to something totally foreign to the way we have been living? Are we ready to graduate from the ignorance of wishful thinking to embrace the certainty of facing the reality of what it means to come out transformed in our way of thinking, doing, and being?

As I meditated on Jesus' question to Bartimaeus, I can see where both approaches could have motivated Jesus' question. I have worked with people who lived in the different homeless shelters of America. For some it is a means to survive hard times until they can get on their feet. In good faith they are trying to gain their footing to change their present status, but there are those who travel from shelter to shelter because it has become a lifestyle. They see no need to change or be revolutionized. At times they might give the impression that they want life differently, but the reality is that they are quite content in their present state of affairs.

Through the years I have had to realistically ask the right questions to see whether those in some type of bondage want relief from their unpleasant circumstances or deliverance from their way of life. Once certain individuals become familiar and comfortable with their status, they have a tendency of seeing no need to come higher in their pursuits. After all, they can get by without exerting much energy, while avoiding changing their lifestyle and sliding by with minimum effort.

The Apostle Paul stated that Christians will actually become new creations where the old ceases to be and a whole new way of living and being will come forth.[1] Such a change does not imply an outward change, but an inward transformation, where an actual metamorphosis takes place. Such a change would be as revolutionary as a caterpillar changing into a butterfly.

As a Christian I have been mindful that even though I have had a genuine encounter and experience with God, there is always the awareness of how far away I am from the mark of what God intended when He formed the first man from the dust of the earth. It is true that dust carries no real worth, but God distinguished man from the earth by blowing into his very nostrils the breath of heaven. The breath of heaven was God's very Spirit. Although man was created from the substance of the earth around him, he was distinguished as being spiritual by the type of breath and life that was pulsating through his very being. It was the air or spirit within man's very being that identified him to an unseen world that was marked by that which was not only excellent, but eternal.

It was clear that man came from the earth, but he was also created to operate in the spiritual realm. In the beginning he had the ability to interact with God because he had the very breath of God operating and pulsating through his spirit and soul. He had the necessary connection to walk with God in a relationship of blessed fellowship and communion. Such a fellowship was obvious when the Lord brought all of the animals to Adam to be named. No doubt there was blessed interaction and exchange between the Creator and the one who He created to manifest His glory to the physical world.

When the first man, Adam, rebelled, the breath of God lifted from him, leaving him spiritually naked, exposed, and empty. Granted, the air of the earth may have filled his lungs, but the breath of God was not present for him to connect to the heavenly life or interact with God on a

---

[1]   2 Corinthians 5:17

spiritual level. Man's spirit was left in an unresponsive spiritual state. In essence, it became dead to the spiritual realm, unable to interact with God in the spiritual arena, while his soul became sensitive and subject to the earthly, worldly, and fleshly arenas. As he succumbed to the soulish aspects of his life, the spiritual world became foreign and foolish to him, causing him to disregard it altogether in pursuit of the temporary physical pleasures of the flesh and world around him.

The further man drifted from God in his fallen state, the more he became earthbound, worldly in his ways and preferences. His inclinations toward the things of God were replaced by an inclination to pursue the things of the world. As his tendency turned from the truth to prefer his own reality, the fleshly lust and attractions became the natural tendency in which he would try to pursue or manipulate the reality around him.

In his inherent fallen state man became utterly lost to God, and God became lost to man. It is hard to imagine how lost man became. After all, if you are born into a certain state it is what becomes "normal" to you. You have no real comparison to understand that you are indeed lost to the very essence of life. You have no sense as to that which is now obscured in a dimension that you have no connection to. Since you have no contrast, you do not know what you are missing. If a person is not aware of missing something then he or she has no sense that it is lost to him or her or the necessity of possessing it. This is what makes man's state of affairs precarious. Once again, I am reminded that a man who is aware of being lost can easily be saved, but he first has to be convinced that he is lost.

The Apostle Paul is clearly calling each of us as believers to come back to the original purpose for which man was created. We may have been sown or conceived in the natural, but we must be made spiritually alive to reach our potential. We may start out from the premise of the worldly, but we must taste of that which is eternal. We may have been bound to the earth, but we must possess the life that will allow us to soar into the very heights of the heavenly. We might be limited by the fleshly, but we have the promise of the glories awaiting us in the world to come.

The question is, what must we do to ensure that the spiritual is brought forth in our life? We know that flesh and blood will give way to corruption. It will never inherit the kingdom of God. For this reason, we must ensure that when our flesh returns to dust, and the part of our life that is associated with the earth gives way to an unseen dimension, that we indeed possess the life that ultimately will identify us to the unseen world that has been promised to those who truly belong to God. In summation, we must become the spiritual man that the Apostle Paul makes reference to in 1 Corinthians 15. We cannot remain in the state we were born into. Our state of affairs must be changed, and transformed by something that not only comes from outside of what is of this earth and belongs to this age, but it comes from above and is stamped with the mark of eternal bliss.

Have you been stamped with the mark of heaven or are you still being identified with the dust of the earth and the mark of the present darkness of this age? Honestly examine yourself as you consider what makes a person a spiritual man.

UNVEILING THE SPIRITUAL MAN

We are told that when we receive what God has for us in light of salvation we will become new creations.[2] The concept of being a new creation points to the work of recreation. In recreation, the old that possesses the seeds of death must give way to the new. Such an exchange is necessary for the seeds of a new life to be brought forth in an arena that was not formerly conducive to receive or produce a life that was contrary to its present state. It is for this reason that the present environment where spiritual ruin reigned must be recreated in order for it to produce a new type of life.

Within the first two verses of Genesis 1, we get glimpses of this recreation in regard to the creation of the earth. We know that God created the earth, but we have to acknowledge that at one point the earth was void of any life. It may have had potential to house life and somehow reproduce life, but it laid in utter darkness. There were no real seeds of life, because the environment was not conducive for such life to come forth. The surroundings had to be completely changed. For example, light had to penetrate darkness. There had to be some type of separation that occurred within the elements of the environment to ensure that the proper laws or principles were in operation so that life could come forth. This

---

[2]   2 Corinthians 5:17

required the terrain to be changed so that it could embrace the seeds of life and reproduce it.

The idea that the world was void of life and lay in utter darkness and ruin is a good description of what sin has done to man. Due to sin, man's spirit laid in utter darkness, as chaos reigned and spiritual ruin became the product. Even though he was a breathing soul, the terrain of his inner man was without form and lifeless. Without life there is no light of understanding, purpose, or hope. He may have had a shell or body in which he somewhat interacted with the world around him, but in all truth the inner terrain of his spirit and soul was void of the life that would truly identify him to the purpose for which he was created. Clearly, man needed to be recreated from within to reach his potential.[3]

This facilitates us coming to terms with being new creations. We know according to John 3:5 that we must be "born again" Once we have the seeds of life in us, we must be transformed within by the life that has been imparted to us. Our inner disposition must be transformed into something that will be the complete opposite of what we have been in our former state. The problem with many people is that they assume they are new creations upon saying the sinner's prayer, changing outward posture, or succumbing to a set or religious rules or practices, but they continue to remain void of understanding of what it entails to ensure that the new life is brought forth. They may have the seeds of new life planted within their spirits, but unless the seeds of life are properly cultivated and nurtured, this new life will never come forth in the arena of their souls. Without this new life being nurtured, these individuals will fail to manifest the new life that will clearly identify them as new creations. Obviously, the inner disposition of the spirit and soul of man must be completely transformed.

Have you ever thought of what it means to take on and possess a new disposition? We have an exemplary example of what it means to take on a complete new disposition. Our example is the Man, Christ Jesus. In fact, His example was outlined in the Old Testament and manifested in the New Testament. The Apostle Paul referred to it as the

---

[3]   If you would like to read more about this subject, see the author's book, *The Principles of the Abundant Life*, in Volume 1 of the foundational series.

mystery of godliness. Throughout his writings he actually unveiled this mystery in an incredible way.

For example, in Romans the apostle first introduces us to this mystery by declaring that creation itself gives us insight into it in relationship to the Godhead. This visible declaration will leave us without any excuse for not recognizing or believing what has been unveiled. He reveals Jesus as the second Adam. Because of the first man's rebellion in the Garden of Eden, death was passed upon all of his seed. But, because of the second man's work on the cross, life has been offered to all who will believe. As the second Adam, Jesus would also become head of the human race. As head of the human race, He would signify a complete change in who man should be and what man can become. For this reason Jesus is also described by the apostle as the first-born among that which will exemplify a new creation.[4]

In 1 Corinthians the apostle adds more insight into Jesus by describing this second Adam who was made a life-giving spirit as the Rock who the children of Israel drank from in the wilderness. He stated of Jesus that He alone is Lord and by Him all things exist, and it is by Him we must obtain life and live accordingly.[5] Since He brought creation into existence, as well as continues to maintain or hold it together, it is obvious that Jesus existed before His entrance into the world as the second man. The Apostle Paul confirms that Jesus was the creator of all things in Colossians 1:16-18, thereby, He alone must hold all preeminence in creation, inclusive of that which is being brought forth.

The apostle's exquisite presentation of Jesus continues in his second letter to the Corinthians. He presents Jesus as God's Lamb who became the substitute sacrifice on the cross for us. The Son of God had to take on a body in order to be offered up on our behalf. Paul said of Jesus' sacrifice that He had to become poor so we could be made spiritually rich. Hebrews describes Jesus' poverty. It states that He was made lower than the angels He had created. Philippians explains that although Jesus was God by nature, He ceased to be equal to the two other persons of the Godhead in order to take on a completely different disposition of

---

4   Romans 5:12-21; 8:29

5   1 Corinthians 8:6; 10:4; 15:45

being a servant.[6] Although He retained His deity, He would also become man.

In Galatians we are told that the Law of God pointed to Jesus as the solution to our sin problem. He became a curse on a tree so that He could redeem us from the curse of death pronounced by the holy Law of God upon those who live according to the fleshly ways of this present world.[7]

In Ephesians, the Apostle Paul reiterates that Jesus is the head of a living body that is unified by the Spirit of God. He tells of how He ascended into glory, but before He ascended, Jesus also descended into the lower parts of the earth. He may have come from the heights above to enter into the human race and descended to the depths below into a grave, but He also ascended back into heaven. He did all these things to fill all things.[8] He must become all that we have need of, and He must be found in all we do to bring order to our lives, allowing us to make sense out of the world around us.

As the Apostle Paul pulls back the curtain to reveal more of Jesus, we must remember that Jesus represents the spiritual man. In Timothy, the apostle tells us that Jesus is the eternal, immortal, invisible King who is also our wise God. Then he makes this statement about Him, "And without controversy great is the mystery of godliness: God was manifest in the flesh, justified in the Spirit, seen of angels, preached unto the Gentiles, believed on in the world, and received up into glory" (1 Timothy 3:16).

To reiterate an important truth, Jesus was and is God by nature, but He took on another disposition. Keep in mind He did not give up being God, but He took on a disposition that was foreign to His nature as God. He took on the disposition of a servant. The One who was served in heaven, would now become a servant on earth. To express His disposition as a servant, He had to be fashioned as a man.[9] In other words, He had to clothe His deity with flesh and blood to serve as a servant who would become a sacrifice.

---

6   2 Corinthians 5:21; 8:9; Philippians 2:6
7   Galatians 3:13, 24
8   Ephesians 4:2-16
9   Philippians 2:6-7

Was Jesus a spiritual man because of His deity, or was He a spiritual man because of the life He chose to live? Since we do not possess a dual nature like Jesus, we must conclude that He was a spiritual man because of how He walked as a man.

By taking on humanity, Jesus became our example as to what it means to be a spiritual man. His deity may have identified Him to the heavenly, but His humanity identified Him to us. In Him heaven was revealed, but in His humanity the mystery of godliness unfolded before us to manifest the ways, truth, and life of a spiritual man. He was subject to the same things we are, but without sin. He experienced the same temptations and challenges, but He overcame them all in His humanity. He put up the mirror to show us that godliness is not some unobtainable concept, but a life that can be possessed and lived in our humanity. We can become a spiritual man even when we are earthbound by natural laws and limited by a world that has no consensus as to who God is.

What separates the earthly man from the spiritual man? Christ reveals that it is a matter of disposition. As Christians our disposition must be transformed. The truth is we are already slaves to sin, subject to the earth, and greatly influenced by the world. However, due to our independence and rebellion, we do not possess the disposition of a servant. In order to change our disposition, we must change our head, master, and source of influence or agreement. For example, we must choose Jesus as our head in order to cease to function according to the fallen disposition that has been passed down by the first head, Adam. We must come into subjection to God in order to change our master of sin, and we must cease to be influenced by the flesh and the world in order to come into agreement with the life and purpose established by our risen Lord, Jesus Christ.[10] As we give way to the second Adam, and become instruments of God and walk in agreement with the life of Christ in us, we become new creations that are marked by something that is not of this present world. This mark clearly identifies us to that which is eternal and heavenly.

Jesus did not belong to this world. He came from outside of this world. His life clearly stipulated that He was from a world that was contrary to the type of world around Him. He gave life, while the world

---

[10]   Romans chapters 5-7

hides the ultimate reality of condemnation and death. Jesus offers hope, while the world offers temporary happiness that will eventually subside into misery, hopelessness, and spiritual ruin. Because Jesus did not belong to the present age, nor was He recognized by it, the world hated Him. He made it clear to His followers that the world would hate them as well.[11] The world would never know or understand the spiritual, and the spiritual would have no part of or agreement with the present world.

Another aspect of Jesus' humanity was His mission. Those of the world live for the purpose of benefitting self, but Jesus revealed that the mission of the spiritual man possesses excellent qualities that cannot be counterfeited. He explained that His mission was threefold: to give life to the hungry and thirsty, to do the will of the Father, and to do the works of the Father.[12]

One would think the will and works of the Father were the same. However, the will of the Father had to do with daily obedience to that which would be perfected in righteousness, while the works of the Father had to do with redemption that would bring about reconciliation between man and God. Jesus would show man that by doing the will of the Father, he would know what it would mean to be satisfied even in the midst of spiritual devastation. And, by doing the works of the Father he would fulfill his ministry and ultimately reach his potential, bringing glory and honor to the Father.

Jesus' invitation was for each of us to come and personally learn of Him.[13] This means that we would be learning how His very disposition of servitude was clearly expressed in His humanity. We would know how a disposition tempered by lowliness would conduct itself in regard to the Father's will, and how a meek attitude would respond when it came to doing the Father's business. However, there is more to the spiritual man than a disposition that is being expressed in service and tempered by humility and meekness. It is vital that we look behind the manifestation of a right disposition and understand what motivates and compels it to give way to something that is contrary to its original state of affairs.

---

[11]   John 17:3, 14-16
[12]   John 4:34; 6:33; 9:4
[13]   Matthew 11:28-29

ANOINTED

Even though Jesus' deity was veiled by His humanity, He could easily be identified as a spiritual man. His disposition set Him apart from the age He lived in, and His mission revealed that He was clearly not of this world. However, there is one other important aspect of His humanity that set Him apart as a spiritual man.

Believing there is a God may make you decent, and being part of some religious group may make you moral, but only the Spirit of God can make you a spiritual man. Jesus stated we had to be "born again" of the Spirit of God. The Apostle Paul made it clear that the Spirit is the one who connects those who are bound by the natural laws of the earth and limited by the function of the world, to that which is spiritual.[14] The earth only allows those who are earthbound to see in part and those who are limited by the world to know in part. And, that which belongs to the world cannot relate to anything that is not of the present age. There is no common ground or connection in which to bring the two dimensions together.

We are told that God is Spirit and truth. The physical and emotional world around us is fleshly and wrapped in lies. It mocks the spiritual and scoffs at the absolutes of truth. It cannot imagine or take serious what it cannot see and know according to the rudiments or fundamental philosophies of the age in which a person lives.[15]

Although Jesus was deity, in His humanity He revealed how man will need the presence, anointing, and power of the Holy Spirit to connect to the unseen, in order to walk through this present age of darkness. In the Gospel of John, John the Baptist explained that the Spirit of God would identify the Son of God by descending on Him.[16]

When Jesus came to John the Baptist to be baptized, He stated that He was fulfilling a requirement of righteousness. In other words He was obeying what He had been instructed to do. The work He was doing also was the means for the Holy Spirit to descend on Him to confirm His identity to John the Baptist. We see Jesus' disposition as a servant before

---

[14]   1 Corinthians 2:10-14

[15]   John 4:24; 1 Corinthians 1:18-24; Colossians 2:8

[16]   Matthew 3:15-17; John 1:29-34

the Father, but such a disposition also serves as a proper environment in which He would be anointed from above to fulfill His purpose.

It was clear that Jesus was sent from heaven to carry out a mission that would secure salvation for those who would believe. His walk would eventually lead Him to giving way to the redemptive work that would close the gap between lost man and his Creator, resulting in reconciliation.

What we learn from Jesus' example as man, is that He did nothing unless He was led to do so by the Holy Spirit. As man, He was tuned into the prompting and leading of the Spirit of God. After being baptized by John, the Holy Spirit came down on Him to not only identify Him as the Son of God, but to anoint Him for service as the Son of man.

There is much conflict surrounding the concept of "anointing." Some portray "anointing" as a mark that points to being spiritually superior and exceptional. However, anointing was to serve as a mark or sign that something or someone has been designated to serve in a certain capacity. For example, kings and priests were anointed in relationship to the position they were to hold. These positions carried certain requirements and responsibilities. Obviously, anointing someone or something in regard to God's kingdom such as priests, sacrifices, and altars pointed to a type of ownership. Since God ordained the person or object, that which was anointed not only was selected for a certain position or work, but it belonged to Him to place it where it needed to be in relationship to the work that needed to be accomplished.

The other aspect of anointing is that it was capable of breaking the yoke. Breaking the yoke was not in relationship to possessing more power, but in relationship to the fact that people would know where they fit, the burden that they were to shoulder in light of God's kingdom, and the freedom and ability to fulfill their mission. The Apostle Paul made mention of the yoke placed on the Jewish people by religious rituals, rules, and traditions that proved to be too heavy. As believers, they were exhorted to stand fast in the liberty that they had in light of Christ and not to be entangled again with the yoke of bondage.[17]

This brings us to the source of real liberty in the Christian life. The Apostle Paul stated that real liberty can only be obtained when the Holy Spirit has the freedom to work in our lives and to lead us where we

---

[17]   Isaiah 10:27; Galatians 5:1

need to go to fulfill the mission that has been entrusted to us.[18] Keep in mind that Jesus stated that by learning of Him, we would take on His disposition that would ensure an easy yoke and a light burden. However, Jesus' disposition was sensitive to the leading of the Holy Spirit. It was lowly; therefore, prepared to always respond. It was meek in attitude, therefore, properly tempered to give way to what was necessary, right, and honorable to carry out the mission regardless of the obstacle or price.

Jesus explained what He was anointed for in the confrontation He had with those of His hometown. Granted, He was anointed as the Messiah. The term "Messiah" points to "The Anointed One" or "The Promised One." As we are about to see, as believers we are "anointed" as well, but there is only one who will fulfill the position of "the Messiah." As "the Messiah" Jesus was set apart to do a specific work that would not only identify Him as the "Promised One" of God but would enable Him in His humanity to carry out His mission. To those of His hometown, He quoted a prophecy taken out of Isaiah to confirm His responsibilities in light of His position,

> The Spirit of the Lord is upon me, because he hath anointed me to preach the gospel to the poor; he hath sent me to heal the brokenhearted, to preach deliverance to the captives, and recovering of sight to the blind, to set at liberty them that are bruised, To preach the acceptable year of the Lord (Luke 4:18-19).

The Lord stated that it was the Spirit who sent Him forth as man and anointed Him to carry out His commission. It was the Spirit that anointed the message, and the same Spirit who enabled Him to heal, make the necessary impact to set enslaved souls free, cause the blind to see, and set at liberty those who had been bruised by the devastation of sin and the world.

Amazingly enough, Christians have a similar commission. The Bible is clear that we have the unction of the Holy One. "Unction" points to endowment. We have been given the endowment of the Holy Spirit. He

---

[18] 2 Corinthians 3:17

is the one who anoints us to carry out our commission as saints, priests, and servants of the Most High God.[19] As saints we have been set apart by Him to represent the kingdom of God, and as God's priests we have been given responsibilities to stand on behalf of others in relationship to God and to represent God to man. As His servants we belong to Him and must carry out our commission to preach the Gospel and make disciples of Jesus.

Although as His saints we all have received the same anointing, the extent in which it influences our lives and impacts others will be determined by how much we give way to the working of the Spirit in our lives. As the giver of spiritual gifts, the Spirit wants to use us as instruments that are available to bring forth the preparation, instruction, and healing of heaven to others. However, if we are unwilling or closed to His ways and working, then the Spirit of God will be unable to impact our lives, as well as those who we come in contact with.[20] Such unwillingness on our part will always point to unbelief. This was brought out by those in Jesus' hometown. Even though He had been anointed to impact their souls, unbelief prevented Him from making the impact He so desired to make in their lives.

There are those in Christendom that hide behind erroneous teachings and concepts about being anointed. These heretical teachings are taken from David's instruction to not "touch the anointed" in relationship to Saul's being the king. This reference had to do with not killing Saul. He had been anointed as king by God, and it was up to God to deal with him. Due to sin, God had already stripped Saul and his descendents of the right to the throne of Israel.[21] It was only a matter of time before God would bring Saul down as king. Until then David would wait for the time that the Lord would exalt him to the throne. He would not take it by force even though he had the opportunity or reason to do so.

These modern day false apostles and prophets most likely have never been anointed by the Holy Spirit. They are simply hiding behind

---

[19] 1 Peter 2:5, 9; 1 John 2:20, 27
[20] If you want to understand the person and working of the Holy Spirit in a constructive way, see the author's book: *For the Purpose of Edification* in Volume 5 of the foundational series.
[21] 1 Samuel 26

the concept of being "the anointed one" presenting themselves as being another "Christ" or "Messiah," something that Jesus and the Apostle Paul emphatically warned those who live in this age to beware of.[22] These individuals imply that since they are another "Christ" or "Messiah" their "anointing" makes them above reproach in light of their claims or to be subjected to testing in light of their credibility. Such erroneous presentations reveal that these individuals are imposters and must be regarded as heretics. Sadly, many of the people who are following these false "Christ's" do so to their own destruction. They are being blinded by a false light and seduced by another spirit into a reality that is void of all truth.

Another challenge that many in Christianity must properly discern is the concept of "spirituality." There are many caught up with some type of spiritual insight or experience. Just because a person has been exposed to some type of spirituality does not make him or her a spiritual person. Once again only the Holy Spirit can make a person a spiritual man. He alone is the only one who is able to reveal the real heart, mind, and thoughts of God. Just because people have trespassed into the unseen world does not mean they have discovered the connection between man and God.

Spiritual enlightenment can also come from the kingdom of darkness. Satan is very spiritual and can be quite religious, but his type of spirituality is darkness wrapped in rhetoric that may appeal to the arrogant conceit of man's pride, but there is no real truth or wisdom in it. Truth never produces confusion and pure wisdom will reveal itself in the form of simplicity that can be understood by those pure in heart, Since heavenly, inspired wisdom is pure it can be applied in practical ways to the matters of life.

The Apostle Paul was clear about what really distinguished the spiritual man from the earthly man. He said although Adam, the first man, was a living soul, the second man, Jesus, was quickened by the Spirit. Adam represented the earthly man, but Jesus the spiritual man.

Believers are clearly identified by a new birth experience that planted the very seeds of life into their souls. This birth experience pointed to the reality that they have been made alive by the Spirit of God with the

---

[22]   Matthew 24:4-5, 11; 2 Corinthians 11:2-14; 1 Timothy 4:1-2

very seeds of eternal life. However, this life must be cultivated by the Spirit to ensure that believers come forth as new creations. The inward environment of their souls must be rendered conducive to God's Spirit to ensure such cultivation by obeying the Word of God. This environment must be maintained by developing a disposition that is sensitive to the Holy Spirit. It is in such sensitivity that the Holy Spirit empowers a person to live the life that he or she has been ordained to live before the very foundations of the world.

EMPOWERED

We know the Holy Spirit sets us apart by anointing us to do the bidding of God, but we must also recognize that He is the one who empowers us to carry out our mission. Jesus was clearly anointed as "the Messiah" or "the Promised One of God" to carry out His responsibilities and mission. Jesus would indeed become the ladder to heaven and the bridge that would reconnect man to the life and purpose that He was predestinated to fulfill. However, it would be the Holy Spirit that would empower Him in His humanity to carry out His commission and endure to the end of His mission.

We have a hard time remembering that Jesus did not accomplish the impossible when it came to our redemption because He was God, but because as man He was being empowered by the Holy Spirit. In fact, what might surprise many believers is that God's capacity is always being tempered by His Spirit. It is His Spirit who executes all matters. The last part of Zechariah 4:6c bears this out, "Not by might, nor by power, but by my Spirit, saith the LORD of hosts." God is mighty, but He does not do anything except through His Spirit, who tempers such strength. Nor, does God take liberty to do things because He is all-powerful and has the means to do it. It is the temperance of the Spirit who ensures the intent of a matter. Obviously, God's power is disciplined by the very character of the Holy Spirit who ensures that the Lord's will is carried out in a manner that will ultimately glorify Him.

If God does nothing but through His Spirit, how could mere man perceive that he is able to carry out a matter in his own strength according to any personal resolution on his part? If the Son of God did nothing in His humanity outside of the prompting, moving, inspiration, and leading of the Spirit, how can we as His people negate our need for the Spirit of God to serve as the compelling inspiration behind all we do?

In His humanity Jesus gave way to the inspiration of the Holy Spirit. This means He followed after the ways of the Spirit, was led by the Spirit in all He did, and walked in the Spirit in carrying out the will of the Father. As you study His life, examples, and teachings, it is obvious that Jesus did not look to His own strength to accomplish a matter, trust in His abilities to see something through, make assumptions about what needed to be done, or make presumptions about the way He should walk because it appeared proper and right. He was totally lining up to every aspect of heaven in light of the leading of the Spirit.

The problem with many Christians is that they are ignorant about the character and work of the Spirit. How can you follow the Spirit when you do not *know His character*? How can you give way to the Holy Ghost when you cannot *properly discern His work*? How can you submit to the leading of the Holy Spirit when you are *ignorant of His ways*? There are so many false assumptions about the character of the Spirit that in many cases, He is being completely ignored due to ignorance. There are also ridiculous presumptions being made in regard to His work, along with erroneous presentations being taught about the intent and purpose of how He manifests Himself. It is no wonder that many find themselves confused, skeptical, and turned off by any reference made to the third Person of the Godhead.

The only way to address confusing, skeptical, and indifferent attitudes about the Holy Spirit is to set the record straight by challenging people to examine their attitudes as they consider a balanced presentation of the Spirit in light of the Word of God. The first notion that many people must rid themselves of is that the Holy Spirit is simply a force. He is a person. This means we can personally know His character, discern His ways, and interact with Him. How do we know He is a person and not some force that is trying to manipulate or influence us against our will? We know that the Holy Spirit can be personally resisted when He is trying to bring conviction causing Him to depart. He can also be vexed by sin causing Him to withdraw, grieved by compromise causing Him to lift, and quenched by another spirit causing Him to turn people over to their preferred fleshly reality or delusion. He can be blasphemed. In other words, He knows whether we are being disrespectful of His person, mocking towards His work, and vilifying Him by giving Him credit for that which is wicked, or accrediting His perfect work as being of the devil.[23]

The Holy Spirit is a gentleman who will not step across our preferred realities or desires. He is the gentle dove from above, and the heavenly dew at the beginning of a new day who refreshes the parched soul after being purged by the heat of the day. His gentleness is the secret behind His greatness and strength. Such gentleness tempers His character, work, and function in our lives. He is sensitive to the heart of God and compassionate towards the plight of man. He is a zealous groomsman who points everyone to the bridegroom, Jesus, as well as serves as the gift of the Father to His children, and the promise of heaven to all those who desire more of God.[24]

The work of the Spirit of God is to recreate that which was void of life and purpose. He flutters over that which is being prepared to be shaken in order to recreate, and moves upon that which is lifeless to bring life. He broods over that which is being brought forth through a new birth experience. He anoints that which has been designated by God, and empowers that which has been commissioned to do the Lord's bidding.

The Holy Spirit also represents the presence of God. He is the presence that abides within every believer. It is for this reason we are referred to as the temple of the Holy Spirit. He is the presence that surrounds God's people. Our responsibility is to follow after Him in the ways of righteousness, be led by Him into a growing relationship with God, and to walk in Him in order for the very life of Jesus to be brought forth.[25] He is also the presence of God that comes from above.

We know that when we are born again the presence of God comes from outside of all fleshly attempts to revive or quicken our spirits and connect us to heaven. At this point the Holy Spirit serves as a seal that identifies us to our future inheritance.[26] As the presence that surrounds us, He moves upon us through conviction, inspiration, and prompting to

---

[23] Genesis 6:3; Isaiah 63:10; Ephesians 4:20; 1 Thessalonians 5:19
[24] 2 Samuel 22:36; Psalm 18:35; 1 Corinthians 2:10; John 14:27; 16:13; Luke 11:13; 24:49; Acts 1:4; 8:17-20
[25] 1 Corinthians 6:19
[26] John 3:3, 5; Ephesians 1:11-14

prepare us to properly respond to that which is necessary as a means to make an eternal difference in our lives and in the lives of others.

This brings us to the matter of being empowered by the Holy Spirit. We are told this empowerment happens when we are baptized by the Holy Spirit. After His resurrection, and before Jesus ascended, He breathed His Spirit on His disciples. His instruction that followed was for them to tarry in Jerusalem until they were endued with the Holy Spirit. It would be the Holy Spirit who would empower them to serve as living witnesses who would boldly and effectively testify of the reality and truth of His redemption. The Apostle Paul later pointed out that believers would also serve as living epistles. As epistles they would be read of men, and as emboldened witnesses they would proclaim the good news of what Jesus accomplished on the cross.[27]

It was clear that Christians could not live the Christian life or be effective witnesses without the presence of God's Spirit. They would become spiritually impoverished, void of any real evidence of life in their activities, and ineffective as to what they proclaimed.

When a person is baptized by the Holy Spirit, he or she will experience what has been referred to as divine invasion. The Living Waters from within the spirit is uncapped breaking forth in the soul, the presence without parts to allow the presence from above to flow downward. As the Water from above flows into the Living Water that is breaking forth in the inner man, it begins to penetrate every area of the soul to not only fill up the clay vessel, but to spill over and out to embrace the fullness of the presence of God from without. In a sense, the flow and function of this water almost forms a cross as man is lifted up in total identification into a new life, while he experiences the rapture that comes with the fullness of God filling every barren, void, and empty area of his heart and soul.

Divine invasion is also known as the filling of the Spirit, commonly called "the Lord's seal" or "the Lord's Signature" by early Christian writers.[28] In his devotion, *The Way,* E. Stanley Jones described this

---

[27]   Luke 24:45-49; John 20:21-23; Acts 1:4-9; 2 Corinthians 3:1-6

[28]   *Deeper Experiences of Famous Christians,* James Gilchrist Lawson, © 2000 by Barbour Publishing, Inc. pg. 50

experience by stating that before Pentecost, the disciples had the Holy Ghost, but after Pentecost, the Holy Spirit had them.

Sadly, man has replaced much of the work of the Spirit with dead-lettered theology that proves ineffective. He has devised worldly evangelistic methods that may impress others, but the various methods lack any power to save or sustain a person. Then, there are those religious, fleshly practices that may stir the emotions, but leaves the spirit empty and the soul unchanged. All of these points of identification identify man to the works of the flesh and the world, and not heaven. They may identify man as being zealously religious, but they do not signify that he is a "spiritual man."

Jesus was sent into the world to accomplish the impossible on behalf of man. In His humanity He represented the spiritual man, made alive by the Spirit who anointed and empowered Him to carry out His mission. He not only had the identifying mark of the Spirit of God upon His life, but He also represented the "spiritual man" by the life He lived, the way He walked, and the attitude in which He carried out His heavenly responsibilities.

As Christians we have been entrusted with a commission. As Jesus proclaimed in John 17:18 in His prayer to the Father, "As thou hast sent me into the world, even so have I also sent them into the world." Jesus was not sent empty handed out into the world to carry out a mission He was not equipped to see through to the end. Likewise, we are not being sent out into the world empty handed.

We have been given the promise of the Father, the gift of heaven. The promise and gift is the Holy Spirit. Upon our spiritual birth experience, as believers we are given the gift of the Holy Spirit as a seal to identify us to our eternal inheritance wrought by redemption. At the point of our birth experience, we are given new life by the Spirit, allowing Him to recreate the terrain of our hearts and souls. However, we also need to be empowered by the throne of God before we can be sent forth in the Spirit to be emboldened witnesses. To be empowered by the throne of heaven requires Jesus to baptize us or immerse us with the Spirit from above.

As we can see, everything in the saint's life would identify him or her as being "a spiritual man". Such identification will point to that which is unseen, eternal, and heavenly. For example, the saint has the unseen breathe of God within, an eternal, abundant life that is being brought forth, and a heavenly commission to complete in regard to the world. To effectively carry out his or her responsibility, as well as reach his or her potential, the saint has to experience a divine invasion of the spirit and soul.

This brings us to the final identifying mark of a "spiritual man." It comes down to what type of glory a person is reflecting in and to this world.

THE GLORIES THAT BE

The Word of God gives us insight into the aspect of our lives that sin has perverted and prevented. Sin has perverted our purpose and prevents us from reaching our potential. What is our purpose and what is our ultimate potential? It has to do with the concept of glory.

The Apostle Paul stated in Romans 3:23 that we have all fallen short of the mark of God for our lives, thereby, missing His glory. When you study the Bible you will realize that our purpose is to bring glory to God and our potential is to reflect His glory to the world. But, what does glory entail?

We know that glory has to do with the type of light or life we are manifesting in this world through attitude and conduct. Such glory will in some way identify us by bringing certain distinction or clarity to our person or character. For example, it will identify us to the kingdom we represent, the type of disposition we are developing, the master we serve, the type of life we live, the attitude in which we express that which is influencing us, and the approach we will take in regard to the matters of life.

"Glory" has to do with that which brings honor or recognition to something. In considering God's glory we know that which brings honor or recognition to Him is His character or attributes. They identify Him as being divine. They reveal His majesty that declares He is wonderful, beyond description. They confirm that He is who the creation identifies as being Creator. The Bible has also confirmed His attributes, unveiling Him as God and Redeemer, and declaring that there is only one entity who can and will be identified as God.

This brings us to the man, Jesus Christ. We have been following Him in relationship to Him being the true example of a "spiritual man." We know that He alone reveals what the spiritual man looks like. Such a man will possess a lowly, humble disposition and a meek attitude. He will bring himself into subjection to the will of the Father, as He gives way to that which is in line with the Father's plan. He will follow after the Spirit in the ways righteousness, be led by the Spirit in that which is worthy and excellent, and will walk in the Spirit in relationship to the life that has been promised. We also see that the man, Jesus, was anointed and empowered by the Spirit to carry out the mission He was sent to do in regard to redemption.

This brings us to the final aspect of being a "spiritual man." It has to do with the glory that was emitted from the life of Jesus. The Apostle Paul stated that in Jesus' humanity dwelled all the fullness of the Godhead bodily. Although His glory was veiled by His humanity, the fullness of the glory of God was still present. We know that His glory as God was seen by men on the Mount of Transfiguration when His flesh parted like the Red Sea to express the brightness of His person to Peter, John, and James.[29]

The Apostle John noted this event in his gospel in this manner, "And the Word was made flesh, and dwelt among us (and we beheld his glory, the glory as of the only begotten of the Father,) full of grace and truth" (John 1:14). Clearly, the glory unveiled on the mount gave the three witnesses glimpses into the eternal beauty of Jesus' grace and truth.

In Hebrews 1:2-3 we read these words,

> Hath in these last days spoken unto us by his Son, whom he hath appointed heir of all things, by whom also he made the worlds; Who, being the brightness of his glory, and the express image of his person, and upholding all things by the word of his power, when he had by himself purged our sins, sat down on the right hand of the Majesty on high.

The first Scripture in the Gospel of John states Jesus made the worlds. The second verse in Hebrews speaks of His majesty or brightness in relationship to His glory as God.

Note the statement in Hebrews 1:2, "Who, being the brightness of his glory, and the express image of his person." There is a difference in being the expressed image of who you are and being conformed to

---

[29]   Matthew 17:1-8; Colossians 2:9

an image. Jesus was the express image of His own person, not of the Father or someone else. This means He was expressing the fact that He was and is divine. Clearly, you cannot express something you are not. His humanity may have veiled the glory of His deity, but He never ceased to express who He was. As man He simply expressed His person or attributes through His disposition, attitude, and conduct. Everything He did in His humanity was according to who He was. He maintained His glory as God, but His divine glory was tempered by His disposition, attitude, and conduct as man.

In her outline of Hebrews, Ruth Specter Lascelle explained that Jesus was the stamp or image of the person or character of God.[30] In Him, the complete likeness of deity had been clearly stamped in the framework of humanity. He was the true representation or reproduction of deity for man to see, observe, and testify as being so to the rest of the world.

When we consider the concept of the "spiritual man," we must realize that such a man will be identified as to the glory that must emulate from his being. Such distinction will ultimately identify God as being the source or origin of the glory that is unfolding in his countenance.

As Christians our potential is to reflect the glory of God to the world. It has been my goal to understand the concept of glory. I have learned that every living thing has some type of glory being emitted that will reveal the type of life that is present. For example, man in an unregenerate state can emit the vainglory of the self-life, the false glory of man's religion, or the temporary glory of the world.

Each of these glories simply reflect the type of life man is giving way to, developing in, or pursing after. When man is emitting the vainglory of the self-life, he is simply giving way to the vanity of limited, fleshly strength and a surface concept of beauty that covers up a prideful selfishness which will fade in due season.

When he is taking on the false glory of man's religion, he is reflecting nothing more than a white-washed sepulcher. The false glory may present an appearance of righteousness, but it is to hide the dead men's bones of dead religious rituals and practices that lay in utter ruin due to decay and death. Unregenerate man may be emitting the reflection of the

---

[30]   We Have a Great High Priest © 1982 by Ruth Specter Lascelle

glory of the world, but it is glitter that will flicker for a short time before the gross darkness it hides will be exposed in judgment. This gross darkness represents emptiness, deception, despair, and death.[31]

The Apostle Paul also gives us another concept of the temporary glory this world offers in his first letter to the Corinthians. He explained how the world's presentation of wisdom, strength, and what is considered acceptable or noteworthy will be brought low, while that which it deemed to be foolish, weak, despised, and base is what God will ultimately exalt and use. The reason for this is because in the end God will be recognized as the source of strength and might operating in these individuals. He will be honor as the One who is bringing forth that which is impossible and excellent, and will receive the glory for what is worthy of real consideration.[32] It is for this reason that the apostle stated that no flesh would be able to glory in His presence, and he ended with this exhortation, "That, according as it is written, He that glorieth, let him glory in the Lord" (1 Corinthians 1:31)"

In 2 Corinthians 3, the Apostle Paul made reference to the glory emitted in the first ministration that was represented by Moses and the Law and the glory that would be reflected by the second ministration that is represented by Christ and a more excellent covenant. Moses had to hide the glory of the first ministration behind a veil. However, Jesus wants to tear the veil away so that His glory can be revealed through the lives of His followers.

It is important to understand that we cannot bring glory to God unless we are reflecting it in our lives. Such glory will not belong to us but to the very life of Christ that is being reproduced in us by the Holy Spirit. In His prayer on the night He was betrayed Jesus gives us some valuable insight into how we will bring glory to Him.[33]

We are told in His prayer that even though He would no longer be physically present, as His disciples, and members of His Body, the Church, He would ultimately be glorified in them. It is by becoming one as He was one with the Father that the world would also believe that He

---

[31]   Matthew 23:26-28; Philippians 2:3; 2 Timothy 3:5; James 4:4, 14; 1 Peter 2:24; 1 John 2:15-17
[32]   1 Corinthians 1:25-31
[33]   John 17

was sent with a life changing message and mission. The Lord also stated that the glory He possessed, He wanted to give to each of us as His followers so that we may be made perfect in that bond of being one in agreement and purpose in regard to our mission and ministry. However, to be glorified in us we must believe Him so that His joy would clearly be fulfilled in us even in the midst of being hated by the world.

The Apostle Paul stated that we have been predestinated to be conformed to the image of Jesus.[34] Remember there is a difference to being the express image of something and being conformed to an image. "Conforming" points to recreating something to reflect a likeness or image. Such recreation points to the concept of taking something that has no real shape or form and reshaping it into the form that will reflect the desired image.

As Christians our inner man must be recreated by the Spirit in order to reflect the very glory that was given to us by Jesus. The more we give way to the work of the Holy Spirit the more He will shape the life of Christ in us to reflect His image or likeness. We will be shaped in such a way we will take on Jesus' disposition, embrace His attitude, and become more like Him in our conduct. Therefore, the more we give way to the masterpiece that the Holy Spirit is creating in regard to the life of Jesus in us, the more Jesus' glory will be unveiled in our lives.[35] The more His glory is unveiled, the more we will become distinguished as a spiritual man that is not of this world.

As I consider the reality of bearing the very image of Jesus in this world, I cannot help but think what a humbling or incredible responsibility we have been entrusted with as Christians. There is a tendency for us to conform to some lifeless religion, rather than to the likeness of Jesus. We want people to admire our cloaks of piousness and become impressed with our masks of plastic presentations, but in such situations, we are simply casting a shadow of something that has no real substance behind it.

As I ponder the reality that I could offer what is real, I had to ask myself why would I settle for casting a mere shadow? Such a shadow

---

[34]   Romans 8:29

[35]   2 Corinthians 3:18

would prove to be empty, illusive, and disappointing to those who desire to encounter what is real and lasting.

While I meditated on settling for a shadow instead of possessing the likeness of Jesus I realized how easy it is to miss the mark in our Christian lives. Sadly, we often become content with the shadows because we can hide in them. But, as saints of the Most High God, we must not be content with such frivolous activities. We must become a spiritual man who is identified by the glory of Jesus as we reflect His life, His very image to a lost, dark world.[36]

Like the Apostle Paul, we must see the need as well as the urgency to press towards the high calling we have in Christ Jesus. We must make sure that we do everything in our power to give way to the image of Christ and bear it in humility. In summation, we must not settle for imitating Him, but we must insist out of love and devotion that we become like Him, allowing His ongoing glory to be unveiled in our lives for the sake and glory of the Father.

---

[36] If you would like to know more about the spiritual man, see the author's book, *Possessing the Soul*, in Volume 6 of her foundational series.

2

THE CALL TO
DISCIPLESHIP

INTRODUCTION

Jesus set forth the criteria to be His disciple. It is easy to romanticize it because we are divorced from the harsh reality of what it meant to forsake all to follow our Lord. However, to forsake the old life involved disowning what was often considered normal. Disowning the normalcy of the old life served as a prelude to picking up an instrument that meant torture and death to those of Jesus' day in order to embark into an unknown life.

In today's Americanized version of Christianity there is no cost involved to follow Jesus. All a person needs to do is wear the title of being a "Christian," give the impression of his or her religious piousness, adorn his or her neck with a cross, and in zeal offer the tainted pabulum to others and all is well. Sadly, the truth is real Christianity is literally being gutted out by such a foolish presentations. It is being stripped of its life and power to radically change a person's life.

The Apostle Paul stated that he did not want to know anything among the followers of Christ except Jesus Christ and Him crucified.[1] Clearly, the cross of Christ is present in the powerful message of the Gospel of Jesus Christ. Even though it presents a harsh picture, it is designed to become a place of liberation to those who are seeking freedom from the torment of their spiritual oppression.

---

[1]   1 Corinthians 2:2

Since Paul pointed to the importance of the work done on the cross by Jesus, I realized that it must become an important focal point to me if I am to understand the Christian life. Even though the Apostle Paul's desire is that Christians would not stray away from the simplicity found in Christ, the simple message of the cross is often shrouded in complication, confusion, and conflict.[2] What I discovered in my search to come to terms with this controversial object was that I cannot obtain, know, or walk out the Christian life apart from the work of the cross.

Clearly, the work of the cross is what brings the Christian life into focus. It connects the dots to what appears to be an unreachable spiritual life. It is also obvious that it is the object that God designed for the specific purpose to bring forth this life.

This small presentation presents a simple picture of the work of the cross as to the profound depth it can arrive at when it comes to the soul of man, the width it can encompass as to its accomplishments, and the heights it can reach into glory.

If this presentation inspires you to consider a different angle of the cross, you can study this subject more by obtaining my book, *Revelation of the Cross* located in Volume Two of the Foundational Series.

THE PRESENTATION
OF THE CROSS

He that saith he abideth
in him ought himself also so
to walk, even as he walked.
1 John 2:6

Jesus' initial call to His disciples was simple. Deny yourself, pick up your cross, and follow Him.[3] If a person failed to adhere to His calling, he or she could not be His disciple. I have meditated on what it means to heed His call. It may seem simple enough, but the reality is

---

2   2 Corinthians 11:3-4
3   Matthew 16:24

that it is a radical way that is intended to revolutionize a person's life in unimaginable aspects.

First of all, to deny self is so contrary to all of the psychobabble nonsense that is being sold as a bill of goods in the Christian realm. Such a contrast would surely be considered repulsive to anyone who is used to the self-serving fluff of the worldly, socially adjusted presentation of the Christian life. The idea of denying self of any exaltation or place of importance instead of esteeming self is unheard of today in many of the "feel good" environments promoted in some of the churches. To disown the right to self is so foreign to those in the social cliques of many church bodies that they have no consensus as to the type of life that they are being called to embrace and experience.

However, Jesus was clear. As His followers we must first disown our right to self and devalue its importance in our lives before we can pick up the cross and follow Him. Without first denying self of its right to survive and call the shots, self will use the cross as a platform to exalt itself to the status of martyrdom, while figuring out how to play dead and maintain its reign. Until self is recognized as a coward, a criminal worthy of death, a traitor to godliness, an enemy of God, a culprit to the disciplined life of a Christian, and denied its right to live, the cross will have no real impact.

When we consider Jesus we see where He first denied Himself of the glories of heaven to take on a body that was subject to the curse brought on by the sin of the first man. He knew what it meant to be hungry, tired, and despairing. He felt pain and tasted death, yet He never sinned.[4] He became our example. We see in 1 John 2:6, we are to walk as He walked. He may have ruled from the glories of heaven, but He also walked the dusty paths of this earth, through the barren wilderness of this world as an obedient Son to His Father and a servant to mankind.

We must follow Jesus. We must understand how Jesus walked and where it ultimately led Him. It is not a popular path that will be attractive to a person who is bound to the earthly ways and the worldly lifestyle of the present age we live in. But, as believers, we cannot ignore or live in denial of His example. He denied Himself of the glories of heaven, to serve in the capacity as a humble servant. He set His face towards His ultimate destination as He set His feet to walk in the way of Calvary, while

---

[4]   Philippians 2:6-9; Hebrews 4:15; 1 Peter 2:21-22

carrying a cross. As man, Jesus was always walking towards His demise. After all, death is what the cross represented to everyone who tasted its indifferent ways.

As we consider what Jesus had to do to prepare for His demise as man, it is both humbling and incomprehensible to our limited understanding. He gave up His glory as God (authority and power), as well as the glory of heaven. He took on the disposition of a servant when He allowed Himself to be formed into the likeness of man. He came into subjection to that which was eternal, submissive towards that which was worthy, and obedient to that which was sacrificial. He not only showed us the way to life, but He became the Way.[5]

We are told that we are to walk as He walked if we are to abide in Him as the source of our life and hope. However, He walked in the way of the cross. We need to not simply become acquainted with the way Jesus' walk led Him, but we must know and experience it in a personal way. His walk always followed the simple outline of the cross as He looked upward for His guidance, while being empowered by the Spirit as He walked it out among humanity. He was always reaching up to embrace the Father's will as He reached out to impart the reality of heaven to lost souls. Consider the following diagram.

---

[5] Philippians 2:6-8

Jesus said that He was the way, the truth, and the life.[6] As you follow Christ in His walk, you can see that this summarized His ministry. He was the way for man to come into a relationship with the Father, He was the truth about the holy character and ways of God, and He was the life that ensured communion with the Father. In Jesus' ministry, we once again can see the outline of the cross. The way He walked revealed the ongoing reality of the cross, while His truth embraced the work of the cross, which always leads to the promised life.

Jesus came to give us eternal life wrought by redemption that possesses the abundance of everlasting hope, heavenly promises, divine authority, and power. This life can only be obtained when we find our life hidden in Christ.[7] The Apostle Paul summarized the fullness of Christ in this way, "But of him are ye in Christ Jesus, who of God is made unto

---

[6]   John 14:6

[7]   Colossians 3:3

us wisdom, and righteousness, and sanctification, and redemption" (1 Corinthians 1:30).

Only the work of the cross can ensure a hidden life in Christ. The cross firmly stands in light of the wisdom of ages. As previously stated, like Jesus, we must bear a personal cross. This cross may take on various forms as it works the very life of Christ into us, but nevertheless it points to some type of death. The death is necessary to ensure life. Through it all, the cross will become the pillar that will brace us while it strikes important blows to all that would hinder us from the life that is promised. Ultimately, it will enable us to stand upright (righteous) before God, as we submit to the work of sanctification. Ultimately, we will experience the fullness of redemption as we come into a right standing in Him.

The cross of Christ made a way for man to come near to the Father. However, man must embrace the work of the cross of redemption to become identified in Christ in order to experience salvation. He must then learn what it means to pick up his own cross.

Consider how the work of Christ's cross will manifest itself in the Christian.

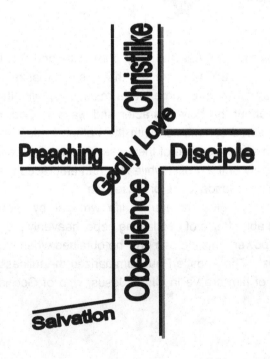

The *vertical* part of the cross represents man's relationship to God, while the *horizontal* points to man's relationship with others. Man must properly line up to God before his relationships with others can become an easy yoke to bear. In fact such relationships can prove to be too burdensome if God's love and power is not present to uphold such a yoke. Remember, Simon was compelled to help Jesus carry His cross, and our Lord will help us carry ours, making it a yoke, rather than a burdensome instrument too great to bear.[8] Even a yoke forms a type of cross, but instead of lifting one up in exaltation, it will humbly rest on the backs of those who shoulder it.

Love from above is what binds the vertical (God) and horizontal (others) relationships together. If I do not love God, my relationship with Him becomes a religious burden that has no life in it. If His love is not flowing through me to others, then my relationship with others will prove to be self-serving and too burdensome to bear rather than honorable and sacrificial.[9]

A person's relationship with the Lord begins at salvation. However, that salvation serves as a foundation in which the very life of Christ will be worked in, through, and out of the believer's life. This working can only occur if a person is walking in obedience to God's Word.[10]

Such obedience entails fulfilling the commission to preach the Gospel and disciple believers in being followers of Jesus.[11] Unless the Christian is compelled by the love of God, led by His Spirit, and a true convert of Jesus, the commission will become too great of a burden to fulfill.

As the cross has its way in our lives, we will be conformed to the very image of Christ. This is what God has predestinated for each of us.[12] We are to take on the very likeness of the Son of God. King David made reference to this in Psalm 17:15, "As for me, I will behold thy face in righteousness; I shall be satisfied, when I awake, with thy likeness."

However, to take on such likeness, Jesus' life must be formed in us by the work of the cross. In essence, our salvation or deliverance from

---

[8]   Matthew 11:28-30; 27:32

[9]   Romans 13:8-10

[10]   Philippians 2:12; James 1:22-25

[11]   Matthew 28:18-20; Mark 16:15-16

[12]   Romans 8:29

the oppressive ways of self and the hopelessness of spiritual death hinges on us living the life of Jesus by faith. Genuine faith leads us to acceptable obedience. Such obedience will allow us to identify with the heart of God towards lost souls as we fulfill our commission in the great harvest field of the world. The Apostle Paul summarized the goal of this work the best in Galatians 2:20, "I am crucified with Christ; nevertheless I live; yet not I, but Christ liveth in me; and the life which I now live in the flesh I live by the faith of the Son of God, who loved me and gave himself for me."

THE CROSS THAT FORMED
GOD'S ALTAR

We have an altar, whereof
they have no right to eat which
serve the tabernacle.
(Hebrews 13:10)

One of my favorite studies in the Bible regards altars. God provided the design for the altars that were used to memorialize His promises, serve as places of covenant, and to offer sacrifices.

The earthen altars that were ordained by God were made by stones that were untouched by man.[13] When it came to the altars of the tabernacle, they were made of the priceless materials the earth had to offer such as gold, brass, and acacia wood. It is important to note that acacia wood was a sturdy wood that was accessible in the barren wilderness during the construction of the tabernacle. These altars had to be constructed according to God's established pattern.

The final altar that God would design and use was the cross. The cross was an earthen altar. It came from the ground, and although roughly shaped by man, he could not pervert its design or intent.

Although death by the cross did not come into being until the Roman Empire, there were already shadows and prophecies of it in the Old Testament. For example, King David spoke of Jesus' death on the cross

---

[13]   Exodus 20:24-25

in the 22nd Psalm, 1,000 years before the cross was used for capital punishment. At Mount Sinai, God laid out the pattern for the furnishings of the tabernacle, which also cast a shadow of the cross. Let us now consider how the cross was foreshadowed in the tabernacle by lightly connecting the furnishings.

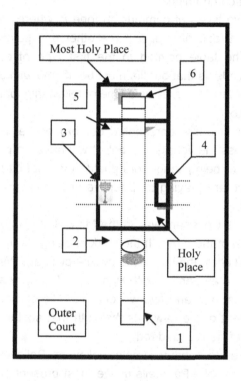

There were three compartments that made up the tabernacle: the outer Court, the Holy Place, and the Most Holy Place. There were two objects located in the outer court: (1) the Altar of Burnt Offering and (2) the Laver. There were three objects in the Holy Place: (3) the Candlestick or Menorah, (4) the Table of Shewbread, and (5) the Altar of Incense. There was only one furnishing in the Most Holy Place, (6) the Ark of the Covenant. The diagram shows us that the pattern of the furnishings formed an outline of the cross.

Note, there are three altars in the tabernacle. There was the Altar of Burnt Offering that pointed to the physical cross of Jesus. This altar dealt with sin. It stood in view of the gate or entrance so people could witness the cost of sin. The Laver pointed to the Word of God that cleanses man once sin has been addressed.

The Altar of Incense pointed to the discipline of the cross. The fire on this altar came from the Candlestick, which represented the walk. Believers must walk in the light of Christ. This light will lead to the table that represented communion.

There are two types of communion: one is where believers partake of Christ as the Bread of Life, and the other one points to agreement and intimacy. The table pointed to the first type of communion. The Candlestick reminds us that our life must be aflame with Jesus' life, while the table of communion serves as a time of fellowship: partaking of Jesus life and learning of Him.

The Altar of Incense represented our prayer life. Prayer will have no authority unless the light is present. It will have no power unless the Lord's will is either being sought or upheld. It will not hit the mark unless we know who we are praying to. Effective prayer must be disciplined to make an impact.

The Ark of the Covenant was in the Most Holy Place, It represented the finished work of the cross. If the work is being brought to fruition, as believers, we will know the Lord's mercy (mercy seat). We will have come into communion or agreement with Him at the Mercy seat. Since our life is hidden in Christ (the ark), we will discover His complete work as the way (the fulfillment of the Law), as the truth that sustains (manna), and as the essence of life (budded rod).

This brings us to another temple: believers. Believers must present a sacrifice. The Apostle Paul tells us we must present our bodies (outer court) as a living or ongoing sacrifice. As we allow the laver, His Word, to cleanse us from all influence, workings, and activities of sin, we will be able to follow Jesus through the door into the Holy Place. There, our inner man will be transformed by the light of Christ's life, enabling us to fellowship at His table and to experience first hand how the fervent prayers of the righteous are effective.[14]

This brings us to the veil that separated the Holy Place from the Most Holy Place. The Altar of Incense stood before this veil. The veil reminds us of another type of veil: That of sin. The veil of sin has been over our

---

[14]   Romans 12:1; 1 Corinthians 3:16-17; James 5:15-16

hearts and minds. However, the work of the cross of Jesus was able to remove this veil, opening a way for us to come into the presence of God in sweet fellowship. It is in such fellowship that we can take on the likeness of our Lord, thereby, establishing the freedom to reflect His glory in this dark world.[15] Such a reflection is a manifestation of the powerful work of the cross that will forever cast its shadow upon, in, and through the lives of God's people.

THE WAY OF THE CROSS

And he bearing his cross
Went forth into a place
Called the place of a skull,
Which is called in the
Hebrew Golgotha
(John 19:17)

The cross has a way about it. It is narrow, unforgiving, and cruel. It is an instrument of discipline that is meant to judge a transgressor. Its ultimate goal was to once and for all silence the transgressor through death. However, in spite of its harsh ways, the cross of Christ leads to real life. It will ultimately lift one above judgment as it is firmly planted and reinforced by the foundation or ground it is planted upon and within.

Jesus came to die as the Lamb of God. This is hard for people of this world to understand. The barren hillside of the earth became the cross' platform, as the ground served as its foundation. It would go downward while pointing man upward. However, it is not man's desire to be planted in death in order to be lifted up to embrace life. His desire is to beat the odds of death so he can continue to live the life he knows or to continue to seek the life he desires.

In His humanity, Jesus was not seeking to live, but to die as a lamb. Sacrificial lambs had to be chosen, prepared, set apart, and anointed. Jesus was no exception. He was chosen in heaven, prepared by the will of God, set apart by the Spirit, and anointed to carry out His mission.

---

[15]   2 Corinthians 3:13-18

Jesus had to travel the way of Calvary to become the sacrifice. The way of Calvary started with a small entrance into the world. He came by way of woman through the narrow door of the manger. Until He entered the door of service, He was veiled by obscurity. For three years He traveled the highways and byways of the harvest field of the world, seeking the lost sheep.

The way to Calvary not only formed the narrow way to the cross, but it embraced the work of the cross. It is vital to understand that the cross was formed by the way of Calvary, and that it constantly marked His life.

The first requirement was *self-denial*. We must always first deny self in obedience to that which is worthy before the cross can have its way. Consider how Jesus' denial of self cast a shadow of the cross.

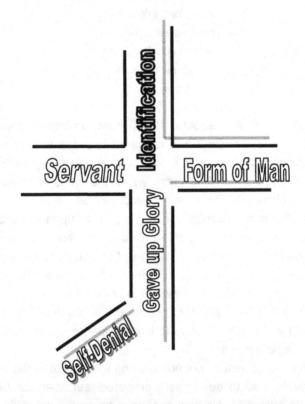

As previously pointed out, Jesus denied self by giving up the glory attached to heaven to take on the disposition of a servant. He was then fashioned as a man. He did this so He could become identified with us as a means to take our place.

Identification is the second requirement to pick up the cross. Jesus had to become man to become the sacrifice. Such identification would serve as a foundation to reach His objective as the Lamb of God. Consider how the cross worked in this area of His walk.

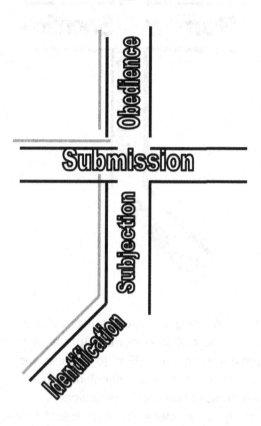

Jesus became identified with us in human form in order to become sin for us. He first had to come into subjection to the will of the Father. This subjection allowed Him to submit to the plan of redemption. Redemption required Him to become the obedient sacrifice to satisfy the death sentence of the Law that hung over all of our heads.[16]

Obedience is the next qualification of the cross of Calvary. Let us consider how this cross transpired for Christ on the road to Calvary.

---

[16]   2 Corinthians 5:21; Philippians 2:8

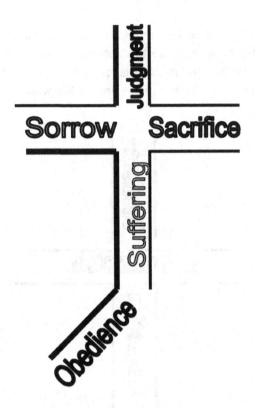

The look, feel, and weight of a cross might change as it cuts deep into the very being and character of man. It is a rough instrument, but it was an instrument designed by God to address each layer of man's inward environment. Clearly, godly obedience must serve as strong foundation for the cross to be effective in its work.

In His humanity, Jesus became totally identified with man as the different works of the cross brought Him close to the abyss of destruction. The last part of the road to Calvary challenged Jesus in a way we will never fully understand in our present state. In our humanity we do not initially, in a gracious manner, give way to the work of the cross as He did.

It is said of Jesus that as man He offered up prayers and supplications with strong crying and tears to the One who was able to take the burden from Him. However, Hebrews 5:8-9 goes on to tell us that even though He was a Son, worthy of such deliverance, He still had to learn obedience by the things He suffered. The deep working of self-denial at this level produced the very suffering that perfected Jesus in His humanity, allowing Him to become the sacrificial Lamb of God.

Even though Jesus suffered and became a man of sorrow, He was perfected as a sacrifice in His humanity that was able to suffice all judgment on sin. We see where He was wounded for our transgressions, bruised for our iniquities, chastised to bring forth peace, and by His stripes we can be healed.[17]

Jesus became acquainted with grief as He bore our sins. He was not esteemed by man, as well as being smitten of God. However, through His suffering and perfect sacrifice He became the author of salvation to those who follow in His steps of obedience.[18]

In obedience Jesus allowed Himself to be led as the Lamb to the slaughter. He was God's Passover Lamb that had been prepared to be offered up as the ultimate sacrifice in our place. This aspect of the cross resulted in three judgments. Judgment represents separation, which can only happen when the cross is properly applied. Let us now consider this particular cross.

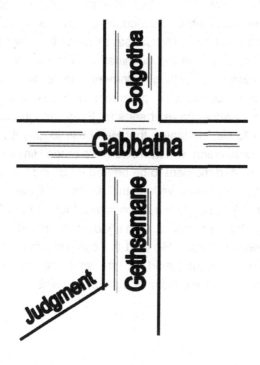

---

[17]   Isaiah 53:5

[18]   Hebrews 5:8-9

As mentioned in the previous paragraph, Jesus faced these three judgments on the way to Calvary. He faced the judgment on His *flesh* in the Garden of *Gethsemane,* as He was crushed by the weight of the ordeal He was about to face. He had to get through the challenge as man, but the flesh was weak.[19] However, the influence and sweat of the flesh was poured out on the ground as He gave way to the Father's will.

As the perfected Lamb of God, He stood in judgment before the Sanhedrin. After examining Jesus, this religious body found Him guilty for being the Son of God. Every Passover Lamb first had to be examined by the priest before it was offered. In a sense, after being examined by these religious men, they found Him worthy to become the Passover Lamb of God. They called for His death.

The Lord would later silently stand before Pilate who could find no fault in Him. He was taken to Herod where He was mocked after refusing to entertain him with miracles. He was then taken back to Pilate, where He was brought before him at *Gabbatha*, the place of judgment. It was here that the religious mob demanded Jesus' crucifixion as they rejected Him as their king and referred to Caesar as being their leader.[20]

"Gabbatha" represented the culmination of the perverted judgments of the world's system of both government and religion. These worldly systems will often prove to bring judgment on the self-life, with its pride and rights to experience life as it sees fit. Even though Jesus appeared to lose His right to life, He stated that He chose to give it up.[21] He never lost control of the situation, which would have made Him a victim. He had come for this time and moment to be offered up as the Lamb of God.

From Gabbatha, Jesus walked the distance to the final judgment, that of *Golgotha*. Golgotha is the Hebrew word for "Calvary", the place of the Skull. Golgotha represented God's judgment on sin. Jesus became a sacrifice on behalf of man. He paid the complete ransom price for our redemption. In death Jesus would take the sin of man to the barren tomb to silence its claims and accusations against mankind.

---

[19] Matthew 26:36-44
[20] John 19:12-15
[21] John 10:18

Clearly, the "old man" that is in existence in each of us, has been thoroughly judged by the cross. When God looks down on the believer He sees the life and glory of His Son, not the pathetic state of fallen man.

The secret for the Christian is to realize that his or her life is hid in Christ. This hidden life means that since believers are dead in Christ, sin has no claims on them. Their sins are not only done away with, but they also possess a resurrected power and life to overcome every aspect of the flesh and the world. However, they must become identified with Christ through the Gospel. They must properly apply the cross to all fleshly influences, and to any claims of the self-life to possess the spiritual and eternal life that has been made available by this old rugged instrument.

THE CROSS THAT SAVES

For by grace are ye saved through
faith; and that not of yourselves,
it is the gift of God: Not of works,
lest any man should boast.
(Ephesians 2:8-9)

The cross stands at the center of the Christian faith. It is a brutal instrument that was designed to torture and eventually kill those who were put upon it. These individuals died a humiliating death. There was no glamour, nobility, or valor in such a death.

Sadly, many people have taken the intent out of the cross. They have made it into jewelry that adorns their necks. They may become sentimental about it when they think of Jesus' sacrifice. They even sing songs about it, but few ever become identified to the cross of Christ or pick up their personal cross. As a result, death does not mark their life, their walk is not disciplined, and they do not abide in Christ.

The Apostle Paul stated that the Jews seek after a sign. However, Jesus' resurrection was the greatest sign they were given. But, instead of receiving God's sacrifice, the cross of Jesus has become a stumbling block they cannot get around.[22]

---

[22]   1 Corinthians 1:21-24

The Greeks seek after wisdom, but the intent of the cross seems too crude, simple, and insulting; therefore, the preaching of the cross seems foolish to such individuals. Let us now consider and compare how this cross operates according to God and man.

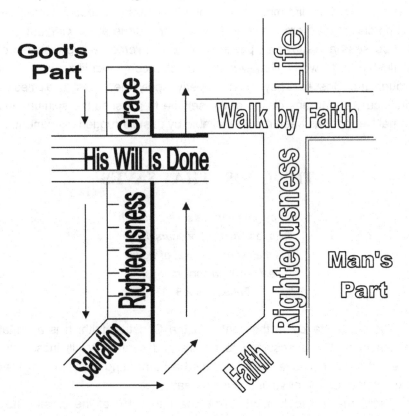

The cross of Christ actually serves as a ladder that lifts up and connects the bridge (Jesus) to heaven. This entryway allows the grace of God to flow downward towards undeserving man, while serving as the entryway in which genuine faith allows a person to begin to identify with its work. The believer's walk of faith allows him or her to proceed upward in his or her life in Christ.

The cross is not meant to be a symbol, but a brutal instrument of God in which God's favor can be shown to man, while His will is being done in saving man from perishing in his sins. In order for God to show such favor, His grace must be reigning through righteousness.[23] As His grace freely flows down through righteousness, salvation will be brought forth in man.

Man's order, when it comes to the cross, is different than God's. Unfeigned faith is reckoned as righteousness by God to the believer. As a result, man is able to walk by faith in obedience to God's Word and reliance on His character. Ultimately, such faith will lead to possessing the gift of life.

The cross cost God His best and Christ His all. It also can cost man his soul, or cost him his self-life and the world. Therefore, it is not meant to bring honor to the matter of lost man, but to judge and strike a death blow to his fallen state. It is not meant to be worshipped as an icon, it is meant to lift up the only real solution in the midst of great darkness and hopelessness.

In order to become identified *by* the work of the cross, man must first become identified *to* it. In some cases people view the cross from a far distance, but have no intention of becoming identified with it. They may admire it, but will not allow it to strike death blows to their old man. They may come to it, but they will remain in the shadow of it to prevent its light from revealing their true condition.

As we can see, men respond to the cross differently. Their attitude towards the real work of the cross will determine how they approach it and the type of impact it will have on their lives.

What is your response towards the work of the cross? What price will you ultimately pay based on the type of attitude you possess towards this instrument of death?

THE VICTORIOUS CROSS

Therefore we are buried with
him by baptism into death: that like
as Christ was raised up from
the dead by the glory of the

---

[23]   Romans 5:21

Father, even so we also should
walk in newness of life.
(Romans 6:4)

Although the cross of Jesus was an instrument of judgment and death, it now clearly serves as a door to life and victory. For this cross to produce a victorious life in a person, it must become a place where the great exchange takes place. The old man with his selfish disposition must be exchanged with the new man, Jesus.

Before this exchange can take place, this tool of judgment must have its way in our lives. To bring judgment to the old, the cross has to be properly applied to bring about the death of the self-serving disposition.

Keep in mind there are two crosses in operation. The cross of Jesus serves as a place of identification to and in Christ. It represents death, but the second cross is the personal cross. It is the means by which the mark of death will be branded into our very being.

The cross of Christ hides us in Him. We cease to be, as we become identified in His work of redemption. However, our personal cross is what works the very life of Jesus in us.

The application of our personal cross must go deep into our being. It must root out and expose sin, cross out all semblance of pride, cut away the profane, kill the influence of the flesh, and cause us to become crucified to the world. Ultimately, it will bring the necessary circumcision of the profane that clings to our very beings, and robs and sucks any life or resolve we may have towards God. This is why the Apostle Paul talked about dying daily. He was concerned that if he did not keep his body in subjection, he would become a castaway or a reprobate. This is why Paul's personal cross was being constantly applied to ensure victory in his walk.[24]

Do we apply this cross to our lives? The answer is no. We must discipline our body by picking up our cross to continually come to a place of death, but we cannot personally apply it. It is the Spirit of God who applies this cross to our lives. We must have His Spirit present, as well as give way to His work. It is only through His Spirit that we can abide in Jesus' life, and it is only by His Spirit that His life can come forth.

---

[24] 1 Corinthians 9:27; 15:31

Consider how the Spirit works Jesus' life in us by way of the cross, and what we must do to give way to the Spirit.

The Christian's victorious route begins with being born again from above. However, this birth cannot occur unless man is first drawn by the Father to the Son. It is only after the Spirit convicts him of sin that he can repent and accept Jesus' invitation to come to Him to receive the Living Water of life (the Spirit).[25]

A person, who is born from above, receives a new disposition (spirit and heart). This new disposition changes an individual's inclinations towards God as it transforms the mind. The transformation of the mind results in a person taking on the very likeness of Jesus. At this point, the person will be inclined to walk or follow after the Spirit. The Holy Spirit's

---

[25] John 6:44; 7:35-39

goal is to lift us up above the judgment that is upon this age, and place us in heavenly places in Christ Jesus.[26]

The Apostle Paul made this statement in Romans 14:17, "For the kingdom of God is not meat and drink; but righteousness, and peace, and joy in the Holy Spirit." If as believers, we walk or follow after the Spirit, we will be following after righteousness, godliness, faith, love, patience, and meekness.[27]

As we come under the leading of the Spirit, our minds will be transformed to consider life from a spiritual perspective in light of an eternal inheritance.[28] Clearly, our relationship as children of God will be established as we learn to walk in His Spirit. The more we give way to the work of the Spirit, the more we will become like Jesus.

Have you made the great exchange of your old former life with the new life? Are you experiencing the victorious life because the Holy Spirit is properly applying your cross to the different layers of your old life?

THE CHALLENGE OF THE CROSS

Let this mind be in you,
which was also in Christ Jesus.
(Philippians 2:5)

Our personal cross must go through layers of the old life in us in order to ensure the resurrection of the new life of Jesus. As the Apostle Paul declared the old will pass away and all things will become new.[29]

The greatest battle with the old surrounds the mind. Mind includes spirit, perception, and attitudes. Being born again ensures a new spirit, which will produce a new perception about God and life. How we perceive something will either change or reinforce our attitudes about a matter.

---

[26]   Ezekiel 36:26-27; John 3:3, 5; 16:11; Ephesians 2:6
[27]   1 Timothy 6:11
[28]   1 Corinthians 2:10-14
[29]   2 Corinthians 5:17

God's Word talks about the influence of the mind. We are told that strongholds are found in our thought processes. These strongholds entail imaginations that exalt themselves against the real knowledge of God.[30]

An unregenerate mind possesses a carnal mind that thinks according to the world's philosophies. It is at enmity with God and ruled by the selfish disposition. Since self has a high opinion of its understanding, it cannot see how it could possibly be wrong in its conclusions. However, the wisest man of the Old Testament warned that there is a way that seems right to a man, but it leads to destruction or death.[31] Let us now consider what the personal cross must address as far as our mind.

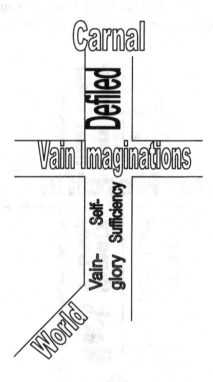

The Apostle Paul tells us the mind has to be transformed.[32] When you consider the idea of something being transformed, it is the same

---

[30]   2 Corinthians 10:5

[31]   Proverbs 14:12; 16:2, 25; Romans 8:5-8; Colossians 2:8

[32]   Romans 12:1-2

as a metamorphosis taking place. It will not be a mind conformed to something, but completely changed into something decisively different than its former disposition.

Man's world is out of order. Nothing really fits or makes sense. Man's mind is defiled and he has become lost to the things of God. The personal cross brings everything back to center in order to properly expose and address the influences of the old life. This is what allows the Spirit to transform the mind.

Scripture tells us that we must bring all thoughts into captivity to the obedience of Christ.[33] Obviously, if we bring all thoughts into captivity and submit them in obedience to what is right, we will begin to take on the mind or attitude of Christ. Consider how this attitude will express itself.

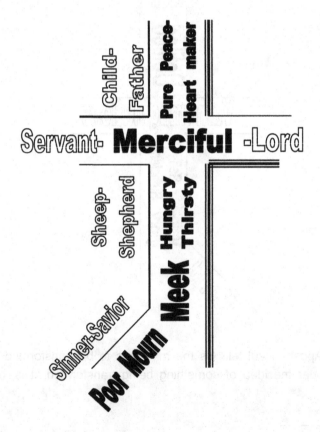

---

[33]   2 Corinthians 10:5

The work of the cross is always calling us to come higher, to a place of excellence. It wants to lift us above this present world to embrace the next one. It must destroy earthly ties and ways so that we can freely reach our heavenly status.

As you follow the work of the cross, you will see that the attitude that is being developed was described in the Beatitudes by Jesus in the Sermon on the Mount in Matthew 5:3-9. Each attitude establishes the person in a more defined relationship with the Lord. For example a convicted sinner will see his or her spiritual poverty and begin to mourn his or her plight and sin. This is where Jesus can meet the sinner as a Savior, and an exchange is made upon the death to the old, with a new life.

Once saved, the new convert can begin to take on the meek disposition of a lamb. This is where he or she learns dependency on the Shepherd to lead him or her to places where he or she will gain a hunger and thirst for righteousness. It is only as the believer follows Jesus as the great Shepherd, that he or she will be satisfied.

As believers allow the cross to address the reign of the self-life, they will take on the disposition of a servant. Such a disposition will express itself in mercy.

Each attitude enlarges us to walk in a more selfless way towards the matters of God. Mercy can't exist as long as self demands that it be regarded in a specific way. Self can only demand judgment when insulted, for it has no concept of true mercy.

The more self is out of the way, the purer our heart becomes allowing us to see the Lord, and the more liberty we will have to move into a relationship as a child to the Father. It is in this relationship that the real source behind true peace is discovered.

What does your attitude say about your relationship with God?

THE FRUIT OF THE CROSS

But the fruit of the Spirit is
love, joy, peace, longsuffering,
gentleness, goodness, faith,
Meekness, temperance: against
such there is no law.
(Galatians 5:22-23)

We already have considered how the Spirit applies the cross to the old life. This cross clearly has to go deep into layers and patterns that are destructive before a person can be established and hidden in a new life. The more believers give way to the new life, the more they will effectively live it out in authority and power. However, the attitude of Christ produces the fruit of the Spirit. We need to see how the life of Christ being worked in us by the cross, expresses itself in the fruit of the Spirit.

The life of Christ may be what is being worked in us, but it will manifest itself through the fruit of the Spirit. Even though the fruit is the product of Jesus life in us, it is also the direct result of the Spirit influencing, leading, guiding, and inspiring us along the way.

The fruit of the Spirit should be what is being reflected from our disposition. In His humanity Jesus was under the leading of the Spirit. The life of the Spirit comes from above to work on, within, and through man. Therefore, it would only make sense that the inner reflection of His life being manifested in us would speak of us partaking of His heavenly nature.[34]

Let us now consider how the cross would cross out an old disposition to ensure the heavenly fruit of a new one. Remember, as you consider the following diagram, God's work comes from above, while our work starts from the foundation or position of humility and need.

---

[34]   2 Peter 1:3-4

Love is what brings our attitudes and relationships together to produce the excellent life of Christ that will display the fruit of the Spirit in attitude and responses. When the Spirit begins to minister to us, joy takes it place as an anchor in our soul. The anchor brings peace, which allows us to know and receive the patience, gentleness, and goodness of God. Such an experience reinforces God's faithfulness towards us, allowing us by good faith to come under the meekness of the Spirit. Meekness produces temperance, which becomes a stable foundation that disciplines our conduct.

Humility serves as temperance or self-control in the soul of believers as they give way to the discipline of the cross according to the sanctifying work of Spirit. As they give way to its work, they will become meek in attitude towards the leadership of God. As they come into obedience to the Lord's way, their faith will be enlarged. As their attitude is fine-tuned, the abiding love of God serves as an environment that will allow them to take on the virtues of patience, gentleness (kindness), and goodness (honorable conduct) towards others, just as Jesus had displayed in His earthly ministry. This type of submission ensures peace with God and the joy of possessing the abundant life.

Although, we possess eternal life, it is the heart of our Shepherd that we also know what it means to experience the abundance of this eternal life.[35] The abundance of the Christian life points to eternal fruits that will bring glory to God. These fruits not only necessitate the life of Christ coming forth, but it also entails this life being multiplied in lost souls.

As Christians we should be fruit bearers that identify us to the powerful life, excellent attitude, and perfect ways of Christ. These fruits should clearly speak of His love, grace, and truth.

What does your fruit say about your life before the Lord?

THE REALITY OF THE CROSS

*For the law of the Spirit of
life in Christ Jesus hath made
me free from the law
of sin and death.
(Romans 8:2)*

There are two types of spiritual laws in operation. There is the law of sin and death. This law judges all transgressions and iniquity, and is known as the Law of God. However, there is also the law of the Spirit of life in Christ Jesus. In other words life reigns instead of death because the Spirit is influencing man, rather than sin.

The law of the Spirit is a more excellent law than the Law of God. God's Law was holy and righteous, but it could not save. The law of the Spirit is able to save man from his plight by establishing a new life in him.

Galatians 5:22-23 tells us that the life in us is identifying us to the Spirit because His fruit is present in our attitude and conduct. However, it is important to point out that you cannot have the fruit of the Spirit if He is not present.

Galatians 5:23 goes on to explain that we are no longer subject to God's Law. There are a couple of reasons for this. God's Law judged the ways of fleshly man, but the law of the Spirit is spiritual, and serves as a

---

[35]   John 10:10

point of identification. Obviously, God's Law has no jurisdiction over that which is of the Spirit.

The second reason we as believers are not subject to the Law is that the Spirit reaps life everlasting, while the flesh, which is under God's Law, will reap corruption because there is no life in it. It cannot please the Law, but the Spirit is in agreement with God and has His approval.

The reality of the cross is that it brings us back to center, by lining us up to God's leadership. Let us now consider man's choice as to the cross he must bear in light of leadership.

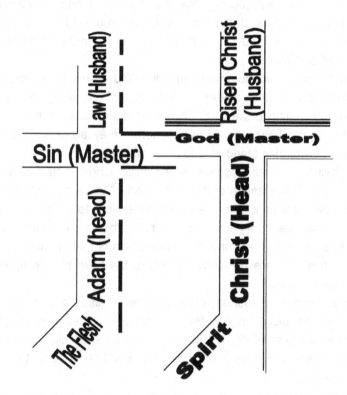

Leadership brings some type of responsibility, service, and identification. It is God's leadership that will lead us to a complete life in Jesus. These two crosses show that there are three levels of leadership that are clearly defined in Romans 5-7. They are the head, master, and husband.

At the base of these leaderships is what is influencing you the most, the flesh or the Holy Spirit. Your influence will determine what head you will come under. "Head" points to how you will view a matter. You will view a matter from Adam's perspective, which will be selfish and perverted, or, you will view it from the basis of the man Christ serving as your head. As your head, Christ will become your point of identification and example, and you will view everything from the premise of His truth.

Head will determine what or who you will serve. Under Adam you will serve sin. It is a tyrant, but it will allow you to give into your fleshly appetites and live according to your own preference or take on life until you taste the bitter consequences of it: that of spiritual death.

If God is your master, you will become His instrument of righteousness. You will count all matters of the flesh dead to you so that you can live unto God. Under His leadership, you will discover not only an abundant life, but a just, caring master who is worthy of consecrated service and devotion.

This brings us to our husband. Husband points to accountability or agreement. For those under the influence of the flesh, they will find that they are bound to the Law. They are accountable to the righteous judgments of the Law regardless of whether they agree with it or not. Under the Law people stand judged and condemned.

For believers, their husband is the risen Christ. It is important to understand the significance of the "risen Christ." We are all bound by the Law. However, it is only when we become identified to Jesus in His death that we are set free from being accountable to the Law. After all, a person cannot seek another mate until there is a death of that spouse. By being dead in Christ, we are no longer bound to the Law; therefore, we can seek a new husband.

Since our new husband, Jesus, has been raised above this world, we also will be raised up with Him in heavenly places in order to walk with Him in newness of life. This will raise us above the claims of the Law upon our lives, allowing us to become accountable to a life that will prove much more excellent.[36]

We are subject to one of these leaderships. The question is, who serves as your head, master, and husband? The answer will show whether you are walking in the ways of corruption or in the ways of life that is being wrought by the Spirit of God.[37]

---

[36]   Galatians 5:23; Ephesians 2:6
[37]   Galatians 6:7-9

THE EXCELLENCE OF
THE CROSS

For if these things be in you,
and abound, they make you that
ye shall neither be barren nor
unfruitful in the knowledge of
our Lord Jesus Christ.
(2 Peter 1:8)

In the last chapter, we discovered that under the law of the Spirit, Jesus has been declared our husband. We are to walk in agreement with Him about all matters. We are to have His mind, display His heart, and manifest His life.

When we think of having a spouse, most would agree that it is vital to know what is important to him or her. This pursuit does not point to serving the whims of our spouses, but sharing an intimacy with those who are committed to the well-being of such a relationship.

In order to discover what is important to our spouses, we must travel the way of the cross. Subsequently, if self is present, it wants to be served or recognized for what it does. It only can prefer its whims and strive for its desire to be honored. Self does not have any concept about self-denial.

Godly love will result in self-denial and sacrificial devotions to ensure the quality of the relationship. Such love allows for agreement where partners feel free to share intimate matters with their spouses.

In the Scripture in 2 Peter 1:8, it tells people that the reason they do not abound in the virtues that would truly identify them to the life of Jesus is because they are barren or unfruitful in the knowledge of Him. How can you love or appreciate someone you do not really know? How can you take on the character of someone you do not respect?

Since the work of the cross is about working Jesus' life into us, we must conclude that it is His very character that is being forged into our life. Granted, we know that the work of the cross transforms our mind to embrace His lowly state, but it also forms His very character in us.

The more His excellent character is worked into our lives, the more we become aware of who He is. Instead of being a sentimental figure or notion at the center of our religious beliefs, His life will take on dimension.

371

His personality will come alive and His ways will become necessary to maintain our conduct.

This brings us to the reality of the excellence of the cross. It points to the ways of death, but in light of gaining Christ. His ways are excellent and worthy of all consideration. The Apostle Paul brought out the excellent way of the cross in Philippians 3:10, "That I may know him, and the power of his resurrection, and the fellowship of his sufferings, being made conformable unto his death." Paul was always being conformed to Jesus' death by his personal cross. However, he understood that in such death he was becoming identified to Jesus in every way.

Let us now consider how the work of the cross conforms us to the likeness of Christ by working His character in us. The Apostle Peter reveals how this life would express itself in 2 Peter 1:5-7.

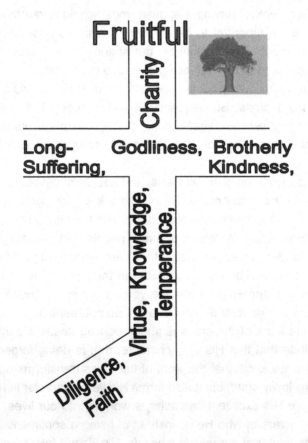

Fruitful

Charity

Long-Suffering,   Godliness, Brotherly Kindness,

Virtue, Knowledge, Temperance,

Diligence, Faith

In order to develop a knowledge of Jesus that will be fruitful, we must be diligent or earnest in our faith to know and please Him. We must insist on being virtuous in our pursuit to honor Him in all we do. The purpose of pursuing Him is so that we can honor Him, but such honor does not mean we will simply know about Him or will remain content in knowing of Him; rather we must know Him in a personal way to do what is right. Knowledge without virtue to temper it will be puffed up by facts and concepts, as well as void of life-changing revelation.

Temperance will produce patience in us as the Spirit develops godliness in our behavior towards others. As godliness is forged into our character, it will express itself in brotherly kindness. This kindness will be a product of a state of charity which will express itself in genuine benevolence. This condition will serve as an open door to acceptable service, and will prove to be fruitful in the knowledge of our Lord Jesus Christ.

Forming the character of Christ in each of us is the excellent work of our personal cross. The result of this work is that we can be assured of being fruitful in our knowledge of Jesus. Such knowledge will translate into a fruitful life that will bring glory to the Father.

Have you allowed the work of the cross to establish you in the excellent way of Christ? If not, perhaps you need to revisit or once again come under the cross that will lead you to being renewed by the quickening of the very life of Jesus that is in you.

THE PURPOSE OF
THE CROSS

*For I determined not to
know any thing among you,
save Jesus Christ, and
him crucified.
1 Corinthians 2:2*

We have been considering the different aspects of the cross. It serves as the narrow gate that leads to the door of Jesus and life. It looms between death and life. It is meant to minister the fatal blows to the old man in order to ensure the resurrection and liberation of a new man. It is where the believer's old life has been crossed out and he or she is now hid in Christ, completely consumed by His life. Rather than seeing the believer's former filthy rags of the old man, the Father sees the wisdom, righteousness, sanctification, and redemption of His Son.

The cross has different angles to it and is meant to take on different intensities in our life to rid us of something in order to work something in us, but we must stand in front where Jesus has been lifted up for the world to see. It is from the heights of redemption that the life of Jesus begins to serve as our light and hope. It is from this premise that His grace flows downward to deposit the measure of faith in our hearts that is necessary for us to receive and possess the gift of life.

Even though the shape and work of the cross has not changed, it will change us. In fact, as the altar of God, we will receive new life from above. Each time our personal cross is applied, it will appear at times to be different, harder, and perhaps formidable. However, the truth is, we are different because of it. It changes us from within as the glory of Jesus is being established in us, preparing us to express even greater glory. Eventually it will become that easy yoke that simply will bring us into step with our Lord as we follow Him in the ways of righteousness. In the end, we will reflect His glory rather than the fading glory of man, the false glory of man's religion, and the temporary glory of the world.

The cross of Christ represents death to the old life where the great exchange is to take place, but our personal cross represents regression to the old way in order to exchange the type of leadership that has been influencing us. Death and regression are necessary if the new life is to come forth, and the work of the Holy Spirit is to bring this new life forth in spiritual perfection.

As we can see, everything in our Christian walk forms the cross. Whether it is a place of self-denial, identification, the deep work of the Spirit, or the type of walk and leadership that ensures we are abiding in Christ, it requires the application of the cross. It is a place of redemption, victory, challenge, and excellence. It encompasses every aspect of the spiritual life, while it narrows and disciplines the walk.

The message of the cross is simple. The work of the cross is straightforward and the product of the cross is glorious. Yet man has a tendency to mock its simplicity, pervert its straightforwardness, and strip it of the glory it is capable of working in each us. Man's rejection is the real tragedy of the cross. In this light it remains a death instrument that is devoid of life, mercy, and grace.

The Apostle Paul stated he did not want to know anything among us except Christ and Him crucified. Clearly the Word of God advocates the cross as a distinct focus, a simple solution, and a realistic presentation of the Christian walk. As the Apostle John explained in 1 John 2:6, such presentation is necessary to assure that a man walks as Jesus did in order to abide in Him.

What is the cross of Jesus to you? Does it represent tragedy or liberation, loss or hope, death or life? What does your personal cross represent to you? Is it too great of a burden to bear, or is it the merciful instrument that will rid you of the insipid burden and harsh demands of the self-life? Your attitude towards it will determine whether you mock it or embrace it, reject it or become identified with it, or hide in its shadows or walk in its glorious, liberating light.

3

WALKING IN
THE LIGHT

INTRODUCTION

In considering the reality of the Christian life, we must note what truly distinguishes people as to the type of life they are embracing. It will be determined by the type of light they are walking in. It is easy to talk about the Christian life, but if a person is not walking according to the light that distinguishes this godly life, there will be much debate as to whether or not he or she is a Christian.

Although there are various lights that abound in the age we live in, there is only one true light that identifies a person to the kingdom of God. This light cannot be counterfeited. After all, light is about exposure and identification. Every light reveals how we will see a matter, ultimately identifying us as to what we understand once the real fruits of the matter have been tested. It is time for those of the Christian realm to understand the type of light that will illuminate the deeds of their lives.

The Lord also made another statement that darkness can serve as a light to those who are in spiritual darkness. He posed the thought that if the darkness is great in light of a person's spiritual condition, just how great will that darkness be?

Meditating upon the reality that what I may perceive as light could in fact be nothing more than darkness is disconcerting to say the least. How can I personally know whether I am groping in spiritual darkness or walking in the light of heaven? Clearly, I cannot assume that the light I am walking in is leading me down the right path. I must be sure that the type of life I am embracing possesses the light that will ultimately identify me to the kingdom of light.

As we come face-to-face with our personal concept of the Christian life we are living, we must evaluate whether we are walking in the true light of God or whether we are walking in a pseudo light that is blinding us to the spiritual darkness that is lurking in our souls.

DIFFERENT LIGHTS

In order to understand what it means to walk in the light, we need to understand what constitutes light. It is vital that each aspect of light is brought out and discussed. There are three types of light that must be properly understood. There is the light from above, the light from without, and the light from within.

Light refers to a type of life that resonates in, through, and from us. For example, the light from above will affect the type of life we end up pursuing. The light from without will determine how we interpret life around us, and the light from within will reveal the life we possess. Notice how light will determine the type of life we desire, how we define life, and the quality of life we develop.

The first light we must consider is the light that comes from above. The light from above is what shines upon us, as well as illuminating the terrain that is before us. Such a light comes from outside of us. It is a light that has been created in some way. It is meant to illuminate our surrounding to reveal the possibilities that are before us. It will either bring clarity or outline what lurks in the shadows of obscurity. Without such an illumination, man would simply grope in darkness, unable to see any danger that might be lurking in front of him. Ultimately, without the light from above man would not be able to function. In fact, without light, man is doomed by the darkness of his environment. He has no means to recognize where he is at and what is required of him to prepare for darkness. He will become lost, and remain lost, as he gropes with the unseen or unknown terrain ahead of him.

The light that comes from above is represented by the natural light provided for the earth, the artificial light developed by man, and the light from heaven. As we meditate on the different types of lights that come from above, we will begin to sense that they each bring light to different terrains. For example, the natural light illuminates the physical terrain of the earth that we are bound to by natural laws. The light developed by man will illuminate those places where he will abide, while the light of God will reveal the activities of an unseen world that surrounds each of us.

There are a couple of aspects about the lights from above that must be considered. In creation, when the Lord created the world, He gave us the intense light of the sun and the lesser light of the moon. The first thing we must understand about the light from above is that it will bring contrast. Light has a great intensity which can overshadow anything that it is directed towards, but a person will determine how intense the light will shine on him or her. As the individual gets further away from the sphere of it, the light's intensity becomes less. Therefore, you can stand in an intense light or you can walk in shadows. Clearly, the shadows represent a cooler environment that will bring relief to man.

With this in mind, let us now consider what the natural light of the earth reveals about the quality of light. There are a couple of aspects we must note about the natural light. Our Creator provided this light so that we could function in this world. Everything is dependent on the light of creation. We know without the light of the sun, nothing could grow, but we also know if it is too intense, and there is no water to cool down the earth it beats down upon, that nothing could live and grow in it.

The lesser light of the moon cools the earth down, regulates the tides of the ocean, and provides the necessary atmosphere where the dew of the morning is able to come forth to revive that which the heat purged the day before. However, without the sun to balance out the moon, the earth would also become uninhabitable. Both lights are necessary, but as noted, in the extremes they can only produce destruction. There is a fine balance that these two lights maintain that enables creation to function properly.

The artificial light provided by man can come in different forms. However, the main purpose for this light was and is to break through the darkness so that man can abide or function in his present atmosphere. Consider the campfire that breaks through the darkness of the forest. It actually will expose, as well as create a circle of protection from that which preys in the night. Consider the lights of a vehicle breaking through the dark night as one heads down a lonely road towards a destination that awaits him. The lights will illuminate the way until he safely reaches his location. Then, you have the lights that light up a dark room. When you turn the light on in such a room, the darkness flees, exposing the contents, familiarity, or the possibilities the room possesses in regard to resting or abiding.

The third light is the light from heaven. The Apostle John reveals this light as being a person. When He came into the world, the brilliance of heaven shone about declaring the glory associated with this light, while a star at night guided the wise men to this particular light.[1] Matthew described this light by quoting the prophet Isaiah, "The people which sat in darkness saw great light; and to them which sat in the region and shadow of death light is sprung up" (Matthew 4:16).

The light of heaven is the person of Jesus Christ. Although obscured by the darkness of the world and veiled by humanity, nothing could extinguish the light of heaven. Jesus possessed the light from above, walked according to a light from without, and offered the life that would penetrate and serve as a light from within.

The light from above penetrates the darkness of the terrain so that man can see, function, and abide in the world in which he lives. We can see how the natural light reveals the terrain of the world, while the light created by man reveals the environment around him. However, the light of heaven can penetrate the natural darkness of the world, the darkness that abides in the midst of man, and the darkness that spiritually engulfs him. The beauty about the light of heaven is that it will never be overcome by the darkness of the world or man's environment. It will never cease to bring the light or illumination to what is before man. It will always bring contrast as it illuminates the terrain, reveals what is in the shadows, and exposes what has been in darkness.

The question we must consider is, how much of the light from heaven have we allowed to penetrate our lives? We can settle for the lesser light while abiding in the shadows, but the reality of it is that we need the light of heaven to not only penetrate our lives, but we need to be assured that we are abiding in it. Are you abiding in the light of heaven?

---

[1]   Matthew 2:1-2; Luke 2:9; John 1:4-5

THE LIGHTS FROM WITHOUT

When we consider the light from without, we must realize it has to do with how we interpret what constitutes life. Our interpretation of life will determine the attitude we take about it. As we consider that the different lights from without can determine the attitude we take towards life, we will realize that such lights will actually determine our reality.

Therefore, we must recognize that life constitutes the reality around us. We must interact with the reality around us to live the life that we desire or that is before us. Many times people are trying to adjust, find, or secure a particular reality based on the type of light that they have adopted towards life. Obviously, this reveals that we all determine the reality we walk in. In some cases, people insist on their particular reality to control or adjust others to their perception of life. Others throw bones to those who would challenge their concept of life so that they can freely live as they chose without much opposition. There are still those who ignore any outside challenges about the reality they are adopting so they can maintain a fragile balance of a false peace or security in their world.

We all maintain our particular realities, revealing that we indeed possess different definitions of life, exposing the diverse attitudes we can have towards it. Attitudes towards life reveal that we perceive it according to some frame of reference or worldview that will determine what we emphasize about it and the approach we make in regard to it. Clearly, we are interacting with our reality based on this perception or frame of reference we have embraced.

The harsh truth about the light we adopt from without is that it may not be truth, but a pseudo environment of superstition that keeps us in ignorance or delusion towards what is real. Such reality will keep us from being prepared to face the constant changes or challenges that life will bring us. Instead of being prepared to face reality, we will be set up to fall into the traps of seduction and delusion that will take us captive and mark us for impending judgment and wrath.

There are four lights that can affect our perception and attitude towards life. These lights will determine our emphasis and approach in regard to life. Keep in mind that what we emphasize is what we will focus on and pursue. Our emphasis will determine the spirit or manner with which we approach something. Our approach may reveal that we are meek in attitude, or we are judgmental, indifferent, and hateful towards what is true and real. We may harbor a love for what is true or a mocking, skeptical, or angry attitude towards any realism that may challenge our desired reality.

The first light we must consider that influences or determines people's reality are the world's philosophies. The world conditions and indoctrinates people according to philosophies that are humanistic in nature. In other words, the world declares that man has the means to determine, control, and establish his own reality, regardless of the challenges life may bring that will prove otherwise.

Man may delude himself about reality, but he cannot control it. He may situate his small selfish world to conform to his desired reality, but the storms of life will eventually intrude into his world to prove how incapable and fragile he is in trying to determine or maintain his desired environment. He may try to establish his particular reality, but the crisis of life will end up shaking every attempt, bringing his world to utter ruin. Each affront that life wields against man's fragile reality based on the deceptive and foolish philosophies of the world reminds him that he is mortal and that his life is but a vapor in light of the changing winds that move in, through, and out of his world. The fruit of his humanistic philosophy is that of ruin and chaos.

It is for this reason that the Apostle Paul gave this warning in Colossians 2:8, "Beware lest any man spoil you through philosophy and vain deceit, after the tradition of men, after the rudiments of the world, and not after Christ." Paul gives us insight to the type of influence the world has on us. First of all, worldly philosophies are presented by men who are trying to change your way of looking at life. They want to influence your thinking through indoctrination. However, such influence will spoil you as to what is true with that which represents vain and deceptive conditioning. This conditioning becomes a set tradition. Tradition is what serves as a foundation that erects a particular worldview as to what is right and wrong. For instance, such traditions can be found in cultural influences and religious practices. The reference to rudiments of the world points to that which serves as man's foundation in which everything he believes or stands for is founded or rooted in. However, Jesus clearly reveals that such foundations represent the shifting sand of the present age and will not stand when the storms of life challenge it.[2]

---

[2]   Matthew 7:24-27; 1 Corinthians 3:11

The Apostle Paul exhorts us to not be conformed to this world's way of thinking, but to be transformed in our perception. For this reason, we are to let the mind of Christ be in us about the matters of God and life.[3] Our thinking must become Christ-centered, not man-centered. We must be rooted in the person of Jesus, grounded in His truth, and established according to His example as the spiritual cornerstone of our lives.

The next light we must consider is the seductive counterfeit light of Satan. We know that in the end days many will depart from the faith, giving heed to seducing spirits and doctrines of devils. The Apostle Paul explained how the seducing light of Satan works. It will present a false Jesus, another spirit, and offer a different gospel.[4] This false Jesus will appear true, the spirit will seem right, and the gospel will be one that will offer greater enlightenment, but such a presentation will lead people away from the simplicity that can be found in the true faith and Gospel message that was first delivered to the saints.

The light of this false presentation will be intense. People will be attracted to it because it seems so real. They will be deluded by it because there will be no shortage of false apostles who hide behind works of deception. These false apostles who cleverly undermine the real Christ will transform themselves into ministers of righteousness. These individuals will be zealous in their proclamations and deeds, but their end shall be according to their reprobate works and heretical claims.[5]

Those beguiled by the light of Satan and seduced by the deceptive presentation of the false ministers will become caught up in the delusion. The main reason people get caught up with such delusion is because the false reality or environment that is created is often reinforced by powerful religious experiences. Such experiences are a result of false realities that have been created by seductive spirits. However, such experiences are to keep seduced souls from seeing that the experiences hide an antichrist spirit. An antichrist spirit will redefine God and will replace Jesus with a counterfeit, as well as proclaim a social gospel of works or a New Age gospel that is mystical.[6]

---

3 Romans 12:2; Philippians 2:5; 1 Peter 2:8
4 2 Corinthians 11:2-3, 14
5 2 Corinthians 11:2-14; Titus 1:15-16
6 1 Timothy 4:1; 1 John 2:22-25; 4:1

The third type of light many walk according to is created by man's religion. This light can tout doctrine that may be founded on truth, but lacks life. It may give an appearance of righteousness by advocating certain rituals or wearing certain cloaks, but lacks the right spirit. It may be disciplined by traditions but it will lack godly love that will nullify the validity of it claims and reveal that is it all quite hypocritical in light of a loving, compassionate God. Jesus contended with the rigid, unloving environment of man's religion when He reminded the religious leaders of His day of these words spoken through the prophet Hosea, "For I desired mercy, and not sacrifice, and the knowledge of God more than burnt offerings".[7]

The truth is that people have the tendency to hide in the shadows of man's religion. They can obscure their lost state with some type of religious cloak. They can hide the arrogance of their ways behind the brushes of religious works. They can conceal their shame behind the fig-leaves of religious business, and they can console themselves in their sins as they recede into the background of some type of religious affiliation. As long as there is some type of religious exposure in their life they can justify their spiritual darkness while falling through the cracks of indifference and complacency. As they spiral into spiritual obscurity, they will console themselves with the argument that at least they tried, but the truth is they have remained hidden from the true light that will make them accountable for their pathetic, irresponsible, and unreceptive spiritual condition.

In regard to other people, they can be like Jonah. These individuals are content to hide in their church pews as the forces of hell rage against the souls and resolve of people in the ocean of humanity. They can sleep in blissful ignorance and indifference as the storms of deception and destruction slams against the immense doors of their religious, worldly based kingdoms. They remain spiritually unaware that they are on sinking ships as they feel secure in their inner sanctuaries that are surrounded by what appears to be worldly success. After all, their immense beautiful church buildings which perhaps houses gymnasiums or the latest programs and attempts that have been designed to appeal to the "unchurched" with modern day entertainment and the most sophisticated

---

[7]   Hosea 6:6; Matthew 9:13; 15:3-9; Romans 7:6; 2 Corinthians 3:6

technology of sound equipment and advertisement, will fortify them against the waves that are slamming against their faulty foundations. As the storm grows they sing songs of victory and declare that the gates of hell will not prevail against them. They refuse to see that they are about to go down into the waters of judgment, while the living Church will raise up out of the ashes of refinement, purified in the fiery ovens like the one that Shadrach, Meshach, and Abednego experienced.[8]

The final light has to do with the truth of God's Word.[9] God's Word has the wisdom to expose the foolishness of the world's light. It contains the light of the real Gospel, which has the power to penetrate the false light of Satan to reveal man's need to be saved. It can become an axe that will cut through the roots of that which is lifeless. It is the fire that purges, the hammer that will tear down, and the sword that will expose. Once it exposes it can impart the incorruptible seed that will produce eternal life in the fertile grounds of open hearts and thirsty souls.[10]

The problem is that people do not approach the Bible to believe it. They will not walk according to its instruction.[11] They will not allow it to be a sword that exposes their inner man or a washing machine that cleanses their way of thinking and being. They constantly fall short of obeying it because they do not properly respect it as being true. Nor, will they tremble before it because it is of God, or value it as their spiritual milk and meat that will bring forth life, ultimately sustaining them and ensuring spiritual growth.[12]

As we consider the three counterfeit lights we must consider why people are so susceptible to be blinded by them. Clearly, the light God has provided from without is able to penetrate those lights which prove to be counterfeit. When it comes to the world, man in his fallen state has been conformed through conditioning and indoctrination to accept the

---

[8]   Daniel 3:8-18

[9]   If you want to understand the authority and power of God's Word can have on those who approach it to believe it, see the author's book: *My Words Are Spirit and Life* in the first volume of the foundational series.

[10]   Jeremiah 23:29; Matthew 3:10; Romans 1:16; 2 Corinthians 4:3-6; Ephesians 5: Hebrews 4:12; 1 Peter 1:22-25

[11]   2 Timothy 2:15; 3:16

[12]   Romans 10:17; Hebrews 12:1-14

world's view. It is for this reason that people must step outside of the former influences of the world by faith to believe God's Word about who He is to develop a proper spiritual emphasis, as well as take on a right attitude towards life.

When it comes to Satan's counterfeit light, the only way to overcome it is by choosing to love the truth.[13] The reality of the spiritual war that rages for man's soul is that only God can penetrate the false seductive light of Satan with His real light. He alone can bring the contrast between that which already stands judged with that which will remain standing when all else is shaken, tested, and proven.

When it comes to the false light of man's religion it is a matter of honestly testing the fruit of it according to God's evaluation set forth in Scripture. The one virtue that truly identifies man to the kingdom of God is godly love. Jesus clearly stated that people will know whether or not we are His disciples if we have love for one another.[14] Much of the self-righteous cloaks that religion uses to impress others hide the harsh truth that godly love is missing from the equation. Religious people blinded by their self-righteousness have an indifference to the real needs of people around them. Granted, they can pick and choose how they want to express their religious piousness, but in most cases it will prove to be sentimental hogwash that is fickle and very self-serving. It will lack real love that proves to be merciful, compassionate, enduring, and sacrificial.

The Word of God tells us that we are to be more than hearers of His Word we must be doers of it. We are commanded to love God, this is our first work in regard to His kingdom. To love someone is not a matter of words, but entails expressing it through honorable actions. If we do not love God, we will be incapable of carrying out our second obligation, which is to love others. This represents the excellent way we must walk if our Christianity is to mean anything in the scheme of eternity.[15]

We must discern what light we are walking according to. The darkness of the present age is ready to consume those who do not walk according to the light provided by God. It is easy to defile the light of His truth with the world's philosophies, pervert it by allowing Satan to

---

[13] 2 Thessalonians 2:8-10

[14] Matthew 7:16-20; John 13:35

[15] Mark 12:29-31; 1 Corinthians 12:3-13; Hebrews 11:22-25; 1 John 3:14-18

undermine it with doubts and unbelief, and render it ineffective with vain traditions. But, as believers, we need to be faithful to it by approaching it to believe it as the only truth that can clearly establish us in reality. Such reality will prepare each of us to face the present, overwhelming challenges of this age in the strength of God's truth and hope.

THE LIGHT FROM WITHIN

We have been considering the different lights that man can abide in as a means to function and walk according to as far as his reality, but he will also walk in some type of light when it comes to the type of life he chooses to live. Such a light points to the life that is being wrought in or brought forth in the inner man.

Jesus talked about the type of light that penetrated the soul of man. He stated the light could, in reality, be darkness.[16] It is hard to believe that the light in us could in fact be a form of darkness that we are unable to recognize or discern. This type of light has to do with our understanding of life.

For some people they are pursuing their *"idea"* of life, while others are trying to establish a certain lifestyle that they feel will represent the pinnacle of *experiencing* life. However, there is a third group that realizes they must truly *seek* out life. It is important to understand that life comes from outside of man. Man in himself has no means to give himself life. His physical life is a matter of conception, the life that is eventually developed and brought to maturity is a matter of outside influences, and his spiritual life comes from heaven.

The reality of life from within also involves the will and intervention of others. When it comes to the physical existence, it entails the will of two people coming together and the constant intervention of those closest to the person to nurture that life. When it comes to how this life is brought forth it entails the influences of those in the environment that surrounds a person. And, when it comes to a person's spiritual life, it is a matter of God's will and intervention to make it a reality.[17]

---

[16] Matthew 6:23

[17] John 1:12-13

This brings us to the need to understand that life is not a simple matter of our heart beating, our lungs inhaling and exhaling the air around us, and our physical bodies moving in some way in our environments. Life also has to do with connecting and interacting with our environments in order to experience some type of emotional awakening whether it is pleasure, happiness, satisfaction, or enlightenment. However, experiencing these different emotions is not enough. In the recesses of people's minds, who are aware that such emotions will prove to be fleeing or temporary, their understanding of life will often become confusing, burdensome, and disappointing. It is not enough to settle for that which is fleeing. Such temporary ecstasy will actually throw a light on the harsh reality that something sustaining and eternal is missing. It is not enough to see the different pieces of the puzzle if there is no pattern or picture that emerges from it to bring understanding or answers to the questions as to our existences or reveal the real reason for us taking up space and time. Although we may experience pinnacles in our adventures, they are short lived and have a downside that will cast us into utter sorrow and despair. Such understanding will leave us perplexed and skeptical towards what will prove to be vain and temporary, often leaving us standing in a stagnant pool of hopelessness.

Without coming to terms with the inner sense that there is more to life than what we can see, know, or experience on a physical and emotional plane, we cannot know the purpose of our journey or where it will lead us. This clearly reveals that man must not only discover life, but ultimately he will choose the type of inner life he will walk in.

The Apostle John pointed out that the light that comes from within represents some type of life in us. If we pursue the idea of life according to worldly attractions, the life in us will prove to be fleshly. In fact, what we end up pursuing will be the knowledge of the world as to how it defines life. Such a pursuit is based on the various possibilities of experiencing some type of happiness or satisfaction in the world, but in many ways such promises never materialized or they proved to be fleeting, leaving the person empty. Granted, the world can offer temporary pleasures, dangle carrots of illusive happiness, and offer various promises or options when it comes to feeding the various lusts of the flesh, but there is nothing sustaining in any of it.

When it comes to pursuing a lifestyle, man associates life with establishing some type of reputation, association, or kingdom that will speak of him in a personal way. In America, the concept of the "American dream" is often lifted up as the essence of life. In many people's mind if they can possess the "American dream" before their journey is up, they will discover that which will bring satisfaction. However, even the "American dream" can prove to be illusive or empty. Even if it is somehow attained, it can show itself to be another pinnacle that allows one to enjoy an accomplishment that may possess a certain height of excitement, but it will only last for a short time. The reality of lifestyles is that they must be maintained. To preserve a particular way of life can become very burdensome and overwhelming if one lacks the means to maintain the quantity or quality of it.

Clearly, people's concepts of satisfying lifestyles will change or vary. One of the pursuits that appear to be prevalent when it comes to lifestyles is that of possessions. It is not unusual for people to perceive that possessions define wealth, add to the quality of their life, or will give satisfaction and security. Jesus challenged such an emphasis with these words, "Take heed, and beware of covetousness: for a man's life consisteth not in the abundance of the things which he possesseth" (Luke 12:15).

As believers we must understand what truly constitutes real life. To pursue an idea of life based on fleshly attractions or some materialistic lifestyle is to pursue the vanity of the world. Such a pursuit can be compelled or driven by idolatrous greed and pagan practices that leave even Christians clamoring for more of the world. However such a pursuit causes people to become indifferent and complacent towards the things of God. As believers we cannot afford to lose our spiritual edge when it comes to having a sense as to the type of life we are developing or nurturing in our inner man.

The Apostle John tells us that the light of the world is Jesus. I love the description Jesus gave of Himself in Revelation 22:16, "I Jesus have sent mine angel to testify unto you these things in the churches, I am the root and the offspring of David, and the bright and morning star." As the bright and morning star, Jesus' light will arise in us at the new birth experience and begin to brighten up our lives with the penetrating, purifying brightness of His life. His light cannot be extinguished, and when He comes back as the victorious King and Righteous Judge the light of His countenance will be as the sun at the height of its brightness.[18]

The Lord's brightness will be so intense that darkness will want to flee from the intensity of it, but it cannot. Wickedness will want to hide from the judgment of it, but there will be no place that will not be illuminated. Evil will want to be hidden from the wrath to come, but it will be exposed as His brightness dissipates all shadows, removes all wicked coverings, and exposes all evil designs and activities.

Nothing will be able to stand in Jesus' brilliance that harbors any darkness. All cloaks and veneers will not withstand the penetration of His radiance as they fall to the wayside to reveal the nakedness and shame of unbelief and iniquity. All reprobate's works will be reduced to ashes in the purifying fire of His holy light. It is only that which is marked with His life, and identified and purified with His brightness that will be left standing in the glow of His countenance.

Jesus' life serves as the light within believers' souls. When it comes to life, we are to pursue or seek the essence of His life by seeking to know, love, serve, and worship Him. We are told that if we seek Him with our whole heart He will be found by us. If we follow Him, He will lead us to spiritual pastures that will satisfy the inner hunger and thirst that is present in our souls. If we abide in Him, we will not only receive an abundance of His life, but we will become an extension of it to others in the world.

Such a light is to guide us in our search to possess Jesus' life in greater measures. It is everlasting and possesses a heavenly inheritance, spiritual blessings, and eternal promises. Although we will catch glimpses of the benefits of this life along the way, the reality of it is that it will be unfolding to us and in us for ages to come. In our finite state we cannot begin to comprehend such a life, but as its light reveals greater revelations of Jesus, His life will become a greater reality to each of us.

The question is, how can each of us be assured that we possess the light of the world to come? It would be easy to embrace another type of life that would leave us spiritually, morally bankrupt. We need to discern our agenda and make sure it is not fleshly. We need to make sure our emphasis is not on tangible things that can only add burdens and not value or worth to our way of living.

---

[18]   Revelation 1:16

The Word of God clearly gave us insight into this matter. Instead of searching to possess an "idea of life", let us be as the Apostle Paul. His agenda was to preach Christ and Him crucified. His emphasis was to gain Him as a prize. In order to gain Christ, he counted all the worldly pursuits and associations as being dung in light of winning Him for himself. The apostle wanted to be completely submerged in Jesus' life and consumed by it to ensure that in the end that he not only possessed Jesus' life, but He was possessed by Jesus.[19]

Instead of pursuing a certain lifestyle we need to be as the Apostle Peter. He strived to live the life he was ordained to live. He mentioned the fact that he had partaken of the divine nature of Christ, as well as escaped the corruption of the world. Peter knew that he was to live the life of Christ by taking on the virtues that exemplified Him. He chose to remember his humble beginnings; that his sins had been purged. By remembering where he came from and insisting on taking on godly virtues he would never become barren in his knowledge of Jesus Christ. Like Paul, he wanted to develop the excellent life of Jesus into his character. He described Jesus in this way, "We have also a more sure word of prophecy; unto where ye do well that ye take heed, as unto a light that shineth in a dark place, until the day dawn, and the day star arise in your hearts" (2 Peter 1:19).

The Apostle Peter understood the light that had penetrated the dark places of his soul. He knew that it was the life of Jesus. The very light of Jesus had dawned in his spirit, and remained the day star that flooded his heart with new life and his soul with incredible hope. He understood the prize and instructed us to become strangers in attitudes and pilgrims in disposition when it came to the age we live in.[20]

As Christians we should be pursuing the Pearl of Great Price, Jesus. We should be willing to sell all to possess this incredible prize of heaven. We should insist on walking in the way of Jesus' light, as well as according to the liberating truth and reality of it. Clearly, we must walk in His light to ensure that it serves as the only life worth finding in this present age. This is the only means to secure our future in the world to come.

---

[19]   1 Corinthians 2:2; Philippians 3:7-14

[20]   1 Peter 2:11; 2 Peter 1:3-12

As a believer, are you seeking Jesus' life, or are you pursuing some "idea" of life or a particular lifestyle? There is only one real life that will bring satisfaction. As believers, we must make sure we are not pursuing some religious idea of it or seeing it as a pious lifestyle; rather, we must choose to live it according to the light that has dawn in our souls.

MAN'S NATURAL PREFERENCE

If I were to ask you if you prefer to walk in blindness, your answer would be that you prefer to see where you are going. I am sure there is not one person that would admit that they prefer to walk in darkness. Such a prospect should not only be foreign to each of us, but would be a foolish preference. Who wants to be blind? However, we must ask ourselves if we are being honest about our preference. We must realize that we do choose what light we walk in.

The light we choose to walk by may represent the gross darkness of the world around us. Such darkness simply serves as our so-called "light," but it reveals that we indeed like to walk in the darkness of ignorance, foolishness, delusion, and according to the outlines and shadows produce by our own perception of reality. The real crux of the matter is that if we did discover that we were blind in some way, would we not want to face such a state and desire to see and walk in the true light?

The truth of the matter is that we all start out blind in some way. When I read about how blind men joyously received their sight after Jesus touched their eyes, it is hard to believe that anybody would prefer any type of darkness brought on by blindness. However, Jesus stated in John 3:18-21 that men prefer spiritual darkness. To prefer spiritual darkness means to favor being spiritually blind to the light of truth. Granted, such men may have their physical sight, but they still prefer to grope in spiritual darkness about matters that will affect their present and eternal state.

The reason that they prefer spiritual darkness makes their preference seem more foolish and ridiculous. They prefer darkness because their deeds are evil. It is amazing to think that people prefer spiritual blindness because they are trying to cover up vain, foolish deeds that in the end will expose their real spiritual condition. Do such individuals perceive that their deeds are hidden away from the penetrating light of truth? In reality, these individuals are thoroughly convinced there is no such light because they walk in the darkness of unbelief. Granted, some have put on the veneer of religion to satisfy any religious concern about the matters of God. At best this outward veneer is their way of sufficing or flattering any religious concerns and judgments. These individuals use such a veneer to deceptively console or sear any personal conscience that may state differently. Such works may delude them, as well as create a false illusion or appearance to others, but they cannot be hidden away from a holy God who one day will not only expose such works for their wicked, reprobate ways, but will judge these individuals in light of the truth.

God is light, and in Him is no darkness. His light will not only penetrate the darkness of man's soul, but it will tear away any veneers that hide such darkness. At such times, the light will dissipate false lights that are nothing more than shadows that shroud any false notion, intention, and hypocrisy on man's part. Jesus made reference to this very fact when He made this statement in John 15:22, "If I had not come and spoken unto them, they had not had sin; but now they have no cloke for their sin."

As I consider how easily it is for each of us to be deceived by a false light, I cannot assume that I possess the necessary sight to see or presume that the illumination in front of me is trustworthy. I must know how to discern the light that is before me, honestly face the light within me, and test the light that I am allowing to illuminate and define my reality.

Jesus gives us the means in which we can discern the type of spiritual light we prefer in His discourse in the Gospel of John concerning this matter. He states that what separates people when it comes to the spiritual light they walk in is that they believe on Him. "Believe" is a strong word. Those who believe on Him have chosen to believe what He has said to be true. In their mind it is the same as saying, *"amen, so be it for it is so."* Notice in this statement, how there are three confirmations as to the light that is being chosen. "Believing" is saying amen to the truth of the light that has penetrated the darkness of the world. It is declaring that the light is the true reality that will establish the life of the believer on what is immovable and unchangeable. In the last part of the declaration it states that no matter what darkness may abide, that a matter has already been established in heaven and it will stand as so, regardless of the darkness that is invading the souls of those who are lost. This light is going to establish these people's premise as to how they look at something, the attitude they adopt towards it, and how they approach it.

The opposite spectrum of the premise of belief is that of unbelief. Unbelief is an actual state of condemnation. Condemnation simply means that the person is under a death sentence. Granted, such an individual may be walking around, but there is no hope for him or her to escape damnation. This person is clearly marked for wrath.

This brings us to the real matter of spiritual blindness. There are people who know they are marked for death. However, the people who are considered spiritually blind are not cognizant that this death sentence exists. They believe they are seeing clearly. They do not believe that the way they are walking in will ultimately lead to eternal damnation. They may think they are seeing clearly, but the reality is that they cannot see because they are spiritually blind. Since they have been born in this state of darkness, they believe that what they perceive is the way things truly are. They have no real contrast, and unless the light of the Gospel penetrates their souls with the truth of their need for salvation from such a state, they will continue to believe that their spiritual darkness is actually light.

The Bible speaks of this state of spiritual blindness in many different ways. In Proverbs 14:12 and 16:25 we are told that there are ways which seem right to the person, but they lead to death. Man can be blinded to the real intentions or motivations behind his ways. Such ways however exclude the wisdom of God that is present in His truth.

When we consider that the people love darkness because it hides their deeds, we must consider what deeds are these individuals trying to hide under the cover of darkness. After all, these deeds possess the fruit of death, are attached to the vanity of the self-life, the corruption of the flesh, and ultimately stand cursed and judged. Keep in mind that regardless of how much these deeds are hidden by darkness, they will manifest themselves in the ways of death by the types of attitudes that these people will adopt and display towards the character, ways, and life of God. For example, intellectually, such individuals will mock and demean the life of God. They will show no consideration for such a life as they operate in lawlessness towards the ways of God. They will rise up in rebellion to oppose the existence of such a life, while showing indifference and cruelty when confronted with it. They will be quick to discard or sacrifice the life of God by insisting that it be aborted along the way because it serves no real purpose.

Isaiah 5:18-24 speaks of these people's reality. They perceive that they are right in their own eyes about a matter, regardless of how God may view it. Obviously, these individuals cannot know anything outside of their spiritual state. They have either forgotten or never known the covenant of God, and can do nothing more than to curse His righteous ways. In their state of unbelief and delusion, they will use the darkness of iniquity and sin to deceive others into their particular reality. They will define righteousness established by God as being sin, and their sin as being the real measure of righteousness. As a result, they will see their deceptive darkness as being light and the light of truth as being darkness. They will conclude that they are being wise to maintain such a reality. However, the Bible warns such individuals that God's fire will devour their works of darkness, revealing that at best that such works are stubble that will quickly be consumed by the fire of God's holiness, reducing them to ashes, and like chaff these ashes will be taken by the winds of judgment and dispersed in all directions. Not only will these individuals experience the affliction of their foolishness, but all memory of their person and ways will be forever be wiped out by God's wrath. [21]

The second aspect to the reference Jesus made in John 3, in regard to walking in spiritual darkness, is that they who prefer such a state do so because they love darkness. The Bible tells us that a man's ways seem clean to him but God weighs the spirits or motivations that influences or inspires such ways. The Word of God speaks of His Spirit, but it also makes reference to man's spirit and the spirit of the world. [22] Man's spirit is subject to the whims of his selfish disposition, while the spirit of the world makes people subject to the god of this world, Satan. Man's spirit will claim independence when it comes to the supremacy and authority of God, while the spirit of the world will influence man to rebel against God's authority and reign. Man's spirit will cause him to become stiff-necked towards God, while the spirit of the world will cause man to rage against God in defiance.

The Word of God instructs God's people to discern the spirit that is compelling them. [23] The wrong spirit drives while the right Spirit convicts,

---

[21] Psalm 6:5; Proverbs 2:17-18; 21:16-17
[22] Proverbs 16:2; 25:28; 1 Corinthians 2:12; Ephesians 2:2
[23] 1 John 4:1

nudges, or encourages people to repent of the direction they are walking, turn from their destructive ways, to follow Jesus into a new life. The wrong spirit will give individuals a false sense of personal righteousness and infallibility, while the right Spirit will give them an inner knowing that a matter is either right or wrong to God. Righteousness will produce sobriety towards the responsibility of doing what is necessary to ensure the integrity of God's instruction and personal conduct and deeds.

Jesus stated that men who prefer darkness do so because they love such darkness. The concept of "love" invokes a description of how powerful the delusion of spiritual blindness can have on man's perception, motives, and conduct. "Love" points to a passion that will drive and cause people to pursue something with the intent of gaining inroads into coming into a place of agreement, loyalty, or possessing that which has caught the attention of their affections. Such a pursuit has no regard as to the price it may cost or the outcome of it.

It is for this reason that Christians are told to love the truth. If we do not love something we will display a non-committal or indifferent attitude towards it. If we lack the passion or fervor to possess it, we will not be compelled to pursue it or desirous of attaining it. Love clearly will determine what our natural preference will be. Jesus confirmed this by stating that wherever our heart is, there will be what we treasure or value.[24] Therefore, if someone loves darkness, he or she will be indifferent, complacent, and negative towards the light of truth. Such a person will never be at home in the light; therefore, he or she will not only choose the way of death but he or she will love it.

Since people who prefer spiritual darkness love it, their natural reaction towards anything that would challenge their love would be that of hatred. As I considered the precarious days we live in, I asked the Lord how He would protect His people from the darkness engulfing this world. He reminded me that the people who are in darkness cannot see even His light. Like the Egyptians who were blinded by the gross darkness they encountered at the Red Sea, these individuals will be unable to see even the light that God's people will be abiding in.[25]

---

[24] Proverbs 23:23; Matthew 6:21; John 14:6, 15; 2 Thessalonians 2:8-10
[25] Exodus 14:14-21

It must be pointed out that the only time the people of gross darkness are stirred up is when the penetrating light of truth pierces their darkness bringing real contrast and challenge to their realities. It is at such times these people are stirred up against the light and will rage and try to destroy it. Subsequently, these people will show their utter hatred towards the light. Jesus stated that those who belong to the present world, regardless of religious influence or affiliation, will show utter contempt towards His light because they have no intention of coming to the light of truth. We once again must remind ourselves that what these people are trying to hide and protect from the penetrating light of truth are their deeds. They do not want the vanity of their wicked deeds being exposed by the light of truth and reproved by the standard of righteousness that has been clearly lifted up for all to see. They do not want to see that their works stand judged and their spiritual state already sealed by condemnation and damnation.

We already know that when the light came into this world to penetrate its darkness, that the cloak that hid and justified sin was taken away. Such a cloak could not stand in the penetrating light of Jesus. Each time the cloak was taken away, man was brought to the place of decision as to how he would respond to such a light. After all, such a light could set him free from the grave of darkness that had so long held him captive.

The truth is, many people were found to fear the liberation the light could bring to them. The revelation of their wretched spiritual condition that had been long hidden under the fig-leaves of shame and the heavy robes of self-righteousness left them feeling naked, vulnerable, and undone. Instead of allowing the light to bring them to a place of liberty, they scrambled to find some other covering that would hide them in the shadows of obscurity and conceal them in some false reality that would allow them to remain in their delusion. After all, in darkness they could believe what they wanted, hold onto whatever reality that fed their flesh and catered to their pride. Subsequently, these individual could maintain that the darkness in them was superior to the light that was personally challenging them.

How will Jesus ultimately address or confront such darkness? Clearly, those who love spiritual darkness are resolved that such darkness will remain true and will be left standing when all else has been shaken and judged. We know that Jesus is capable of taking away any false, dark covering or veil upon the hearts and minds of men, but they must first repent of such darkness. [26]

This brings us to how the Lord will deal with the darkness that men insist on maintaining. He will become a Rock of judgment that will break through the darkness, causing each wicked kingdom, false reality, and wicked deed to crumble into millions of pieces as it is being ground into powder. Then the powder will be blown away by the winds of judgment to be no more. Even though such people will ask the mountains to fall on them to hide them from His wrath, the mountains will flee, leaving them exposed. Even though they scramble for cover, His intense light will become a spotlight that will be cast upon them as He brings an end to the wicked reign of their darkness upon the face of this world. It will mark a terrible time for these individuals as they fall into the hands of the living God, but it will be a glorious time of veneration and restoration for those who love His light.[27]

As Christians, we must not lightly assume we are walking in Jesus' light. We must become sober about the light that we abide in, as well as serve as our reality and life. We must repent of any darkness, choose to embrace and love the penetrating, piercing light of His truth, and insist on testing the integrity and virtue of the light that resides in us. We must not presume that our light constitutes reality regardless of how religious or right it seems, or maintain that it must or will serve as truth for others. We must make sure that the light from without and within is truly the light that was sent from heaven to penetrate through the great darkness of this world into our very souls to set us free to discover the gift of eternal life.

WALKING ACCORDING TO
AN EXCELLENT VOCATION

The more I understand the characteristics of the light of Jesus, the more I become aware that unless God's light penetrates my hard heart, I would never be able to receive its truths in simple faith. Unless His light

---

[26]   Isaiah 25:7; 30:1; Daniel 7:27; John 15:22; 2 Corinthians 3:13-16; Hebrews 10:31; 12:25-29

[27]   Daniel 2:44-45; Matthew 21:42-44; Revelation 6:14-17

floods my soul, I would remain lost in the darkness of the delusion that is prevalent in my soul and the world. If God's light could not transform my mind, I would remain content in my ignorance. If His light did not reveal the depths of my depravity and inability to be right before Him, I would remain blinded by my prideful ways that would ultimately leave me in spiritual ruin, as well as vulnerable to the changing tides of the age I live in. And in the end, if I am not founded and established in His light, eventually the tides of the world will sweep me out into the ocean of judgment to taste His wrath that abides on each age. It is the power of His light that enables me to see the foolishness that blinds me to the arrogance that is always ready to set me up to fall into the destructive traps of the age I live in.

The truth is, God's light does not have to penetrate my spiritual darkness. It is only by His mercy that it ever has pierced the darkness of my soul with the Gospel that saves. It does not have to bring conviction to the destructive path that seems so attractive to my selfish disposition, but because of His grace the veil over my mind could be taken from my spiritual eyes to see my need to repent of the direction I am going. Once the veil was taken away, I could then be converted to the narrow path of righteousness that can only be revealed by His Word. It is because of His love that He sent forth the light into the dark world to save me from my wretched state of spiritual darkness.

This brings me to what it means to walk in God's light. God's Word has not remained mute or abstract about this important subject, leaving me to second guess or speculate about what it means to walk in His light. It has indeed presented a clear picture of what it means to walk in and according to His illumination. It has revealed the attitude that I need to adopt towards my responsibility of ensuring the integrity of such a walk.

To ensure the integrity of my preference and walk, I must first come to terms with the attitude I must have in regard to walking in the true light of heaven. I have been given insight as to the attitude I must adopt in relationship to walking in the light in Ephesians 4:1, "I therefore, the prisoner of the Lord, beseech you that ye walk worthy of the vocation wherewith ye are called." The Christian life must be considered a vocation. The only way I can maintain the excellence of my profession, occupation, or responsibility is by walking in the true light of heaven.

It is easy to become divorced to the reality that our Christianity is a life we must personally experience and live. It is vital, as believers, that each of us keep in mind that it is not some religious exercise that we practice on Sunday and leave at the door of the church building, allowing us to live like the devil the rest of the week. Such a life is not a matter of works that are designed to impress or fool others to prevent them from seeing that behind such a pious presentation there is no real Christian substance or character to sustain us the rest of the time. The Christian life was and is never meant to serve as a form of hypocrisy that is simply being acted out on the stage of the world according to some Hollywood script. The Apostle Paul made it clear that it is a life to be lived out daily. He stated that the life in him that he was living was the life of Christ in him. He was living this life by faith in the Son of God and not according to his strength.[28]

The Christian life is a high calling that must be lived out on a daily basis. As saints, it must be obvious at every level of our lives. For example, as Christians we hold the official position of an ambassador in relationship to this world, and a royal position as an heir to a heavenly kingdom where we are being prepared to one day reign and rule with our King. We hold an honorable position as soldiers of the cross who must endure hardship in this present world as overcomers. We also have been placed in an invaluable position as being part of a lively priesthood that stands between God and others, and as living epistles who bear record of the eternal life within, a record that will be read by those around us. We are to serve as sanctified vessels who possess a valuable treasure that will clearly identify us to the Potter, the Creator of the universe. We also are to serve as righteous instruments that will be used by God to proclaim His glory, His Gospel, and His truths to the world that lies in utter darkness and spiritual ruin and damnation.[29]

Sadly, many Christians do not understand their high calling. They drift according to the different religious waves of the world because they are not anchored to the Rock of ages. Because many are not properly discipled, they find themselves confused and lost among the different ideas or concepts of those who have no real knowledge of the true God. As a result, they are often left to define Christianity according to

---

[28]   Galatians 2:21

[29]   Romans 6:12-14; 9:20-23; 2 Corinthians 3:1-3; 4:7; 5:18-20; 2 Timothy 2:3-5, 11-12, 19-21; 1 Peter 2:5, 9; Revelation 1:6; 20:4-6

their way of thinking because there is no real contrast being presented. The standard of righteousness clearly established by the Holy Spirit is missing; therefore, these poor uninformed souls do not realize that what they often hold to be true, stands judged with the rest of the foolishness of the world.[30]

People must first realize who they are intended to be before they can have any real vision as to where they are going. The Word tells us that people without vision will perish.[31] There are those in the Christian realm that have no vision because they have no sense as to who they are in light of eternity. Without the sense of their high calling, they have no real direction or means to test the way in which they are walking.

This brings us back to the importance of the light believers must walk in. We must discern the character of the light that is truly influencing our lives. In other words, we must honestly consider how the light we are walking in is truly impacting us on a personal level. In order to know how the light is impacting us, we must understand the purpose of the light we need to walk according to. Purpose will also define the characteristic of the light we must be walking in.

The main purpose of the light from above is to expose our spiritual condition. It must reveal all darkness in our lives in order to make us transparent before God. Once we become transparent, then we will be able to not only freely walk in the light, but properly reflect it to the rest of the world. In a sense, we will become the means in which God will attract those who are seeking the true light.

Keep in mind that the light is meant to bring contrast between what is of the light and what is in darkness. The Apostle John tells us in his first epistle that if we declare we have fellowship with God, but walk in darkness, we are lying to ourselves. However, if we walk in the light of God we have fellowship with Him and others believers. We also are assured that the blood of Jesus cleanses us from all sin.[32]

God will never have fellowship or agreement with darkness because there is no darkness in Him. He can only meet us when we are in His light. However, His light will expose all sin. There is only one way to

---

[30]   John 16:7-13; Ephesians 4:14

[31]   Proverbs 29:18

[32]   1 John 1:5-7

address sin: repent, confess it, and seek God's means of mercy and forgiveness that can only be obtained in Christ.[33] It is from this premise that fellowship is established with God and other believers.

Fellowship represents what is influencing us the most and ultimately what type of light we will be reflecting to the world. We must be in fellowship with God if we are going to reflect His light. The ultimate goal of any light is to reflect the glory of something. If our lives do not ultimately bring glory to God, we can know that we are not walking by, accordingly to, or in His light. We see this truth throughout Scripture.

After being on the mountain with God for forty days and night, Moses came down from his time of fellowship reflecting the glory of God. There was no doubt to those who encountered him that the brilliance was not his or that it was not of the world. After Jesus exhorted people to not hide their light under a bushel, He gave this command, "Let your light so shine before men, that they may see your good works, and glorify your Father, which is in heaven" (Matthew 5:16).

This brings us to how sin affects us. Remember, light is about contrast. It will always bring dimension to a matter. Such dimension allows us to see that in light there are different shades that will be revealed if we are hiding in the dark to conceal a matter, walking in shadows of compromise to obscure a matter, or walking in the light to ensure the integrity of our life and conduct. Or, perhaps we are being challenged by the intensity of a light because it has become a searchlight that is pinpointing that part of the terrain in our lives that must be revealed, cleansed of unrighteousness, revived, and recreated by the work of sanctification done by the Holy Spirit.

It is important to point out that when the ways of death are illuminated by the light, we must respond to the light by making sure that such ways are declared dead, and bury them. Granted, there may be a struggle with the "old man" in us that is playing dead. Such a struggle points to travailing until new life comes forth, but we must take all that is of the "old man" and put it to death in order to bury him. Once he is buried, then we can ensure that new life will be brought forth out of the barren wilderness of death, decay, and utter ruin.

---

[33]   Luke 13:3, 5; 1 John 1: 9

Without putting off and burying the old, the new man cannot be awakened or quickened in us to properly respond to the light. The ways of the "old man" often serves as our grave clothes that bind us to the stench and decaying conduct of the old life. Like the raising of Lazarus in John 11, Jesus may raise us out of the grave with resurrection power, but we cannot walk in the new way until we are loosed from the old. Such rotting clothing will cause us to be spiritually inept to properly see, hear, or know the life that awaits us. For this reason, the Bible clearly tells us we must put off the old in order to put on the new.[34]

The light of Jesus will always expose the presence and working of the ways of the "old man." Such illumination is not meant to bring condemnation to us; rather, its purpose is to awaken us to the urgency and need to realize that the "old man" with his destructive, gross ways will never benefit us. The old sinful disposition is not only walking in condemnation, but it will seal our doom. It will not only keep us from the best, but it will take us down into the miry pit of the grave to taste the consequences of separation from that which entails life.

It is for this reason that Christians are reminded that they used to live in darkness that possessed the ways and fruits of death, but that such works are not to even be mentioned among them, let alone be part of their conduct. The works from the old life have been done away with by the work and life of Jesus. If any work of darkness is exposed, it must be reproved and dealt with quickly. It must never be given any opportunity to work its deception on us, thereby, taking root in our vulnerable souls so that like leaven it can take captive our inner man.

As Christians we must remind ourselves and insist that we walk as children of light. We must not assume we are walking in the light or presume we are being transparent about our spiritual condition. We have to partake of that which is divine to keep our spiritual edge as a means to avoid being put to sleep by the spiritual dullness of sin. We must be quick to do as Scripture instructs which is to test the fruits of our lives. We must make sure that the fruit of the Spirit is present in our attitude, walk, and preferences. Foremost, we must be able to discern sincere love in our hearts towards God that will be expressed in sacrificial love towards others. Obviously, we must be walking in righteousness in

---

[34]   Ephesians 4:22-25; Colossians 3:5-12

regard to God, while we conduct ourselves in honorable ways towards others. We must walk circumspectly by being transparent about personal struggles to ensure that our ways and deeds are made manifest by the light of Christ to ensure that fellowship is maintained with God and those of the household of faith. We must insist on understanding the will of God for our lives so that we do not waste our life or time on those things that ultimately will prove to be inspired by that which is evil and frivolous.[35]

It is only by walking in the light of Jesus that we can be assured that the darkness of this present age will not overtake us as a thief. The Apostle Paul tells us that it is the light that will keep us alert, prepared, and sober in regard to the age we live in. It is for this reason that we must not be flippant, assume, or presume anything about our spiritual lives. We must be spiritually awake and alert to properly and soberly discern the days and times we live in. The apostle assures us that if we are in the light, the day of the Lord will not overtake us as a thief.

As children of the light, we can and will know the times and seasons we live in. We will be prepared as we put on the breastplate of faith to confidently stand in darkness and the helmet of salvation to not only know what is truly upon us, but that which also awaits us in the next age to come.[36]

The beauty about being the children of the light is that we know our identity is not attached to the present world of darkness. Our Christian life is a vocation that defines our responsibility, a high calling that distinguishes us, a way of walking that leads us, and a way of living that will bring satisfaction and contentment to our very souls. We know because of the light of this life, that we will not be caught off guard by the present deception encroaching upon this world, and that a glorious future awaits us.

Clearly, the *light from above* assures us that we are not bound to this age; rather, we are being prepared for the next. The *light from without* confirms that we do not walk in condemnation of the past, but in light of the resurrection power that will raise us up above the judgment that is already upon the world. The true *light from within* brings an inner knowing that we are not groping in darkness, while walking according to a false light that blinds us to God's wrath. Rather, we are walking in a light that

---

[35]   Ephesians 5:1-17

[36]   1 Thessalonians 5:1-8

will never be extinguished. This light will guide us through the terrain of the world, bring understanding from without as to what is really going on in the matters of the present age we live in, and serve as the inner life that will cause us to walk according to the Spirit of God to our final destination.

There is no doubt as to the type of life the light of Christ will produce in us.[37] There can be no debate as to how it will express itself. There will be no second guessing as to the preference, quality, or fruit that will be produced in our lives. The Bible is explicit about what it means to be children of the light. Such a light cannot be imitated or counterfeited. In the end, it will reveal all other lights to be darkness as it prepares us as saints to be lifted up into the unfolding glorious brightness of the bright and morning star who not only has arisen in us to serve as our day star, but continues to shine in us and through those works that will bring glory and honor to God.

As we come to a close of this presentation, we must soberly examine our lives to determine the light that illuminates the way for us. We must discern the source of it, the reality it reveals, and the life it is producing. We must allow it to make known to each of us whether we are on the broad road of destruction or the narrow path that leads to life. If the light we possess is the light of Christ we can be assured that we will not see any need to hide it under a bushel. After all, those in spiritual darkness will not see it, but those who are searching for the light of truth will see it through the darkness and seek it out to find refuge for their weary souls. It is in light of such understanding that we will have the liberty to joyously let the illumination of our souls so shine before men that they will see the wondrous work and ways of God, even in the midst of the greatest type of darkness. At such times those seeking the truth will give the Father glory for the gift of His ever-abiding, eternal light.

---

[37] If you would like to know more about this subject, see the book, *The Many Faces of Christianity,* in Volume 6 of the foundational series.

BEING CONFORMED TO THE IMAGE OF CHRIST

INTRODUCTION

Have you ever encountered a situation where it was not just enough to know about a Scriptural truth or acquire a certain amount of understanding about it? In your spirit you were aware that there was a definite need to know how God perceived the matter in question. The subject I want to address in this particular presentation produced such an attitude in me. I needed to understand what it meant to be conformed to the image of Christ. After all, the Apostle Paul stated that we have been predestinated to be conformed to this image. Clearly, such a predestination points to potential. I don't know about you, but I have been aware that in order to make a difference in the harvest field of humanity, I must reach and fulfill my heavenly potential.

I realized there were different ways in which I could approach this subject. I could be sentimental about imitating Christ, but such sentiment never produced any real change. I could approach it from a theological basis, which might add some interesting facts to my understanding, but would there be any life in it? I did not want to settle for a silly, unrealistic fickleness or an intellectual, but lifeless understanding. I wanted to have a heart revelation about this subject that would actually produce the right results.

At different times I would come across a word that would cause me to study or meditate on being conformed in such a manner. Each glimpse into the study gave me another piece of the puzzle. However, such pieces had to fit nicely together if they were going to present a life-changing mosaic.

To some extent, I do feel that I have this mosaic before me. Granted some of the areas lack details, while other parts of it are still taking on shape, but I believe that this presentation is sufficient enough to understand what it means to be conformed to the image of Christ.

I also realized that the image being brought forth in this mosaic is Christ Himself. But, the real issue to me is not the image but what it means to be conformed to this incredible image. Truly, as the Potter, God would know what it would take to conform each of us to His Son's image. As the great artist or sculptor, He would understand what results He is after, but we must realize that we are the clay, the canvas, and the instruments. Our responsibility is to submit to the process while trusting Him to work out the details.

However, as the clay, canvas, or instrument I want to rejoice in the work being done in me. I want to share in admiring the beauty that is being brought forth from our skillful Artist. I want to glory in the abilities of my great Creator to bring the best out in my life. Clearly, I am aware that it is His work, but I want to come to full age during such work. I want to come out seasoned and ready to express the image of the Son of God in a powerful way.

It is for these reasons, that I had to know what it meant to be conformed to the image of Christ, and it is for the same reasons I feel compelled to share with you what I have discovered about this subject. If enough of us in Jesus' living Church truly became conformed to the heavenly image, the more Jesus could be found and beheld by those poor, searching souls who are in seeking for what is real and lasting.

CREATED WITH A PURPOSE

If we are going to understand the desired results of our life on earth, we must first come to terms with why we are here. Although complicated by lifeless religion and the rhetoric of the world, the answer to this question is quite simple. However, one's starting point must be right before the answer can make any sense. The premise people must start from in order to come to terms with this challenge is God.

God is our Creator. However, the typical response of the world is to deny that man has been created in spite of the insurmountable evidence.

This is a surprise because being created allows man to understand his reason for being. Yet, those foolish individuals of past ages right up to the present age continue to loudly deny the truth of a Creator or Designer, while hiding behind their imprudent logic. Clearly, we must consider why there are people who are so vehement in denying that man has been created. After all, if man has been created, he would have an ordained purpose in this world.

While meditating on the dichotomy of this matter, I had to conclude that the problem rests with the concept of "purpose." If man has a "purpose" then one must reason that he will be made accountable and possibly rejected by his Creator for failing to reach his potential and fulfilling his purpose.

Obviously, as you watch how man handles sin, his blatant independence often causes him to refuse to be accountable. On the other hand, if man believes he evolved out of nothing, there is no reason or point of accountability. This makes him the master, designer and ruler of his world. He has no purpose but to live for self. He has no future except that which he forges out for himself. He is the master of his own ship, of his world, and of his destiny. For this reason, he will not concede that in the end he will answer to someone who might hold him accountable for failing to recognize the inevitable.

The truth is, man has been created with a purpose in mind. Romans 8:29 tells us that man has been predestinated. "Predestinated" points to something being ordained or designed with a purpose in mind. It specifies something as a means to determine or make a decree. The idea of predestination also points to man being appointed. We know that this appointment was in place before man was ever created. After all, man had to be designed according to specifications to ensure that he was complete and capable of fulfilling his purpose.

Since man was designed with some type of specifications, we must come to terms with those qualifications to understand man's purpose. We must begin in the Garden of Eden. The Bible starts with God creating the heavens and the earth. This is pretty significant when you realize that man's environment was brought forth first. However, this shows the wisdom of God. For man to survive, he had to be put in a place that was conducive to his well-being.

Let us consider what kind of environment God created for man. First of all, he created the heavens so man could consider the vastness of His

Creator. He created the earth in which man could tabernacle with Him. He gave light so man could experience his Creator's beauty through creation. He created the night so man could learn how to rest in his Provider and Protector as he ceased from his work.

God then divided the firmament so there would be a separation between that which would recycle and move water and the water itself in order to ensure life. In the separation He also created land to ensure the maintenance of life. Then the Creator brought forth the seed, distinguished the seasons, days, and years, followed by the creatures of both water and land.

Clearly, God is a God of order, but as someone once said, "God left the best for last." That is when he took the essence of man from the ground and created him into a living soul. He brought forth the best of creation, man, as a means to complete creation. He then put man into a paradise where he could walk with Him in sweet fellowship.[1]

When God created man, He formed within him a capacity to serve as His crowning glory in the midst of creation. In other words, man would have the ability to reflect the glory of God to the rest of creation. Granted, creation spoke of God's incredible majesty, but man would reflect it.

For man to reflect the glory of his Creator, God had to distinguish man from the rest of His creation. First of all, He would make him an eternal being by marking his life with eternity. In fact, man would be marked in two ways. He would house the very life and Spirit of God. Since man would be connected to God by His Spirit, man's inclination would be spiritual. He would be able to partake of God's divine life in sweet fellowship. Housing the life and Spirit of God enabled the second mark to come forth in man, allowing him the means to reflect God's glory.

When we consider the tabernacle of the Old Testament, we can get a sense as to what kind of creature God made man. He had to be pure (innocent) within, and he had to be able to house the glory of God to ensure interaction and fellowship with Him.

Man was therefore, given a spirit to interact with God, a soul to enjoy his life in God, and a body that would express His glory, as well as serve and worship God. In a way the three aspects of man's makeup pointed to

---

[1]   Genesis 1:26-31; 2:7-9

the Godhead, but there was an occurrence in Adam's life that pointed to the type of relationship God desired with man.

Man was put into a deep sleep in the garden. From his side, God formed a woman.[2] In a sense, He made man incomplete in order to complete him once again in an ordained union. God knew that His fellowship with Adam would be broken by transgression. The heart of Adam's oneness with God would be ripped from him by his rebellious actions. As a result, man would become incomplete. Granted, he may have had a wife and a physical wholeness as such, but spiritually he would discover himself to be incomplete.

God had to send forth His Son to reconcile creation back to Him. This reconciliation involved redeeming man so he could once again be brought back into fellowship with his Creator. God would work from three angles to accomplish this feat. The Father would draw lost man to His Son, the Son would invite lost man to partake of the rivers of Living Water, and the Holy Spirit would convict man of his need to be saved. Once man responded to the salvation being offered to him, he would be brought back to a place of fellowship with God. It was at this place that man would once again experience a spiritual completeness or wholeness.[3]

It is important to point out that marriage points to man being made whole in the physical and emotional arenas, but it is only when he is brought back into a relationship with God that he will experience a wholeness; that of body, soul, and spirit. In spirit he would once again have fellowship with God, in soul he would once again be able to interact with His Creator at the point of agreement, and in body he would be able to come to a place of oneness in service and worship.

When we consider the unregenerate man, we can see how incomplete he is. His world is chaotic, he is mostly at odds with those in his world, and he appears lost and uncertain in his walk.

Obviously, man must become spiritually whole to come to terms with his purpose for being. He must see beyond his present status to understand the status that was prepared for him before the foundations

---

2   Genesis 2:18-24

3   John 3:16; 6:44; 7:37; 16:7-11; 2 Corinthians 5:18-19; Ephesians 2:13-18

of the world. He must embrace this position by faith if he is ever going to reach the potential that God had ordained.

Before we can come to a clear understanding of our individual potential in Christ, we must understand what happened to mankind that now hinders him from reaching his original potential. Granted, it is not a politically correct subject, and it is one that can cause people to gnash their teeth in hatred when speaking of it. However, the fact is that something happened to man, and it is not going away until it is properly dealt with.

THE TAINTED, CRACKED MIRROR

As students of the Bible, we know that we were created in the image of God, but we need to understand what happened to the image. Most of us know that Adam sinned in the Garden of Eden. However, what most people do not understand is just how that sin really affected man's potential. We know that it changed man's relationship with his Creator, but most do not understand to what extent it changed it.

First of all, it broke relationship between God and man. This may not seem too important, but it basically cut man off from his Creator. God is holy and will have no part in the perverse ways of sin.[4] Without God being present in the midst of man, satisfying life would become elusive to mankind and death would reign.

Secondly, man would never be able to reach his potential. Man was made in the image of God in order to reflect Him to the rest of creation. In summation, man would reflect the life and glory of His Creator. However, sin perverted this potential.[5]

In order to understand how man was to reflect the glory of God, we must consider the man, Jesus Christ. Jesus in His humanity represented what man was meant to be before Adam's fall. Even though He was deity, He also reflected what man was ordained to become in relationship to his humanity.

---

[4]   Isaiah 59:1-2

[5]   Romans 3:23

It is important to understand that there is a difference between being conformed to the image of Christ and being the express image of God.[6] To conform man into the likeness of Jesus implies shaping or molding him into His likeness. It is the same concept as molding or shaping a piece of clay into the likeness of someone. However, for Jesus to serve as the express image of God, means that He was simply expressing His own Person. In other words, Jesus was expressing His deity through His humanity. He did not have to be shaped in the image of God, for He already was deity; and He did not need to be formed in the likeness of deity because He is deity. Deity was stamped on every part of His life, from His attributes, His attitude, and His behavior to the miracles He performed.

For individuals to be conformed to the image of Jesus means they will take on Jesus' likeness by taking on His disposition, attitude, and behavior. Even though they may be able to partake of Jesus' deity through faith, identification, and obedience, it does not make them divine. They will simply be like the man, Christ, in how they think, walk, and conduct themselves.

This brings us back to the fact that man was made in the image of God. Christ in His humanity was the natural express image of God because He was and is deity, while man had to be made in the image of God. In other words, man has the capacity or potential to reflect the glory of God. His very soul was stamped with this image. This implies he has the potential of coming into subjection to God's will, while his emotions have the capacity of expressing God's heart, and potentially his mind could be reasoned with to express the thoughts and ways of God, thereby, reflecting his Lord's image

Before this heavenly image could come forth, man would have to be properly shaped and molded. For man to be properly shaped he would have to subject himself to the work of the Potter to bring forth that image. And, in order to be molded, he would have to submit himself to the example that was stamped on the inner conscience of his soul by God. For God to have such influence on man, man had to be in fellowship with Him. He had to allow the reality and working of God to bring to life the image that would reflect His glory.

---

[6]   Hebrews 1:3

Clearly, man was designed to reflect his Creator. Another way of putting it is that man was created to mirror the reflection of God. In a sense, the light or life of God working in man would simply be reflected from the arena of man's soul. He would mirror the life that was present as he reflected the light of it to the rest of creation.

When Adam sinned, he fell into darkness. The breath and life of the Spirit of God lifted from him, leaving him in darkness. Instead of mirroring the glory of God, he would begin to mirror the fading light of man's vainglory, the temporary light of the world, and the antichrist light of man's religion. Such light would prove to be darkness that would blind these individuals as to the path of destruction they were on.[7]

Clearly, sin tainted and cracked the mirror that held the stamped image of the Creator. The light in man's soul became nothing more than encroaching darkness of the present age that was resonating in him. Because of this darkness, man would not be able to see the destructive path he was on, hear the warnings, smell the stench of death, touch the ugliness, or taste the bitterness of the darkness that surrounded him. Man would prove to be clueless, lost, and hopeless. The darkness of sin would cause him to fall short of the glory of God.[8]

Man is clearly missing the mark. Instead of finding and knowing life, he walks in the state of death.[9] He is under a death sentence, and there is no way to get around it. He can try to conform the outside to some religious idea, but the inside remains unchanged. He can try to reform his actions, but the attitude of the heart remains the same. He can comply to get along with others, but he is still at odds with God. He can perform according to some script, but he remains on the path of destruction.

This is the harsh reality of man's condition. There is no clarity to his life. He remains lost to what is real and true. He has no hope in his abyss of vanity, and no way out of the death march he is on. His soul is a spiritual vacuum that can never be satisfied with the things of the present age.

There was only one person who could intervene on man's behalf and that was God. He was the only one who could bring the image back

---

7   Matthew 6:22-23; John 3:18-21

8   Romans 3:23

9   Romans 6:23

into the world. However, He would have to recreate the mirror. After all, there was not, and never will be, any value found in a mirror that has been tainted by sin and cracked by broken fellowship. The mirror would have to be completely broken in order for God to refurbish it to its original specificity.

RECREATING THE MIRROR

The mirror of man had become tainted and cracked by sin. Man's soul no longer had the means to reflect the glory of the Creator. As a result, man would fall short of ever reaching his potential.

It was clear that the tainted and cracked mirror of man's soul would have to be discarded if it was not restored. What good is a mirror that perverts the image? No one wants to look into a mirror and see some type of silhouette or see a fragmented image of self. Yet, due to sin, this is what man would see of his person. Everything would be shrouded in confusion or appear as abstract or disjoined. Nothing would make sense, causing hopelessness, frustration, and sorrow to nag at his heels.

God described the state that man fell into because of sin. He referred to it as a curse that would set up an environment of vanity, sorrow, and toil.[10] Man who was formed from dust would return to dust. Death had made its entrance. The state of lifelessness would work within two arenas, physical death where the body would be separated from the spirit and soul to be consumed in the dust or grave of the world, and spiritual death where man would be separated from the essence of eternal life and well-being. In spiritual death man would taste the bitterness of the curse of death in utter isolation, torment, and despair.

It is important to understand that any great inventor, artist, sculptor, composer, etc. will put his or her whole heart in ensuring the integrity of his or her creation. After all, it is going to speak of personal abilities and devotion. As Creator, God was no exception. He had put His best in the creation of man, and He was not about to let that creation fall into obscurity because of the presence of sin. He would take the steps to restore His creation to its original design.

---

[10] Genesis 3:17-18

The question is, what would it take for God to recreate a work that had been totally ruined by sin? Upon meditating on this reality many times through the years, I realized that God had already worked out the details. He had a plan. It would begin with redeeming man back from the tyrannical master of sin and the curse of the Law.[11]

Hence, enters the Son of God. Jesus admitted that He came to ransom mankind back from the bondage of slavery. As Christians, we know that the taskmaster is sin. The Apostle Paul clearly made mention of this in Romans 6:20, "For when ye were the servants of sin, ye were free from righteousness."

In order to ransom us, Jesus had to first become identified with us in our plight. He took on the disposition of a servant and allowed Himself to be fashioned as a man. Eventually, He would offer His life as the actual payment or ransom for our release. This required Him to become sin for us so we could be made in the righteousness of God.[12]

Jesus died for us, but we must recognize that we must first receive the payment to be released from the curse. For us the payment came in the form of a pardon. Our sins had to be remitted before God could restore us.[13] However, we first must recognize our need to be pardoned and receive it for ourselves.

I remember a story about a Civil War hero who had fought on the side of the Union. In a fit of anger he had killed someone. The death sentence had been pronounced on him for his crime. His family pleaded his case with President Lincoln. Because of his service and his seeming remorse for his actions, the President granted him a pardon. However, this former hero would not receive it for himself. He was an honorable man who felt his sentence was just and he needed to pay the price for his unacceptable act. Since he refused the pardon, the sentence was carried out.

Jesus paid the necessary price for everyone's redemption, but according to the Bible, few will receive it. Sadly, it is not that such people perceive that they rightly deserve the sentence; rather, they do not believe that such a sentence is hanging over their heads.

---

[11]   Galatians 3:13
[12]   2 Corinthians 5:21; Philippians 2:6-8
[13]   Hebrews 9:22

Those who received the pardon are given a new life from above. Instead of being defined by the old condemned man, they are now being defined by a complete new life. They have in fact been justified by Christ and now stand justified in Him.[14] Such justification declares that it is as though they have never sinned.

God desires to make each of us alive with the life of His Son. The new life coming from above and imparted in us is known as the born-again experience. This is when the seed of His Son's life is planted within our spiritual ground (the heart) by the Holy Spirit, giving us a new heart and spirit to respond to God. After all, in the old state our hearts were inclined towards a make-believe god that would serve selfish purposes. Such a state was incapable of responding to the one true God of the universe on a spiritual level.[15]

It is important to realize that the seed of this life has been imparted to believers, but it must be nurtured and cultivated for the new life to come forth, and to actually reproduce itself in others. This brings us to the concept of being conformed by this new life to reflect the author of it.

BEING CONFORMED

The new life that has been imparted to us from above had to come from outside of the old life. In fact, the old life has no part with the new life. They are both contrary to one another. One comes from the earth and carries the seed of death, while the other one comes from above and possesses eternal life. However, the old opposes the new; therefore, the new must be forged in us, as our way of thinking is reshaped to embrace the new, and our way of doing is molded according to the pattern and example set forth by Jesus.[16]

Another important aspect of this new life is to understand what it will look like. There are many images that we can be mistaken for the original image. There is the image of man's religion. On the outside it looks pious, but it often falls short of what the new life will look like. There is the pious

---

[14] Romans 5:1

[15] Ezekiel 36:26-27; John 3:3, 5; 1 Corinthians 2:10-14

[16] John 13:15; Romans 5:14-21; 1 Peter 2:21

look produced by good works. Such works may have an appearance of representing the new life, but still be void of it.

What will this new life look like? That answer is Jesus. But, what did Jesus look like in His walk, attitude, and ways? After all, Jesus warned us of the many counterfeits who would try to take center stage and ride high on His reputation and credentials. They would claim that they were "the Messiah" or "the Anointed One" sent from God. He exhorted His disciples not to accept or follow such counterfeits.

Clearly, we must know how Jesus looked. We know what He looked like as far as His disposition. He was lowly in disposition, which was expressed in His servitude before God and man. How would this be expressed in the life of a believer? It would be expressed in humility. Instead of pride reigning, a believer would operate from a state of humility that would be quick to respond to a matter in an honorable way. Even though believers are given such a disposition at their new-birth experience, the state of humility must be forged in them because of pride.

What did Jesus look like as far as His attitude? He loved the Father, which brought Him into obedient subjection. He loved you and me, causing Him to operate from the premise of submission. He was always giving way to that which was worthy and beneficial for the cause and work of our salvation. His attitude is summarized by one word: meekness.

"Meekness" is controlled strength or rage. In other words, it is strength that is completely under control and submitted to the authority of that which is worthy and honorable. What will meekness look like in believers? It is important to point out that there is no meekness in the selfish disposition. It might give the appearance of subjection while maintaining its fierce independence. It might act like it is coming into submission, but it is an outward show that hides obstinacy. The truth is, the old life is unmanageable in its thinking, undisciplined in its emotions, unyielding in its ways, and unruly in its plans. It may appear as if it is under control, but it is only a matter of outward compliance, reformation, performance, and conforming. Sadly, without transformation the inward man continues to be ruthless and treacherous as it watches out for its own self-interest and purpose.

In order to bring change to man's attitude, it must be transformed. The only way the Holy Spirit can transform each of our attitudes or minds about a matter is to totally reshape it by working the mind of Christ into our way of thinking and perceiving. The Apostle Paul makes reference to letting the mind of Christ reshape our way of thinking. Clearly the carnal mind must be regenerated by the Holy Spirit and cleansed by the Water of the Word in order to be reshaped and transformed by the mind of Christ.[17]

For believers a meek attitude will express itself in faith that manifests itself in submission to the work of the Spirit and obedience to the Word of God. As the mind of Christ shapes the believers' way of thinking, they will begin to reflect His attitude in their service to God and others

How did Jesus walk? After all, Jesus set before us a pattern that we must follow. The Apostle John said it best when he exhorted believers that if they are going to abide in Christ, they must, ". . . walk, even as he walked" (1 John 2:6).

It is interesting to follow Jesus in His walk before the Father. He walked according to the life the Father put in Him, as He lined up to the plan of the Father in relationship to redemption. Keep in mind that Jesus was fully God and fully man. In Him was the fullness of deity, but, as man, all matters including His life had to come from the Father. Granted, His deity identified Him to heaven, but His humanity identified Him to us. It was in His humanity that He would be offered up as the Lamb of God.

Jesus' tests and walk did not come along the lines of His deity, but along the lines of His humanity. He came in the form of man to serve as our example. He actually set forth a pattern. He walked according to the life of the Father in Him. He was led by the Spirit as He walked in the light of the Father's plan for humanity and in obedience to the Word. As a result, He became our example of what constitutes real righteousness.

As believers, we are to walk according to the light of the life of Christ in us. We are to walk after, be led by, and walk in the Spirit. We are to walk in the ways of Christ's righteousness.

If you study the Word of God in light of how we are to walk, live, or respond to a matter, there is one common word that will tie all of these aspects of the Christian life together, and that is righteousness. Let me

---

[17]   Romans 8:6-7; 12:2; Philippians 2:5

give you a couple of examples. Remember what we are to first seek as believers: The kingdom of God and His *righteousness*.[18]

Consider what the Apostle Paul said in 2 Corinthians 5:21. He stated that Christ became sin for us so we could be made the *righteousness* of God. The word "made" in this text points to coming into a place of righteousness, or to be brought to a position of righteousness to fulfill a requirement or an ordination.

We must understand what it means to be made the righteousness of God. Isaiah 64:6 states that man's best is as filthy rags. Clearly, this means that man does not have, in and of himself, anything that could be considered righteous to God. Therefore, he must be made the righteousness of God.

This brings us back to being conformed to the image of God. To be made the righteousness of God means to become a visible, living expression of right standing before God. The Bible tells us that as believers we have been placed in Christ who is made unto us wisdom, *righteousness,* sanctification, and redemption. In other words, we have been placed in Christ, who serves as our place of righteousness. Because of Christ, we have right standing or stand upright before God.

We are told that the kingdom of God is not food or drink but *righteousness,* peace, and joy in the Holy Spirit. We are to follow *righteousness,* as well as yield ourselves up as instruments of *righteousness.* We cannot do what is right unless we are Spirit led. We cannot be right or honorable unless we follow after the ways of *righteousness.* We will not be considered upright before God unless we yield our ways to His *righteousness.*[19]

Obviously, there is nothing *righteous* in us or springing from us unless it finds its origins in God. The only way that such *righteousness* will be brought forth in us is if we believe God in the first place.

God cannot count or reckon a matter *righteous* unless it is a product of unfeigned faith. Faith approaches the Word to believe a matter as being true, just, and right. As a result, it will respond in obedience to what is true, to ensure just, honorable actions and right standing before God. When God sees a person responding towards Him and His Word with

---

[18] Matthew 6:33

[19] Romans 6:13; 14:17; 1 Timothy 6:11

unfeigned faith, He counts it as *righteousness*, causing the response or act to become acceptable to Him.[20]

To be conformed to the image of Christ means being conformed by and to His *righteousness*. As we yield to the *righteous* pattern of Christ, His disposition, attitude, and life will be forged in us. It will shape how we think, influence how we walk, and mold us to His very likeness.

BEING PLANTED IN HIS DEATH

Christ's life must be forged in us. To forge something implies forcing it against its natural grain to adjust and change it into something else. It also means to copy something in such a way that is so close to the real thing, that it cannot be distinguished by the naked or experienced eye. This brings us to the process it will take to shape and mold the life of Christ in each of us.

We know that the process begins with being born again, but the new life in us must be nurtured, cultivated, and brought to maturity. For Christians it is a lifetime work, but at different intervals such a process can seem to be long and drawn out. The determination for how long a particular process takes comes down to how fast the old ways die in order to give way to the new. This part of the process points to the dying out process.

In Romans 6:1-3, the Apostle Paul begins to present an important case about what it means for the life of Christ to come forth. Keep in mind it is Christ's life that will serve as the light to our spiritual eyes. It is only as we walk in the light of His life that we will discover what it means to live His life in our physical bodies. The more we walk according to the life of Christ, the more we will allow the Holy Spirit to recreate the mirror that will reflect Jesus' very image or likeness.

In order to be fair about the case that the Apostle Paul was presenting in Romans 6, we must go back to Romans 5:20-21. The apostle explained how the Law of God entered because of offences committed towards Him. This law showed how offences abounded because of sin. However, where sin once abounded, grace can much

---

[20]   Romans 4:3, 9; 10:17; 14:23

more abound. He then goes on to explain how sin reigns unto death, but grace reigns through righteousness unto eternal life by Jesus Christ.

Once again, righteousness is taking center stage to bring a contrast between the Law which can only pronounce death where sin still reigns, and grace which can only reign through righteousness. We must remember that positionally we stand upright before God because we are in Christ. But, we are also in right standing before the Lord because our unfeigned faith is counted to us as righteousness; and, we stand right in regards to others due to godly obedience and benevolence. When a Christian has righteousness in all three areas, God's grace or favor is able to reign in us unto eternal life by Jesus Christ.

It is from this premise that the Apostle Paul challenges the reader in regard to abusing God's grace. Shall a person who is in sin convince self that it is alright to continue in it because of grace? The apostle's resounding reply is, "God forbid!" If we are dead to the influence, workings, and activities of sin, how can we live any longer in it?

When we consider how sin reigns, we must realize that sin influences us through our selfish dispositions, works in the flesh, and operates according to the activities of this present age. The Apostle Paul clearly states that we are to be dead to the ways of sin in all three arenas.

How can we be dead to sin when we are quite alive? The Apostle Paul explains that we are dead through identification with Christ.

> Know ye not that, so many of us as were baptized into Jesus Christ were baptized into his death? Therefore, we are buried with him by baptism into death: that like as Christ was raised up from the dead by the glory of the Father, even so we also should walk in newness of life (Romans 6:3-4).

The concept of baptism in Romans implies total immersion in Christ's death, burial, and resurrection. In this text, "death" points to death to the old way or old man, burial points to the old being put off, and resurrection points to a new life immerging.

In Romans 6:5, Paul takes us one step further in understanding identification to Christ through total immersion into His work of redemption. He explains that we have been planted together (the Body or Church of Jesus) in the likeness of His death.

When we think about Jesus' death on the cross we can get quite sentimental about it. The idea that Jesus died for my sin and your sin is humbling. Since we are to be planted in the likeness of His death, there must be something far greater for each of us to realize. After all, we cannot die for sin; therefore, there must be another aspect of His death that we must be able to identify with. It is true that Jesus died _for_ our sin as the substitute Passover Lamb of God, but Jesus in His humanity also died _to_ the influence, workings, and activities of sin so we could be made the righteousness of God.[21]

To be identified or planted in the likeness of Jesus' death means we must also die _to_ sin. Sin must not have any more influence over our self-life, work within our fragile, weak flesh, or cause us to be attracted to the world's activities. If we are dead _to_ sin, then we will be able to walk in the ways of righteousness.

Sadly, Christians experience defeat in their spiritual lives because they have not become planted in the likeness of Jesus' death. Sin in some way continues to rule from different arenas of their life. Obviously in such a state, they will not know, nor will they understand, the liberty that is attached to such a death.

Such a death means that like Jesus, our former life that identifies us to this present world, will fall into the ground as a lifeless seed so that it will be able to give way to a new life.[22] Since we have been planted in the likeness of Jesus' death, we no longer are subject to the torment and consequences of sin upon our souls.

As I meditated upon this concept of being planted in the likeness of Jesus' death, I began to see glimpses into His death. He died _for_ us so we could have life, but He died _to_ sin as our example so that we could be made the righteousness of God. Through identification with His death _to_ sin, we can be totally immersed into the grave, where death will release us from any claims that the old ways had upon our lives.

Keep in mind, Satan wants to wipe out any image and reflection of Jesus in the world. He wants to abort any image from ever coming forth in our lives. We have to make sure we have been planted in the death of

---

[21]   2 Corinthians 5:21

[22]   John 12:23-25

Jesus to ensure His likeness comes forth. Have you been planted in the likeness of Jesus' death?

BEING PLANTED IN THE LIKENESS OF HIS LIFE

In Romans 6, the Apostle Paul continues to present his case concerning our immersion or total identification with Jesus in His death, burial, and resurrection. In fact, we have been planted in the likeness of His death _to_ sin in order to experience the next aspect of the very life of Christ being worked in us.

It is only reasonable that if we have been planted in the likeness of His death, we will also be planted in likeness of His powerful life. The Apostle Paul confirms this. He states, "For if we have been planted together in the likeness of his death, we shall be also in the likeness of his resurrection" (Romans 6:5).

The idea of planting something is so that life can take root and produce fruit. In the ground (heart) of our soul the very life of Jesus is planted by the Spirit of God. But, for the fruit of His life to come forth, the old must go into the ground and die. Keep in mind that death points to decay and ruin, but remember what is used to fertilize the ground? That which is dying, rotting, and decaying is what fertilizes the ground to ensure new life comes forth. Therefore, the death of our old life allows us to be planted in the likeness of His resurrection. This is called the great exchange.

We give up a life that was subject to sin and made powerless by death. By becoming totally immersed and identified in the death of Jesus, we can also be immersed into His life. We can be planted in the likeness of His life. This likeness will make itself known through the power of resurrection.

The beauty of Jesus' life is that it possesses resurrection power. His physical body was completely transformed, as well as raised again in the newness of life by the power of resurrection. Even though the life of Christ is eternal, it also possesses the power from above to raise it out of the grave.

Once we are planted in the likeness of Jesus' resurrection, we will take on the likeness of His life. We will actually take on His disposition, attitude, and ways. Do not be mistaken as some have been, we will become *like* Him, but we will not *become* Him. We will never be "little christ's" or "little gods". We will simply be mirroring Him to the world. His life will actually be raised up in us to express His likeness to others. As a result, we will discover what it means to walk in the power of His resurrection, knowing that without such power, we would not be able to walk out this life.

Clearly, the Christian life must be walked out in order to take on the likeness of Christ. As we walk this life out, it will be worked in us by the Spirit, worked through us as we come into submission to Jesus' Lordship, and worked out of us through obedience to the Word. This life will reveal itself through deliverance from the old, salvation unto the new, and the liberty to mirror the image of Jesus.

As we become like Jesus, we will begin to bear His image. The Apostle Paul talks about bearing the image of Christ in 1 Corinthians 15:49-50. Let us consider what he said about this subject, "And as we have borne the image of the earthly, we shall also bear the image of the heavenly. Now this I say, brethren, that flesh and blood cannot inherit the kingdom of God; neither doth corruption inherit incorruption."

When we were born into this world, we bore the image of the earthly. In other words, we expressed the image of the first Adam. We know that this image had been darkened by sin, was cracked by the judgment of death, and was doomed for destruction. However, we have the potential to bear the image of the heavenly man, Jesus, the second Adam.

In order to bear the image of the heavenly, we must be born again from above, and immersed into Jesus' death, burial, and resurrection. The old must be crucified and buried in order for the new to be resurrected in the empty or vacated tombs of our souls.

Once the new life begins to develop in us, we will begin to bear the image of Christ. "Bear" implies shouldering a burden. Our burden as Christians is that we must constantly reflect the disposition, attitude, and life of Christ in this world. This is the essence of reaching our potential of serving as the crowning glory of God's creation. It is reminding all of creation that God did keep the best for the last when He spoke all of creation into being.[23]

---

[23] Hebrews 1:2-3

In order to bear this image we must put Jesus on daily. The Apostle Paul made this statement in Romans 13:14, "But put ye on the Lord Jesus Christ, and make not provision for the flesh, to fulfill the lust thereof."

To put Jesus on means to place Him before us, set our focus and affections on Him, and lay all aside that would hinder us from rightfully taking our position in Him. We must take these measures while situating our priorities, agendas, and emphasis to line up to His purpose and will for our lives. We must plant ourselves upon His truth, as we avail ourselves to deposit His life into others.

It is important to point out that to clothe ourselves with Jesus, we must recognize that such heavenly clothing comes from above as we reach up in complete humility and surrender to the work of the Spirit to bring forth Jesus' life in us. In Christ, we will not fulfill the lusts of the flesh. As we walk forth in the very life of Christ, it will become our armor allowing us to stand against enemy attacks, to withstand the darts of the enemies, and to continue to stand when it seems as if defeat is imminent.[24]

Clearly, the life of Christ must consume us. We not only have the life of Christ being established within us, but we are also being clothed by it. As a result, we can truly mirror the very image of Christ. In fact, the life of Christ in us will serve as the light that will take the image we are bearing and reflect it to the world.

When you take the light of the life within and the life of Christ that is being put on, a person will ultimately reflect or mirror His glory. The Apostle Paul also talked about this subject in 2 Corinthians 3:18, "But we all, with open face beholding as in a glass the glory of the Lord, are changed into the same image from glory to glory, even as by the Spirit of the Lord."

"Glory" points to the distinction that Jesus' person, life, and work brings Him. This distinction clearly exalts Him, revealing that He is worthy of all praise, worship, and adoration. In his book, *"Full Life in Christ,"* Andrew Murray brings this principle into perspective by explaining that being saved is one aspect of the Christian life, while the other one is being conformed to the image of Christ. He quoted an old saying that

---

[24] Ephesians 6:10-17

best summarizes the urgency of truly being made in the likeness of Christ: *"Embodiment is the end of the ways of God."*

It is true that God's great desire and will are to save each of us. However, the flip-side of salvation is that God also wants to bring us from simply receiving salvation to being restored back unto our original state before the fall of Adam. At our salvation Christ rises in our life as the bright and morning star, but He also must become the light from within, and the glory that is being reflected from our lives.[25]

Murray explained that the glory of God had to do with God's holiness, and that His holiness is redeeming love. His love brings it back to that which was manifested in Jesus' humanity. He was the manifestation of divine perfection in human form. The chief marks of the image of His divine glory were His humiliation and love. In humanity, humiliation is seen as the true glory of the expression of Christ, while godly, sacrificial love serves as the highest or more excellent manifestation of His glory.

Clearly, the more we are exposed to our Lord Jesus, the more we are going to reflect the glory of His likeness. In fact, as we give way to His life within, while daily putting on His life in our walk, His reflection will become clearer and clearer. The Apostle John said it best when he made this declaration, "Beloved, now are we the sons of God, and it doth not yet appear what we shall be, but we know that, when he shall appear, we shall be like him; for we shall see him as he is" (1 John 3:2).

His image in us will change as His glory or distinction is unveiled in greater ways. As His glory is reflected from our lives, we will fulfill the original purpose behind what man was originally predestinated for by his Creator. Like King David we will be able to make this declaration, "As for me, I will behold thy face in righteousness: I shall be satisfied, when I awake, with thy likeness" (Psalms 17:15).

---

[25]   Revelation 22:16

BIBLIOGRAPHY

Strong's Exhaustive Concordance of the Bible; Word Bible Publishers

A Dwelling Place for God, Ruth Specter Lascelle, © 1990 by Hyman Israel Specter

Deeper Experiences of Famous Christians, James Gilchrist Lawson,© 2000 by Barbour Publishing Inc.

The Way, E. Stanley Jones, Abingdon-Cokesbury Press, New York.

We Have A Great High Priest, © 1982 by Ruth Specter Lascelle

Full Life In Christ, Andrew Murray, © 2000 by Whitaker House

Other books by Rayola Kelley:
Hidden Manna
Battle for the Soul
Nuggets From Heaven
More Nuggets From Heaven
The Leadership Series
Volume One: Establishing Our Life in Christ
My Words are Spirit and Life
The Anatomy of Sin
The Principles of the Abundant Life
The Place of Covenant
Unmasking the Cult Mentality
Volume Two: Putting on the Life of Christ
He Actually Thought it Not Robbery
Revelation of the Cross
In Search of Real Faith
Think on These Things
Follow the Pattern
Volume Three: Developing a Godly Environment
Godly Discipline
Prayer and Worship
Don't Touch That Dial
The Face of Thankfulness
ABC's of Christianity
Volume Four: Issues of the Heart
Hidden Manna (Revised)
Bring Down the Sacred Cows
The Manual for the Single Christian Life
Parents are People Too
Volume Five: Challenging the Christian Life
The Issues of Life
Presentation of the Gospel
For the Purpose of Edification
Whatever Happened to the Church?
Women's Place in the Kingdom of God
Volume Six: Developing Our Christian Life
The Many Faces of Christianity
Possessing Our Souls

Experiencing the Christian Life
The Power of our Testimonies
The Victorious Journey
Devotions
Devotions of the Heart: Book One & Two
Daily Food for the Soul
Gentle Shepherd Ministries Devotion Series:
Being a Child of God
Disciplining the Strength of our Youth
Coming to Full Age